Status, Distribution and Biogeography of the Birds of Paraguay

Floyd E. Hayes

Department of Natural Sciences
Loma Linda University
Loma Linda, CA, 92350, USA

Present address:
Department of Biology
Caribbean Union College
P.O. Box 175, Port of Spain
Trinidad and Tobago

Monographs in Field Ornithology

This series of occasional monographs, published by the American Birding Association, has been established for original scholarly contributions to field ornithology. Possible subject matter may include studies of distribution and abundance, population dynamics, identification, behavior, conservation, migration, and life history.

Correspondence concerning manuscripts for publication in the series should be addressed to the Editor, Dr. Kenneth P. Able, Department of Biology, State University of New York, Albany, New York 12222.

Monographs in Field Ornithology, No. 1, 224 pages

Editor of Monographs in Field Ornithology, Kenneth P. Able

Author, Floyd E. Hayes

Manuscript received 18 June 1993; revised 26 September 1994; accepted 10 October 1994.

Issued, May 1995

Price, $29.95

Library of Congress Catalog Card Number, 95-75102

ISBN: 1-878788-30-2

Cover photo: *Greater Rhea (*Rhea americana*), a near-threatened resident of grasslands in Paraguay. Parque Nacional Ybucuí, Dpto. Paraguarí, July, 1987. Photo by the author.*

TABLE OF CONTENTS

1. Abstract/Resumen 7

2. Introduction 9

3. Geography, Climate and Vegetation

   A. Introduction 10

   B. Geological History 12

   C. Geographical Regions 14

      1. The Paraguay River 15

      2. The Chaco 15

         a. Alto Chaco 16

         b. Matogrosense 17

         c. Bajo Chaco 17

      3. The Orient 18

         a. Campos Cerrados 19

         b. Central Paraguay 19

         c. Ñeembucú 20

         d. Alto Paraná 20

4. Ornithological History

   A. Introduction 23

   B. Pre-Columbian Period 23

   C. Colonial Period, 1524-1811 24

   D. Early Independence Period, 1811-1870 25

   E. Between Wars Period, 1870-1935 25

   F. Post Chaco War Period, 1935-1972 28

   G. Modern Period, 1972-present 30

5. Methods

   A. Compilation of Data 43

   B. Evaluation of Records 44

   C. Systematic Treatment 46

   D. Biogeographical Analyses 46

      1. Regional Comparisons 47

         a. Species Richness 47

         b. Faunal Similarity 47

         c. Faunal Uniqueness 47

         d. Regional Affinities 47

         e. Body Size 49

      2. Dispersal Barriers 49

         a. Regional Cluster Prediction 50

         b. Distributional Limits Prediction 50

         c. Faunal Similarity Prediction 50

        d. Body Size Prediction 51
        e. Migrant Prediction 51
        f. Distributional Crossover Prediction 51
        g. Phenotypic Differentiation Prediction 52
        h. Contact Zone Prediction 52
        i. Limitations of Predictions 52
    3. Computation of Data 52
 6. Annotated Checklist 53
 7. Distributional Notes 85
 8. Taxonomic Notes 119
 9. Hypothetical Species
    A. Possible Species 125
    B. Doubtful Species 131
10. Biogeography
    A. Introduction 135
    B. Origins 135
    1. Biological Diversification 135
    2. Centers of Endemism 138
    C. Regional Comparisons 140
    1. Species Richness 140
    2. Faunal Similarity 142
    3. Faunal Uniqueness 144
    4. Regional Affinities 146
    5. Body Size 148
    D. Dispersal Barriers 148
    1. Paraguay River vs Forest-Savanna Barriers 148
        a. Regional Cluster Prediction 150
        b. Distributional Limits Prediction 150
        c. Faunal Similarity Prediction 151
        d. Body Size Prediction 153
        e. Migrant Prediction 156
        f. Distributional Crossover Prediction 156
        g. Phenotypic Differentiation Prediction 158
        h. Contact Zone Prediction 160
    2. Alternative Ecological Barriers 161
        a. West/East Contact Zones 161
        b. North/South Contact Zones 161
    3. Conclusions 163
11. Conservation 164
    A. Environmental Threats 164

    B. Distribution of Threatened Species 165

12. Acknowledgments 168

13. Literature Cited 169

14. Appendices

    1. Chronological Sequence of Publications 186

    2. Summary of Field Work 188

    3. Forest Understory Species of Birds 192

    4. Eastern Distributional Limits of Western Birds 193

    5. Western Distributional Limits of Eastern Birds 196

    6. Distributional Crossover of Paraguay River 205

    7. Threatened and Near-threatened Species of Birds 208

    8. Gazetteer of Localities 209

15. Tables

    1. Environmental Characteristics of Geographical Regions 14

    2. Environmental Gradients in Paraguay 14

    3. Ecological/taxonomic Groups of Birds by Family 48

    4. Species Richness in Geographical Regions 140

    5. Percentage of Birds in Geographical Regions Also Occurring in Other Regions of
        South America 146

    6. Mean Body Size Class of Birds in Geographical Regions 147

    7. Frequency of Birds in Body Size Classes in Geographical Regions 149

    8. Jaccard Coefficients for Adjoining Geographical Regions 153

    9. Mean Body Size Class of Shared and Non-shared Birds in Adjoining Geographical Regions 154

   10. Jaccard Coefficients of Migrants and Non-Migrants in Adjoining Geographical Regions . . . 157

   11. Numbers of Threatened Species in each Geographical Region 166

   12. Protected Areas of Paraguay 167

16. Figures

    1. Map of Departments 10

    2. Map of Major Rivers 10

    3. Map of Elevation 11

    4. Map of Mean Annual Temperature 11

    5. Map of Mean Annual Precipitation 12

    6. Map of Vegetation 12

    7. Map of Geographical Regions 14

    8. Map of Political Features 33

    9. Photo of Paraguay River 34

   10. Xeromorphic Features of Chaco Vegetation 16

   11. Photo of Thorn Scrub Forest in Alto Chaco Region 34

   12. Photo of Flooded Forest in Matogrosense Region 35

   13. Photo of Small Stream in Matogrosense Region 35

   14. Photo of Palm Savanna in Bajo Chaco Region 36

15. Photo of Flooded Grassland in Bajo Chaco Region 36

16. Photo of Campos Cerrados Vegetation in Campos Cerrados Region 37

17. Photo of Hills and Vegetation in Campos Cerrados Region 37

18. Photo of Humid Deciduous Forest in Central Paraguay Region 38

19. Photo of the Bahía de Asunción 38

20. Photo of Grasslands in Ñeembucú Region 39

21. Photo of Marshes and Scrub Forest in Ñeembuú Region 39

22. Photo of Humid Deciduous Forest in Alto Paraná Region 40

23. Photo of Salto Ñacunday 40

24. Faunal Similarity Between Regions for Breeding Birds 142

25. Faunal Similarity Between Regions for Ecological/Taxonomic Groups 142-143

26. Distributional Limits of Eastern and Western Birds 151

27. Eastern Limits of Western Bird Groups and Western Limits of Eastern Bird Groups 152

17. Species Index. 218

ABSTRACT

The Paraguay River divides the Republic of Paraguay into two distinct regions: the Chaco to the west and the Orient to the east. The relatively flat Chaco is characterized by semiarid thorn scrub forest in the west, subhumid forests in the northeast and palm savannas in the southeast. The topographically diverse Orient is characterized by campos cerrados in the northeast, savannas in the west and southwest, and humid forest elsewhere that increases in height toward the east. None of the hills exceeds 800 m in height. Paraguay's climate is subtropical; rainfall increases roughly fourfold from west to east.

Previous studies of the birds of Paraguay have focused primarily on the distribution and taxonomy of resident species. There have been no thorough reviews of the avifauna of Paraguay since 1940. This monograph summarizes the status and distribution of the birds of Paraguay, documents patterns of bird distribution, and attempts to analyze the factors affecting bird distribution. It is based on a review of the available literature, examination of thousands of Paraguayan specimens in major American museums, and extensive field work in Paraguay by myself (1987-1989, briefly in 1993 and 1994) and others.

The avifauna of Paraguay includes 645 species that have been reliably recorded. An annotated checklist summarizes the status, habitats and relative abundance of each species in seven geographical regions of Paraguay. Distributional notes are provided for the more unusual bird records, taxonomic notes are provided for species whose taxonomic status requires clarification, and additional information is provided for species whose occurrence in Paraguay is regarded as hypothetical.

Species richness in Paraguay increases from west to east. Faunal similarity between regions is best explained by habitat similarity, with the avifauna of the Chaco-like southwestern Orient being more similar to that of Chaco regions than to other Orient regions. The avifauna of each region has high affinities with adjacent areas of South America, except that few Andean birds occur in Paraguay. No species is endemic to Paraguay. Tests of a suite of predictions suggest that the forest-savanna transition, which roughly coincides with the upper Paraguay River but shifts eastward in the southern Orient, is the most effective barrier to bird dispersal in Paraguay. There is little evidence that the relatively broad Paraguay River is an effective dispersal barrier. The Pilcomayo River may have formed a forest bridge between Yungas and Paranense forests, and subdivided the Chaco avifauna, during more humid interglacial periods.

Key words: avifauna; biogeography; conservation; dispersal barriers; distribution; gazetteer; Neotropics; ornithological history; Paraguay; seasonality; status; South America; taxonomy

RESUMEN

La República del Paraguay está dividida por el Río Paraguay en dos regiones diferentes: el Chaco al oeste y el Oriente al este. El Chaco, que es relativamente plano, se caracteriza por selva espinosa semiárida al oeste, bosques subhúmedos al noreste y sábanas de palma al sureste. El Oriente, que es topográficamente diverso, se caracteriza por campos cerrados al noreste, sábanas al oeste y suroeste, y selvas húmedas en otras partes que aumentan en altura hacia el este. Ninguno de los cerros sobrepasa los 800 m de altura. El clima del Paraguay es subtropical. El promedio de lluvia en el Paraguay aumenta aproximadamente en un cuádruplo de oeste a este.

Estudios anteriores de las aves del Paraguay han enfocado principalmente en la distribución y taxonomía de las especies residentes. No se han publicado revisiones minuciosas de la avifauna del Paraguay desde 1940. Esta monografía resume el estado y la distribución de las aves del Paraguay, documenta patrones de la distribución de las aves, y esfuerza analizar los factores que afectan la distribución de las aves. Se ha basado en una revisión de la literatura disponible, investigación de miles de ejemplares paraguayos en museos norteamericanos, y amplio trabajo en el campo del Paraguay por mi persona (1987-1989, brevemente en 1993 y 1994) y otros.

La avifauna del Paraguay incluye 645 especies que han sido registradas confiablemente hasta el presente. Una lista anotada resume el estado, hábitat y la abundancia relativa de cada especie en siete regiones geográficas del Paraguay. Notas distribucionales son suministradas por los registros de aves más raras, notas taxonómicas son proporcionadas por especies cuya condición taxonómica requiere clarificación, e información adicional es suministrada por especies cuya presencia en el Paraguay es estimada como hipotética.

La riqueza de especies en el Paraguay aumenta de oeste a este. La similitud de la fauna entre regiones es mejor explicada por la similitud de hábitat, con la avifauna de la región suroeste del Oriente, una región parecida al Chaco, siendo más parecida a las regiones del Chaco que a otras regiones orientales. La avifauna de cada región tiene altas afinidades con las áreas adyacentes de América del Sur, con la excepción que pocas aves andinas existen en el Paraguay. Ninguna especie es endémica en el Paraguay. Pruebas de una serie de predicciones sugieren que la transición selvática-sabana, que coincide aproximadamente con la región superior del Río Paraguay, pero cambia en dirección este al sur del Oriente, parece ser la barrera más efectiva en la emigración de las aves del Paraguay. Existe poca evidencia que el Río Paraguay, que es relativamente ancho, es una barrera efectiva de emigración. El Río Pilcomayo posiblemente formó un puente selvático entre las selvas Yungas y Paranense, y subdividió la avifauna del Chaco, durante los períodos interglaciales más húmedos.

INTRODUCTION

"The ornithological exploration of the Republic of Paraguay has been achieved with greater difficulties than that of any other South American country..."

H. von Ihering (1904:310), translated from Portuguese

The Republic of Paraguay is a small land-locked country, roughly the size of California, located to the east of the Andes in south-central South America. In comparison with most other South American countries, the avifauna of Paraguay has been relatively ignored by ornithologists and birders alike. This is probably due to its long history of political and geographical isolation, and to its relatively featureless terrain which lacks the endemic species eagerly sought by collectors. But as a result of the country's gradual modernization during the last few decades, an intricate network of paved and dirt roads now connects many formerly inaccessible areas, thus providing access for an increasing number of adventurous ornithologists.

During the past two centuries there have been numerous attempts at compiling lists of the avifauna of Paraguay (Azara 1802a, 1805a,b, Berlepsch 1887, Bertoni 1901, 1914a, 1939, Ihering 1904, Laubmann 1939, 1940, Podtiaguin 1941, 1944, 1945, Schade and Masi Pallares 1967, 1968, 1969, 1970, 1971, Mason and Steffee 1982, Wendelken 1983, Altman and Smith 1986, 1989, 1993, Contreras et al. 1990, Hayes et al. 1991). However, all have erroneously incorporated many species whose distribution has not been adequately documented, and none has adequately accounted for all of the available literature. The only review that adequately summarized all known locality records for each species was that of Laubmann (1939, 1940) more than half a century ago. Another weakness with these earlier attempts is that they relied primarily on published reports and specimen records, which provided relatively little information on the true status of the birds of Paraguay. The latest attempt (Hayes et al. 1991), based on five years of field work (combined for two authors) and an extensive review of the literature, provided information on the relative abundance of 622 species of birds in three broad geographical areas, but still had numerous errors (mostly of omission) and was merely a precursor to the Annotated Checklist section of this monograph.

The primary purposes of this monograph are to summarize our current knowledge of the status and distribution of the birds of Paraguay, and to analyze the patterns and processes affecting the distribution of birds in Paraguay. I first describe the geography, climate and vegetation of Paraguay, and review the history of Paraguayan ornithology. I discuss how I compiled and evaluated data on the distribution of birds, define my positions on taxonomy and systematics, and describe my methods of biogeographical analysis. I then present information on the status of each species in different geographical regions of Paraguay in the form of a checklist, followed by distributional notes for the more unusual records, taxonomic notes for species whose taxonomic status requires clarification, and additional information for species that are considered hypothetical. I proceed to an analysis of the patterns of bird distribution in Paraguay and the processes affecting their distribution, followed by a brief discussion of the conservation of birds in Paraguay. A bibliography of Paraguayan ornithology is incorporated into the Literature Cited section, and eight appendices provide a chronology of publications on Paraguayan ornithology, a summary of my field work during 1987-1989 and briefly during 1993 and 1994, documentary information on patterns of bird distribution, and a gazetteer of localities mentioned in the text.

I hope that this review of Paraguayan ornithology will stimulate others to help expand our knowledge of Paraguayan birds, for by doing so we can all contribute to the preservation of Paraguay's rich but increasingly threatened birdlife.

GEOGRAPHY, CLIMATE AND VEGETATION

"From the point of view of its geological formation and the consequent composition of its terrain, the territory of Paraguay appears divided into two large areas, the Oriental and the Occidental, more or less demarcated by the course of the Paraguay River... The differences between these areas are large and very marked..."

M. S. Bertoni (1918:17), translated from Spanish

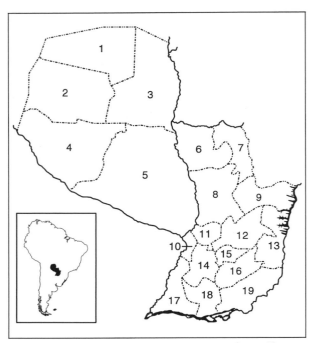

Figure 1. Map of Paraguay showing location within South America and the location of 19 political departamentos (including two that have been recently merged with others), based on Dirección del Servicio Geográfico Militar (1989, 1992). Departamentos: 1=Chaco (part of Alto Paraguay since 1992); 2=Nueva Asunción (part of Boquerón since 1992); 3=Alto Paraguay; 4=Boquerón; 5=Presidente Hayes; 6=Concepción; 7=Amambay; 8=San Pedro; 9=Canindeyú (formerly Canendiyú); 10=Central; 11=Cordillera; 12=Caaguazú; 13=Alto Paraná; 14=Paraguarí; 15=Guairá; 16=Caazapá; 17=Ñeembucú; 18=Misiones; 19=Itapúa.

Figure 2. Map of Paraguay showing major rivers, based on Dirección del Servicio Geográfico Militar (1992).

Straddling the Tropic of Capricorn in the heart of South America, the Republic of Paraguay encompasses an area of 406,752 km^2. The country is situated east of the Andes between 54°19' and 62°38' west longitude, and between 19°18' and 27°30' south latitude (Fig. 1). Its northern and northwestern borders, which are shared with Bolivia, are delineated by 11 boundary markers arcing northwestward between the upper reaches of the Pilcomayo and Paraguay rivers (Fig. 2). To the northeast, Paraguay is bordered by Brazil along the Paraguay and Apa rivers, and farther south along the Amambay and Mbaracayú cordilleras. To the southeast, Paraguay

is separated from Brazil and Argentina by the Paraná River. The western and southwestern border with Argentina is formed by the Pilcomayo and Paraguay rivers.

Paraguay's borders with Argentina and Brazil were disputed until the War of the Triple Alliance (1865-1870), which pitted Paraguay against Brazil, Uruguay and Argentina. After losing the war, Paraguay ceded over 150,000 km^2 of territorial claims. Paraguay's borders remained unchanged until the aftermath of the Chaco War with Bolivia (1932-1935), when Paraguay gained disputed territory in the northern Chaco.

The word "Paraguay" is derived from the Guaraní language, and can be translated as "source of water." This metaphor presumably refers to the Paraguay River, which led the early European explorers to the region and historically has been Paraguay's primary connection to the outside world. The river still remains the major artery of com-

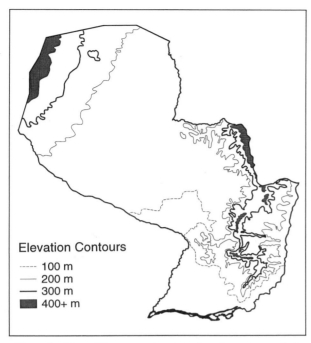

Figure 3. Map of Paraguay showing elevation contours (m), based on Lisboa (1991).

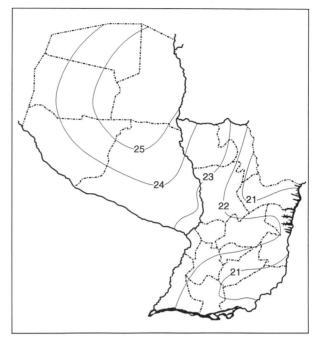

Figure 4. Map of Paraguay showing mean annual temperature isotherms (C). Data from 1951-1980, based on Anonymous (1985).

merce, and is vital to the cultural and political institutions of "the riverside nation."

The southward-flowing Paraguay River divides Paraguay into two distinct regions: the relatively flat Chaco to the west and the topographically diverse Orient to the east (Figs. 2 and 3). Until recently, the country has been subdivided into 19 political *departamentos* (departments), with five large ones in the Chaco and 14 smaller ones in the Orient (e.g., Dirección del Servicio Geográfico Militar 1989). However, due to their sparse human populations, Dpto. Nueva Asunción was annexed to Dpto. Boquerón and Dpto. Chaco was annexed to Dpto. Alto Paraguay in November 1992 for political reasons (e.g., Dirección del Servicio Geográfico Militar 1992; see Fig. 1). Paraguay's capital, Asunción, is situated on the east bank of the Paraguay River in Departamento (hereafter abbreviated as Dpto.) Central, in the southwestern portion of eastern Paraguay. Asunción is by far the largest city in Paraguay, with about 631,300 residents in 1992 (Dibble and Webb 1992). Paraguay's human population numbered slightly more than 4.5 million in 1992 (Dibble and Webb 1992).

Paraguay's continental climate varies from tropical to subtropical, with mean annual temperatures ranging from over 25°C in the north to less than 21°C in the east (Fig. 4). The climate of Paraguay

is dominated by the subtropical anticyclone of the Atlantic Ocean. The weather is invariably hot and humid during the austral summer, and relatively mild and dry during the winter, with temperatures occasionally dipping below 0°C. Because winds are usually northeasterly or southeasterly, dramatic changes in temperature are common as warm or cold fronts pass through. Precipitation is concentrated during the summer months and increases more than fourfold from west to east (Fig. 5).

General aspects of the geography, climate and vegetation of Paraguay have been summarized by various authors (e.g., M. S. Bertoni 1918, Krieg 1931, Gorham 1973a, Paiva 1977, Anonymous 1985). Atlases providing descriptions and maps of the country have been published by Emategui (1977) and Lisboa (1991). The geological history and present structural geology of Paraguay have been reviewed by Eckle (1959), Putzer (1962), Boettner (1973) and Palmieri and Velázquez (1982). The climate of Paraguay has been described in detail by Gorham (1973b), Fariña Sánchez (1973) and Prohaska (1976). The dominant plant communities of Paraguay have been reviewed by Hueck (1966), Cabrera (1970) and Esser (1982); the distribution of trees in Paraguay was reviewed by Bernardi (1984, 1985) and López et al. (1987). The most accurate map of the vegetation of Paraguay was provided by

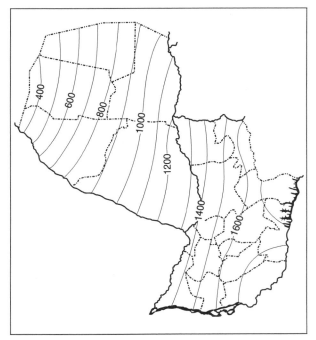

Figure 5. Map of Paraguay showing mean annual precipitation isohyets (mm). Data from 1941-1983, based on Anonymous (1985).

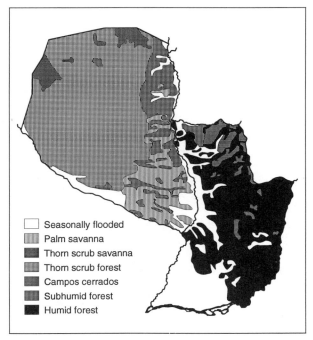

Seasonally flooded
Palm savanna
Thorn scrub savanna
Thorn scrub forest
Campos cerrados
Subhumid forest
Humid forest

Figure 6. Map of Paraguay showing major vegetation units. Data from 1966 satellite photos, based on vegetation map of Esser (1982). Cultivated areas in the central Chaco (Esser 1982) are interpreted as originally being covered by thorn scrub forest; cultivated areas in the Orient (Esser 1982) are interpreted as originally being covered by humid forests. Most of the humid forest of the Orient has been subsequently cleared. (Figure reproduced on back cover.)

Esser (1982), based on satellite photographs (Fig. 6). The following descriptions of the geology, geography, climate and vegetation of Paraguay are drawn primarily from these sources.

GEOLOGICAL HISTORY

The early Paleozoic history of Paraguay was characterized by several marine invasions, resulting in the deposition of limestone, sandstone and shale beds that are presently exposed over wide areas of eastern Paraguay and in isolated outcrops of western Paraguay. The last of marine conditions in Paraguay occurred during the Silurian (Putzer 1962) or Devonian (Eckle 1959). Deposition of tillites occurred during the late Paleozoic; these tillites are thought to have been deposited by glaciers (Eckle 1959, Putzer 1962), but have been reinterpreted as impact crater deposits (Oberbeck et al. 1993).

The Mesozoic history of Paraguay was characterized by deposition of red sandstones in eastern Paraguay during the Triassic, which were subsequently buried by intermittent basaltic lava flows during the remainder of the Mesozoic. These lava flows did not extend much farther west than the major cordillera ranges of the central Orient (Eckle 1959). The landscape of the Orient was punctuated

by volcanic eruptions at various periods during the Mesozoic and Cenozoic (Comte and Hasui 1971).

The Chaco basin began filling with alluvial sediments as a result of erosion in the Andes during most of the Cenozoic. As a consequence of the eastward movement of these sediments, which still continues, the course of the sluggish and sinuous Paraguay River has been shifting eastward, as evidenced by lateral cutting into the Paleozoic limestones on the east bank of the river in Dpto. Concepción (Eckle 1959).

Although little is known about the paleoecology of Paraguay during the Cenozoic, an abundance of geological, biological and paleoecological evidence from elsewhere indicates that the Quaternary history of South America was characterized by alternating periods of relatively cool, semiarid conditions during glacial phases, followed by warm, humid conditions during interglacial phases (e.g., see reviews by Prance 1982, Vogel 1984, Whitmore and Prance 1987, Vanzolini and Heyer 1988, Garleff and Stingl 1991). In response to climatic fluctuations during the Quaternary, the forests of South

América contracted and expanded several times. During the interglacial phases there were periods when the temperatures and humidity were apparently higher than today.

The impact of climatic fluctuations on the topography and vegetation of Paraguay is uncertain. There is no evidence that glacial ice sheets extended as far as Paraguay during the Quaternary (Eckle 1959, Putzer 1962, Vuilleumier 1971). Embayment of the lower Paraná River likely occurred during early interglacial phases (e.g., Vuilleumier 1971) and may have extended northward along the Paraguay River as high ground water flooded lowland areas adjacent to the Paraguay River and in the Pantanal of Bolivia and Brazil (Short 1975). During the more humid interglacial phases, humid forests evidently invaded the Chaco, at least along the major

river courses (e.g., Pilcomayo River), as suggested by relict patches of forest along presently dry riverbeds (Nores 1992). A subsurface podzolic soil horizon near Filadelfia (Dpto. Presidente Hayes) suggests more humid conditions in the more xeric portions of the Chaco (Lüders 1961). The more arid conditions during glacial phases may have connected the Chaco with the Cerrado and semiarid Caatinga of eastern Brazil, and isolated the humid forest biotas of southeastern South America from the Amazon basin (e.g., Short 1975, Brown and Prance 1987). Although patches of humid forests may have persisted in the Orient during glacial phases (Brown and Prance 1987), relict patches of cacti suggest more arid conditions than at present (Esser 1982).

Eared Dove (*Zenaida auriculata*)　　　　　　　　　　　　　Dan Brown

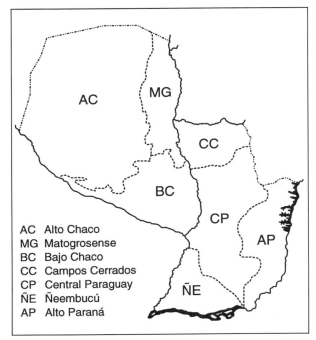

AC Alto Chaco
MG Matogrosense
BC Bajo Chaco
CC Campos Cerrados
CP Central Paraguay
ÑE Ñeembucú
AP Alto Paraná

Figure 7. Map of Paraguay showing the seven geographical regions used in this study, based primarily on major vegetation units and geographical features (rivers and mountain ranges).

GEOGRAPHICAL REGIONS

For the purposes of this monograph, I have subdivided Paraguay into seven geographical regions (Fig. 7; Fig. 8, page 33), based primarily on vegetation and geographical features. A summary of the dominant environmental features of each region is provided in Table 1. Before describing these regions, I must emphasize that the boundaries between the regions are usually ecotonal, characterized by gradual, mosaic changes in the dominant plant communities. These gradual changes result from complex interactions between a variety of environmental gradients (Table 2). As a consequence, the borders between these different regions are somewhat arbitrary and subject to revision with further study. Nevertheless, I feel that these regions are sufficiently distinct, at least from an ornithological perspective, to warrant recognition and further study by biogeographers.

Because the Paraguay River divides the Chaco from the Orient and borders five of the seven geographical regions, I will describe it separately.

Table 1: Summary of environmental characteristics for the seven geographical regions of Paraguay

Variable	Matogro-sense	Alto Chaco	Campos Cerrados	Campos Cerrados	Central Paraguay	Alto Paraná	Ñeem-bucú
Topographic relief	flat	flat	flat	hills	hills	hills	flat
Dominant vegetation	forest	forest	palm/grass	forest	forest	forest	grass
Forest humidity	subhumid	semiarid	subhumid	semihumid	humid	humid	semihumid
Precipitation	meduim	low	medium	high	high	very high	high

Table 2: Major environmental gradients in Paraguay

	Direction of Increase	
Variable	Chaco	Orient
Precipitation	west to east	west to east
Temperature	southwest to northeast	southeast to northwest
Potential evapotranspiration	southwest to northeast	southeast to northwest
Humidity	west to east	west to east
Seasonality	east to west	east to west
Plant species richness	west to east	west to east
Forests	southeast to northwest	southwest to northeast
Grasslands/wetlands	west to east	east to west
Xeromorphism	east to west	east to west
Elevation	southeast to northwest	southwest to northeast

The Paraguay River

Originating from surface waters in the Pantanal region of eastern Bolivia and southwestern Brazil, the Paraguay River flows southward through south-central South America to its confluence with the Paraná River at the southwestern corner of eastern Paraguay. It forms a part of the La Plata River basin, which encompasses both the Paraguay and Paraná river basins and constitutes the largest and most important watershed of South America south of the Amazon River, draining an area of approximately 3,100,100 km^2 (Anonymous 1985).

Because the Paraguay River passes through relatively flat terrain, it is shallow and sluggish, and meanders considerably. Oxbow lakes, channels, islands, sandbars and mudflats are ubiquitous along the river's course (Fig. 9). Riparian forests apparently once lined the river's banks (e.g., Page 1859:131), but have been largely cleared during the past few centuries and exist today only as isolated patches. The river's depth and width vary greatly between seasons; at a given locality, extremes in water levels during a single year may exceed 5 m, and the width may vary from several hundred m to several km, but is usually less than 1 km (Hayes 1991). However, day-to-day changes are small and usually unidirectional, with water level changes rarely exceeding 10 cm (Hayes and Fox 1991). Water levels along the Paraguay River are generally highest during the dry winter months, from May to August, and are lowest during the rainy summer months, from November to February (Anonymous 1985, Hayes 1991, Hayes and Fox 1991). This phenomenon has been attributed to the "sponge effect" of the Pantanal just north of Paraguay, where wetlands absorb excess water and delay the release of flood waters into the Paraguay River by about six months (Bucher et al. 1993). Since 1978, flooding of the Paraguay River has reached unprecedented proportions, perhaps due to the increased runoff of precipitation resulting from extensive deforestation in the river's watershed (Hayes 1991, Hayes and Fox 1991); a similar situation exists along the upper Amazon River (Gentry and López Parodi 1980). Increased flooding may also be due to siltation of the Pantanal wetlands as a result of erosion, thus reducing the effectiveness of the "sponge effect."

The Chaco

The Chaco basin is formed by a deep syncline that arcs upward toward the Andes in the west and toward the Paraguay and Paraná rivers in the east. The basin is filled with unconsolidated Tertiary and Quaternary sediments, which are several hundred m deep in the Paraguayan Chaco (Eckle 1959). At the surface the Chaco comprises a vast, relatively flat, alluvial plain that gradually slopes downward toward the Paraguay and Paraná rivers. However, isolated outcrops of older sedimentary deposits are exposed in several areas in the form of hills.

The "Gran Chaco" encompasses large portions of northern Argentina, southern Bolivia and western Paraguay. The expanse of the Chaco to the north of the eastward-flowing Bermejo River, in northern Argentina, is often referred to as the "Chaco Boreal"; to the south of the Bermejo River it is generally referred to as the "Chaco Austral" (Gorham 1973b). The entire Paraguayan portion of the Chaco thus lies within the Chaco Boreal.

The Paraguayan Chaco, sometimes referred to as Paraguay Occidental (Western Paraguay), comprises 246,925 km^2 and occupies 61% of Paraguay's total area (Anonymous 1985). Its elevation ranges from over 400 m above sea level along the Bolivian border to less than 100 m along the Paraguay River; the elevation gradient from west to east is roughly 1 m/2 km (Myers 1982), but increases in the northwest (Fig. 3). Mean annual temperatures are highest in the northeastern Chaco (>25°C), lower in the west (<24°C), and lowest in the southeastern Chaco (<23°C; Fig. 4); temperatures often exceed 40°C (maximum of 44°C) during summer, and occasionally dip below freezing (minimum of -5°C) during winter in most areas of the Chaco (Fariña Sánchez 1973, Anonymous 1985). The Chaco of Argentina and Paraguay is subject to the highest temperatures in South America (Prohaska 1976).

Mean annual precipitation varies from about 35 cm along the Bolivian border to about 140 cm in the southeastern Chaco, with isohyets running in a SSW-NNE direction (Anonymous 1985; Fig. 5). This climatic gradient is reflected by a decrease of xeromorphic features in Chaco plants from west to east (Sarmiento 1972; Fig. 10). Precipitation patterns are highly seasonal and unpredictable, with most rain falling during the summer months (Gorham 1973b). Up to 21 cm of rain has fallen within a 24 hr period (Fariña Sánchez 1973). Long

16

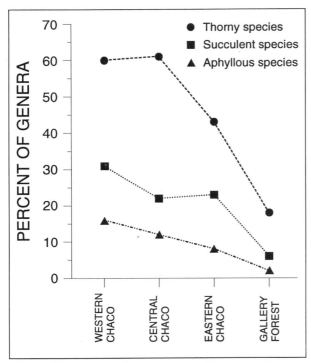

Figure 10. Percent of plant genera with species showing xeromorphic features (thorns, succulence and aphylly) along a west-east transect of the Gran Chaco and in gallery forest along the Paraguay/Paraná Rivers, based on Sarmiento (1972). Comparative data for the Orient are lacking.

periods of drought often occur during the winter months (May-September), especially in the western Chaco; during extreme droughts, 6-9 months have passed without rainfall (Gorham 1973b).

The soils of the Chaco are characterized by dense clays that are impervious to water. There is relatively little humus, especially toward the west. Because of the unusually flat terrain, which prevents runoff of surface water, and the imperviousness of the soils, extensive flooding occurs after heavy rains. Portions of the Chaco may remain flooded for several months, or even during most of the year.

The Paraguayan Chaco is sparsely inhabited by humans (0.26/km^2 in 1992); hence, much of it remains pristine wilderness. Only 1.4% of Paraguay's human population lives there. Until recently, the Paraguayan Chaco was so little known by biologists that the Chacoan Peccary (*Catagonus wagneri*), previously known only from fossils, was found alive in Paraguay in 1972 (Wetzel et al. 1975). A paved road, the Ruta Trans Chaco, currently extends about 425 km from Asunción (Dpto. Central) to Filadelfia (Dpto. Boquerón). Filadelfia and Loma Plata (both in Dpto. Boquerón) are the largest of several modern

Mennonite colonies in the central Paraguayan Chaco. Puerto Bahía Negra and Fuerte Olimpo (both in Dpto. Alto Paraguay) represent the largest urban centers in the northeastern Chaco, and Benjamin Aceval and Villa Hayes (both in Dpto. Presidente Hayes) are the largest in the southern Chaco. Large *estancias* (ranches) and military outposts are scattered throughout the Chaco, especially along the major roads. Indigenous communities occur in many areas, and in the northern Chaco a small band of Ayoreo indians still roams free.

The Paraguayan Chaco may be divided into three ecological regions (Fig. 7), based on the dominant plant communities identified from satellite photographs in the vegetation map of Esser (1982; see Fig. 6).

Alto Chaco. Literally meaning "Upper Chaco," this large but relatively homogeneous region encompasses the western portion of the Paraguayan Chaco, well to the west of the Paraguay River. It is sometimes referred to as the Chaco Boreal (Northern Chaco), Chaco Seco (Dry Chaco) or Chaco Occidental (Western Chaco). The Alto Chaco includes Dpto. Boquerón, and the western portions of Alto Paraguay and Presidente Hayes. The region is semiarid and dominated by relatively short, xerophytic, thorn scrub forests (5-10 m high; Fig. 11); these forests are generally dense, and often have heavy undergrowth (e.g., terrestrial bromeliads) and arborescent cacti (Esser 1982). A taller "monte alto" formation, composed of xerophytic thorn scrub and more mesophytic elements, occurs at the southern and eastern limits (transition zone) of the Alto Chaco (Esser 1982), but is not depicted in Fig. 6 (shown as thorn scrub forests). Palm savannas are relatively rare, occurring mostly along the eastern fringes of the region (Esser 1982). Farther west the forests become shorter and increasingly dominated by cacti. Near the Bolivian border the forest is sometimes broken by extensive sand dunes and grasslands (Myers 1982); these are referred to as thorn scrub savannas (Esser 1982; Fig. 6). Artificial grasslands and artificial ponds occur in areas where the forest has been cleared by man, especially near the major roads and in the vicinity of the Mennonite colonies in the central Chaco.

The few rivers extending westward into the region are generally narrow and usually temporary. An exception is the upper Pilcomayo River, which flows profusely and continuously in western Dpto. Boquerón, but diffuses into the swampy environs of

Laguna Escalante and Estero Patiño (both in western Dpto. Presidente Hayes) farther downstream (Krieg 1931). However, its flow has been recently diverted into canals for agriculture in both Paraguay and Argentina. In many areas of the Alto Chaco, salts are drawn up from the subsoil in large, bare depressions that often form shallow saline lakes after heavy rains. Less salty lakes occur in many areas, particularly in the eastern portion of the region.

In Dpto. Alto Paraguay, Cerro León is an enormous hill formed of Devonian sandstones (Eckle 1959). The subhumid forests in the vicinity of Cerro León are generally taller than elsewhere in the Alto Chaco (Esser 1982; Fig. 6). Elsewhere the Alto Chaco is relatively flat.

The boundary between the Alto Chaco and Matogrosense region is marked by a fairly abrupt (e.g., Conover 1950:359) transition from thorn scrub forest to taller subhumid forests (Esser 1982; Fig. 6). From the Bolivian border it generally runs from about 58°45'W longitude southward to a point about 100 km west of Puerto La Victoria, and then meanders somewhat to the south and east to about 58°30'W, 23°00'S (Esser 1982; Fig. 6).

The boundary between the Alto Chaco and Bajo Chaco is marked by the zone where continuous thorn scrub forest becomes broken up by extensive palm savannas (Esser 1982; Fig. 6). This zone is imprecisely defined; from the north it begins at about 58°30'W, 23°00'S, crosses the Ruta Trans Chaco just north of Pozo Colorado (Dpto. Presidente Hayes), and meanders westward along the northern edges of Estero Patiño and Laguna Escalante (Dpto. Presidente Hayes), which are two large wetland areas on the north bank of the Pilcomayo River (Esser 1982; Fig. 6).

Matogrosense. This region, literally meaning "pertaining to the Mato Grosso," includes most of Dpto. Alto Paraguay and northeastern Dpto. Presidente Hayes, in the northeastern portion of the Paraguayan Chaco. It is sometimes referred to as Alto Paraguay (Upper Paraguay). The region is characterized by subhumid, medium-height forest (10-20 m high) with dense undergrowth (primarily bromeliads), and periodically inundated forest (Fig. 12) and wetlands (Fig. 13) along the Paraguay River that are contiguous with the extensive Pantanal ecosystem of adjacent Bolivia and Brazil. Although palm savannas are present, especially along the river and increasingly so toward the south, this region is more heavily forested and more humid than other areas of the Paraguayan Chaco (Esser 1982; Fig. 6). Explorers have often referred to the Pantanal/Chaco area as "the green hell of South America."

The Paraguay River, which forms its eastern boundary, is narrower in this region than it is farther south, and in many places it is bordered by extensive marshes. Numerous small streams, most of which are temporary, flow eastward through the region. The largest rivers are the Melo and the lower portion of the Verde (Fig. 2). In the western part of the region there are several lakes. Although the region is very flat (Fig. 3), there are several small hills along the western bank of the Paraguay River, most notably at Fuerte Olimpo (Dpto. Alto Paraguay), Cerrito (Dpto. Alto Paraguay; an extension of the Pao de Açúcar massif of adjacent Brazil) and Cerro Galván (Dpto. Presidente Hayes). The subhumid forests in the vicinity of these hills tend to be taller than in surrounding areas.

The western boundary of this region is marked by the transition from taller semihumid forests to the shorter scrub forests of the Alto Chaco region farther west (Esser 1982), as described above. The southern boundary is marked by the gradual transition from subhumid forests to the palm savannas that are prevalent in the Bajo Chaco region. The boundary meanders to the south and east from 58°30'W, 23°00'S to the south bank of the Verde River, and then eastward to the Paraguay River (Esser 1982; Fig. 6).

Bajo Chaco. This region, literally the "Lower Chaco," includes the southeastern portion of the Paraguayan Chaco in southeastern Dpto. Presidente Hayes. It is sometimes referred to as the Chaco Húmedo (Humid Chaco) or Chaco Oriental (Eastern Chaco). The region is characterized by extensive palm savannas (Fig. 14), interspersed with patches of medium-height, xerophytic scrub forest (8-15 m high) on slightly elevated terrain. The dominant palm in the savannas is *Copernicia alba*, which is interspersed among grasses and patches of herbaceous trees. Belts of taller, subhumid riparian forest (10-20 m high) border highly convoluted rivers, which flow eastward to the Paraguay River; in some areas these rivers are bordered by extensive marshes. The most extensive marshes away from the Paraguay River are found at Laguna Escalante and Estero Patiño, on the north bank of the Pilcomayo River in western Dpto. Presidente Hayes. The

18

vegetation in these marshes is typical of the Paraguay River floodplain (Krieg 1931, Esser 1982; Fig. 6).

The rivers in this region are generally wider and extend farther west than the rivers in the Matogrosense region (Fig. 2). Nevertheless, water levels fluctuate greatly in these rivers; the larger rivers (*ríos*) are usually permanent, whereas the smaller ones (*riachos*) are temporary. Major rivers include (from north to south) the Verde, Siete Puntas, Montelindo, Negro, Aguaray Guazú and Confuso (Fig. 2). The Paraguay River, which forms the eastern boundary of the region, is generally wider here than it is farther north. The Pilcomayo River, which forms the southern boundary of the region and borders Argentina, is choked with vegetation and is thus not navigable. The ubiquitous palm savannas of the region are often inundated following rain, creating temporary wetlands attractive to hordes of waterbirds (Fig. 15). There are few natural lakes. However, numerous artificial ponds occur along the major roads and in estancias, and in some areas (e.g., Estancia La Golondrina, Dpto. Presidente Hayes) the streams have been dammed to provide permanent water for livestock. Although the region is relatively flat, gently rolling hills are present in the southeastern corner in the vicinity of Benjamin Aceval and Villa Hayes (both in Dpto. Presidente Hayes). The boundaries between this region and the Alto Chaco and Matogrosense regions were defined above.

The Orient

The structural geology of eastern Paraguay is more complex than that of the Chaco. Just east of the Paraguay River the strata form a gentle north-south anticline that parallels the course of the Paraguay River. The western side of the anticline appears steeper than the eastern side, apparently due to faulting or folding (Eckle 1959). Farther east the anticline dips gently downward toward the Paraná basin, gradually exposing younger sediments.

The topographically diverse Orient covers an area of 159,827 km^2, comprising 39% of Paraguay's total area (Anonymous 1985). In Spanish it is often referred to as Paraguay Oriental (Eastern Paraguay), and is here abbreviated and anglicized as "Orient." Extensive lowlands less than 100 m above sea level border the Paraguay River and Paraná River in the southern Orient, whereas several hilly *cordilleras* in

the northeast and central Orient range up to 760 m in height (Fig. 3). Mean annual temperatures are highest in the northwestern Orient (about 24°C), and lowest in both the northeastern and southeastern Orient (about 21°C; Anonymous 1985; Fig. 4). As with the Chaco, temperatures regularly exceed 40°C during summer (maximum of 44°C), and occasionally plunge below 0°C (minimum of -6°C) during winter, especially in the southeast (Fariña Sánchez 1973). Mean annual precipitation ranges from about 120 cm in the northwest to about 170 cm in the east, with isohyets running in a SSW-NNE direction (Anonymous 1985; Fig. 5). Precipitation is usually heaviest during the summer months, but is more evenly distributed throughout the year than in the Chaco. Precipitation can be quite heavy during storms, with up to 27 cm being recorded within a 24 hr period (Fariña Sánchez 1973).

In comparison with the Chaco, the Orient is densely populated by humans (27.9/km^2 in 1992). Most of the population is concentrated in the west-central Orient, especially near Asunción; in 1992, roughly a third of Paraguay's population lived in Dpto. Central alone, at a density of 550.8/km^2. However, the majority of the human population in the Orient remains rural. Until recently the eastern Orient was sparsely populated. But during the last two decades the construction and completion of the Itaipú hydroelectric dam, just north of Ciudad del Este (Dpto. Alto Paraná), has stimulated a dramatic increase in immigration, primarily from Brazil. Paraguay's human population has remained relatively low due to its inland location, the high number of casualties incurred during its two major wars, a repeated history of civil strife, an impoverished economy, and a high rate of emigration during the mid-1900s, primarily to Argentina (Anonymous 1985). In addition to Asunción (Dpto. Central), the major urban centers of the Orient include Concepción (Dpto. Concepción) in the northwest, Pedro Juan Caballero (Dpto. Amambay) in the northeast, Ciudad del Este (Dpto. Alto Paraná) in the east, and Encarnación (Dpto. Itapúa) in the south; these urban centers are all connected by recently paved roads. Small Mennonite colonies are scattered throughout the region. The few remaining indigenous colonies of the Orient are concentrated primarily in the central and eastern portions of the region.

The spatial distribution of dominant plant communities in the Orient is far more complex than that of the Chaco (Esser 1982). Furthermore, much of the original vegetation has been cleared and re-placed by cash crops, making it difficult to subdivide the region on the basis of dominant plant communities. As a consequence my division of the Orient into four regions is based primarily on geographical features. For an alternative division into six regions, see Acevedo et al. (1990).

Campos Cerrados. This region, literally meaning "Closed Fields" or "Closed Country," includes Dpto. Concepción and the northern half of Dpto. Amambay, in the northern Orient. It includes the Aquidibán ecoregion and the northern portion of the Amambay ecoregion of Acevedo et al. (1990). In many areas it is dominated by a unique scrub forest/grassland formation, referred to as *campos cerrados* (or simply *cerrado*), which also covers an extensive area in adjacent Brazil. Campos cerrados is a savanna formation characterized by a mosaic of xerophytic woodlands and grasslands (Fig. 16). The woodlands are relatively open, but sometimes dense, with twisted, semideciduous trees of short or medium height (8-20 m high); the ground is usually covered by an assortment of bromeliads, shrubs and coarse grasses. Other forest formations are present in the region, and often intermingle with campos cerrados. The western portion of the region has extensive patches of xerophytic Chaco-like forests, subhumid forests and palm savannas resembling the adjacent portions of the Chaco. Taller, humid deciduous forests (20-50 m high) occur in many areas, particularly in the highlands of Dpto. Amambay. The vegetation of the region was described in further detail by Sanjurjo (1976).

The northern boundary of this region is formed by the westward-flowing Apa River; the western boundary is formed by the Paraguay River; and the southern boundary is formed by the westward-flowing Ypané River (coinciding with the southern border of Dpto. Concepción), and Arroyo Ypané-mi (a stream) farther upstream (Fig. 7). The transition in plant communities between the Campos Cerrados region and Central Paraguay is rather gradual; hence, the river boundary between the two regions is arbitrary (Fig. 6). The only other major river of the region is the Aquidabán, which flows westward through the middle of the region (Fig. 2). These major rivers, all of which are relatively sluggish, are irregularly bordered by riparian forests, sandy beaches and marshes. Numerous streams, which are sometimes bordered by marshes, flow through the region.

The eastern boundary is formed by the Brazilian border along the divide of the Cordillera de Amambay, a range of tall hills (up to 650 m in elevation) which is oriented north-south (Fig. 3). Precipitous hills punctuate the landscape in many areas of Dpto. Amambay, such as at Parque Nacional Cerro Corá (Fig. 17). Elsewhere the region is characterized by gently rolling hills. The Serranía San Luis protrudes above the landscape in northwestern Dpto. Concepción (Fig. 3). These hills are mostly covered by subhumid forests and campos cerrados. Along the east bank of the Paraguay River, precipitous limestone bluffs tower 100 m or so above the river near Puerto Valle Mí (Dpto. Concepción).

Central Paraguay. As its name implies, this region is situated in the central part of the Orient, and includes the Dptos. San Pedro, Cordillera, Central, and portions of Amambay (southern), Canindeyú (western), Caaguazú (western), Paraguarí (eastern), Guairá (western), Caazapá (all but northeast) and Itapúa (central). Ecologically it is the most heterogeneous of the seven regions. Relatively flat marshes, palm savannas and patches of relatively low, humid deciduous forest occur in the vicinity of the Paraguay River, gradually yielding to taller humid forests (Fig. 18) on rolling terrain toward the east. Humid forests once covered most of the region, but have been extensively cleared and now occur in most areas as isolated patches; these forests represent the westernmost extension of the Paranense forest of adjacent Brazil and Argentina. The humid forests of several localities were described in further detail by Keel et al. (1993). Campos cerrados occur in a few areas, but are not as extensive as in the Campos Cerrados region (Esser 1982; Fig. 6).

Acevedo et al. (1990) divided this region into two ecoregions, Litoral Central and Selva Central, but the west-east transition from lower forests to higher forests is so gradual and interrupted by agriculture that a natural boundary cannot be discerned. The northern boundary is formed by the Ypané River and Arroyo Ypané-mi, but the distinction between the plant communities of this region and the Campos Cerrados region is also gradual. The southwestern boundary is imprecisely marked by the zone where relatively flat grasslands and marshes of the Ñeembucú region meet gently rolling hills and taller deciduous forests of the Central Paraguay region to the northeast; the line generally runs southeastward from Villeta (Dpto. Central) to Cerro Acahay (Dpto. Paraguarí), to the triple junction of the Dptos. Paraguarí, Caazapá and Misiones, and to Encarnación (Dpto. Itapúa; Fig. 7).

The eastern boundary of the region is formed by the hilly divide between the Paraguay and Paraná river watersheds, which includes (from north to south) the Cordillera de Amambay, Cordillera de Mbaracayú, Sierra de San Joaquín, Cordillera de Ybytyruzú, and Cordillera de San Rafael (Fig. 3). The highest point along this divide is Cerro Amor, which rises 760 m above sea level in the Cordillera de Ybytyruzú, in Dpto. Caazapá. Several series of hills formed by extrusive volcanic rocks are found in the western portion of the region. These include the precipitous Cordillera de los Altos, which arcs toward the southeast from Dpto. Cordillera into northern Dpto. Paraguarí; the eroded volcanic cone Cerro Acahay, in the middle of Dpto. Paraguarí; and the undulating Serranía de Ybycuí, in eastern Dpto. Paraguarí.

The major rivers of the region, all of which flow westward into the Paraguay River, include (from north to south) the Ypané, Aguary-Guazú/Jejuí-Guazú, Manduvirá, Piribebuy, and the upper reaches of the Tebicuary (Fig. 2). Marshes often border these rather sluggish rivers, especially farther downstream near the Paraguay River. An extensive area of lowland marshes extends to the north and southeast of the Manduvirá River (Fig. 6). The only large lake in the region (and the largest natural lake in Paraguay) is Lago Ypacarai, situated in a downfaulted depression on the border of the Dptos. Central and Cordillera. Lago Ypacarai drains into an extensive marsh bordering the Río Salado at its northern terminus. Lago Verá, in southwestern Dpto. San Pedro, is probably the second largest lake in the region. The Bahía de Asunción, on the northern outskirts of Asunción (Dpto. Central), is perhaps the largest "bay" of the Paraguay River and represents an important stopover site for resident and migratory waterbirds (Fig. 19).

Ñeembucú. This distinctive region occupies the southwestern corner of the Orient. It includes the Dptos. Ñeembucú and Misiones, and portions of Dptos. Central (southern), Paraguarí (western), and Itapúa (western). It is characterized by vast grasslands (Fig. 20) and extensive periodically inundated wetlands (Fig. 6). Palm savannas typical of the Chaco occur in some areas. The landscape is dotted by small patches of low, subhumid Chaco-like forest (8-15 m high) on slightly higher terrain (Fig. 21). The region's terrain is generally flat and low in ele-

vation (Fig. 3); near the confluence of the Paraguay and Paraná rivers the elevation is slightly less than 50 m above sea level. The region superficially resembles the Chaco, as does the adjacent portion of Corrientes Province, Argentina. Short (1975:169) suggested that "possibly the southwestern corner of eastern Paraguay, south of Asunción, should be included" as the Chaco. The Ñeembucú region is contiguous with the western portions of Corrientes and Entre Ríos Provinces, Argentina (east of the Paraná River); these areas are regarded as transitional between the Chaco (west of Paraná River) and Mesopotamia (east of Paraná River; Nores 1987, 1989). Short (1975) considered the western third of Corrientes and northwestern corner of Entre Ríos as pertaining to the Chaco.

The western boundary of the region is delimited by the Paraguay River, and the southern boundary by the Paraná River; both of these boundaries form the border with Argentina. The northeastern boundary is shared with the Central Paraguay region; it is imprecise and was described above. The only other major river in the region is the Tebicuary, which flows westward to the Paraguay River (Fig. 2). In some areas the Tebicuary River is bordered by broad sandy beaches (except when flooded) and dunes, such as at Villa Florida (Dpto. Misiones). In this region the Paraná River widens greatly and is broken up by numerous islands, some of which are very large with extensive sand dunes. The largest islands on the Paraguay side of the river include Yacyretá and Talavera; Apipé Grande, farther downstream, belongs to Argentina. Numerous streams feed extensive marshes and several lakes. The largest lakes are Lago Ypoá (Dptos. Central and Paraguarí) and Lago Verá (Dptos. Ñeembucú and Paraguarí), in the northern part of the region. Although slightly undulating hills occur in the region, none are very high or precipitous.

The Yacyretá hydroelectric dam, completed in 1994, was built across the Paraná River just upstream from Ayolas (Dpto. Misiones). The dam spans Isla Yacyretá (Dpto. Itapúa) and extends eastward along the north bank of the river toward San Cosme y Damián (Dpto. Itapúa). The reservoir (Brooks and Esquivel 1994) holds back 2.1×10^{6} m^3 of water covering a surface area of 1,600 km^2, and extends upstream beyond Encarnación (Dpto. Itapúa).

Alto Paraná. This region, literally the "Upper Paraná," encompasses the upper Paraná River basin in the eastern Orient. It includes Dpto. Alto Paraná and the eastern portions of Dptos. Canindeyú, Caaguazú, Caazapá and Itapúa. It is characterized by rolling hills that are deeply cut by fast-flowing tributaries of the Paraná River. The region was originally covered by tall, humid deciduous forests (often 25 m high; Fig. 22), but most of these forests have been cleared by humans or flooded by hydro-electric dams since 1975. Isolated patches of campos cerrados occur in a few areas (Fig. 6).

The northern boundary of the region is formed by the divide of the Cordillera de Mbaracayú, which also forms the border with Brazil. The western boundary of the region is defined primarily by a se-ries of hilly ranges (up to 760 m in elevation) that divide the Paraguay River and Paraná River water-sheds; these ranges include (from north to south) the Sierra de San Joaquín, Cordillera de Ybytyruzú, and Cordillera de San Rafael (Fig. 3). From the southern terminus of the Cordillera de San Rafael the bound-ary extends southward to Encarnación (Dpto. Itapúa). The southern and eastern boundaries of the region are delimited by the southwestward-flowing Paraná River, which borders Brazil and Argentina.

The major rivers of the region, all of which flow east or southeast toward the Paraná River, include (from north to south) the Piratíy, Carapá, Ytambey, Acaray/Yguazú, Monday, Ñacunday, Yacuy Guazú

Toco Toucan *(Ramphastos toco)*   Dan Brown

and Tembey (Fig. 2). These rivers and other smaller streams generally flow fast, sometimes over rapids and waterfalls of varying height. Some of the rapids and waterfalls were covered when Itaipú Reservoir (Embalse de Itaipú) was formed subsequent to the completion of the Itaipú hydroelectric dam (Represa de Itaipú). The Salto del Guairá (Dpto. Canindeyú), a tremendous waterfall along the Paraná River, was covered by this reservoir. Large waterfalls are still present near the mouths of the Monday, Ñacunday (Fig. 23) and Tembey rivers. Small marshes occur in many areas throughout the region, but are extensive only in the upper portions of the Monday River and its tributaries, where they meander through a relatively flat area (Figs. 2 and 6).

In contrast with the Paraguay River, the channel of the Paraná River in the Alto Paraná region is relatively narrow. Hence, the Paraná flows rapidly (except where it has been dammed), often over large rapids. The volume of water flowing through the Paraná River is estimated to exceed fourfold that of the Paraguay River (Anonymous 1985), but the Paraná is not appreciably wider until it reaches flatter terrain west of Encarnación. Water levels in the Paraná River and its tributaries are generally highest toward the end of the wet season, from February to April, whereas the lowest levels tend to occur at the end of the dry season, from August to October (Anonymous 1985). Day-to-day changes in water levels often fluctuate dramatically as the river quickly drains runoff precipitation.

The Paraná River has been dammed at a point just north of Ciudad Este (Dpto. Alto Paraná) by the Itaipú hydroelectric dam, which generates more electricity than any other dam in the world. The reservoir behind the dam, created in 1982, holds approximately 29×10^9 m^3 of water, and covers a surface area of 1,350 km^2; the reservoir extends upstream above Salto del Guairá (Dpto. Canindeyú), into Brazil. Smaller hydroelectric dams have been built along the Yguazú River just above its confluence with the Acaray River, and along the Acaray River just north of Ciudad del Este; of these, the reservoir behind the Yguazú Hydroelectric Dam is much larger than that of the Acaray. Additional hydroelectric dams are planned for construction along the Paraná River south of Ciudad del Este.

ORNITHOLOGICAL HISTORY

"But I, without having arrived at a visible employment, and without occasion to make myself known to you or anyone else, have spent the twenty best years of my life in the farthest corner of the earth, forgotten even by my friends, without books or rational conversation, and traveling continually through immense and terrifying wildernesses and forests, communicating only with the birds and wild beasts."

F. de Azara (1802b:dedication to brother Nicolás),
translated from Spanish by Beddall (1983:225)

A pervasive feeling of isolation has permeated the history of Paraguayan ornithology. Early naturalists in Paraguay, such as Félix de Azara, often expressed their feelings of isolation. These feelings have been echoed in the writings of later naturalists in Paraguay, who generally worked alone and lacked access to the extensive museum collections and ornithological literature of Europe and North America. Even today, in the age of computers, fax machines and satellite communications, the handful of ornithologists working in Paraguay continue to feel isolated from the international scientific establishment.

The ornithological history of Paraguay is a mixture of contributions by early Spanish explorers and Jesuit missionaries, later American, English and German explorers, visiting American and Argentine ornithologists, and resident Paraguayan naturalists. Much of the basic ornithological exploration of Paraguay was accomplished by foreigners, who often carted away large numbers of collected specimens to distant countries. However, a much greater quantity of specimens was sold to foreign museums by Paraguayan residents who made a living by collecting birds. Many contributions to Paraguayan ornithology were made by foreign ornithologists who had never been there, but nevertheless had access to specimens of birds from Paraguay and other countries in South America.

Although a few ornithologists living in Paraguay amassed considerable specimen collections and made important contributions to the taxonomy and distribution of Paraguayan birds, several of these collections have subsequently perished through neglect. As a consequence, the largest extant collections of Paraguayan birds are located in North America and Europe. Because ornithologists in Paraguay and in foreign countries were often ignorant of each others' publications and viewed the birds of Paraguay from a different perspective, the literature of Paraguayan ornithology is plagued with a confusing plethora of taxonomic names, inconsistent locality spellings, incorrect citations, omissions of earlier literature, and outright errors. Nevertheless it contains a wealth of information on the birds and the people who studied them, and has not been adequately reviewed for more than half a century (Laubmann 1939, 1940, Podtiaguin 1941).

This section reviews the ornithological history of Paraguay, focusing primarily on the background and contributions of people who studied the birds. For organizational purposes I have divided the history of Paraguayan ornithology into six distinct periods. A chronology of publications dealing primarily with Paraguayan ornithology is provided in Appendix 1.

Pre-Columbian Period

The first humans acquainted with Paraguay's birdlife were the various indigenous tribes who arrived in Paraguay several millennia prior to the Europeans' "discovery" of South America. As hunters and gatherers, these tribes were utterly dependent upon birds and other animals and plants for their survival. As a consequence, they acquired extensive first-hand knowledge regarding the customs of the local birds. Even today many indigenous people remain intimately familiar with Paraguay's birds, but little has been published regarding their knowledge and folklore. Earlier explorers frequently commented upon the indians' names and knowledge of birds (e.g., Sánchez Labrador *in* Castex 1968), and modern ornithologists (e.g., Bertoni 1901, Wetmore 1926) and anthropologists (e.g., Cadogan 1973, G. Sequera unpubl.) have done likewise, but no systematic study of the ornithological knowledge and folklore has been published for any indigenous group in Paraguay.

Perhaps the most enduring contribution of the indigenous people to modern ornithology is the names by which many birds are known. Many scientific names and even some English names have a Guaraní origin. For example, the Guaraní word for bird is *guyrá*, from which Guira Cuckoo and its scientific name, *Guira guira* (literally "bird bird"), are derived. The Rosy-billed Pochard (*Netta peposaca*) is known in Guaraní as *ypé pepó sacá*, literally meaning "duck" (*ypé*) with "wings" (*pepó*) that are "transparent" (*sacá*; Schade and Masi Pallarés 1967). Surucua Trogon (*Trogon surrucura*) and other trogons are collectively referred to as *surucuá* in Guaraní. The Crested Caracara (*Polyborus plancus*) is known in Guaraní as *caracará*. In fact, most of the vernacular bird names in both Paraguay and Argentina are derived in part from Guaraní (Schade and Masi Pallarés 1967, 1968, 1969, 1970, 1971, Narosky and Yzurrieta 1987, Navas et al. 1991). Many of these names are based on linguistic imitations of a bird's vocalization (onomatopoeia).

Colonial Period, 1524-1811

The first Spanish explorers arrived in Paraguay in 1524, and discovered that the indigenous Guaraní farmers of eastern Paraguay were far less hostile than the various tribes of hunters and gatherers in surrounding areas. They quickly formed an alliance with the Guaraní and returned to establish the city of Asunción on the east bank of the Paraguay River in 1537. Within a few years Paraguay became the center of a Spanish colonial province that encompassed most of southern South America, and lasted until Paraguay achieved independence from Spain during a bloodless revolution in 1811.

During the first few centuries of the colonial period, Jesuit missionaries successfully established numerous agricultural colonies in eastern Paraguay in an effort to convert the Guaraní indians to Christianity. Several of the priests recorded their observations on the region's natural history (Ferreiro 1965, Gorham 1973b, Argüello M. de Masulli 1983). For example, José Guevara studied the habits of the Scale-throated Hermit (*Phaethornis eurynome*), and Miguel Marimón collected and classified about 200 species of animals, including birds. However, the most energetic natural historian among the Jesuits was Francisco José Sánchez Labrador, who arrived in South America in 1734 and remained until the Jesuits were expelled from Paraguay by royal decree in 1767.

Sánchez Labrador wrote extensively about virtually every subject regarding Paraguay, which at that time encompassed a much larger geographical area than it does today. Although numerous volumes of his writings have appeared in print, most of his six volumes titled "Paraguay Natural" remain unpublished, with the original manuscript archived in Rome. However, Sánchez Labrador's entire manuscript (127 hand-written pages) on the birds of Paraguay was published by Castex (1968). Sánchez Labrador first addressed general subjects regarding birds (e.g., anatomy, nesting, etc.) and then wrote extensively about the names, customs and culinary uses of Paraguayan birds, and even included a discussion of bats within the chapter on night birds. Although Sánchez Labrador provided the first ornithological summary for southern South America, his unpublished writings have long been overlooked by historians, who generally credit Félix de Azara as the "father of ornithology" in southern South America (Argüello M. de Masulli 1983).

The most influential natural historian in South America during the eighteenth century was Félix de Azara (Beddall 1975, 1983, Fernández Pérez 1992), a Spanish soldier who arrived in Buenos Aires in 1781 to assist in delineating the boundaries between the Spanish and Portuguese colonies in South America. In 1784 Azara was reassigned to Asunción, where he waited 13 years for the Portuguese to send their representatives. During this period Azara occupied himself by mapping the region and studying its flora and fauna. Azara's extensive collections and observations of birds were aided by Pedro Blás Noseda, a priest at San Ignacio (Dpto. Misiones), whose contributions were summarized by Selva (1917). By 1796 the Portuguese representatives still had not arrived, so Azara was reassigned to Buenos Aires and returned to Spain in 1801. Azara's collections, most of which have subsequently perished, were sent to Madrid, and his writings were soon published in Spanish and French. Azara (1802a, 1805a, b) described 448 different birds, a number later reduced to 381 when duplications of sex, age and plumage were taken into account (Beddall 1983). These were assigned numbers and descriptive vernacular names rather than binomial scientific names, and were later identified or properly named by Temminck, Viellot and Lichtenstein (Berlepsch 1887). After more information became available, Azara's bird list was further revised by Hartlaub (1847), Berlepsch (1887), Bertoni (1901),

Podtiaguin (1941), Pereyra (1945) and Fernández Pérez (1992).

Early Independence Period, 1811-1870

Paraguay's first six decades of "independence" were characterized by an isolationist policy imposed by José Gaspar Rodríguez de Francia, Paraguay's first president and undisputed dictator. Although his policies were softened somewhat by his successors, first Carlos Antonio López and then Francisco Solano López, they were hardly conducive to the study of natural history.

In 1853, the United States government dispatched Captain Thomas J. Page on a naval expedition to explore the tributaries of the La Plata River and to establish diplomatic relations and commerce with the neighboring countries, including Paraguay, then ruled by Francisco López. Between 1853 and 1856, William H. Powell and Robert Carter collected birds for the expedition while aboard the steamer *Water Witch*. They cruised through Paraguay intermittently from late September 1853 to early October 1854. The birds collected were sent to the Academy of Natural Sciences of Philadelphia and were briefly described by Cassin (1859). A full account of the expedition was published by Page (1859).

Captain Page apparently returned to Argentina and Paraguay in 1859 and 1860 (specimens in National Museum of Natural History, Collar et al. 1992:247), but no details of the expedition were published.

Between Wars Period, 1870-1935

In spite of the political chaos following the disastrous War of the Triple Alliance (1865-1870), much progress was made in the study of natural history during the succeeding years. With its male population decimated and the economy in shambles, Paraguay opened up its borders to the outside world. As a consequence, educated immigrants and visiting scholars contributed substantially to the country's intellectual development.

From December 1885 to February 1886, Ricardo Rohde, a German traveler who studied ethnology in Paraguay, collected 229 birds of 116 species in the vicinity of Lambaré (Dpto. Central), and also along the Pilcomayo River. Rohde's collection,

which was sent to the Berliner Museum in Germany, was described by Berlepsch (1887).

In 1889, the British ornithologist J. J. Dalgleish published a report on a collection of eggs sent to the British Museum (Natural History) in London by an unnamed collector at Estancia Ytañú, Dpto. Central (Dalgleish 1889).

In March 1890, the British naturalist J. Graham Kerr accompanied a detachment of British and Argentinian soldiers on a reconnaissance of the Pilcomayo River aboard the steamer Bolivia. The river's narrow course was tortuous and practically unnavigable. After great hardships they reached their farthest point along the river's northern branch, naming it Fortín Page (north bank of river in Dpto. Presidente Hayes), in June, but then became stranded as the river dried up. A series of disasters befell the expedition, culminating in the tragic death of Captain Juan Page, an Argentinian, in August. A military relief expedition rescued them in October, but Kerr remained with the garrison at Fortín Page until March 1891. Kerr (1891, 1892) described the birds observed and collected during the expedition, and vividly recounted their epic adventures. The collection was sent to the British Museum.

During the 1890s, the Italian collector Alfredo Borelli traveled extensively in Bolivia, Brazil, Paraguay and Argentina. In Paraguay, Borelli collected roughly 145 species of birds in areas to the east of Asunción (Dpto. Central) between June and August 1893, and to the north of Concepción (Dpto. Concepción) from August to November 1893. Borelli's collections, which were deposited in the Museo Zoologico di Torino (in Italy), were described by Salvadori (1894, 1895, 1900).

In September 1896, J. Graham Kerr left Asunción on yet another expedition, this time traveling northward on a steamer up the Paraguay River, accompanied by J. S. Budgett. After a pause at Concepción (Dpto. Concepción), they traveled to Puerto Carayá Vuelta (Dpto. Presidente Hayes) and then overland toward the southwest, arriving a week later at the mission station Waikthlatingmayalwa (possibly Misión Inglesa, Dpto. Presidente Hayes). They remained in the area and collected birds and other animals for the British Museum until at least May 1897 (Sclater 1897, Kerr 1901).

The most productive ornithologist in Paraguay during the early twentieth century was Arnaldo de Winkelried Bertoni, a young Swiss immigrant who arrived with his family in Buenos Aires in 1884. Bertoni's wealthy family soon established Puerto Bertoni on the west bank of the Paraná River (Dpto. Alto Paraná). Winkelried's father, Moisés Santiago Bertoni, became well known for his publications in botany, agriculture and other subjects. Winkelried followed his father's footsteps as a natural historian, but found his own niche by specializing in the vertebrates of Paraguay.

Winkelried Bertoni began collecting birds and other vertebrates in 1890. In 1897, Bertoni spent several months in Caaguazú (Dpto. Caaguazú) collecting birds with Natalicio Noce. Shortly afterward they sent a collection of over 100 species to a museum somewhere in Europe (Robebar 1930, Podtiaguin 1941), but the sources do not specify where. Bertoni quickly recognized the usefulness of many species of birds to agriculture, and published a catalog of these species (Bertoni 1898, 1900).

After accumulating material for a decade, Bertoni published a volume describing many species of birds that he thought were new to science, and appended a catalog listing each species recorded in Paraguay and the number, when appropriate, of each species described by Azara (Bertoni 1901). In his introduction, Bertoni lamented the fact that he lacked access to the specimens and literature of the European museums, and stated that his volume was written to the best of his ability with what little material he had available. Nevertheless, Enrique Lynch Arribálzaga, an Argentinian ornithologist, published a critique of Bertoni's volume in which he identified most of Bertoni's "new" species as previously described species (Lynch Arribálzaga 1902). Shortly afterward, the Brazilian ornithologist H. von Ihering published a revised list of the birds of Paraguay (Ihering 1904), including the species described by Bertoni (1901) and identified by Lynch Arribálzaga (1902).

Resolved to be more cautious, Bertoni continued to publish papers on Paraguayan birds (Bertoni 1903a, b, 1904, 1907, 1913) and other vertebrates, but he avoided describing new species of birds. In 1914, Bertoni published the first catalog of the vertebrates of Paraguay, which included a section on birds (Bertoni 1914a). During the next few decades Bertoni published many other papers on Paraguayan ornithology (Bertoni 1914b-d, 1918a-e, 1919a, b, 1922a, b, 1923a, b, 1924, 1925a, b, 1926, 1927, 1928a-c, 1929, 1930a, b), including a revised index of his 1901 volume (Bertoni 1918e). Bertoni's stud-

ies eventually culminated in a complete revision of his catalog of the vertebrates of Paraguay (Bertoni 1939). Tragically, his collections, which were maintained at the family's estate at Puerto Bertoni, have disappeared.

Bertoni was not the only active collector in Paraguay during the early twentieth century. The British immigrant William T. Foster arrived in Paraguay in 1894, and resided in Sapucái (Dpto. Paraguarí), where he obtained large collections of vertebrates and invertebrates. Portions of his bird collections were sent to the United States National Museum in Washington, D.C. (78 specimens reported by Oberholser 1901, 1902), the British Museum (several hundred specimens reported by Sharpe 1905, Chubb 1910) and the Museo Nacional de Buenos Aires (Argentina, now the Museo Nacional de Ciencias Naturales "Bernardino Rivadavia"; several specimens reported by Partridge [1954]). Foster also established the Museo de Historia Natural de la Escuela Normal de Asunción (Dpto. Central; Robebar 1930), but this museum no longer exists (Podtiaguin 1941). Although Foster published papers on many natural history subjects (Robebar 1930), he apparently published nothing on birds.

Another contemporary of Bertoni was Félix Posner, a Hungarian immigrant who collected birds for many years, beginning in 1907 (Robebar 1930). Posner began collecting birds in the vicinity of Villarrica (Dpto. Guairá), and a sample of 86 species was sent to the Museo Nacional de Buenos Aires and described by Dabbene (1912). Posner later obtained a collection of 350 birds of 141 species in the vicinity of Villa Hayes (Dpto. Presidente Hayes); this collection was deposited in the Museo de Historia Natural de la Sociedad Científica del Paraguay in Asunción (Dpto. Central), and described by Bertoni (1930a) and Podtiaguin (1944).

Between July and November 1909, the British ornithologist Claude H. B. Grant collected birds in Paraguay while traveling along the Paraguay River northward to Mato Grosso, Brazil. His collections were deposited in the British Museum (Grant 1911).

At some time prior to 1914, Lord Brabourne spent 15 months in Paraguay, mostly in the vicinity of Villarrica (Dpto. Guairá). Brabourne obtained a variety of live birds that were apparently taken to England (Brabourne 1914).

In November 1913, the American naturalists George K. Cherrie, an ornithologist, and Leo E. Miller, a mammalogist, spent two weeks collecting birds in the vicinity of Asunción (Dpto. Central) during the Roosevelt Expedition. The expedition traveled northward along the Paraguay River and continued on through the interior of Brazil. Cherrie returned to Paraguay in September and October 1916, and collected Chaco birds at Fort Wheeler (presumably near Fortín Guaraní, Dpto. Presidente Hayes) and Puerto Pinasco (Dpto. Presidente Hayes). Their collection of about 477 specimens from Paraguay (data from unpublished catalogs) was taken to the American Museum of Natural History in New York City, and several new species and subspecies were described by Cherrie and Reichenberger (1921, 1923). A more detailed account of the 1913 trip was published by Cherrie (*in* Naumburg 1930).

In 1914 the Paraguayan botanist Carlos Fiebrig established the Jardín Botánico in Asunción (Dpto. Central). The Jardín Botánico is a large park with botanical gardens, a zoo, and a small building known as the Museo de Historia Natural del Paraguay. The museum's small collection of mounted bird skins was obtained primarily by Juan B. Caballero, who collected birds throughout the country (Podtiaguin 1941). Some of the museum's specimens were described in an essay on Paraguay's birds by Fiebrig (1921). The collection still exists, and is displayed in glass cabinets. However, it is in poor condition and has few locality data.

In 1920, Roberto Redder collected birds along the Apa River in Dpto. Concepción. One of his specimens, deposited in the Museo Argentino de Ciencias Naturales, was reported by Zotta (1940).

Francisco H. Schade, an Austrian immigrant, initially resided in Villarrica (Dpto. Guairá), where he collected birds as well as other animals during the 1920s and 1930s. Some of his specimens were sent to foreign museums. The Field Museum of Natural History in Chicago received 199 specimens collected by Schade between 1922 and 1931 (data from unpublished catalogs), and the University of Michigan Museum of Zoology at Ann Arbor received 105 specimens (Storer 1989) collected by Schade between 1922 and 1929 (data from unpublished catalogs). Schade and his son continued collecting birds in Paraguay for many decades, and eventually moved to San Lorenzo, where Schade held several government posts. His personal collection formed the nucleus of the Museo de Zoología de la Facultad de Agronomía y Veterinaria on the campus of the Universidad Nacional de Asunción, in San Lorenzo (Dpto. Central). Schade curated the museum's collection.

Although Schade's research focused primarily on invertebrates (Ferreiro 1965, Gorham 1973, Argüello M. de Masulli 1983), he and parasitologist R. Masi Pallarés eventually published an annotated checklist of the birds of Paraguay, in which they noted the specimens present at the university's Museo de Zoología (Schade and Masi Pallarés 1967, 1968, 1969, 1970, 1971). Schade's massive collection still exists at the university, where it is displayed on tables in a large, open room. However, it is rapidly deteriorating and will eventually perish if not salvaged soon.

During 1920 and 1921, the American ornithologist Alexander Wetmore spent nearly a year collecting birds in Paraguay, Chile, Argentina and Uruguay, for the United States National Museum (Wetmore 1926). Wetmore arrived by ship in Asunción (Dpto. Central) in late August 1920, and shortly afterward traveled northward to Puerto Pinasco (Dpto. Presidente Hayes). During the next month, Wetmore collected birds in nearby areas on both banks of the river and traveled by rail 200 km west of Puerto Pinasco. He returned to Asunción in early October and then traveled toward Buenos Aires by train. Wetmore's collection of about 206 specimens (data from unpublished catalogs) from Paraguay was described in several publications (Wetmore 1922, 1926, 1927).

In August 1928, the Argentinian ornithologist J. B. Daguerre collected 138 specimens of birds at Puerto Guaraní (Dpto. Alto Paraguay) for the Museo Argentino de Ciencias Naturales. Several specimen records were reported by Zotta (1938, 1940, 1950) and Partridge (1954).

During the late 1920s and early 1930s, Emil Kaempfer collected over 10,000 specimens of birds in South America (mostly in Brazil) for the American Museum of Natural History. In Paraguay, Kaempfer collected in Dpto. Concepción from late July to late September 1930, and again in May 1931; in Dptos. Caaguazú, Guairá and Caazapá from late September 1930 to early February 1931; and to the west of Puerto Pinasco (Dpto. Presidente Hayes) during March and April 1931 (Naumburg 1935). Although Kaempfer collected about 1575 specimens from Paraguay (data from unpublished catalogs), relatively few specimen records were published in Naumburg's (1937, 1939) studies of part of Kaempfer's collection. However, data for other Kaempfer specimens are widely scattered in the ornithological literature (e.g., Zimmer 1950, 1953a, 1955, Short 1975, Hayes et al. 1994).

The Museo de la Sociedad Científica del Paraguay was established by Andrés Barbero in 1929 at Avenida España in Asunción (Dpto. Central). The museum included a natural history section referred to as the Museo de Historia Natural de la Sociedad Científica del Paraguay (Podtiaguin 1941). Although an ethnological museum and library still occupy the site, the bird collection apparently no longer exists. Nevertheless, the museum and the society quickly became the country's center of ornithological activity, but only for a few decades. During its heyday several Paraguayan naturalists were associated with the society and collected specimens for the society's museum. As the society's first president, Barbero's personal contribution to Paraguayan ornithology comprised a list of birds observed along the Confuso River in southern Dpto. Presidente Hayes (Bertoni 1930b).

Facundo R. Insfran, a young Paraguayan naturalist, accumulated observations on Paraguay's birds from as early as 1914 (Insfran 1931) until his premature death in 1936 (Podtiaguin 1941). His observations formed the basis of several short notes in the society's journal (Insfran 1929, 1930, 1931, 1936).

Juan C. Vogt, another Paraguayan naturalist, traveled to Caaguazú (Dpto. Caaguazú) with collectors from the Jardín Botánico in Asunción (Dpto. Central). Vogt published a note on his observations of toucans (Vogt 1931), and later joined the staff of the Museo de Historia Natural de la Sociedad Científica del Paraguay (Podtiaguin 1941).

During the 1920s and early 1930s, the German scholar Hans Krieg led several scientific expeditions to the interior of South America. During Krieg's third expedition in 1931 and 1932, approximately 1300 specimens of birds were obtained in Paraguay by Krieg, Michael Kiefer and Eugen Schuhmacher. The expedition arrived in Asunción (Dpto. Central) during May 1931, and collected along the west bank of the Paraguay River while working its way northward. During the next several months they collected birds as far north as Puerto Sastre (Dpto. Alto Paraguay), and traveled 145 km west into the central Paraguayan Chaco, where Mennonites of German descent had recently established a colony. From September 1931 to the middle of January 1932, they collected in areas to the east of the Paraguay River in Dpto. Concepción, and then spent the latter half of January and all of February in Dpto. San Pedro. After a brief stay in Asunción in early March, the expedition traveled east into Dpto. Guairá, where they continued collecting until returning to Asunción in April. The specimens obtained during Krieg's expeditions were deposited in the Münchener Museum in Germany, and were reported by Alfred Laubmann (1930, 1933a, b, 1935, 1937, 1939, 1940) and by Krieg and Schuhmacher (1936). Laubmann's final two volumes (1939, 1940) provided the most detailed accounts of bird distribution in Paraguay. An excellent overview of the expeditions was provided by Krieg (1948).

Post Chaco War Period, 1935-1972

Paraguay suffered immensely during the Chaco War with Bolivia (1932-1935), and ornithological exploration was curtailed as a result. Some workers, such as Alberto Schulze, somehow managed to collect birds throughout the war.

Schulze was possibly the most ambitious bird collector ever in Paraguay. He apparently began collecting around 1930 and continued through at least 1941. Unfortunately, little is known about Schulze; even less is known about most of his coworkers, who included Loesch, López, Haack, Huber (first names not known) and Jakob Unger. Between 1931 and 1942, Schulze and his coworkers sent 4942 specimens to the University of Michigan Museum of Zoology (Storer 1989) and about 542 specimens to the Field Museum of Natural History (data from unpublished catalogs). An additional collection of 44 specimens, collected by Schulze, Huber and López, was purchased from Major L. R. Wolfe by the National Museum of Natural History (formerly the United States National Museum; data from unpublished catalogs). Schulze's specimens were reported in publications by Brodkorb (1934, 1935, 1937a-c, 1938a-c, 1939a-c, 1941a, b), Conover (1934, 1937), Zimmer (1953b), Weller (1967) and Short (1972b, c).

An examination of the unpublished catalogs of the University of Michigan Museum of Zoology indicates that Schulze apparently lived in Horqueta

(Dpto. Concepción), where he collected intermittently from December 1930 through July 1938. Schulze's name came first on all specimen labels, but apparently his coworkers did much of the collecting because birds were often obtained simultaneously in different parts of the country.

In the Chaco, collecting by Schulze et al. took place at the following places and periods: to the west of Puerto La Victoria (Dpto. Alto Paraguay) during May 1934, January 1935, 7-9 months per year during 1936-1939 and during March and October 1940 (Schulze, López and Unger); at Puerto Pinasco (Dpto. Presidente Hayes) from late October 1937 to early January 1938 (Schulze and López); at Riacho Caballero (Dpto. Presidente Hayes) from late January to early February 1938 and in June 1938 (Schulze and Haack); at Campo Esperanza (Dpto. Presidente Hayes) during September 1936, June 1938, April, May and October 1940 (Schulze and Unger); at Estero Patiño and "235 km W of the Riacho Negro" (Dpto. Presidente Hayes) from June to September 1939 (Schulze and Haack; see Methods section for further details); and at Colonia Fernheim (Dpto. Boquerón) during March 1940 (Schulze and Unger).

In the Orient, collecting by Schulze et al. took place at the following places and periods: within 70 km of Rosario (Dpto. San Pedro) during February, March and August 1935, the latter half of 1937, intermittently during six months of 1938, and during January and February 1939 (Schulze, Loesch, Huber and Haack); at Cordillera de Amambay, near Capitán Bado (Dpto. Amambay) from August to November 1938 (Schulze); and at Puerto Gibaja (Dpto. Alto Paraná) from July to October 1940 (Schulze). At some time around 1940, Schulze apparently moved to Areguá (Dpto. Central), where he collected intermittently during 1940 and 1941.

Between 1934 and 1938, the German immigrant Adolfo Neunteufel and his companion Gröpel (first name not known) collected birds in southern Dpto. Itapúa. Several specimens sent to the Münchener Museum were reported by Laubmann (1935, 1937, 1939, 1940). Other specimens sent to the Museo Argentino de Ciencias Naturales were reported by Giai (1949) and Partridge (1953, 1954, 1956).

In December 1939, the zoologist B. Podtiaguin, a Russian immigrant employed by the Ministerio de Agricultura, led an expedition under the auspices of the Sociedad Científica del Paraguay to the Apa River in northern Dpto. Concepción. A collection of 65 specimens representing 32 species was deposited in the Museo de Historia Natural de la Sociedad Científica del Paraguay (Podtiaguin 1941). Podtiaguin later published a series of three detailed papers on the ornithology of Paraguay (Podtiaguin 1941, 1944, 1945). The series was apparently intended to represent a comprehensive catalog of records for each species, but unfortunately Podtiaguin did not even finish with the non-passerines. Nevertheless, the series contains a wealth of information on ornithological history, biogeography, distribution, systematics, behavior, nesting, and the results of the 1939 expedition to the Apa River, all arranged in an amazingly haphazard fashion.

Pedro Willim, a resident of Nueva Italia (Dpto. Central), was another Paraguayan collector who was active during this period. At some time prior to 1941, Willim obtained a collection of 127 specimens that was obtained by Barbero for the Museo de Historia Natural de la Sociedad Científica del Paraguay (Podtiaguin 1941). Between 1939 and 1945, Willim collected extensively at Nueva Italia and at numerous localities in the Chaco. Most of his collecting in the Chaco took place between June and September 1945, when he and Jakob Unger began collecting to the west of Puerto La Victoria (Dpto. Alto Paraguay), continued southwestward through Colonia Menno (Dpto. Boquerón), and eventually reached Fortín Guachalla (Dpto. Boquerón) on the north bank of the Pilcomayo River. Willim sent roughly 283 specimens to the American Museum of Natural History and 502 specimens to the Field Museum of Natural History (data from unpublished catalogs). The specimens collected by Willim formed the basis of several publications (e.g., Podtiaguin 1941, 1944, 1945, Willim 1947, Blake 1949, Conover 1950, Short 1975).

In October and November 1944, Andrés G. Giai and his companion Cranwell (first name not known) collected birds for the Museo Argentino de Ciencias Naturales at Puerto La Victoria (Dpto. Alto Paraguay). Some of their specimen records were reported by Zotta (1950) and Partridge (1954).

The Mennonite naturalist Jakob Unger, another energetic bird collector in Paraguay, appears to have been the only active collector in Paraguay between 1950 and 1975. Unger immigrated to Paraguay in 1932 (Steinbacher 1962) and initially resided at Orloff, a subdivision of Colonia Fernheim (Dpto. Boquerón) in the central Paraguayan Chaco. During the next few decades Unger collected extensively in the Paraguayan Chaco, mostly in the vicinity of Orloff and, after 1960, at Lichtenau, a subdivision of Colonia Menno (Dpto. Boquerón), where he apparently moved. Nearly all of Unger's specimens were sold to foreign museums. Although a small museum in Filadelfia (Dpto. Boquerón) is named in his honor, it has only a few dozen of Unger's bird specimens, which lack dates and localities.

Unger collected birds in the Alto Chaco region with Schulze in 1938 and 1939 (specimens sent to the University of Michigan Museum of Zoology), and with Willim in 1945 (specimens sent to the Field Museum of Natural History). According to Steinbacher (1962), Unger sent a collection of birds to Bethel College in Kansas. Presumably part (or all) of this collection was purchased from H. S. Bender of Goshen College, Indiana, by the National Museum of Natural History. The latter collection includes about 316 specimens obtained in the vicinity of Orloff during 1939 and 1940 (data from unpublished catalogs). The specimen labels do not give Unger's name, but the handwriting appears identical to Unger's handwriting on specimen labels in other museums (pers. obs.). Between 1944 and 1948, Unger obtained a collection of 1050 bird specimens that was sent to the Field Museum of Natural History (data from unpublished catalogs). Between 1955 and 1957, Unger collected 666 specimens that were sent to the Senckenberg Museum in Frankfurt (Germany), and another 641 specimens that were sent to the Museum Alexander Koenig in Bonn (Germany); these specimens were reported by Steinbacher (1962). Another collection of 266 specimens, obtained during 1960, 1962, 1963 and 1966, was sent to the Senckenberg Museum and reported by Steinbacher (1968). A final collection of 723 specimens, obtained from 1960 to 1974 (Short 1976a), was sent to the American Museum of Natural History and reported by Short (1972a, 1975, 1976a, b).

During the 1960s and early 1970s, the Paraguayan parasitologist R. Masi Pallarés, of the Facultad de Agronomía y Veterinaria of the Universidad Nacional de Asunción, published several papers on the parasites found in Paraguayan birds (e.g., Masi Pallarés 1969, Masi Pallarés and Usher 1972a, b). Masi Pallarés also collaborated with F. Schade on a

summary of the birds in Paraguay (Schade and Masi Pallarés 1967, 1968, 1969, 1970, 1971).

Raúl Leonardo Carman, a correspondent for the Argentinian magazine *Camping*, reported his observations of Troupials (*Icterus icterus*) in the Paraguayan Chaco during August 1969 (Carman 1971).

Modern Period, 1972-present

Beginning in the 1970s, collectors began to record more than just the date, locality and sex on specimen labels. During August and September 1972 and September 1973, the mammalogist Philip Myers collected 23 specimens of birds for the University of California's Museum of Vertebrate Zoology in Berkeley (data from unpublished catalogs). In 1973 he was joined by his brother, the ornithologist John P. Myers, who added another 16 specimens to the museum's collection (data from unpublished catalogs). J. P. Myers's observations on shorebirds in Paraguay were published in Myers and Myers (1979); some of the specimen records were published later by Hayes et al. (1990a).

In August 1972, Gregory Schmitt, John P. Hubbard and Juan Guggiari briefly collected birds for the Denver Museum of Natural History in the Paraguayan Chaco (Schmitt and Hubbard 1974).

A dramatic increase in ornithological investigation commenced during the late 1970s, when several field parties led by Philip Myers, who had become a curator at the University of Michigan Museum of Zoology, collected 1167 bird specimens throughout Paraguay during the austral winters of 1976-1979 (Storer 1989). The field parties were accompanied by the ornithologist Robert W. Storer, also from the University of Michigan, during 1978 and 1979. The ornithologist Ned K. Johnson of the University of California at Berkeley joined the University of Michigan group during 1979, and collected 64 specimens of birds for the Museum of Vertebrate Zoology (data from unpublished catalogs). The specimens obtained during the University of Michigan expeditions formed the basis of several publications (Myers and Hansen 1980, Storer 1981, 1989, Goodman and Glynn 1988, Hayes et al. 1990a).

Up until 1980, virtually all papers on Paraguayan ornithology focused primarily on distributional records and systematics of birds, with only a few anecdotal accounts of their behavior and ecology. This changed when the biologist Mercedes S. Foster, of the United States Fish and Wildlife Service, intermittently studied the ecology of frugivorous birds at Hotel El Tirol (Dpto. Itapúa) during 1976-1983. Her studies resulted in several publications (Foster 1981, 1985, 1987a, b, 1990, Foster et al. 1989). On occasion Foster was accompanied by N. K. Johnson; the birds collected by Foster and Johnson were deposited at the National Museum of Natural History and the Museum of Vertebrate Zoology.

In 1977, the American ornithologist Robert S. Ridgely, then at Yale University, spent most of July and August observing birds throughout Paraguay. Ridgely subsequently moved to the Academy of Natural Sciences of Philadelphia, and returned to Paraguay in August and September 1982, this time with bird photographer John Dunning. A few collected specimens were donated to the National Museum of Natural History. Ridgely returned to Paraguay again in May and June 1992, traveling with Louis Bevier, Timothy Burke and Paul Scharf. Some of Ridgely's observations were incorporated into several publications (Ridgely 1981, Ridgely and Tudor 1989, 1994, Hayes et al. 1994).

Also in 1977, the American ornithologist Raymond A. Paynter, Jr., of Harvard University, published the first ornithological gazetteer of Paraguay, which included coordinates and other details for the various collecting sites in Paraguay, plus a bibliography of Paraguayan ornithology (Paynter and Caperton 1977). This initial gazetteer was later revised and expanded by Paynter (1989).

Theo Kleefisch, Jr., a German traveler, visited the Paraguayan Chaco during the late 1970s or early 1980s, and briefly reported his observations on birds in the vicinity of Filadelfia (Dpto. Boquerón) and Puesto Estancia-í (Dpto. Presidente Hayes; Kleefisch 1983).

Mercedes S. Foster became involved in a cooperative project with the Paraguayan government, which was initiated in 1979 when United States Peace Corps Volunteers David and Diane Wood urged administrators of Paraguay's Servicio Forestal Nacional to request assistance from the United States government in establishing a permanent biological inventory and natural history museum in Paraguay. After agreements were worked out between the Servicio Forestal Nacional (a branch of the Ministerio de Agricultura y Ganadería) and the U. S. Fish and Wildlife Service, a group of prospective Paraguayan biologists joined professional American biologists on several field trips to Paraguayan national parks, beginning in 1980, where the Paraguayans were trained in biological field techniques (Foster 1983). Several U. S. Peace Corps Volunteers accompanied the field trips, and an agreement was made whereby U. S. Peace Corps biologists would assist the project's personnel during the first ten years. A small museum collection was subsequently established in the offices of the Servicio Forestal Nacional in Asunción (Dpto. Central). Some of the bird specimens collected during the project were deposited at the National Museum of Natural History and at the Museum of Vertebrate Zoology.

The project became known as the Inventario Biológico Nacional and received assistance from numerous international institutions. The ornithology section was organized by Foster, and specimens were initially collected throughout the country by Christian Bogado, María Elena Escobar E., Nancy E. López (de Kochalka), Mario Rolón and Peace Corps Volunteer Richard White. López received a scholarship for several months of training in the United States and became employed as the project's official ornithologist. López eventually received a Master's degree in wildlife management from the Universidad Nacional in Costa Rica, and became Paraguay's only professionally trained ornithologist.

Because of financial constraints, only López remained permanently on the project's ornithology staff. Peace Corps Volunteer White left in late 1982 and was briefly replaced by Peter W. Wendelken in 1983. By 1986 the project had outgrown its cramped offices in Asunción (Dpto. Central), and moved into a vacant building on the campus of the Universidad Nacional de Asunción in San Lorenzo (Dpto. Central). When López left Paraguay for two years of graduate studies in early 1987, Felicita E. Areco de Medina was hired to be the counterpart of arriving Peace Corps Volunteer Floyd E. Hayes. In 1989, John Luís Ramírez joined the ornithology staff, Areco de Medina left for another government post, and Hayes left for graduate studies at the end of the year. During 1988 and 1989, two of the museum's personnel, Nora Neris and Flavio Colmán, were employed by the American mammalogist Andrew Taber to assist with his studies of the Chacoan

Peccary (*Catagonus wagneri*) in the Alto Chaco region. During the project Neris and Colmán collected specimens for the ornithology section.

In 1989 the official name of the Inventario Biológico Nacional was briefly changed to Centro de Estudios y Colecciones Biológicas para la Conservación. In 1990 its name was changed again to Museo Nacional de Historia Natural del Paraguay. Since its inception, the Inventario Biológico Nacional/Museo Nacional de Historia Natural del Paraguay has accumulated a rapidly growing collection of plants and animals that are maintained in modern museum cabinets. The bird collection now includes roughly a thousand specimens. The ornithology section has conducted field projects that have resulted in numerous publications (e.g., Anonymous 1982a, Foster and Fitzgerald 1982, Wendelken 1983, Anonymous 1985, López 1985, 1986a, b, undated, Contreras et al. 1988a, b, Hayes and Areco de Medina 1988, Hayes and Escobar Argaña 1990, Hayes et al 1990a, b, Hayes 1991, Hayes and Fox 1991, Neris and Colmán 1991, Hayes 1992, in press, Hayes and Granizo Tamayo 1992, López 1992, 1993, Hayes et al. 1994).

Other Paraguayan institutions were also active during this period. Itaipú Binacional, the entity responsible for the Itaipú hydroelectric dam, initiated a faunal survey of the Alto Paraná region in 1977. The Museo de Historia Natural de Itaipú Binacional was subsequently established at Vivero Forestal, in Hernandarias (Dpto. Alto Paraná), and numerous collecting trips were made in Dptos. Alto Paraná and Canindeyú. Most of the specimens were collected by two technicians, Andrés Colmán and Nelson Pérez, who became well acquainted with the region's birdlife. The museum's bird collection includes over 700 specimens (Cabrera and Escobar 1991), but little has been published on the results of the museum's work. Perez et al. (1988) summarized the first decade of Itaipú Binacional's faunistic studies, and various records have been published by Colmán and Pérez (1991) and Contreras et al. (1992a, b).

During the 1980s, various faculty members and students of the Instituto de Ciencias Básicas of the Universidad Nacional de Asunción in San Lorenzo (Dpto. Central), under the leadership of Narciso González Romero, participated in several field projects with other institutions. Lists of species for various localities formed the basis of several publications (e.g., Escobar and Salomón 1983, González Torres and González Romero 1985, Contreras and González Romero 1988, 1989a, b, 1991, González Romero et al. 1988, J. R. Contreras et al. 1989, González Romero and Contreras 1989, Contreras et al. 1990).

The Centro de Datos para la Conservación was jointly established in 1986 by The Nature Conservancy and Paraguay's Ministerio de Agricultura y Ganadería, with offices in downtown Asunción (Dpto. Central). The primary purpose of the Centro de Datos was to establish a comprehensive data base aimed at promoting conservation in Paraguay. Three of their biologists, Celeste Acevedo Gómez, Tarsicio Granizo Tamayo and Peace Corps Volunteer Jennifer A. Fox, became involved in ornithological studies, and often worked in conjunction with Hayes and the Argentinian biologist Julio Rafael Contreras (see below). Several publications (e.g., J. R. Contreras et al. 1988a, b, 1989, Acevedo Gómez 1989, Acevedo et al. 1990, Granizo and Hayes 1989, Hayes and Fox 1991, Hayes and Granizo Tamayo 1992) and unpublished technical reports by Centro de Datos staff included pertinent data on the birds of Paraguay. Fox left in 1989, and Granizo Tamayo departed in 1990 to establish a new Centro de Datos in Ecuador, his native country.

The Fundación Moisés Bertoni para la Conservación de la Naturaleza was established in 1988 as a private conservation organization, with its headquarters in Asunción (Gauto 1989). Its primary contribution to ornithology stems from its involvement in the establishment, management and biological exploration of Reserva Natural del Bosque Mbaracayú (Brooks et al. 1993), and its publication of a preliminary list of birds in the reserve (Meisel et al. 1992).

Visiting scientists and birders contributed substantially to Paraguayan ornithology during the 1980s and early 1990s. During portions of 1983 and 1984, the Spanish biologists Salvador J. Peris, from the Universidad de Salamanca, and Francisco Suarez, from the Universidad Cumpletense, studied the birds of the Bajo Chaco in conjunction with the Paraguayan biologist Luis Cabello of the Instituto de Ciencias Básicas. Their studies resulted in several publications (Peris and Suarez 1985a, 1985b, Peris et al. 1987, Peris 1990).

The Argentinian biologist Julio Rafael Contreras, together with his son, Andrés Oscar Contreras, and adopted daughter, Yolanda Ester Davies,

Figure 8. Geographical regions shown in relation to Paraguay's major cities and highways. Map by Cindy Lippincott.

34

Figure 9. Channels and islands along the Paraguay River at Concepción, Dpto. Concepción. Photo by Floyd E. Hayes, May 1989.

Figure 11. Thorn scrub forest typical of the Alto Chaco region, east of Fortín Toledo, Dpto. Boquerón. Partial defoliation of the vegetation is typical during the dry winter season. Photo by Floyd E. Hayes, August 1994.

Figure 12. Scrub forest flooded by Paraguay River in the Matogrosense region, west of Puerto 14 de Mayo, Dpto. Alto Paraguay. Photo by Floyd E. Hayes, August 1989.

Figure 13. A small stream (*riacho*) near the Paraguay River in the Matogrosense region, north of Puerto Bahía Negra, Dpto. Alto Paraguay. Photo by Floyd E. Hayes, January 1989.

Figure 14. Flooded palm savannas typical of the Bajo Chaco region, west of Puente Remanso, Dpto. Presidente Hayes. Photo by Floyd E. Hayes, June 1987.

Figure 15. Flooded grassland with scrub forest (background) in the Bajo Chaco region, west of Estancia Pozo Azul (Dpto. Presidente Hayes). Temporary wetlands attract hordes of waterbirds, including the Jabiru (*Jabiru mycteria*), Wood Stork (*Mycteria americana*) and Maguari Stork (*Ciconia maguari*). Photo by Floyd E. Hayes, September 1989.

 37

Figure 16. Campos cerrados vegetation typical of the Campos Cerrados region, with savanna and forest (background), east of Estancia San Luis, Dpto. Concepción. Photo by Floyd E. Hayes, May 1989.

Figure 17. Precipitous hills and campos cerrados vegetation in the Campos Cerrados region, at Parque Nacional Cerro Corá, Dpto. Amambay. Photo by Floyd E. Hayes, July 1988.

38

Figure 18. Humid deciduous forest typical of the Central Paraguay region, at Parque Nacional Ybycuí, Dpto. Paraguarí. Photo by Floyd E. Hayes, March 1987.

Figure 19. The Bahía de Asunción, a large "bay" of the Paraguay River on the outskirts of Asunción, Dpto. Central. Extensive mudflats during low water levels attract resident and migratory waterbirds, including Bare-faced Ibis (*Phimosus infuscatus*), American Golden-Plover (*Pluvialis dominica*), Hudsonian Godwit (*Limosa haemastica*) and White-rumped Sandpiper (*Calidris fuscicollis*). Photo by Floyd E. Hayes, Nov. 1988.

Figure 20. Extensive grasslands typical of the Ñeembucú region, northwest of Ayolas, Dpto. Misiones. Photo by Floyd E. Hayes, March 1989.

Figure 21. Marshes and scrub forest typical of the Ñeembucú region, north of Villa Florida, in Dpto. Paraguarí. Photo by Floyd E. Hayes, April 1988.

40

Figure 22. Humid deciduous forest typical of the Alto Paraná region, west of Puerto San Rafael, Dpto. Itapúa. Landless *campesinos* are waiting to claim portions of this privately-owned tract of forest. Photo by Floyd E. Hayes, September 1989.

Figure 23. Salto Ñacunday, a large waterfall in Alto Paraná region, near the mouth of the Ñacunday River, Dpto. Alto Paraná. Waterfalls such as this provide important habitat for the Great Dusky Swift (*Cypseloides senex*) and Black-collared Swallow (*Atticora melanoleuca*), which were both present when this photograph was taken. Photo by Floyd E. Hayes, September 1989.

made numerous short visits to Paraguay during the 1980s and 1990s, and collected a large number of specimens of birds for the Museo Félix de Azara in Corrientes, Argentina. Their expertise in the field contributed to several projects coordinated by the Instituto de Ciencias Básicas and the Centro de Datos para la Conservación. The Contreras family initiated an annual series of binational and multinational ornithological meetings with Paraguayan ornithologists, beginning with the Primer Simposio Ornitológico Argentino-Paraguayo at Corrientes in 1988 (see Contreras 1988). During the 1989 meeting in Asunción, Contreras initiated the formation of the Sociedad Ornitológica del Paraguay, which will likely be a focal point in the future for Paraguayan bird enthusiasts. The Contreras family has authored numerous papers on the birds of Paraguay (e.g., Contreras and Mandelburger 1985, J. R. Contreras 1986a, b, 1988, 1989, 1992, Contreras and Contreras 1986, 1993a, b, 1994, Contreras et al. 1988a, b, J. R. Contreras et al. 1989, 1990, 1992a, b, 1993a, b, Contreras and González Romero 1988, 1989a-c, 1991, González Romero et al. 1988, González Romero and Contreras 1989, A. O. Contreras 1993, Contreras and Argaña 1993), and continues doing research in Paraguay.

Avicultural enthusiasts Tony Silva, George Smith and Ron van Leeuwen briefly studied the status of parrots in the Chaco and Alto Paraná region at some time during the 1980s. Their observations were reported by Silva (1988, 1989).

During August and September 1988, Steven M. Goodman and Michael W. Nachman spent a month collecting vertebrates, including about 350 birds (Storer 1989), along the upper Paraguay River for the University of Michigan Museum of Zoology. Several of their specimen records were published by Storer (1989) and Hayes et al. (1990a, b, 1994).

Alberto Madroño Nieto, a Spanish student, traveled extensively in the Chaco during the austral winters of 1989 and 1990, and took excellent notes on his ornithological observations, which included a new species for Paraguay (Madroño Nieto 1991, Madroño Nieto and Pearman 1993).

Paul A. Scharf, a colonel of the United States Army, served at the United States Embassy from July 1989 to June 1991. An avid birder, Scharf kept meticulous lists of birds observed during his travels throughout the country, which included several trips with Hayes in 1989, and with Ridgely in 1991. Scharf became a coauthor on several publications (Hayes et al. 1991, 1994, Hayes and Scharf 1993).

From August 1989 to August 1990, the American biologist Daniel M. Brooks managed the San Diego Zoo's captive breeding program for the Chacoan Peccary (*Catagonus wagneri*) at Fortín Toledo (Dpto. Boquerón). Brooks published two papers on his ornithological observations (Brooks 1991a, b).

During July-September 1992, undergraduate student Thomas M. Brooks of Emmanuel College in Cambridge, United Kingdom, led an intensive biological survey of several private nature reserves in Dptos. Canindeyú, Caaguazú, Caazapá and Alto Paraná, and in the recently established Reserva Natural del Bosque Mbaracayú (Dpto. Canindeyú). A few days were spent on Isla Yacyretá (Dpto. Ñeembucú) in September. The expedition, dubbed CANOPY `92 (Conservation Assessment of Northern Oriental Paraguay Year 1992), included five other British participants, Roger Barnes, Stuart H. M. Butchart, Robert P. Clay, James C. Lowen and Jon Vincent, and three Paraguayan participants, Lucia Bartrina, Estela Z. Esquivel and Nubia I. Etcheverry. The project was coordinated in Paraguay by Antonio van Humbeeck and Miguel Morales of the Fundación Moisés Bertoni, and by Nancy E. López (de Kochalka) of the Museo Nacional de Historia Natural del Paraguay. The results of the expedition's studies were published by Brooks et al. (1993) and Brooks and Esquivel (1994).

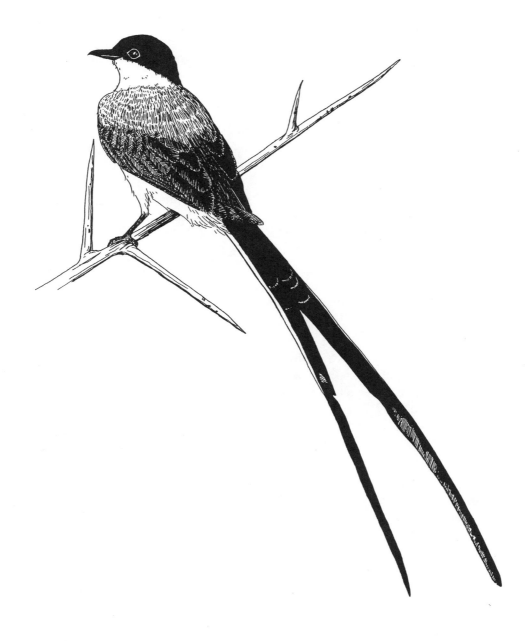

Fork-tailed Flycatcher *(Tyrannus savana)*

Dan Brown

METHODS

"To do science is to search for repeated patterns, not simply to accumulate facts, and to do the science of geographical ecology is to search for patterns of plant and animal life that can be put on a map."

R. H. MacArthur (1972:1)

COMPILATION OF DATA

My introduction to Paraguayan ornithology began in January 1987, when I arrived as a U. S. Peace Corps Volunteer assigned to work in the Inventario Biológico Nacional (subsequently renamed the Museo Nacional de Historia Natural del Paraguay; see Ornithological History section) on the campus of the Universidad Nacional de Asunción in San Lorenzo (Dpto. Central). During the next three years (through November 1989) and briefly during 1993 and 1994, I recorded my observations of birds (about 500 species seen or heard) while traveling extensively throughout the country (see Appendix 2). I also began the task of compiling data from literature records, which I did not complete until long after my departure from Paraguay.

During 1992 I spent six weeks examining bird specimens from Paraguay in the American Museum of Natural History, Field Museum of Natural History, National Museum of Natural History and University of Michigan Museum of Zoology. These four American museums house roughly 13,000 specimens of birds from Paraguay, and include many new or unusual specimen records for which no information had been previously published. The University of Michigan Museum of Zoology alone has well over 6500 specimens of birds from Paraguay (Storer 1989), and apparently represents the largest collection of birds from the country.

In this monograph I have incorporated information from my own observations and those reported to me by others (see Acknowledgments section), from all of the published sources that I could find, and from bird specimens in the four American museums mentioned above. I also examined bird specimens (fewer than 1000) in the Museo Nacional de Historia Natural del Paraguay, and briefly examined specimens in several other Paraguayan museums and an Argentinian museum, but due to local sensitivities I have incorporated only the data that have been published thus far on these specimens. Because of financial constraints, I have not

been able to examine specimens in the museums of Europe and in other South American countries; however, information on a large number of their specimens from Paraguay is available in the published literature (see Ornithological History section).

I initially compiled a checklist of species whose occurrence in Paraguay had been adequately documented on the basis of one or more of the following criteria: (1) a published record of a specimen (unless questionable; see below); (2) an unequivocal photographic record; or (3) an acceptable description of a sight record by one or more experienced observers (see below). I have not attempted to write separate accounts on the status and distribution of each species, primarily because I designed the checklist and accompanying distributional notes to summarize this information. The resulting Annotated Checklist provides a maximum amount of information in a minimum amount of space and facilitates comparisons. Additional information on the status of species that are rare (recorded five or fewer times in either the Chaco or Orient), migratory, threatened with extinction (Collar et al. 1994), or need clarification for miscellaneous reasons, are presented in the Distributional Notes section. Further information on species represented by two or more closely related taxa in Paraguay that may or may not represent distinct species, or whose taxonomic status requires clarification, is presented in the Taxonomic Notes section. The species treated in these two sections are indicated in the checklist.

In preparing the checklist I attempted to estimate the relative abundance of birds in each of the seven geographical regions described earlier (see Geography, Climate and Vegetation section), based primarily on my experiences and those of others (see Acknowledgments section) in the field. My estimates of relative abundance were based on the frequency of detection (seen or heard) by an experienced observer in the habitat(s) where the species were most likely to be encountered. For migratory birds, relative abundance was based on the frequency of detection during the season in which the species were most common. My estimates of relative abundance are defined as follows: abundant, 10 or more recorded daily; common, usually recorded daily; uncommon, recorded every 2-10 days; rare, recorded at intervals of 11 or more days.

In the checklist I have also attempted to evaluate the breeding or migratory status of each species in Paraguay. For some species, such as the North American migrants (see Hayes et al. 1990a), this has been relatively easy to determine. However, the status of many resident South American species, even some of the common ones, is poorly known. Many species resident in South America exhibit clear patterns of migration to and from Paraguay, and are collectively referred to as austral migrants; however, other species that do not exhibit such a clear pattern of seasonality may also be austral migrants (Hayes et al. 1994). Some of these migrants nest in Paraguay whereas others apparently do not. The few published studies on nesting birds in Paraguay indicate that the breeding season occurs during late spring and summer, primarily from October to December (Dalgleish 1889, Chubb 1910, Hayes in prep.). Because of a paucity of information on nesting in Paraguay for most species of South American birds, species present during the summer months or not known to be migratory were assumed to breed. Species distributed primarily to the south or west of Paraguay that were present during the winter months but absent during the summer months were assumed not to breed in Paraguay. Although the designation of breeding or migratory status is probably accurate for most species in the checklist, the designated status of many species, particularly the rarer ones, should be viewed with caution. Much more information is needed before the status of many species can be clarified.

EVALUATION OF RECORDS

In the absence of a formal rare bird committee, I have used my own judgment to critically evaluate the validity of published and unpublished bird records. This has not been an easy task, and undoubtedly other ornithologists will disagree with some of my decisions. Accounts for the species whose occurrence in Paraguay has not been adequately documented or whose occurrence is of questionable origin (i.e., escaped cagebirds) are provided in the Hypothetical Species section.

Although specimen records are generally considered to provide "proof" of a species' occurrence, specimens are sometimes misidentified, especially by ornithologists who are unfamiliar with the species or who lack access to adequate collections. Specimens deposited in well curated museums can always be reexamined, but even when correctly identified, the locality data on the specimen label may be vague or unreliable; this problem is especially acute on older specimens. Another problem is that the present location of numerous specimens reported in the literature, such as the Common Miner (*Geositta cunicularia*) specimen reported by Vaurie (1980:16), is uncertain or unknown. Although some of these specimens are probably lost (e.g., Bertoni's collection; see below), others may turn up and should be reexamined.

Sight records pose another set of problems. Because the identification of the birds cannot be verified by physical evidence, sight records must be subjectively evaluated on the basis of published or unpublished (when available) descriptions, the experience and credibility of the observer(s), the potential for misidentifying the species, and the plausibility of the species occurring where and when it was seen. Although some species of birds in Paraguay pose difficult field identification problems, most species can be accurately identified in the field *with experience*. This has been facilitated by recent advances in the field identification of South American birds.

In the absence of more detailed information, I have tentatively regarded numerous specimen and sight records as hypothetical on the basis of questionable identification, locality, or origin. However, some of these records may be regarded as valid after the questionable specimens have been reexamined or after the distribution of the species in Paraguay and adjacent countries becomes better known. Nevertheless, further documentation is needed for each of these species.

Many older published records are problematic. For example, the reports of birds in Paraguay prior to the War of the Triple Alliance (1865-1870) occurred at a time when Paraguay's borders extended well beyond the present (e.g., Azara 1802a, 1805a, b, Cassin 1859, Schlegel 1863, 1867, Sánchez Labrador *in* Castex 1968). Furthermore, most of these reports give no specific localities other than "Paraguay." For this reason I have regarded all species recorded prior to 1870, but not subsequently, as hypothetical.

Bertoni (1899-1939) reported many rare birds, but generally gave scant details for most species. Furthermore, his extensive collection in Puerto Bertoni (Dpto. Alto Paraná) has rotted away; hence it is impossible to evaluate further his published records. For the species reported in Paraguay by Bertoni but not reported subsequently, I have accepted only those accompanied by a description that adequately eliminates other similar species; the rarer species reported without details are accepted only if other workers have reported those species subsequently. A cautious approach is warranted because Bertoni reported numerous species whose present distributions are located far from Paraguay (see Hypothetical Species section).

The accuracy of localities on specimen labels poses a few problems unique to Paraguay. For example, several species of birds generally restricted to the humid forests of the Orient are represented by one or a few specimens from localities on the west bank (in the Chaco) of the Paraguay River, such as Puerto La Victoria (Dpto. Alto Paraguay) and Puerto Pinasco (Dpto. Presidente Hayes). Were these birds actually collected at these localities, or across the river on the east bank (in the Orient)? In most cases I have accepted the locality as correct, especially when there are several records from different west bank localities. Most of these areas have small hills that are (or were) covered with taller mesophytic vegetation similar to that of the east bank; hence some "eastern" birds might be expected. Furthermore, because these areas on the west bank had facilities where the collectors were able to stay, the workers probably did most of their collecting on the west bank of the river. Nevertheless, these records should be viewed with caution.

By far the most notorious labeling problem in Paraguay concerns numerous specimens collected by Schulze and Haack at a point "235 km W of the Riacho Negro." Short (1972b:46-49) discussed this problem at length, but did not pinpoint the locality. Although there are several ríos (rivers) or riachos (seasonal or temporary streams) that this vague description may refer to, it is virtually certain that the locality refers to a point somewhere in western Dpto. Presidente Hayes. The Chaco river generally thought to have been the collecting locality is the Río Negro (on modern maps) which empties into the Paraguay River just above Rosario (Dpto. San Pe-

dro; Short 1972b, Paynter 1989). Based on an examination of the unpublished catalogs of the University of Michigan Museum of Zoology (UMMZ), Short (1972b) found that specimens from "235 km W of the Riacho Negro" were obtained between 19 June and 7 September 1939. However, the same catalogs indicate that Schulze and Haack also collected birds at "Estero Patiño" between the dates of 20 June and 8 September 1939. Estero Patiño is an extensive marsh just north of the Pilcomayo River, with vegetation resembling that of the Paraguay River floodplain (Esser 1982). The vicinity of Fortín General Caballero (Dpto. Presidente Hayes) is on the fringe of Estero Patiño, roughly 235 km W of the mouth of the Río Negro opposite Rosario, and is just off the main road paralleling the Pilcomayo River. Because the collecting dates at "Estero Patiño" and "235 km W of the Riacho Negro" coincide, it can be concluded that these two localities refer to the same general area, most likely near Fortín General Caballero. This conclusion is further supported by a Cock-tailed Tyrant (*Alectrurus tricolor*) specimen (UMMZ 105415), whose label indicates it was collected "235 km W of Puerto Rosario" on 1 September 1939 (see Distributional Notes section).

Short (1972b) also pointed out that several species and subspecies typical of the Orient but previously unrecorded in the Chaco were collected at the "235 km W of the Riacho Negro" locality. Furthermore, a few species typical of the Chaco were collected in 1940 by Schulze and coworkers in humid forests along the bank of the Paraná River at Puerto Gibaja (Dpto. Alto Paraná). Short (1972b) found that some field numbers of the "Riacho Negro" specimens were out of sequence by as much as nine days, and that the field numbers of these specimens follow consecutively those of Schulze and Unger, who collected to the west of Puerto La Victoria (Dpto. Alto Paraguay) at the same time that Schulze and Haack collected to the west of the Río Negro (was Schulze with Haack or Unger, or somewhere else?). Furthermore, the specimen labels were typewritten, suggesting that the original field labels (if there were any) were discarded at some time after collecting-unless they carried a typewriter in the field, which seems improbable. Although the vast majority of "Riacho Negro" and "Estero Patiño" specimens were undoubtedly obtained in the Chaco, and virtually all of the "Puerto Gibaja" specimens were collected near the Paraná River, some specimens may have been mixed up. In recognizing this possibility, I have regarded several extreme specimen records at each of these localities as hypothetical. Nevertheless, a corridor of subhumid riparian forest penetrates the Chaco along the Pilcomayo River and other tributaries of the Paraguay River (Esser 1982, Nores 1992; Fig. 6); hence some "eastern" birds may be expected to occur in these areas (Nores 1992).

A more recent problem concerns a published list of birds observed in the vicinity of the Itaipú Reservoir (Dptos. Canindeyú and Alto Paraná), which borders Brazil (Perez et al. 1988). Unfortunately the authors did not specifically state whether the birds were all recorded on the Paraguayan side. Because many of the species listed have not been recorded previously from Paraguay, I assume that the list includes species recorded only from Brazil, and therefore I have not included these species in the Hypothetical Species section.

SYSTEMATIC TREATMENT

I have used the traditional biological species concept (BSC) in evaluating the taxonomic status of species that are represented by two or more forms in Paraguay (e.g., see Taxonomic Notes section). The BSC, which views species as "groups of interbreeding natural populations that are reproductively isolated from other such groups" (Mayr 1970:12), has been generally accepted by ornithologists. However, a major weakness of the BSC is that the criterion of reproductive isolation is difficult to evaluate, especially in the case of allopatric populations (e.g., McKitrick and Zink 1988). Although a number of alternative species concepts have been proposed by critics of the BSC (e.g., see Ereshefsky 1992), the BSC still remains the species concept most widely accepted by ornithologists.

The phylogenetic arrangement of higher avian taxa is currently in a state of flux, with several proposed classification schemes. The most revolutionary is that of Sibley and Monroe (1990), based on the results of extensive DNA-DNA hybridization studies (Sibley and Ahlquist 1990). Because their methods of phylogenetic reconstruction are essentially phenetic (based on genetic similarity) rather than cladistic (based on shared derived characters), and have not been unanimously accepted by ornithologists (e.g., Siegel-Causey 1992), I have chosen to follow a more traditional arrangement. The taxonomy and sequence of birds in this monograph pri-

marily follow the American Ornithologists' Union (1983, 1985, 1987, 1989, 1991, 1993), with some exceptions (e.g., Cathartidae is placed after Ciconiidae, different sequence within Psittacidae). For species not included in the above reference, the taxonomy and sequence of species mostly follow Meyer de Schauensee (1970) and Traylor (1979). The English names of Meyer de Schauensee have been in use for several decades and are used in this monograph to promote stability (e.g., see Remsen and Traylor 1989). To facilitate the use of this monograph by those unfamiliar with either scientific or English bird names, I have included both names at every mention of each species.

A recent surge in ornithological research in the Neotropics has resulted in numerous taxonomic changes at the species level; many of these changes have been incorporated by Ridgely and Tudor (1989, 1994) and Sibley and Monroe (1990), and are included in this monograph. These authors have further proposed a number of splits of Paraguayan species with sister taxa occurring elsewhere; in several cases, particularly those in which the data supporting these taxonomic changes have not been published, I have followed the traditional taxonomic treatment. I realize that many of my taxonomic decisions will soon be rendered obsolete by further research. Rather than discussing the potential splits of various taxa and the controversial placement of species into genera and families, the Taxonomic Notes section of this monograph is restricted to the more relevant discussion of the taxonomic status of taxa represented by two or more forms in Paraguay whose taxonomic status requires clarification.

BIOGEOGRAPHICAL ANALYSES

Although much remains to be learned about the distribution of birds in Paraguay, the available data are adequate to reveal distinctive patterns of distribution and to evaluate the processes affecting their distribution in Paraguay. Additional field work will undoubtedly add new species to the various regions, but probably will not significantly alter the conclusions of biogeographical analyses based on current data.

I use the species as the unit of analysis, except in the analyses of contact zones between closely related taxa (including subspecies) of birds (see below). Several of these analyses are based upon regional comparisons. Although some biogeographers criticize the "reality" of vague transitional boundaries (e.g., Peters 1955, Simpson 1977) such as those used in this study (see Geography, Climate and Vegetation section), others maintain that "in principle, boundaries need not be real and sharp" for biogeographical analyses, and that "drawing such lines is the actual start of biogeographical research" (Hengeveld 1990:59, 62).

Regional Comparisons

I began my biogeographical analyses by comparing the breeding bird faunas for each pair of regions. I included all species regarded as breeding in the Annotated Checklist section, with the exception of the Glaucous Macaw (*Anodorhynchus glaucus*), for which there are no specific locality records (see Distributional Notes section). A potential problem is that some species do not necessarily breed in each region where recorded. However, rather than attempt to guess which species breeds in which region, I have included all regions in which each "breeding" species has been recorded (see Annotated Checklist section). The species regarded as non-breeding Nearctic migrants, southern austral migrants and tropical vagrants (see Annotated Checklist section) are not included in the analyses.

Species Richness. I compared species richness between regions for all breeding birds combined. For more detailed comparisons of species richness, I subdivided the avifauna into eight ecological/taxonomic groups: (1) ground-dwelling non-passerines; (2) waterbirds; (3) raptors/scavengers; (4) frugivorous non-passerines; (5) insectivorous non-passerines; (6) nectarivorous non-passerines; (7) insectivorous passerines; and (8) omnivorous passerines (Table 3). I also distinguished a ninth group of birds, composed of forest understory species that do not typically occur in aquatic habitats (see list in Appendix 3). This group of birds spans a diversity of taxonomic groups and life history traits, sharing only an affinity for forest undergrowth. This group of birds is considered less likely to disperse across open water than are forest canopy birds and birds of open country (e.g., Capparella 1988), and is useful for testing predictions regarding the efficacy of the Paraguay River as a dispersal barrier (see below).

Faunal Similarity. I compared faunal similarity between the regions by using the Jaccard, Simpson and Dice coefficients of similarity, which are the most frequently used measures of faunal similarity in biogeographic studies (Brown and Gibson 1983). The Jaccard coefficient emphasizes difference, whereas the Simpson and Dice coefficients emphasize similarity (Cheetham and Hazel 1969). Theoretical and empirical evaluations of 43 similarity coefficients ranked the Jaccard and Dice coefficients, but not the Simpson coefficient, among the four most useful (Hubálek 1982).

The Jaccard, Simpson and Dice coefficients were compared by computing Pearson product-moment correlation coefficients (*r* statistic; Zar 1984). The coefficients of similarity were used to cluster the seven geographical regions by using the unweighted pair-group method using arithmetic averaging (UPGMA; Sneath and Sokal 1973). Comparisons using coefficients of similarity and clustering were made for all breeding birds combined, for each ecological/taxonomic group and for forest understory birds.

Faunal Uniqueness. I compared faunal "uniqueness" among regions by compiling lists of breeding birds whose distribution within Paraguay is restricted to a single region. Patterns of faunal uniqueness may be indicative of the affinities of these regions with other areas of South America.

Regional Affinities. The Chaco's climate is harsher and less predictable, with more pronounced cycles of rainfall and drought, than that of the Orient (e.g., Gorham 1973b, Myers 1982, Anonymous 1985). As a result, the Chaco's relatively xeric vegetation is more characteristic of temperate climates, whereas the Orient's relatively mesic vegetation is more characteristic of tropical climates. Myers (1982) predicted that the Chaco should be inhabited by mammal species whose closest relatives occur in strongly seasonal environments, such as in the Andean highlands and in the temperate latitudes of South America, whereas the Orient should be inhabited by species whose closest relatives occur in tropical or subtropical regions. Determining the closest relative of each bird species in Paraguay is currently unfeasible. However, many species of birds in Paraguay are represented by two or more recognized subspecies (e.g., Howard and Moore 1991), and an examination of each species' distribution in different regions of South America would include the sister taxon/taxa for most species of Paraguayan birds.

Table 3: Ecological/taxonomic groups of birds by family or subfamily

GROUND-DWELLING NON-PASSERINES

Rheidae	Odontophoridae
Tinamidae	Cariamidae

WATERBIRDS

Podicipedidae	Heliornithidae
Phalacrocoracidae	Aramidae
Anhingidae	Charadriidae
Ardeidae	Recurvirostridae
Threskiornithidae	Jacanidae
Ciconiidae	Rostratulidae
Anhimidae	Scolopacidae
Anatidae	Laridae
Rallidae	Alcedinidae

RAPTORS/SCAVENGERS

Cathartidae	Tytonidae
Accipitridae	Strigidae
Falconidae	

FRUGIVOROUS NON-PASSERINES

Cracidae	Psittacidae
Columbidae	Ramphastidae

INSECTIVOROUS NON-PASSERINES

Cuculidae	Trogonidae
Caprimulgidae	Momotidae
Nyctibiidae	Bucconidae
Apodidae	Picidae

NECTARIVOROUS NON-PASSERINES

Trochilidae

INSECTIVOROUS PASSERINES

Furnariidae	Hirundinidae
Dendrocolaptidae	Troglodytidae
Formicariidae	Sylviinae (of Muscicapidae)
Rhinocryptidae	Motacillidae
Tyrannidae	Parulinae (of Emberizidae)
Oxyruncidae	

OMNIVOROUS PASSERINES

Cotingidae	Vireonidae
Pipridae	Emberizidae (except Parulinae)
Corvidae	Fringillidae
Turdinae (of Muscicapidae)	Passeridae
Mimidae	

To test Myers's (1982) hypothesis with distributional data for birds, I compiled lists of breeding species of Paraguayan birds that are resident in eight broad geographical regions of South America, and then calculated the percentage of birds in each region of Paraguay that also occur in the broader geographical regions of South America. Three of these regions comprise tropical lowlands: (1) Amazonia (mostly forests of the Amazonian basin in northern South America); (2) Cerrado (savannas and savanna forests of central Brazil); and (3) Caatinga (thorn scrubland of northeastern Brazil). One region, (4) Southeastern Brazil (humid forests of southeastern Brazil and adjacent Misiones Province, Argentina), is subtropical, and includes lowlands as well as highlands. The remaining four regions are temperate: (5) Andean Highlands (mountains from Colombia to Argentina in western South America, with elevation >2000 m); (6) Chaco Austral/Pampas (scrublands and grasslands west of the Paraná River from the Pilcomayo River to the Negro River of southern Argentina); (7) Mesopotamia (temperate grasslands and forests of Corrientes and Entre Ríos, Argentina, and Uruguay); and (8) Patagonia (lowland steppes and forests south of the Negro River, Argentina). Data on bird distribution in these regions were obtained primarily from Meyer de Schauensee (1970), Blake (1977), Narosky and Yzurieta (1987, 1989), Ridgely and Tudor (1989, 1994), and Sibley and Monroe (1990).

Body Size. I compared the body sizes of birds in each region. Body weight is generally considered to be the best univariate measure of body size (e.g., Rising and Somers 1989, Freeman and Jackson 1990) and the most readily available (Dunning 1992). Storer (1989) provided data on weights for 273 species of birds in Paraguay. Additional data on weights of birds occurring in Paraguay, but obtained from other countries, have been published for most species of birds that occur in Paraguay (Dunning 1992).

Comparisons of exact weights of birds are difficult because of geographical variation, variability in nutritional status (affected by factors such as time of day, season, migration, age, sex, reproductive status, etc.) and measurement error (e.g., Clark 1979). To minimize the potential effects of weight variability, I placed each breeding species into one of ten non-overlapping weight classes, with each successive body size class being approximately 1.5 times larger than the previous one (Gotelli and Graves 1990): 1=0-10 g; 2=10-25 g; 3=25-47 g; 4=47-81 g; 5=81-130 g; 6=130-204 g; 7=204-314 g; 8=314-479 g; 9=479-726 g; 10=>726 g. When weight data were available for both sexes of a given species, I used the mean of the two sexes. The body size classes of species for which there are no published data were estimated by comparing published body length data (e.g., Meyer de Schauensee 1970, Narosky and Yzurieta 1987, Ridgely and Tudor 1989, 1994) with closely related species (usually within the same genus) of known weight. The accuracy of placement into a given body weight class should be ±1 for most species.

Kruskal-Wallis tests (H statistic; Zar 1984) were computed to determine whether the mean body size class varied between geographical regions for all breeding birds combined, for each ecological/taxonomic group and for forest understory birds. A Pearson correlation coefficient (r statistic; Zar 1984) was computed to determine whether the mean body size class of birds for each region was correlated with the number of species in each region.

Dispersal Barriers

The presence of geographical or ecological barriers to bird dispersal may have influenced the composition of species in each region of Paraguay. Because of Paraguay's low topographic relief (<800 m), there are no montane barriers to plant and animal dispersal; hence the degree of faunal similarity between the seven geographical regions might be expected to be correlated with habitat similarity. However, the fairly broad Paraguay River may form a geographical barrier to plant and animal dispersal (e.g., Short 1975). Alternatively, other ecological factors, such as an abrupt transition from forest to savanna, may be more important than a river barrier in explaining bird distribution in Paraguay.

To assess the relative importance of geographical and ecological barriers to bird dispersal in Paraguay, I tested eight predictions of the hypothesis that the Paraguay River forms a barrier to bird dispersal in Paraguay. Although each prediction is framed to evaluate the role of the river as a dispersal barrier, alternative predictions are made to evaluate the relative importance of the river and the forest-savanna transition as dispersal barriers. These predictions are discussed below in further detail.

Prediction 1: Regional Cluster Prediction. If the river forms a substantial barrier to bird dispersal, the regional avifaunas on each side of the river should be more similar to each other than to regional avifaunas on the opposite side. This would be demonstrated if the faunal similarity of the Chaco and Orient regions clustered separately for all breeding birds combined, especially if this occurred for each of the eight ecological/taxonomic groups and for forest understory birds. Although such a pattern would be consistent with the hypothesis that the Paraguay River forms a barrier to bird dispersal, it might also be expected if faunal similarity is due to habitat similarity, independent of a river barrier. However, because the physiography of the Ñeembucú region appears similar to the Chaco, its avifauna might be more similar to the Chaco regions than to other Orient regions. If this were the case, it would suggest that habitat similarity is a more important factor than a river barrier in explaining faunal similarity between regions. The same would be suggested if the regions in the western Orient (Campos Cerrados, Central Paraguay and Ñeembucú) were more similar to the Chaco regions than to the Alto Paraná region, or if the regions of the eastern Chaco were more similar to the Orient regions than to the Alto Chaco region.

Prediction 2: Distributional Limits Prediction. If the river forms a substantial barrier to bird dispersal, the eastern distributional limits of "western" species (occurring primarily in the Chaco) should occur most frequently within a short distance of the river on the western side, with relatively few species reaching their eastern limits on the eastern side of the river. Similarly the western distributional limits of "eastern" birds (occurring primarily in the Orient) should occur most frequently within a short distance of the river on the eastern side, with relatively few species reaching their western limits on the western side of the river. This is analogous to the situation in which the ranges of species coincide with rivers, but only considers the ranges of these species across a limited portion of the river (i.e., in Paraguay). If a relatively abrupt change in vegetation occurs near the Paraguay River and roughly coincides with the river's course, as appears to be the case (e.g., Esser 1982; Fig.6), the species whose distributional limits occur near the river (e.g., within 10 km) should not be concentrated on one side of the river because a change in habitat is unlikely to coincide exactly with the river's course.

The eight ecological/taxonomic groups and forest understory birds presumably differ in their average dispersal abilities. Ground-dwelling non-passerines include species that are relatively weak flyers (e.g., tinamous; rheas cannot fly at all); hence they presumably have low over-water dispersal abilities. Forest understory birds do not necessarily have low dispersal abilities, but are presumably less likely to cross wide rivers than are canopy forest birds and open country birds (e.g., Capparella 1988). In contrast, many species of waterbirds and raptors/scavengers are widely distributed in South America; hence they presumably have relatively high dispersal abilities. Other groups of non-passerines and passerines presumably have dispersal abilities somewhere between these extremes.

I compared data on distributional limits for all breeding birds combined, for each ecological/taxonomic group and for forest understory birds. If the river forms a barrier to bird dispersal, a more abrupt change across the Paraguay River should occur for the ecological/taxonomic groups that are poorer dispersers (e.g., ground-dwelling non-passerines) and for forest understory birds.

Prediction 3: Faunal Similarity Prediction. Several predictions can be tested by comparing the dispersal abilities of birds in three pairs of adjoining regions (sharing a common border) divided by the Paraguay River (Matogrosense/Campos Cerrados, Bajo Chaco/Campos Cerrados, Bajo Chaco/Central Paraguay) with six pairs of adjoining regions not divided by the Paraguay River (Alto Chaco/Matogrosense, Alto Chaco/Bajo Chaco, Matogrosense/Bajo Chaco, Campos Cerrados/Central Paraguay, Central Paraguay/Ñeembucú, Central Paraguay/Alto Paraná). I also compared the physiographically and ecologically similar Bajo Chaco and Ñeembucú regions, which do not share a common border but are nevertheless on opposite sides of the Paraguay River. Each pair of adjoining regions divided by the Paraguay River excludes most species in western and eastern Paraguay that do not occur within ≈150 km of the Paraguay River. The pairs of adjoining regions not divided by the Paraguay River were used as controls to evaluate whether the observed pattern among the pairs of adjoining regions divided by the Paraguay River differed from the controls.

If the Paraguay River forms a barrier to bird dispersal, faunal similarity should be reduced between regions for the pairs of adjoining regions divided by the Paraguay River (*n*=3) relative to the other pairs of adjoining regions not divided by the Paraguay River (*n*=6), especially for ground-dwelling passerines and forest understory birds. If a relatively abrupt forest-savanna transition forms a barrier to bird dispersal, faunal similarity between adjoining regions should be lowest for the Bajo Chaco/Central Paraguay regions and the Central Paraguay/Ñeembucú regions (see Figs. 6 and 7).

Prediction 4: Body Size Prediction. Body size may be considered a rough indicator of dispersal ability, because larger species of birds generally have larger geographical ranges than smaller species (Brown and Maurer 1987, Maurer et al. 1991). A Spearman rank correlation coefficient (r_s statistic; Zar 1984) was computed to determine whether body size was correlated with the number of regions in which each breeding species occurred in Paraguay. A significantly positive correlation would indicate that large-bodied species are more widespread in Paraguay than small-bodied species, and would justify the assumption that large-bodied birds are better dispersers.

If the Paraguay River forms a barrier to bird dispersal, a relatively lower proportion of small-bodied birds should be shared between regions for each pair of adjoining regions divided by the Paraguay River than for the pairs of adjoining regions not divided by the river. If this were the case, the three pairs of adjoining regions divided by the Paraguay River would have a higher ratio of mean body size for shared:non-shared species than that of the six pairs of adjoining regions not divided by the river.

Mann-Whitney *U* tests (*z* statistic; Zar 1984) were computed to compare the body sizes of shared and non-shared species between regions for each pair of adjoining regions; the tests were computed for all breeding birds combined, for each ecological/taxonomic group and for forest understory birds. These tests can only detect differences between shared and non-shared species for a single pair of regions; differences between two pairs of regions cannot be tested. A potentially complicating factor is that significant variation between regions in the distribution of body size would complicate the interpretation of results. Kruskal-Wallis tests (*H* statistic; Zar 1984) were computed to determine whether the mean body size class varied between geographical regions for all breeding birds com-

bined, for each ecological/taxonomic group and for forest understory birds.

Prediction 5: Migrant Prediction. Species that are long-distance migrants are presumably more likely to disperse across geographical barriers and unfavorable habitats than non-migratory species. Although the long-distance migration of resident birds in South America is poorly documented, the data presented by Hayes et al. (1994) and summarized in the Annotated Checklist and Distributional Notes sections indicate that at least 48 species of birds that presumably breed in Paraguay are probable long-distance migrants.

To determine whether migrant species are more widespread in Paraguay than the relatively sedentary species, a Mann-Whitney *U* test (*z* statistic; Zar 1984) was computed to compare the mean number of regions occupied by migrant and non-migrant species. A significantly higher mean value for migrant species would indicate that migrants are more widespread in Paraguay than non-migrants, and would justify the hypothesis that migrant species are better dispersers.

If the Paraguay River forms a barrier to bird dispersal, the three pairs of adjoining regions divided by the Paraguay River should have reduced values of faunal similarity of non-migrant species compared to that of the six pairs of adjoining regions not divided by the river. If this were the case, the three pairs of adjoining regions divided by the Paraguay River would have a higher migrant:non-migrant ratio of faunal similarity compared with the six pairs of adjoining regions not divided by the river. This was tested for all breeding birds combined and for insectivorous passerines and omnivorous passerines. The latter two groups represent the only ecological/taxonomic groups of birds with more than five species of breeding long-distance migrants; hence comparisons using other groups of birds could not be made.

Prediction 6: Distributional Crossover Prediction. If the Paraguay River forms a barrier to bird dispersal, the distribution of bird species restricted primarily to one side of the river would be more likely to cross over the river farther north, where the river is narrower, than farther south, where the river is wider (e.g., Haffer 1974). Such a pattern might also be expected for species restricted primarily to the Orient because of the absence of humid or semi-humid forest to the west of the Paraná River in Argentina (e.g., Nores 1987, 1989) and the presence of semihumid forest in southeastern Bolivia (e.g., Remsen and Traylor 1989). However, if relatively more species occurring primarily in the Chaco cross the Paraná River to the south of Paraguay than cross the Paraguay River to the north of Paraguay, the forest-savanna transition would appear to be a more important barrier to bird dispersal than the Paraguay River. Extensive Chaco-like habitats occur to the east of the Paraná River in Argentina (e.g., Nores 1987, 1989) and in the adjacent Ñeembucú region of Paraguay; hence Chaco species might be expected to cross over the river into these habitats. However, extensive semiarid forest and savanna also occur in the *campos cerrados* of Brazil to the north and east of Paraguay; hence Chaco species might also be expected to cross the Paraguay River to the north of Paraguay.

I examined the distribution of each species restricted primarily to one side of the Paraguay River to quantify the number of species whose distribution crosses over the northern part of the Paraguay River or the southern part of the Paraguay/Paraná Rivers. Data on the distribution of birds were obtained primarily from Short (1975), Narosky and Yzurieta (1987, 1989), Remsen and Traylor (1989), Ridgely and Tudor (1989, 1994) and Sibley and Monroe (1990).

Prediction 7: Phenotypic Differentiation Prediction. The Paraguay River may form a partial barrier to bird dispersal by reducing, rather than preventing, dispersal (and gene flow). If this were the case, populations of closely related taxa (at the species or subspecies level) occurring on opposite banks of the river should be phenotypically (or at least genotypically) differentiated, with an abrupt change coinciding with the course of the Paraguay River. Although a relatively abrupt forest-savanna transition occurs along the upper part of the Paraguay River, this transition shifts to the east of the Paraguay River in the Ñeembucú region (Esser 1982; Fig. 6) and occurs well to the east of the Paraná River in Argentina (e.g., Nores 1987, 1989). If the forest-savanna transition is a more effective barrier to gene flow than the Paraguay and Paraná Rivers, the contact zones between closely related taxa (including subspecies) should coincide with the forest-savanna transition rather than the course of the Paraguay and Paraná Rivers.

I examined the published literature to compile lists of closely related pairs of subspecies whose contact zones roughly coincide with the Paraguay River. Because limited gene flow is feasible between closely related species, I also compiled lists of closely related species (within the same genus) whose contact zones roughly coincide with the Paraguay River. I used the available information to judge whether the contact zones coincided more with the course of the Paraguay and Paraná Rivers or with the forest-savanna transition.

Prediction 8: Contact Zone Prediction. If either (or both) the Paraguay River or forest-savanna transition constitutes the most effective barrier to dispersal (and gene flow) in Paraguay, the majority of the contact zones between closely related taxa in Paraguay should roughly coincide with either (or both) of these potential barriers.

I compiled lists of closely related taxa (at the species or subspecies level) with contact zones occurring anywhere in Paraguay. The presence of contact zones not coinciding with the Paraguay River or forest-savanna barriers may be indicative of other ecological barriers in Paraguay, and the number of contact zones occurring along the potential barriers may indicate their relative effectiveness.

Limitations of Predictions. A weakness of most of these predictions is that they can be evaluated only by visual inspection of tabular or graphic data, and cannot be rigorously tested by statistical methods that are currently available. Nevertheless, each prediction is potentially useful for evaluating the relative importance of geographical and ecological barriers to the dispersal of birds and other organisms.

Computation of Data

The Jaccard, Simpson and Dice coefficients were computed with Biosim software (Gibson 1990). The cluster analyses were computed with SPSS/PC+ Advanced Statistics V2.0 software (Norusis 1990). Pearson product-moment correlation coefficients, Spearman rank correlation coefficients, Mann-Whitney U tests and Kruskal-Wallis tests were computed with Statistix 3.1 software (Anonymous 1990), with two-tailed probabilities and $\alpha = 0.05$.

ANNOTATED CHECKLIST

This checklist includes 645 species of birds that have been reliably recorded in Paraguay. Of these, 576 presumably breed in the country, 34 are Nearctic migrants, 32 are non-breeding austral migrants and four are regarded as tropical vagrants. The Peregrine Falcon (*Falco peregrinus*) is counted above as both a Nearctic migrant and a southern austral migrant (see Distributional Notes section).

I have accepted eight species on the basis of recent sight records alone. These include Lake Duck (*Oxyura vittata*), Semipalmated Sandpiper (*Calidris pusilla*), Blue-crowned Motmot (*Momotus momota*), Many-colored Rush-Tyrant (*Tachuris rubrigastra*), Black-collared Swallow (*Atticora melanoleuca*), Palm Tanager (*Thraupis palmarum*), Temminck's Seedeater (*Sporophila falcirostris*), and Yellow-winged Blackbird (*Agelaius thilius*). Most of these species are sufficiently distinct to preclude the possibility of confusion by experienced observers, and those which are similar to closely related species (e.g., Semipalmated Sandpiper) have been evaluated on the basis of written observations from experienced observers (see Distributional Notes section). I have accepted 15 species on the basis of adequate descriptions of lost specimens (some with subsequent sight records): Brazilian Merganser (*Mergus octosetaceus*), Mantled Hawk (*Leucopternis polionota*), White-rumped Hawk (*Buteo leucorrhous*), Eskimo Curlew (*Numenius borealis*), Scaled Pigeon (*Columba speciosa*), Purple-winged Ground-Dove (*Claravis godefrida*), Blue-and-yellow Macaw (*Ara ararauna*), Tawny-browed Owl (*Pulsatrix koeniswaldiana*), Brazilian Pygmy-Owl (*Glaucidium minutissimum*), Black-billed Scythebill (*Campylorhamphus falcularius*), Large-tailed Antshrike (*Mackenziaena leachii*), Bertoni's Antbird (*Drymophila rubricollis*), Speckle-breasted Antpitta (*Hylopezus nattereri*), Shear-tailed Gray-Tyrant (*Muscipipra vetula*), and Buffy-fronted Seedeater (*Sporophila frontalis*). All other species are accepted on the basis of extant specimens or photographs.

The symbols used in this checklist are summarized as follows:

STATUS (present breeding or seasonal status)

BR   Breeding permanent resident.

BN   Breeding resident but northern austral migrant; less abundant or absent during austral winter, when resident birds migrate northward toward the tropics.

BS   Breeding resident but southern austral migrant; less abundant during austral summer, when wintering birds migrate southward to breed.

IB   Introduced (non-native) breeding resident.

XB   Extirpated formerly breeding resident.

NM   Nearctic migrant; breeds in North America, but migrating or wintering birds present during austral spring, summer and fall.

TV   Tropical vagrant; breeds in tropics north of Paraguay, but occasionally strays to Paraguay; no clear pattern of migration established, but possibly a post-breeding wanderer.

AM   Austral migrant; breeds south of Paraguay, but wintering birds present during austral fall, winter and spring.

HABITAT (generalized habitat where species typically occurs)

GL   Grasslands; normally dry open areas with short vegetation, including palm/grass savannas.

WL   Wetlands; open water, wet margins and marshes, including rivers and riverbanks.

SF   Subhumid and scrub forests; relatively short and dry (usually xerophytic), including forest edges.

HF   Humid forests; relatively tall and humid (mesophytic), including forest edges.

CL   Cliffs; usually in vicinity of rocky cliffs.

WF   Waterfalls; usually in the vicinity of waterfalls.

RE   Residential; usually in areas densely populated by humans.

GEOGRAPHICAL REGION (described in
Geography, Climate and Vegetation section;
see Fig. 3)

AC Alto Chaco
MG Matogrosense
BC Bajo Chaco
CC Campos Cerrados
CP Central Paraguay
ÑE Ñeembucú
AP Alto Paraná

A   Abundant; 10 or more recorded daily in
appropriate habitat.
C   Common; usually recorded daily in
appropriate habitat.
U   Uncommon; recorded every 2-10 days
in appropriate habitat.
R   Rare; recorded at intervals of 11 or
more days.
H   Hypothetical; questionable,
unsubstantiated record(s).
-   Absent; not yet recorded or unlikely
to be recorded.

RELATIVE ABUNDANCE (frequency of
detection within geographical region by
experienced observer during appropriate
season)

NOTES (indicated within parentheses at end of
English name; additional details provided in
the following sections).

Numbers refer to Distributional Notes section

Letters refer to Taxonomic Notes section

Family/Species	Status	Habitat	AC	MG	BC	CC	CP	ÑE	AP
RHEIDAE (1 species)									
Greater Rhea *Rhea americana*	BR	GL	C	R	C	C	R	R	R
TINAMIDAE (10 species)									
Solitary Tinamou (1) *Tinamus solitarius*	BR	HF	-	-	H	-	R	R	R
Brown Tinamou *Crypturellus obsoletus*	BR	HF	-	-	-	-	U	R	U
Undulated Tinamou *Crypturellus undulatus*	BR	SF,HF	-	C	R	C	U	-	-
Small-billed Tinamou (2) *Crypturellus parvirostris*	BR	HF	R	-	R	R	R	R	R
Tataupa Tinamou *Crypturellus tataupa*	BR	SF,HF	U	-	C	C	C	C	C
Red-winged Tinamou *Rhynchotus rufescens*	BR	GL	-	-	U	C	C	C	C
Brushland Tinamou (3) *Nothoprocta cinerascens*	BR	SF	U	-	-	-	-	-	-
Spotted Nothura (A) *Nothura maculosa*	BR	GL	C	R	C	C	C	C	C
White-bellied Nothura *Nothura boraquira*	BR	SF	R	-	-	-	-	-	-
Quebracho Crested-Tinamou *Eudromia formosa*	BR	SF	R	-	-	-	-	-	-

Family/Species	Status	Habitat	AC	MG	BC	CC	CP	ÑE	AP
					Geographical Regions				
PODICIPEDIDAE (5 species)									
Least Grebe *Tachybaptus dominicus*	BR	WL	C	-	R	R	U	-	R
Pied-billed Grebe *Podilymbus podiceps*	BR	WL	C	R	U	-	R	R	R
White-tufted Grebe (4) *Rollandia rolland*	BR	WL	U	H	R	-	R	R	R
Silvery Grebe (5) *Podiceps occipitalis*	AM	WL	-	-	-	-	-	-	R
Great Grebe (6) *Podiceps major*	BR	WL	R	-	R	-	-	R	R
PHALACROCORACIDAE (1 species)									
Neotropic Cormorant *Phalacrocorax brasilianus*	BR	WL	U	A	A	A	A	A	C
ANHINGIDAE (1 species)									
Anhinga *Anhinga anhinga*	BR	WL	R	C	C	C	C	U	C
ARDEIDAE (14 species)									
Pinnated Bittern (7) *Botaurus pinnatus*	BR	WL	R	-	-	-	-	R	-
Stripe-backed Bittern (8) *Ixobrychus involucris*	BR	WL	R	-	R	-	R	R	R
Least Bittern (9) *Ixobrychus exilis*	BR	WL	R	-	R	-	-	-	-
Rufescent Tiger-Heron *Tigrisoma lineatum*	BR	WL	U	C	C	U	U	U	R
Whistling Heron *Syrigma sibilatrix*	BR	WL	C	C	C	C	C	C	U
Cocoi Heron *Ardea cocoi*	BR	WL	C	C	C	C	C	C	U
Great Egret *Casmerodius albus*	BR	WL	C	A	A	A	A	A	U
Snowy Egret *Egretta thula*	BR	WL	C	A	A	A	A	A	U
Little Blue Heron (10) *Egretta caerulea*	TV	WL	-	R	R	-	-	-	-
Cattle Egret (11) *Bubulcus ibis*	BR	WL	C	A	A	C	C	U	U
Striated Heron *Butorides striatus*	BR	WL	U	C	C	C	C	C	U
Capped Heron (12) *Pilherodius pileatus*	BR	WL	R	R	H	R	-	-	-
Black-crowned Night-Heron *Nycticorax nycticorax*	BR	WL	C	C	C	C	C	C	R

Family/Species	Status	Habitat	Geographical Regions						
			AC	MG	BC	CC	CP	ÑE	AP
Boat-billed Heron (13) *Cochlearius cochlearius*	BR	WL	-	R	R	R	R	-	-

THRESKIORNITHIDAE (6 species)

Bare-faced Ibis *Phimosus infuscatus*	BR	WL	A	A	A	A	A	A	R
White-faced Ibis *Plegadis chihi*	BR	WL	C	U	A	A	A	A	-
Green Ibis (14) *Mesembrinibis cayennensis*	BR	WL	-	R	R	R	R	R	R
Plumbeous Ibis (15) *Theristicus caerulescens*	BR	WL	C	C	C	-	-	R	-
Buff-necked Ibis *Theristicus caudatus*	BR	GL	C	U	C	C	R	R	R
Roseate Spoonbill *Ajaia ajaja*	BR	WL	C	U	C	U	U	U	R

CICONIIDAE (3 species)

Jabiru *Jabiru mycteria*	BR	WL	C	C	C	R	R	U	R
Wood Stork *Mycteria americana*	BR	WL	C	C	A	C	C	C	-
Maguari Stork *Ciconia maguari*	BR	WL	C	A	A	C	C	C	R

CATHARTIDAE (5 species)

Black Vulture *Coragyps atratus*	BR	GL,SF,HF	C	C	A	A	A	C	C
Turkey Vulture *Cathartes aura*	BR	GL,SF,HF	C	U	U	C	U	U	U
Lesser Yellow-headed Vulture *Cathartes burrovianus*	BR	WL	U	C	C	C	C	C	U
Andean Condor (16) *Vultur gryphus*	AM	GL,SF	R	-	-	-	H	-	-
King Vulture *Sarcoramphus papa*	BR	SF,HF	R	R	R	R	R	-	U

PHOENICOPTERIDAE (1 species)

Chilean Flamingo (17) *Phoenicopterus chilensis*	AM	WL	C	-	R	-	R	-	-

ANHIMIDAE (1 species)

Southern Screamer *Chauna torquata*	BR	WL	C	C	C	C	C	U	R

Family/Species	Status	Habitat	Geographical Regions						
			AC	MG	BC	CC	CP	ÑE	AP
ANATIDAE (18 species)									
Fulvous Whistling-Duck *Dendrocygna bicolor*	BR	WL	U	R	R	R	R	R	-
White-faced Whistling-Duck *Dendrocygna viduata*	BR	WL	C	U	C	U	U	U	-
Black-bellied Whistling-Duck *Dendrocygna autumnalis*	BR	WL	C	U	C	U	U	R	-
Coscoroba Swan (18) *Coscoroba coscoroba*	BR	WL	U	R	-	H	-	-	-
Orinoco Goose (19) *Neochen jubata*	TV	WL	R	-	-	-	-	-	-
Muscovy Duck *Cairina moschata*	BR	WL	U	U	U	U	U	U	U
Comb Duck *Sarkidiornis melanotos*	BR	WL	U	R	U	R	R	R	R
White-cheeked Pintail (20) *Anas bahamensis*	BR	WL	C	-	-	-	R	-	-
Silver Teal *Anas versicolor*	BR	WL	U	-	U	-	U	U	-
Cinnamon Teal (21) *Anas cyanoptera*	BR	WL	R	-	H	-	H	-	-
Red Shoveler (22) *Anas platalea*	BR	WL	R	-	R	-	R	-	-
Ringed Teal *Callonetta leucophrys*	BR	WL	A	U	C	-	U	-	-
Rosy-billed Pochard (23) *Netta peposaca*	BR	WL	R	-	R	-	R	R	R
Brazilian Duck *Amazonetta brasiliensis*	BR	WL	C	C	C	C	C	C	U
Brazilian Merganser (24) *Mergus octosetaceus*	XB	WL	-	-	-	-	-	-	R
Lake Duck (25) *Oxyura vittata*	BR	WL	-	-	R	-	-	-	-
Masked Duck *Oxyura dominica*	BR	WL	U	-	R	R	R	R	-
Black-headed Duck (26) *Heteronetta atricapilla*	BR	WL	R	-	-	-	-	-	-
ACCIPITRIDAE (34 species)									
Osprey (27) *Pandion haliaetus*	NM	WL	-	C	C	C	C	R	-
Gray-headed Kite *Leptodon cayanensis*	BR	SF,HF	-	R	-	R	U	-	U
Hook-billed Kite (28) *Chondrohierax uncinatus*	BR	SF,HF	R	-	-	R	R	-	R

Family/Species	Status	Habitat	Geographical Regions						
			AC	MG	BC	CC	CP	ÑE	AP
American Swallow-tailed Kite (29) *Elanoides forficatus*	BN	HF	-	-	-	U	U	R	U
Pearl Kite *Gampsonyx swainsonii*	BR	SF,HF	R	R	R	R	R	R	R
White-tailed Kite *Elanus leucurus*	BR	GL	U	R	U	U	U	R	C
Snail Kite (30) *Rostrhamus sociabilis*	BS	WL	C	A	A	A	A	A	R
Rufous-thighed Kite (31) *Harpagus diodon*	BN	HF	R	-	-	R	R	-	R
Mississippi Kite (32) *Ictinia mississippiensis*	NM	GL,SF	-	R	R	R	R	R	-
Plumbeous Kite (33) *Ictinia plumbea*	BN	SF,HF	R	-	U	C	C	U	C
Cinereous Harrier (34) *Circus cinereus*	BR	GL,WL	-	-	H	-	R	R	-
Long-winged Harrier *Circus buffoni*	BR	GL,WL	R	R	R	R	U	U	R
Gray-bellied Hawk *Accipiter poliogaster*	BR	HF	-	-	-	-	-	-	R
Tiny Hawk (35) *Accipiter superciliosus*	BR	HF	-	-	-	-	H	-	R
Sharp-shinned Hawk *Accipiter striatus*	BR	SF,HF	U	R	R	R	R	R	R
Bicolored Hawk *Accipiter bicolor*	BR	SF,HF	R	U	R	R	R	-	R
Crane Hawk *Geranospiza caerulescens*	BR	GL,SF	U	U	U	R	R	R	R
Mantled Hawk (36) *Leucopternis polionota*	BR	HF	-	-	-	-	-	-	R
Great Black-Hawk *Buteogallus urubitinga*	BR	GL,SF,HF	U	U	U	U	U	U	U
Savanna Hawk *Buteogallus meridionalis*	BR	GL,WL	C	U	A	C	U	C	U
Harris' Hawk *Parabuteo unicinctus*	BR	SF	U	R	R	R	R	-	-
Black-collared Hawk *Busarellus nigricollis*	BR	WL	R	U	C	U	U	C	-
Black-chested Buzzard-Eagle *Geranoaetus melanoleucus*	BR	GL,SF,HF	R	-	R	-	R	R	R
Crowned Eagle (37) *Harpyhaliaetus coronatus*	BR	SF,HF	R	-	R	R	R	-	R
Gray Hawk (38) *Buteo nitidus*	BR	SF,HF	-	R	-	-	-	H	R
Roadside Hawk *Buteo magnirostris*	BR	SF,HF	C	C	C	C	C	C	C
White-rumped Hawk (39) *Buteo leucorrhous*	BR	HF	-	-	-	-	-	R	R

Family/Species	Status	Habitat	Geographical Regions						
			AC	MG	BC	CC	CP	ÑE	AP
Short-tailed Hawk (40) *Buteo brachyurus*	BR	SF,HF	R	-	R	-	-	R	R
Swainson's Hawk (41) *Buteo swainsoni*	NM	GL,SF,HF	R	-	-	R	R	-	-
White-tailed Hawk *Buteo albicaudatus*	BR	GL,SF,HF	U	-	U	R	R	U	R
Zone-tailed Hawk (42) *Buteo albonotatus*	BR	GL,SF	U	R	U	R	-	-	-
Harpy Eagle (43) *Harpia harpyja*	BR	HF	-	H	-	R	R	H	R
Black-and-white Hawk-Eagle (44) *Spizastur melanoleucus*	BR	SF, HF	R	-	-	-	R	-	R
Ornate Hawk-Eagle (45) *Spizaetus ornatus*	BR	HF	-	-	-	R	R	-	R

FALCONIDAE (12 species)

Family/Species	Status	Habitat	AC	MG	BC	CC	CP	ÑE	AP
Crested Caracara *Caracara plancus*	BR	GL,WL,SF	C	C	A	C	C	C	C
Yellow-headed Caracara *Milvago chimachima*	BR	GL,WL,SF	R	U	U	C	C	U	U
Chimango Caracara *Milvago chimango*	BR	GL,WL	R	-	U	-	C	A	R
Laughing Falcon *Herpetotheres cachinnans*	BR	SF,HF	U	R	U	U	R	-	R
Barred Forest-Falcon *Micrastur ruficollis*	BR	HF	-	-	-	R	R	-	R
Collared Forest-Falcon (46) *Micrastur semitorquatus*	BR	SF,HF	-	R	-	R	R	-	R
Spot-winged Falconet (47) *Spiziapteryx circumcinctus*	BR	SF	R	-	-	-	-	-	-
American Kestrel *Falco sparverius*	BR	GL,SF	C	R	C	C	C	C	C
Aplomado Falcon *Falco femoralis*	BR	GL,SF	U	R	U	R	R	U	R
Bat Falcon *Falco rufigularis*	BR	SF,HF	R	R	R	R	U	-	U
Orange-breasted Falcon (48) *Falco deiroleucus*	BR	SF,HF	R	R	-	R	-	-	R
Peregrine Falcon (49) *Falco peregrinus*	NM,AM	GL,WL	R	U	U	U	U	-	R

CRACIDAE (5 species)

Family/Species	Status	Habitat	AC	MG	BC	CC	CP	ÑE	AP
Chaco Chachalaca *Ortalis canicollis*	BR	SF	C	U	C	C	R	-	-
Rusty-margined Guan *Penelope superciliaris*	BR	HF	-	-	-	R	U	-	U

Family/Species	Status	Habitat	Geographical Regions						
			AC	MG	BC	CC	CP	ÑE	AP
Blue-throated Piping-Guan (50,B) *Pipile pipile*	BR	SF,HF	-	-	H	R	R	-	-
Black-fronted Piping-Guan (51) *Pipile jacutinga*	BR	HF	-	-	-	-	R	-	R
Bare-faced Curassow *Crax fasciolata*	BR	SF,HF	-	R	R	R	R	R	R

ODONTOPHORIDAE (1 species)

Spot-winged Wood-Quail *Odontophorus capueira*	BR	HF	-	-	-	U	U	-	U

RALLIDAE (20 species)

Speckled Crake (52) *Coturnicops notata*	BR	WL	R	-	-	R	-	-	R
Red-and-white Crake (53) *Laterallus leucopyrrhus*	BR	WL	-	-	R	-	R	-	-
Rufous-sided Crake (54) *Laterallus melanophaius*	BR	WL	R	-	R	R	R	R	R
Rufous-faced Crake (55) *Laterallus xenopterus*	BR	WL	-	-	-	R	R	-	-
Gray-breasted Crake (56) *Laterallus exilis*	TV	WL	-	-	R	-	-	R	-
Gray-necked Wood-Rail *Aramides cajanea*	BR	WL	R	R	R	R	R	R	R
Giant Wood-Rail *Aramides ypecaha*	BR	WL	C	U	C	U	U	C	R
Slaty-breasted Wood-Rail (57) *Aramides saracura*	BR	HF	-	-	H	-	R	H	U
Ash-throated Crake *Porzana albicollis*	BR	WL	-	-	-	R	U	U	R
Yellow-breasted Crake (58) *Porzana flaviventer*	BR	WL	R	R	-	R	R	R	-
Paint-billed Crake (59) *Neocrex erythrops*	BN	WL	R	-	R	R	R	-	R
Spotted Rail (60) *Pardirallus maculatus*	BN	WL	R	-	R	R	R	R	R
Plumbeous Rail (61) *Pardirallus sanguinolentus*	BR	WL	R	-	-	R	R	R	R
Blackish Rail *Pardirallus nigricans*	BR	WL	-	-	-	R	R	-	R
Purple Gallinule (62) *Porphyrula martinica*	BN	WL	U	R	U	R	R	R	R
Azure Gallinule (63) *Porphyrula flavirostris*	BN	WL	R	-	R	R	R	-	-
Spot-flanked Gallinule (64) *Gallinula melanops*	BR	WL	U	-	R	-	-	H	-

Family/Species	Status	Habitat	Geographical Regions						
			AC	MG	BC	CC	CP	ÑE	AP
Common Moorhen *Gallinula chloropus*	BR	WL	C	H	U	U	U	U	U
White-winged Coot (65) *Fulica leucoptera*	BR	WL	U	R	R	-	R	-	-
Red-fronted Coot (66) *Fulica rufifrons*	BR	WL	R	-	R	-	-	-	-
HELIORNITHIDAE (1 species)									
Sungrebe (67) *Heliornis fulica*	BR	WL	-	-	-	-	R	-	R
ARAMIDAE (1 species)									
Limpkin *Aramus guarauna*	BR	WL	U	A	A	C	C	C	R
CARIAMIDAE (2 species)									
Red-legged Seriema *Cariama cristata*	BR	GL	C	R	C	C	-	R	H
Black-legged Seriema (68) *Chunga burmeisteri*	BR	GL	U	-	-	-	-	-	-
CHARADRIIDAE (5 species)									
Pied Lapwing (69) *Hoploxypterus cayanus*	TV	WL	R	-	-	R	R	-	R
Southern Lapwing *Vanellus chilensis*	BR	WL	C	C	C	C	C	C	C
Black-bellied Plover (70) *Pluvialis squatarola*	NM	WL	-	-	-	-	R	-	-
American Golden-Plover (71) *Pluvialis dominica*	NM	GL,WL	U	U	U	U	C	-	R
Collared Plover *Charadrius collaris*	BR	WL	C	C	C	C	C	C	R
RECURVIROSTRIDAE (1 species)									
Black-necked Stilt *Himantopus mexicanus*	BR	WL	A	C	C	R	C	U	R
JACANIDAE (1 species)									
Wattled Jacana *Jacana jacana*	BR	WL	A	A	A	A	A	A	A
ROSTRATULIDAE (1 species)									
South American Painted-Snipe (72) *Rostratula semicollaris*	BR	WL	R	-	R	-	-	R	R

Family/Species	Status	Habitat	Geographical Regions						
			AC	MG	BC	CC	CP	ÑE	AP
SCOLOPACIDAE (20 species)									
Greater Yellowlegs (73) *Tringa melanoleuca*	NM	WL	U	-	U	-	U	U	-
Lesser Yellowlegs (74) *Tringa flavipes*	NM	WL	A	A	C	C	C	U	-
Solitary Sandpiper (75) *Tringa solitaria*	NM	WL	C	A	C	C	C	C	R
Spotted Sandpiper (76) *Actitis macularia*	NM	WL	R	U	R	-	R	-	-
Upland Sandpiper (77) *Bartramia longicauda*	NM	GL	R	-	R	R	U	-	R
Eskimo Curlew (78) *Numenius borealis*	NM	GL	No locality records						
Hudsonian Godwit (79) *Limosa haemastica*	NM	WL	R	-	R	R	U	-	-
Red Knot (80) *Calidris canutus*	NM	WL	-	-	-	-	R	-	-
Sanderling (81) *Calidris alba*	NM	WL	R	-	-	-	R	H	-
Semipalmated Sandpiper (82) *Calidris pusilla*	NM	WL	R	R	-	-	-	-	-
Least Sandpiper (83) *Calidris minutilla*	NM	WL	R	-	-	-	R	-	-
White-rumped Sandpiper (84) *Calidris fuscicollis*	NM	WL	C	R	U	U	A	-	R
Baird's Sandpiper (85) *Calidris bairdii*	NM	WL	R	H	H	-	-	R	-
Pectoral Sandpiper (86) *Calidris melanotos*	NM	WL	A	C	A	C	A	U	R
Stilt Sandpiper (87) *Calidris himantopus*	NM	WL	R	R	U	-	U	-	-
Buff-breasted Sandpiper (88) *Tryngites subruficollis*	NM	GL,WL	R	R	R	-	C	-	R
South American Snipe *Gallinago paraguaiae*	BR	GL,WL	R	-	U	U	U	U	R
Giant Snipe *Gallinago undulata*	BR	WL	-	-	-	R	R	H	R
Wilson's Phalarope (89) *Phalaropus tricolor*	NM	WL	R	-	-	-	R	-	-
Red Phalarope (90) *Phalaropus fulicaria*	NM	WL	R	-	-	-	-	-	-
LARIDAE (6 species)									
Gray-hooded Gull (91) *Larus cirrocephalus*	AM	WL	R	H	-	-	-	H	-
Brown-hooded Gull (92) *Larus maculipennis*	AM	WL	-	-	-	-	R	-	R

Family/Species	Status	Habitat	Geographical Regions						
			AC	MG	BC	CC	CP	ÑE	AP
Large-billed Tern (93) *Phaetusa simplex*	BR	WL	R	C	A	A	A	C	R
Arctic Tern (94) *Sterna paradisaea*	NM	WL	-	-	-	-	R	-	-
Yellow-billed Tern (95) *Sterna superciliaris*	BR	WL	R	C	C	C	C	C	-
Black Skimmer (96) *Rynchops niger*	BR	WL	U	C	C	C	C	R	R

COLUMBIDAE (16 species)

Family/Species	Status	Habitat	AC	MG	BC	CC	CP	ÑE	AP
Rock Dove (97) *Columba livia*	IB	RE	C	C	C	C	C	C	C
Scaled Pigeon (98) *Columba speciosa*	BR	HF	-	-	-	-	R	-	R
Picazuro Pigeon (99) *Columba picazuro*	BS	SF,HF	A	U	C	C	C	C	C
Spot-winged Pigeon (100) *Columba maculosa*	BR	SF	R	-	R	H	H	-	-
Pale-vented Pigeon *Columba cayennensis*	BR	SF,HF	R	C	U	U	U	U	C
Eared Dove *Zenaida auriculata*	BR	GL,SF	A	U	C	U	U	A	U
Scaled Dove *Columbina squammata*	BR	SF	R	U	R	C	R	-	R
Plain-breasted Ground-Dove (101) *Columbina minuta*	BR	SF,HF	R	-	H	R	R	-	R
Ruddy Ground-Dove *Columbina talpacoti*	BR	SF,HF	U	U	U	U	U	C	C
Picui Ground-Dove *Columbina picui*	BR	SF,HF	A	C	A	U	A	C	U
Blue Ground-Dove *Claravis pretiosa*	BR	SF,HF	R	U	R	R	R	R	R
Purple-winged Ground-Dove (102) *Claravis godefrida*	BR	HF	-	-	-	-	-	-	R
White-tipped Dove *Leptotila verreauxi*	BR	SF,HF	C	C	C	C	C	C	C
Gray-fronted Dove (103) *Leptotila rufaxilla*	BR	HF	-	-	-	R	U	R	U
Ruddy Quail-Dove *Geotrygon montana*	BR	HF	-	-	-	R	R	-	R
Violaceous Quail-Dove *Geotrygon violacea*	BR	HF	-	-	-	R	R	R	R

PSITTACIDAE (19 species)

Family/Species	Status	Habitat	AC	MG	BC	CC	CP	ÑE	AP
Hyacinthine Macaw (104) *Anodorhynchus hyacinthinus*	BR	SF	-	R	-	R	H	-	-

Family/Species	Status	Habitat	Geographical Regions						
			AC	MG	BC	CC	CP	ÑE	AP
Glaucous Macaw (105) *Anodorhynchus glaucus*	XB	SF,HF	-	-	-	-	-	H	H
Blue-and-yellow Macaw (106) *Ara ararauna*	XB	SF,HF	-	-	-	R	R	H	R
Red-and-green Macaw (107) *Ara chloropterus*	BR	SF,HF	-	R	H	C	U	H	R
Golden-collared Macaw *Ara auricollis*	BR	SF	-	R	H	R	-	-	-
Blue-winged Macaw (108) *Ara maracana*	BR	SF,HF	-	-	H	R	R	-	R
Blue-crowned Parakeet *Aratinga acuticaudata*	BR	SF,HF	C	R	U	U	R	-	R
White-eyed Parakeet *Aratinga leucophthalmus*	BR	SF,HF	R	R	R	U	U	R	U
Peach-fronted Parakeet (109) *Aratinga aurea*	BR	SF	-	R	R	A	R	R	-
Black-hooded Parakeet *Nandayus nenday*	BR	GL,SF	R	A	A	A	C	U	R
Blaze-winged Parakeet (110,C) *Pyrrhura devillei*	BR	SF	-	R	-	U	-	-	-
Reddish-bellied Parakeet (111) *Pyrrhura frontalis*	BR	SF,HF	R	R	R	C	C	R	C
Monk Parakeet *Myiopsitta monachus*	BR	SF	A	A	A	U	C	C	R
Blue-winged Parrotlet (112) *Forpus xanthopterygius*	BR	SF,HF	-	R	R	R	U	U	U
Yellow-chevroned Parakeet *Brotogeris chiriri*	BR	SF,HF	-	C	R	C	C	-	C
Red-capped Parrot *Pionopsitta pileata*	BR	HF	-	-	-	-	R	-	C
Scaly-headed Parrot *Pionus maximiliani*	BR	SF,HF	R	C	U	C	C	U	C
Turquoise-fronted Parrot *Amazona aestiva*	BR	SF,HF	C	C	U	C	U	R	R
Vinaceous-breasted Parrot (113) *Amazona vinacea*	BR	HF	-	-	-	R	R	H	C

CUCULIDAE (11 species)

Family/Species	Status	Habitat	AC	MG	BC	CC	CP	ÑE	AP
Ash-colored Cuckoo (114) *Coccyzus cinereus*	BR	SF,HF	R	-	H	-	-	R	R
Black-billed Cuckoo (115) *Coccyzus erythropthalmus*	NM	SF	R	-	-	-	-	-	-
Yellow-billed Cuckoo (116) *Coccyzus americanus*	NM	SF,HF	U	-	R	R	R	R	R
Dark-billed Cuckoo (117) *Coccyzus melacoryphus*	BN	SF,HF	U	R	U	U	U	U	U

Family/Species	Status	Habitat	Geographical Regions						
			AC	MG	BC	CC	CP	ÑE	AP
Squirrel Cuckoo	BR	SF,HF	R	R	R	C	C	U	C
Piaya cayana									
Striped Cuckoo	BR	WL,SF	U	U	C	U	U	U	R
Tapera naevia									
Pheasant Cuckoo (118)	BR	HF	-	-	-	-	R	H	H
Dromococcyx phasianellus									
Pavonine Cuckoo (119)	BR	HF	R	-	-	-	R	-	R
Dromococcyx pavoninus									
Greater Ani	BN	WL,SF,HF	R	U	R	R	R	R	R
Crotophaga major									
Smooth-billed Ani	BR	GL,WL	C	U	A	A	A	A	A
Crotophaga ani									
Guira Cuckoo	BR	GL	C	C	C	A	A	A	A
Guira guira									

TYTONIDAE (1 species)

Family/Species	Status	Habitat							
Barn Owl	BR	GL	U	-	U	U	U	U	R
Tyto alba									

STRIGIDAE (15 species)

Family/Species	Status	Habitat							
Tropical Screech-Owl	BR	SF,HF	U	U	U	C	C	U	C
Otus choliba									
Variable Screech-Owl	BR	SF,HF	-	-	-	R	R	-	-
Otus atricapillus									
Spectacled Owl (120)	BR	SF	-	-	H	R	R	-	-
Pulsatrix perspicillata									
Tawny-browed Owl (121)	BR	HF	-	-	-	-	-	-	R
Pulsatrix koeniswaldiana									
Great Horned Owl (122)	BR	SF	U	U	U	R	-	R	-
Bubo virginianus									
Brazilian Pygmy-Owl (123)	BR	HF	-	-	-	-	-	-	R
Glaucidium minutissimum									
Ferruginous Pygmy-Owl	BR	SF,HF	U	U	U	U	U	U	C
Glaucidium brasilianum									
Burrowing Owl	BR	GL	U	-	U	U	U	C	U
Speotyto cunicularia									
Mottled Owl (124)	BR	HF	-	-	-	-	R	-	R
Ciccaba virgata									
Rusty-barred Owl (125)	BR	HF	-	-	-	-	H	-	R
Strix hylophila									
Rufous-legged Owl	BR	SF	C	R	-	-	-	-	-
Strix rufipes									
Stygian Owl (126)	BR	SF,HF	-	-	R	-	R	-	R
Asio stygius									
Striped Owl	BR	SF,HF	R	R	R	R	R	-	R
Asio clamator									

Family/Species	Status	Habitat	Geographical Regions						
			AC	MG	BC	CC	CP	ÑE	AP
Short-eared Owl (127) *Asio flammeus*	BR	GL,WL	R	-	R	R	-	H	-
Buff-fronted Owl (128) *Aegolius harrisii*	BR	SF,HF	R	-	-	-	R	-	R
CAPRIMULGIDAE (11 species)									
Short-tailed Nighthawk *Lurocalis semitorquatus*	BR	HF	-	-	-	R	C	-	C
Common Nighthawk (129) *Chordeiles minor*	NM	GL,SF,HF	C	U	U	C	C	-	U
Nacunda Nighthawk *Podager nacunda*	BR	GL,WL,SF	R	U	U	R	U	U	U
Pauraque *Nyctidromus albicollis*	BR	SF,HF	-	U	-	C	C	R	C
Ocellated Poorwill (130) *Nyctiphrynus ocellatus*	BR	HF	-	-	-	-	R	-	R
Rufous Nightjar *Caprimulgus rufus*	BR	SF,HF	-	-	-	U	U	R	U
Silky-tailed Nightjar *Caprimulgus sericocaudatus*	BR	HF	-	-	-	-	R	-	R
Band-winged Nightjar (131) *Caprimulgus longirostris*	AM	SF	U	-	-	-	-	-	-
Little Nightjar *Caprimulgus parvulus*	BR	SF,HF	C	U	U	U	U	U	R
Scissor-tailed Nightjar *Hydropsalis brasiliana*	BR	GL,WL,SF	R	C	R	U	R	R	R
Sickle-winged Nightjar (132) *Eleothreptus anomalus*	BR	GL,WL	-	-	-	R	R	R	-
NYCTIBIIDAE (2 species)									
Long-tailed Potoo (133) *Nyctibius aethereus*	BR	HF	-	-	-	R	R	-	R
Gray Potoo *Nyctibius griseus*	BR	SF,HF	R	R	R	U	U	-	U
APODIDAE (4 species)									
Great Dusky Swift *Cypseloides senex*	BR	GL,HF,WF	-	-	-	-	R	-	C
White-collared Swift (134) *Streptoprocne zonaris*	BR	GL,HF,WF	-	-	-	-	U	-	R
Ashy-tailed Swift (135) *Chaetura andrei*	BN	GL,SF,HF	C	R	U	U	U	R	U
Gray-rumped Swift (136) *Chaetura cinereiventris*	BR	GL,HF	-	-	-	-	U	-	U

Family/Species	Status	Habitat	AC	MG	BC	CC	CP	ÑE	AP
TROCHILIDAE (16 species)									
Scale-throated Hermit *Phaethornis eurynome*	BR	SF,HF	-	-	-	R	U	-	U
Planalto Hermit *Phaethornis pretrei*	BR	SF,HF	-	-	-	U	U	-	R
Swallow-tailed Hummingbird (137) *Eupetomena macroura*	BR	SF	-	-	-	R	-	-	-
Black Jacobin (138) *Melanotrochilus fuscus*	BR	HF	-	-	-	-	-	-	R
White-vented Violet-ear (139) *Colibri serrirostris*	BR	SF	-	-	-	-	R	-	H
Black-throated Mango (140) *Anthracothorax nigricollis*	BR	SF,HF	R	-	R	R	R	R	R
Black-breasted Plovercrest *Stephanoxis lalandi*	BR	HF	-	-	-	R	R	-	U
Glittering-bellied Emerald *Chlorostilbon aureoventris*	BR	SF,HF	C	C	C	C	C	C	U
Fork-tailed Woodnymph *Thalurania furcata*	BR	SF,HF	-	-	-	R	R	-	R
Violet-capped Woodnymph *Thalurania glaucopis*	BR	HF	-	-	-	-	U	R	U
Gilded Sapphire *Hylocharis chrysura*	BR	SF,HF	U	U	U	U	U	U	U
White-throated Hummingbird (141) *Leucochloris albicollis*	BR	SF,HF	R	-	-	-	R	H	R
White-tailed Goldenthroat (142) *Polytmus guainumbi*	BR	SF	-	-	R	R	R	R	R
Versicolored Emerald *Amazilia versicolor*	BR	HF	-	-	-	R	U	-	U
Blue-tufted Starthroat *Heliomaster furcifer*	BR	GL,SF	U	U	U	U	U	R	R
Amethyst Woodstar *Calliphlox amethystina*	BR	HF	-	-	-	R	R	-	R
TROGONIDAE (3 species)									
Black-throated Trogon *Trogon rufus*	BR	SF,HF	-	-	-	R	U	-	U
Surucua Trogon (143) *Trogon surrucura*	BR	SF,HF	-	-	H	C	C	U	C
Blue-crowned Trogon *Trogon curucui*	BR	SF	R	U	U	U	R	R	-
MOMOTIDAE (2 species)									
Blue-crowned Motmot (144) *Momotus momota*	BR	SF	-	R	-	-	-	-	-
Rufous-capped Motmot *Baryphthengus ruficapillus*	BR	HF	-	-	-	U	U	R	U

Family/Species	Status	Habitat	Geographical Regions						
			AC	MG	BC	CC	CP	ÑE	AP

ALCEDINIDAE (5 species)

Family/Species	Status	Habitat	AC	MG	BC	CC	CP	ÑE	AP
Ringed Kingfisher *Ceryle torquata*	BR	WL	U	C	C	C	C	C	C
Amazon Kingfisher *Chloroceryle amazona*	BR	WL	R	C	C	C	C	C	C
Green Kingfisher *Chloroceryle americana*	BR	WL	R	U	U	U	U	U	U
Green-and-rufous Kingfisher(145) *Chloroceryle inda*	BR	WL	-	-	-	R	R	-	-
Pygmy Kingfisher (146) *Chloroceryle aenea*	BR	WL	-	R	-	-	-	-	-

BUCCONIDAE (4 species)

White-necked Puffbird (147) *Notharchus macrorhynchos*	BR	SF,HF	-	-	H	R	U	-	U
White-eared Puffbird (148) *Nystalus chacuru*	BR	SF,HF	-	-	R	U	U	R	U
Spot-backed Puffbird *Nystalus maculatus*	BR	SF	U	-	R	U	-	-	-
Rusty-breasted Nunlet *Nonnula rubecula*	BR	HF	-	-	-	R	R	-	R

RAMPHASTIDAE (5 species)

Chestnut-eared Aracari *Pteroglossus castanotis*	BR	SF,HF	-	-	-	U	C	R	C
Spot-billed Toucanet (149) *Selenidera maculirostris*	BR	HF	-	-	-	-	R	-	R
Saffron Toucanet *Baillonius bailloni*	BR	HF	-	-	-	-	R	-	R
Red-breasted Toucan (150) *Ramphastos dicolorus*	BR	SF,HF	-	R	-	U	U	H	U
Toco Toucan *Ramphastos toco*	BR	SF,HF	R	U	U	C	U	U	C

PICIDAE (21 species)

Ochre-collared Piculet (D) *Picumnus temminckii*	BR	HF	-	-	-	-	R	R	U
White-barred Piculet *Picumnus cirratus*	BR	SF,HF	U	C	U	C	C	U	R
White-wedged Piculet (151,E) *Picumnus albosquamatus*	BR	HF	-	-	-	-	-	-	R
White Woodpecker *Melanerpes candidus*	BR	GL,SF	U	R	U	U	U	U	U
Yellow-fronted Woodpecker *Melanerpes flavifrons*	BR	HF	-	-	-	R	U	-	C

Family/Species	Status	Habitat	Geographical Regions						
			AC	MG	BC	CC	CP	ÑE	AP
White-fronted Woodpecker *Melanerpes cactorum*	BR	SF	C	R	R	-	-	-	-
Checkered Woodpecker *Picoides mixtus*	BR	SF	U	R	R	R	R	R	H
Little Woodpecker *Veniliornis passerinus*	BR	SF,HF	-	R	R	U	U	U	-
White-spotted Woodpecker *Veniliornis spilogaster*	BR	HF	-	-	-	-	U	-	U
Golden-green Woodpecker (152) *Piculus chrysochloros*	BR	SF	R	C	R	-	R	R	-
White-browed Woodpecker *Piculus aurulentus*	BR	HF	-	-	-	-	R	-	R
Green-barred Woodpecker (F) *Colaptes melanochloros*	BR	SF,HF	R	R	U	U	U	U	R
Campo Flicker (G) *Colaptes campestris*	BR	GL,SF	R	R	C	C	C	C	C
Pale-crested Woodpecker (153) *Celeus lugubris*	BR	SF,HF	-	C	R	U	U	R	H
Blond-crested Woodpecker (153) *Celeus flavescens*	BR	HF	-	-	-	H	R	-	R
Helmeted Woodpecker (154) *Dryocopus galeatus*	BR	HF	-	-	-	R	R	-	R
Lineated Woodpecker (155) *Dryocopus lineatus*	BR	SF,HF	-	H	R	U	U	R	U
Black-bodied Woodpecker (H) *Dryocopus schulzi*	BR	SF	R	H	R	-	-	-	-
Robust Woodpecker *Campephilus robustus*	BR	HF	-	-	-	R	U	-	U
Crimson-crested Woodpecker (156) *Campephilus melanoleucos*	BR	SF,HF	-	R	R	U	R	R	-
Cream-backed Woodpecker (157) *Campephilus leucopogon*	BR	SF	U	U	R	H	H	H	H

FURNARIIDAE (38 species)

Family/Species	Status	Habitat	AC	MG	BC	CC	CP	ÑE	AP
Chaco Earthcreeper *Upucerthia certhioides*	BR	SF	R	-	-	-	-	-	-
Bar-winged Cinclodes (158) *Cinclodes fuscus*	AM	GL	-	-	-	-	-	R	-
Canebrake Groundcreeper (159) *Clibanornis dendrocolaptoides*	BR	HF	-	-	-	-	-	-	R
Rufous Hornero *Furnarius rufus*	BR	SF,HF	U	A	A	A	A	A	A
Crested Hornero *Furnarius cristatus*	BR	SF	C	-	-	-	-	-	-
Wren-like Rushbird (160) *Phleocryptes melanops*	AM	WL	R	H	R	-	-	-	H

Family/Species	Status	Habitat	Geographical Regions						
			AC	MG	BC	CC	CP	ÑE	AP
Tufted Tit-Spinetail (161) *Leptasthenura platensis*	BR	SF	R	-	-	-	-	R	-
Chotoy Spinetail *Schoeniophylax phryganophila*	BR	GL,WL,SF	C	U	C	U	U	U	-
Rufous-capped Spinetail *Synallaxis ruficapilla*	BR	HF	-	-	-	R	U	-	C
Sooty-fronted Spinetail *Synallaxis frontalis*	BR	SF,HF	U	C	C	R	U	U	-
Chicli Spinetail *Synallaxis spixi*	BR	HF	-	-	-	H	R	-	R
Pale-breasted Spinetail *Synallaxis albescens*	BR	SF	U	C	C	U	U	U	R
Plain-crowned Spinetail *Synallaxis gujanensis*	BR	SF	-	A	H	U	-	-	-
Gray-bellied Spinetail *Synallaxis cinerascens*	BR	HF	-	-	-	R	U	-	U
Yellow-throated Spinetail *Certhiaxis cinnamomea*	BR	WL	C	C	C	C	C	C	-
Olive Spinetail (I) *Cranioleuca obsoleta*	BR	HF	-	-	-	-	R	R	R
Stripe-crowned Spinetail *Cranioleuca pyrrhophia*	BR	SF	U	U	R	-	-	-	-
Lesser Canastero (162) *Asthenes pyrrholeuca*	AM	SF	R	-	R	-	-	R	H
Short-billed Canastero (163) *Asthenes baeri*	BR	SF	U	-	U	-	-	R	-
Little Thornbird (164) *Phacellodomus sibilatrix*	BR	SF	C	-	R	-	R	-	-
Rufous-fronted Thornbird (165) *Phacellodomus rufifrons*	BR	SF	-	C	R	C	-	H	-
Greater Thornbird *Phacellodomus ruber*	BR	WL,SF	R	R	C	R	U	U	R
Lark-like Brushrunner (166) *Coryphistera alaudina*	BR	GL,SF	A	-	R	-	-	R	-
Firewood-gatherer *Anumbius annumbi*	BR	GL	U	-	U	U	U	C	-
Rufous Cacholote *Pseudoseisura cristata*	BR	SF	-	R	-	-	-	-	-
Brown Cacholote *Pseudoseisura lophotes*	BR	SF	U	-	R	-	-	-	-
Buff-browed Foliage-gleaner(167) *Syndactyla rufosuperciliata*	BR	SF,HF	-	R	-	R	R	R	R
Black-capped Foliage-gleaner *Philydor atricapillus*	BR	HF	-	-	-	-	R	-	R
Russet-mantled Foliage-gleaner(168) *Philydor dimidiatus*	BR	SF	-	-	-	R	-	-	-
Ochre-breasted Foliage-gleaner *Philydor lichtensteini*	BR	SF,HF	-	-	-	U	C	-	C

Family/Species	Status	Habitat	Geographical Regions						
			AC	MG	BC	CC	CP	ÑE	AP
Buff-fronted Foliage-gleaner *Philydor rufus*	BR	HF	-	-	-	R	U	-	U
White-eyed Foliage-gleaner *Automolus leucophthalmus*	BR	HF	-	-	-	R	C	-	C
Chestnut-capped Foliage-gleaner(169) *Hylocryptus rectirostris*	BR	SF	-	-	-	-	R	-	-
Sharp-billed Treehunter *Heliobletus contaminatus*	BR	HF	-	-	-	-	R	R	R
Streaked Xenops *Xenops rutilans*	BR	SF,HF	-	U	-	U	R	-	U
Plain Xenops *Xenops minutus*	BR	HF	-	-	-	-	R	-	R
Rufous-breasted Leaftosser *Sclerurus scansor*	BR	HF	-	-	-	-	R	-	R
Sharp-tailed Streamcreeper *Lochmias nematura*	BR	WL	-	-	-	-	U	-	U

DENDROCOLAPTIDAE (12 species)

Family/Species	Status	Habitat	AC	MG	BC	CC	CP	ÑE	AP
Thrush-like Woodcreeper *Dendrocincla turdina*	BR	HF	-	-	-	R	R	-	R
Olivaceous Woodcreeper *Sittasomus griseicapillus*	BR	SF,HF	R	C	U	C	C	U	C
Scimitar-billed Woodcreeper(170) *Drymornis bridgesii*	BR	SF	U	-	-	-	-	-	-
White-throated Woodcreeper *Xiphocolaptes albicollis*	BR	HF	-	-	-	U	U	R	U
Great Rufous Woodcreeper *Xiphocolaptes major*	BR	SF	U	R	U	C	R	R	-
Black-banded Woodcreeper (171) *Dendrocolaptes picumnus*	BR	SF	U	U	R	-	-	-	H
Planalto Woodcreeper (172) *Dendrocolaptes platyrostris*	BR	SF,HF	-	-	R	R	R	R	U
Narrow-billed Woodcreeper *Lepidocolaptes angustirostris*	BR	SF	C	A	C	C	U	C	R
Scaled Woodcreeper *Lepidocolaptes squamatus*	BR	HF	-	-	-	-	U	-	U
Lesser Woodcreeper *Lepidocolaptes fuscus*	BR	HF	-	-	-	-	U	R	U
Red-billed Scythebill *Campylorhamphus trochilirostris*	BR	SF	R	U	U	U	U	U	-
Black-billed Scythebill (173) *Campylorhamphus falcularius*	BR	HF	-	-	-	-	-	-	R

FORMICARIIDAE (24 species)

Family/Species	Status	Habitat	AC	MG	BC	CC	CP	ÑE	AP
Spot-backed Antshrike *Hypoedaleus guttatus*	BR	HF	-	-	-	R	U	H	U

Family/Species	Status	Habitat	Geographical Regions						
			AC	MG	BC	CC	CP	ÑE	AP
Giant Antshrike (174) *Batara cinerea*	BR	SF	R	-	-	R	R	-	-
Large-tailed Antshrike (175) *Mackenziaena leachii*	BR	HF	-	-	-	-	-	-	R
Tufted Antshrike *Mackenziaena severa*	BR	HF	-	-	-	-	C	-	C
Great Antshrike *Taraba major*	BR	SF,HF	C	C	C	U	U	U	R
Barred Antshrike *Thamnophilus doliatus*	BR	SF,RE	U	C	C	C	C	C	R
Variable Antshrike (J) *Thamnophilus caerulescens*	BR	SF,HF	U	C	U	C	C	U	C
Rufous-capped Antshrike (176) *Thamnophilus ruficapillus*	BR	SF	-	-	H	-	H	-	R
Plain Antvireo *Dysithamnus mentalis*	BR	HF	-	-	-	R	C	R	C
Stripe-backed Antbird *Myrmorchilus strigilatus*	BR	SF	C	U	R	-	-	-	-
Black-capped Antwren *Herpsilochmus atricapillus*	BR	HF	-	-	-	R	U	-	R
Rufous-winged Antwren *Herpsilochmus rufimarginatus*	BR	HF	-	-	-	-	C	-	U
Black-bellied Antwren (177) *Formicivora melanogaster*	BR	SF	R	-	-	-	-	-	-
Rusty-backed Antwren (178) *Formicivora rufa*	BR	SF	-	-	R	R	R	-	-
Bertoni's Antbird (179) *Drymophila rubricollis*	BR	HF	-	-	-	-	-	-	R
Dusky-tailed Antbird *Drymophila malura*	BR	HF	-	-	-	-	R	-	U
Streak-capped Antwren *Terenura maculata*	BR	HF	-	-	-	-	U	-	R
Mato Grosso Antbird *Cercomacra melanaria*	BR	WL,SF	-	C	-	-	-	-	-
White-backed Fire-eye (180) *Pyriglena leuconota*	BR	SF	-	R	-	-	-	-	-
White-shouldered Fire-eye *Pyriglena leucoptera*	BR	HF	-	-	-	R	U	-	U
Short-tailed Antthrush *Chamaeza campanisona*	BR	SF,HF	-	-	-	U	C	-	C
Variegated Antpitta *Grallaria varia*	BR	HF	-	-	-	-	R	-	R
Speckle-breasted Antpitta (181) *Hylopezus nattereri*	BR	HF	-	-	-	-	-	-	R
Rufous Gnateater *Conopophaga lineata*	BR	HF	-	-	-	-	U	-	U

Family/Species	Status	Habitat	Geographical Regions						
			AC	MG	BC	CC	CP	ÑE	AP
RHINOCRYPTIDAE (3 species)									
Crested Gallito (182) *Rhinocrypta lanceolata*	BR	SF	R	-	-	-	-	-	-
Collared Crescentchest (183) *Melanopareia torquata*	BR	GL	-	-	-	-	R	-	-
Olive-crowned Crescentchest(184) *Melanopareia maximiliani*	BR	GL	U	-	R	-	-	-	-
TYRANNIDAE (101 species)									
Planalto Tyrannulet *Phyllomyias fasciatus*	BR	HF	-	-	-	R	R	-	R
Rough-legged Tyrannulet *Phyllomyias burmeisteri*	BR	HF	-	-	-	-	R	-	R
Greenish Tyrannulet *Phyllomyias virescens*	BR	HF	-	-	-	-	R	-	R
Reiser's Tyrannulet (185,K) *Phyllomyias reiseri*	BR	SF	-	-	-	R	-	-	-
Southern Beardless-Tyrannulet *Camptostoma obsoletum*	BR	SF,HF	U	C	C	C	C	C	U
Mouse-colored Tyrannulet (186) *Phaeomyias murina*	BN	SF,HF	-	R	R	R	R	-	R
Yellow Tyrannulet *Capsiempis flaveola*	BR	HF	-	-	-	-	U	-	U
Southern Scrub-Flycatcher (187) *Sublegatus modestus*	BN	SF	R	R	R	R	R	R	-
Suiriri Flycatcher (L) *Suiriri suiriri*	BR	SF	U	U	U	R	R	U	R
Gray Elaenia *Myiopagis caniceps*	BR	HF	-	-	-	R	R	-	U
Greenish Elaenia (188) *Myiopagis viridicata*	BN	HF	-	-	R	R	U	R	U
Yellow-bellied Elaenia (189) *Elaenia flavogaster*	BR	HF	H	H	-	R	U	U	U
Large Elaenia (190) *Elaenia spectabilis*	BN	SF	U	R	U	R	R	R	R
White-crested Elaenia (191) *Elaenia albiceps*	AM	HF	-	-	H	R	R	-	R
Small-billed Elaenia (M) *Elaenia parvirostris*	BR	SF,HF	R	-	U	U	U	R	U
Olivaceous Elaenia (192) *Elaenia mesoleuca*	BR	HF	-	-	H	-	R	-	R
Lesser Elaenia (193) *Elaenia chiriquensis*	BN	SF,HF	-	-	-	-	H	-	R
Highland Elaenia *Elaenia obscura*	BR	HF	-	-	-	-	R	-	R
Sooty Tyrannulet (194) *Serpophaga nigricans*	BR	WL	R	-	R	-	U	U	R

Family/Species	Status	Habitat	Geographical Regions						
			AC	MG	BC	CC	CP	ÑE	AP
White-crested Tyrannulet (195) *Serpophaga subcristata*	BS	SF,HF	C	C	C	U	U	U	R
White-bellied Tyrannulet (196,N) *Serpophaga munda*	BS	SF	U	U	U	R	R	H	-
Plain Tyrannulet (197) *Inezia inornata*	BN	SF	R	R	R	R	-	-	H
Greater Wagtail-Tyrant *Stigmatura budytoides*	BR	SF	U	-	R	-	-	-	-
Many-colored Rush-Tyrant (198) *Tachuris rubrigastra*	BR	WL	-	-	-	-	-	R	-
Sharp-tailed Tyrant (199) *Culicivora caudacuta*	BR	GL,WL	-	-	R	R	R	R	R
Bearded Tachuri *Polystictus pectoralis*	BR	GL,WL	R	R	R	R	R	U	-
Crested Doradito (200) *Pseudocolopteryx sclateri*	BR	WL	R	R	R	R	R	U	-
Dinelli's Doradito (201) *Pseudocolopteryx dinellianus*	AM	WL	R	-	-	-	-	-	H
Subtropical Doradito (202) *Pseudocolopteryx acutipennis*	BR	WL	R	-	R	-	-	-	-
Warbling Doradito (203) *Pseudocolopteryx flaviventris*	AM	WL	R	R	R	R	R	R	R
Tawny-crowned Pygmy-Tyrant *Euscarthmus meloryphus*	BR	SF	R	R	R	-	U	R	R
Rufous-sided Pygmy-Tyrant (204) *Euscarthmus rufomarginatus*	BR	SF	-	-	-	R	-	-	-
Gray-hooded Flycatcher *Mionectes rufiventris*	BR	HF	-	-	-	R	U	-	R
Sepia-capped Flycatcher (205) *Leptopogon amaurocephalus*	BR	HF	-	R	-	R	U	R	U
Southern Bristle-Tyrant *Phylloscartes eximius*	BR	HF	-	-	-	-	U	-	U
Mottle-cheeked Tyrannulet (206) *Phylloscartes ventralis*	BR	HF	-	-	H	-	U	R	U
Sao Paulo Tyrannulet (207) *Phylloscartes paulistus*	BR	HF	-	-	-	-	R	-	R
Bay-ringed Tyrannulet *Phylloscartes sylviolus*	BR	HF	-	-	-	-	R	-	R
Southern Antpipit *Corythopis delalandi*	BR	HF	-	-	-	R	U	-	C
Eared Pygmy-Tyrant *Myiornis auricularis*	BR	HF	-	-	-	R	U	R	U
Drab-breasted Pygmy-Tyrant *Hemitriccus diops*	BR	HF	-	-	-	-	R	-	U
Pearly-vented Tody-Tyrant *Hemitriccus margaritaceiventer*	BR	SF,HF	C	C	C	C	C	C	R
Ochre-faced Tody-Flycatcher *Todirostrum plumbeiceps*	BR	HF	-	-	-	-	U	-	R

Family/Species	Status	Habitat	Geographical Regions						
			AC	MG	BC	CC	CP	ÑE	AP
Common Tody-Flycatcher (208) *Todirostrum cinereum*	BR	WL,SF	-	U	-	H	-	-	-
Large-headed Flatbill (209) *Ramphotrigon megacephala*	BR	HF	-	-	-	-	R	-	R
Yellow-olive Flycatcher *Tolmomyias sulphurescens*	BR	SF,HF	R	A	C	C	U	U	U
White-throated Spadebill (210) *Platyrinchus mystaceus*	BR	SF,HF	-	R	R	R	R	-	R
Russet-winged Spadebill (211) *Platyrinchus leucoryphus*	BR	HF	-	-	-	-	R	-	-
Bran-colored Flycatcher (212) *Myiophobus fasciatus*	BN	SF,HF	H	-	-	R	R	R	U
Tropical Pewee *Contopus cinereus*	BR	HF	-	-	-	R	R	-	R
Euler's Flycatcher (213) *Lathrotriccus euleri*	BN	SF,HF	R	R	R	R	U	U	U
Fuscous Flycatcher (214,O) *Cnemotriccus fuscatus*	BN	SF,HF	R	R	R	R	U	R	U
Vermilion Flycatcher (215) *Pyrocephalus rubinus*	BS	WL,SF	U	C	C	C	C	C	U
Gray Monjita *Xolmis cinerea*	BR	GL,SF	R	-	C	C	U	C	U
Black-crowned Monjita (216) *Xolmis coronata*	AM	GL,SF	U	-	R	-	R	-	-
White-rumped Monjita *Xolmis velata*	BR	GL,SF	-	-	-	C	-	-	-
White Monjita *Xolmis irupero*	BR	GL,SF	C	C	C	U	C	C	-
Gray-bellied Shrike-Tyrant (217) *Agriornis microptera*	AM	GL,SF	R	-	-	-	-	-	-
Mouse-brown Shrike-Tyrant (218) *Agriornis murina*	AM	GL,SF	R	-	-	-	-	-	-
Austral Negrito (219) *Lessonia rufa*	AM	GL,WL	R	-	-	-	-	R	R
Cinereous Tyrant (220) *Knipolegus striaticeps*	BS	SF	U	R	U	R	R	-	-
Hudson's Black-Tyrant (221) *Knipolegus hudsoni*	AM	SF	R	R	R	-	-	-	-
Blue-billed Black-Tyrant (222) *Knipolegus cyanirostris*	AM	SF,HF	-	-	H	R	R	R	R
White-winged Black-Tyrant (223) *Knipolegus aterrimus*	AM	SF	R	-	H	-	-	-	-
Crested Black-Tyrant (224) *Knipolegus lophotes*	BR	HF	-	-	-	-	R	-	-
Spectacled Tyrant (225) *Hymenops perspicillatus*	BS	GL,WL	U	U	U	U	U	C	R
Black-backed Water-Tyrant *Fluvicola albiventer*	BR	WL	C	C	C	C	C	C	-

Family/Species	Status	Habitat	AC	MG	BC	CC	CP	ÑE	AP
White-headed Marsh-Tyrant *Fluvicola leucocephala*	BR	WL	R	R	U	R	R	C	R
Long-tailed Tyrant (226) *Colonia colonus*	BR	HF	-	-	R	U	C	R	C
Cock-tailed Tyrant (227) *Alectrurus tricolor*	BR	GL,WL	-	-	H	U	R	R	H
Strange-tailed Tyrant (228) *Alectrurus risora*	BR	GL,WL	-	-	U	-	R	C	R
Streamer-tailed Tyrant (229) *Gubernetes yetapa*	BR	GL,WL	-	R	-	C	C	C	C
Yellow-browed Tyrant *Satrapa icterophrys*	BR	WL,SF	R	R	U	R	U	U	R
Cliff Flycatcher (230) *Hirundinea ferruginea*	BR	SF,CL	-	R	-	R	C	-	R
Cattle Tyrant *Machetornis rixosus*	BR	GL,WL,SF	C	A	A	C	C	A	C
Shear-tailed Gray-Tyrant (231) *Muscipipra vetula*	BR	HF	-	-	-	-	R	-	R
Rufous-tailed Attila (232) *Attila phoenicurus*	AM	SF	R	-	-	-	H	-	H
Rufous Casiornis *Casiornis rufa*	BR	SF,HF	U	C	U	C	U	R	R
Sirystes *Sirystes sibilator*	BR	HF	-	-	-	C	C	R	C
Swainson's Flycatcher (233) *Myiarchus swainsoni*	BN	SF,HF	R	R	R	R	R	R	R
Short-crested Flycatcher (234) *Myiarchus ferox*	BR	SF,HF	R	R	R	U	U	R	U
Brown-crested Flycatcher *Myiarchus tyrannulus*	BR	SF,HF	C	A	C	C	C	C	U
Great Kiskadee *Pitangus sulphuratus*	BR	WL,SF,HF	A	A	A	A	A	A	A
Boat-billed Flycatcher *Megarynchus pitangua*	BR	SF,HF	R	R	R	R	U	R	C
Social Flycatcher *Myiozetetes similis*	BR	WL	-	-	-	R	R	H	C
Three-striped Flycatcher *Conopias trivirgata*	BR	HF	-	-	-	-	U	-	U
Streaked Flycatcher (235) *Myiodynastes maculatus*	BN	SF,HF	C	U	C	U	U	U	U
Piratic Flycatcher (236) *Legatus leucophaius*	BN	HF	H	-	-	R	R	-	R
Variegated Flycatcher (237) *Empidonomus varius*	BN	SF,HF	R	-	R	U	U	U	C
Crowned Slaty Flycatcher (238) *Griseotyrannus aurantioatrocristatus*	BN	SF,HF	A	C	C	R	R	U	R
Tropical Kingbird (239) *Tyrannus melancholicus*	BN	SF,HF	A	A	A	A	A	A	A

Family/Species	Status	Habitat	Geographical Regions						
			AC	MG	BC	CC	CP	ÑE	AP
Fork-tailed Flycatcher (240) *Tyrannus savana*	BN	GL,WL,SF	U	C	C	U	U	C	U
Eastern Kingbird (241) *Tyrannus tyrannus*	NM	WL,SF	R	U	-	-	R	-	-
White-naped Xenopsaris (242) *Xenopsaris albinucha*	BR	SF	R	-	-	-	R	-	-
Green-backed Becard *Pachyramphus viridis*	BR	SF,HF	R	U	U	U	U	R	U
Chestnut-crowned Becard *Pachyramphus castaneus*	BR	HF	-	-	-	R	R	R	R
White-winged Becard (243) *Pachyramphus polychopterus*	BN	SF,HF	R	R	R	R	R	R	R
Crested Becard *Pachyramphus validus*	BR	SF,HF	R	R	R	R	U	R	R
Greenish Schiffornis *Schiffornis virescens*	BR	HF	-	-	-	R	U	-	C
Black-tailed Tityra (244) *Tityra cayana*	BR	SF,HF	R	-	R	U	U	R	U
Black-crowned Tityra (245) *Tityra inquisitor*	BR	SF,HF	-	-	R	U	U	R	C

COTINGIDAE (3 species)

Family/Species	Status	Habitat	AC	MG	BC	CC	CP	ÑE	AP
Swallow-tailed Cotinga (246) *Phibalura flavirostris*	BR	HF	-	-	-	-	R	-	R
Red-ruffed Fruitcrow *Pyroderus scutatus*	BR	HF	-	-	-	R	U	-	U
Bare-throated Bellbird *Procnias nudicollis*	BR	HF	-	-	-	R	C	-	R

PIPRIDAE (5 species)

Family/Species	Status	Habitat	AC	MG	BC	CC	CP	ÑE	AP
Helmeted Manakin (247) *Antilophia galeata*	BR	HF	-	-	-	R	R	-	-
Swallow-tailed Manakin (248) *Chiroxiphia caudata*	BR	HF	-	R	R	R	C	R	C
White-bearded Manakin *Manacus manacus*	BR	HF	-	-	-	-	R	-	U
Wing-barred Manakin *Piprites chloris*	BR	HF	-	-	-	-	U	-	U
Band-tailed Manakin (249) *Pipra fasciicauda*	BR	HF	-	R	R	R	U	-	R

OXYRUNCIDAE (1 species)

Family/Species	Status	Habitat	AC	MG	BC	CC	CP	ÑE	AP
Sharpbill *Oxyruncus cristatus*	BR	HF	-	-	-	R	R	-	R

Family/Species	Status	Habitat	Geographical Regions						
			AC	MG	BC	CC	CP	ÑE	AP
PHYTOTOMIDAE (1 species)									
White-tipped Plantcutter (250) *Phytotoma rutila*	AM	SF	R	-	U	-	R	-	R
HIRUNDINIDAE (13 species)									
Purple Martin (251) *Progne subis*	NM	GL,WL	R	C	-	-	R	-	-
Gray-breasted Martin (252) *Progne chalybea*	BN	GL,WL,RE	R	-	U	U	C	C	U
Brown-chested Martin (253) *Phaeoprogne tapera*	BN	GL,WL	U	C	A	C	C	A	U
White-winged Swallow *Tachycineta albiventer*	BR	WL	-	U	-	R	-	-	R
White-rumped Swallow (254) *Tachycineta leucorrhoa*	BS	GL,WL	A	A	A	A	A	A	C
Chilean Swallow (255,P) *Tachycineta meyeni*	AM	GL,WL	-	R	-	-	R	U	-
Blue-and-white Swallow (256) *Notiochelidon cyanoleuca*	BS	SF,HF	R	-	-	-	R	R	R
Black-collared Swallow (257) *Atticora melanoleuca*	BR	WF	-	-	-	-	-	-	R
Tawny-headed Swallow *Alopochelidon fucata*	BR	GL,WL	-	-	U	U	U	U	R
Southern Rough-winged Swallow(258) *Stelgidopteryx ruficollis*	BN	WL	R	R	R	R	U	R	C
Bank Swallow (259) *Riparia riparia*	NM	GL,WL	R	R	U	R	U	R	-
Cliff Swallow (260) *Hirundo pyrrhonota*	NM	GL,WL	R	R	R	-	C	U	-
Barn Swallow (261) *Hirundo rustica*	NM	GL,WL	C	A	A	A	A	A	U
CORVIDAE (3 species)									
Purplish Jay *Cyanocorax cyanomelas*	BR	SF,HF	R	U	U	C	C	U	C
Curl-crested Jay *Cyanocorax cristatellus*	BR	SF	-	-	-	U	-	-	-
Plush-crested Jay *Cyanocorax chrysops*	BR	SF,HF	U	U	U	C	C	U	C
TROGLODYTIDAE (5 species)									
Black-capped Donacobius *Donacobius atricapillus*	BR	WL	-	R	U	U	U	U	U
Thrush-like Wren (262) *Campylorhynchus turdinus*	BR	WL	-	C	U	U	R	R	-
Fawn-breasted Wren (263,Q) *Thryothorus guarayanus*	BR	SF	-	A	-	-	-	-	-

Family/Species	Status	Habitat	Geographical Regions						
			AC	MG	BC	CC	CP	ÑE	AP
House Wren *Troglodytes aedon*	BR	SF,HF	C	C	C	C	C	C	C
Sedge Wren (264) *Cistothorus platensis*	BR	WL	-	-	-	-	R	-	-
MUSCICAPIDAE (8 species)									
Cream-bellied Gnatcatcher *Polioptila lactea*	BR	HF	-	-	-	-	U	-	U
Masked Gnatcatcher *Polioptila dumicola*	BR	SF	C	U	C	C	U	C	R
Yellow-legged Thrush (265) *Platycichla flavipes*	BN	HF	-	-	-	-	-	H	R
Slaty Thrush (266) *Turdus nigriceps*	BR	HF	-	-	-	R	R	-	R
Rufous-bellied Thrush *Turdus rufiventris*	BR	SF,HF	R	C	U	C	C	C	U
Pale-breasted Thrush (267) *Turdus leucomelas*	BR	SF,HF	-	-	R	C	C	U	U
Creamy-bellied Thrush *Turdus amaurochalinus*	BR	SF,HF	C	U	C	C	C	C	U
White-necked Thrush *Turdus albicollis*	BR	HF	-	-	-	R	U	R	U
MIMIDAE (2 species)									
Chalk-browed Mockingbird *Mimus saturninus*	BR	GL,SF	U	R	C	C	C	C	C
White-banded Mockingbird (268) *Mimus triurus*	AM	GL,SF	C	U	R	U	R	U	R
MOTACILLIDAE (5 species)									
Short-billed Pipit (269) *Anthus furcatus*	AM	GL,WL	-	-	-	-	-	R	H
Yellowish Pipit *Anthus lutescens*	BR	GL,WL	C	C	C	C	C	C	R
Chaco Pipit (270,R) *Anthus chacoensis*	BR	GL	-	R	-	R	R	R	-
Correndera Pipit (271) *Anthus correndera*	AM	GL	-	-	-	-	R	-	-
Ochre-breasted Pipit (272) *Anthus nattereri*	BR	GL	-	-	H	-	R	R	-
VIREONIDAE (3 species)									
Red-eyed Vireo (273) *Vireo olivaceus*	BN	SF,HF	C	U	C	U	C	U	U
Rufous-crowned Greenlet *Hylophilus poicilotis*	BR	HF	-	-	-	-	U	R	U

Family/Species	Status	Habitat	Geographical Regions						
			AC	MG	BC	CC	CP	ÑE	AP
Rufous-browed Peppershrike *Cyclarhis gujanensis*	BR	SF,HF	U	R	C	U	U	U	U

EMBERIZIDAE (105 species)

Family/Species	Status	Habitat	AC	MG	BC	CC	CP	ÑE	AP
Tropical Parula *Parula pitiayumi*	BR	SF,HF	U	C	C	C	C	C	C
Masked Yellowthroat *Geothlypis aequinoctialis*	BR	WL	R	R	U	U	U	U	U
Flavescent Warbler *Basileuterus flaveolus*	BR	SF	R	R	R	C	R	-	-
Golden-crowned Warbler (274) *Basileuterus culicivorus*	BR	SF,HF	-	-	R	C	A	U	A
White-bellied Warbler (275,S) *Basileuterus hypoleucus*	BR	SF	-	R	-	R	-	-	-
White-browed Warbler (276) *Basileuterus leucoblepharus*	BR	HF	-	-	R	R	C	U	C
River Warbler *Basileuterus rivularis*	BR	WL	-	-	-	-	R	-	U
Bananaquit *Coereba flaveola*	BR	HF	-	-	-	-	-	-	R
Chestnut-vented Conebill *Conirostrum speciosum*	BR	SF,HF	-	C	R	C	C	U	C
Fawn-breasted Tanager *Pipraeidea melanonota*	BR	SF,HF	-	-	-	U	U	R	U
Green-headed Tanager *Tangara seledon*	BR	HF	-	-	-	-	R	-	U
Chestnut-backed Tanager (277) *Tangara preciosa*	BR	HF	-	-	-	-	R	-	R
Burnished-buff Tanager *Tangara cayana*	BR	SF,HF	-	-	-	U	U	U	U
Blue Dacnis *Dacnis cayana*	BR	SF,HF	-	-	-	U	C	-	C
Blue-naped Chlorophonia *Chlorophonia cyanea*	BR	HF	-	-	-	-	R	-	U
Purple-throated Euphonia *Euphonia chlorotica*	BR	SF,HF	U	C	C	C	C	C	C
Violaceous Euphonia *Euphonia violacea*	BR	HF	-	-	-	U	U	-	U
Green-throated Euphonia (278) *Euphonia chalybea*	BR	HF	-	-	-	-	R	-	R
Golden-rumped Euphonia *Euphonia cyanocephala*	BR	HF	-	-	-	-	R	R	R
Chestnut-bellied Euphonia *Euphonia pectoralis*	BR	HF	-	-	-	R	U	-	U
Diademed Tanager (279) *Stephanophorus diadematus*	BR	HF	-	-	-	-	-	-	R

Family/Species	Status	Habitat	Geographical Regions						
			AC	MG	BC	CC	CP	ÑE	AP
Sayaca Tanager *Thraupis sayaca*	BR	SF,HF	U	C	C	C	C	C	C
Palm Tanager (280) *Thraupis palmarum*	BR	SF,HF	-	H	-	R	-	-	R
Blue-and-yellow Tanager (281) *Thraupis bonariensis*	BS	SF	U	R	U	-	R	-	R
Gray-headed Tanager (282) *Eucometis penicillata*	BR	SF,HF	-	-	-	R	-	-	-
White-lined Tanager *Tachyphonus rufus*	BR	WL,SF	U	C	U	U	U	U	R
Ruby-crowned Tanager (283) *Tachyphonus coronatus*	BR	SF,HF	-	-	R	U	C	-	C
Red-crowned Ant-Tanager *Habia rubica*	BR	HF	-	-	-	-	U	-	U
Hepatic Tanager (284) *Piranga flava*	BS	SF,HF	U	R	U	U	-	R	R
Silver-beaked Tanager (285) *Ramphocelus carbo*	BR	SF,HF	-	R	-	-	-	-	R
Black-goggled Tanager (286) *Trichothraupis melanops*	BR	SF,HF	-	-	R	R	C	R	C
White-rumped Tanager (287) *Cypsnagra hirundinacea*	BR	SF,HF	-	-	-	R	R	-	-
Chestnut-headed Tanager *Pyrrhocoma ruficeps*	BR	HF	-	-	-	-	R	-	U
Hooded Tanager *Nemosia pileata*	BR	SF	R	R	R	U	U	U	U
Guira Tanager (288) *Hemithraupis guira*	BR	SF,HF	-	R	H	U	C	U	C
Orange-headed Tanager *Thlypopsis sordida*	BR	SF	R	-	R	-	R	U	R
White-banded Tanager (289) *Neothraupis fasciata*	BR	HF	-	-	-	-	R	-	R
Magpie Tanager (290) *Cissopis leveriana*	BR	HF	-	R	-	-	U	-	C
Black-faced Tanager (291) *Schistochlamys melanopis*	BR	HF	-	-	-	-	-	-	R
Swallow-Tanager (292) *Tersina viridis*	BN	WL,HF	R	-	-	U	U	H	U
Grayish Saltator *Saltator coerulescens*	BR	SF	U	C	C	U	U	C	R
Green-winged Saltator *Saltator similis*	BR	WL,SF	-	U	U	R	R	R	U
Golden-billed Saltator (293) *Saltator aurantiirostris*	BR	SF	A	-	R	R	H	-	H
Black-throated Saltator (294) *Saltator atricollis*	BR	SF	-	R	-	C	U	-	-
Black-throated Grosbeak (295) *Pitylus fuliginosus*	BR	HF	-	-	-	-	H	-	R

Family/Species	Status	Habitat	Geographical Regions						
			AC	MG	BC	CC	CP	ÑE	AP
Black-backed Grosbeak *Pheucticus aureoventris*	BR	SF	R	-	-	-	-	-	-
Ultramarine Grosbeak *Cyanocompsa brissonii*	BR	SF,HF	U	U	R	-	R	-	R
Indigo Grosbeak (296) *Cyanoloxia glaucocaerulea*	AM	SF,HF	-	-	H	R	R	R	R
Red-crested Cardinal *Paroaria coronata*	BR	WL,SF	A	A	C	C	C	A	R
Yellow-billed Cardinal *Paroaria capitata*	BR	WL	U	A	C	C	C	C	-
Red-crested Finch *Coryphospingus cucullatus*	BR	GL,SF,HF	C	C	C	C	C	C	C
Many-colored Chaco-Finch *Saltatricula multicolor*	BR	GL	A	R	R	-	-	-	-
Black-masked Finch (297) *Coryphaspiza melanotis*	BR	GL	-	-	-	-	-	-	R
Saffron-billed Sparrow *Arremon flavirostris*	BR	SF,HF	-	U	R	U	U	U	C
Blue-black Grassquit *Volatinia jacarina*	BR	WL,SF,HF	U	U	U	U	U	U	U
Buffy-fronted Seedeater (298) *Sporophila frontalis*	BR	HF	-	-	-	-	-	-	R
Temminck's Seedeater (299) *Sporophila falcirostris*	BR	HF	-	-	-	-	-	-	R
Plumbeous Seedeater *Sporophila plumbea*	BR	GL,WL	-	-	-	R	-	-	R
Rusty-collared Seedeater *Sporophila collaris*	BR	WL	R	R	C	U	U	U	-
Lined Seedeater (300) *Sporophila lineola*	BN	WL,SF	U	U	R	R	R	-	-
Double-collared Seedeater *Sporophila caerulescens*	BR	GL,WL,SF	U	U	U	U	U	U	U
White-bellied Seedeater *Sporophila leucoptera*	BR	GL,SF	R	U	U	R	U	-	R
Capped Seedeater (301) *Sporophila bouvreuil*	BR	GL,WL	-	-	H	R	R	U	R
Tawny-bellied Seedeater *Sporophila hypoxantha*	BR	GL,WL	R	R	U	U	U	U	R
Dark-throated Seedeater (302) *Sporophila ruficollis*	BN	GL,WL	R	-	R	-	R	R	H
Marsh Seedeater (303,T) *Sporophila palustris*	AM	GL,WL	-	-	-	H	R	R	-
Rufous-rumped Seedeater (304) *Sporophila hypochroma*	BN	GL,WL	-	-	R	-	R	R	-
Chestnut Seedeater (305,U) *Sporophila cinnamomea*	BS	GL,WL	-	-	-	-	R	R	-
Lesser Seed-Finch (306) *Oryzoborus angolensis*	BR	SF,HF	-	-	R	R	U	R	R

Family/Species	Status	Habitat	Geographical Regions						
			AC	MG	BC	CC	CP	ÑE	AP
Blackish-blue Seedeater	BR	HF	-	-	-	-	-	-	R
Amaurospiza moesta									
Sooty Grassquit (307)	BR	GL	-	-	-	-	R	-	-
Tiaris fuliginosa									
Uniform Finch	BR	HF	-	-	-	-	R	-	R
Haplospiza unicolor									
Saffron Finch	BR	GL,SF	A	C	A	C	C	A	C
Sicalis flaveola									
Grassland Yellow-Finch (308)	AM	GL,SF	R	R	R	R	R	R	R
Sicalis luteola									
Great Pampa-Finch (309)	BR	WL	R	R	C	U	U	C	R
Embernagra platensis									
Wedge-tailed Grass-Finch	BR	GL,WL	-	-	U	U	C	C	R
Emberizoides herbicola									
Lesser Grass-Finch (310)	BR	GL,WL	-	-	-	R	R	U	-
Emberizoides ypiranganus									
Ringed Warbling-Finch (311)	AM	SF	U	-	-	-	-	-	-
Poospiza torquata									
Black-capped Warbling-Finch	BR	SF	C	R	C	C	R	U	-
Poospiza melanoleuca									
Black-and-rufous Warbling-Finch(312)	AM	SF,HF	-	-	-	-	R	R	R
Poospiza nigrorufa									
Red-rumped Warbling-Finch (313)	BR	HF	-	-	-	-	R	-	R
Poospiza lateralis									
Long-tailed Reed-Finch (314)	BR	WL	-	-	R	R	R	U	R
Donacospiza albifrons									
Black-crested Finch (315)	BS	SF	R	-	-	-	-	-	-
Lophospingus pusillus									
Stripe-capped Sparrow (316)	BR	GL	R	-	-	-	-	-	-
Aimophila strigiceps									
Grassland Sparrow	BR	GL	C	R	U	C	U	C	U
Ammodramus humeralis									
Rufous-collared Sparrow	BR	GL,SF,RE	C	C	C	C	C	C	C
Zonotrichia capensis									
Bobolink (317)	NM	GL,WL	R	R	R	R	R	-	R
Dolichonyx oryzivorus									
Yellow-winged Blackbird (318)	AM	WL	-	-	R	-	-	R	R
Agelaius thilius									
Chestnut-capped Blackbird	BR	WL	U	C	C	U	U	U	-
Agelaius ruficapillus									
Unicolored Blackbird	BR	WL	C	C	C	C	C	C	-
Agelaius cyanopus									
Saffron-cowled Blackbird (319)	BR	GL,WL	-	-	H	-	R	R	R
Agelaius flavus									
Chopi Blackbird	BR	GL,SF	U	A	A	A	A	A	A
Gnorimopsar chopi									
Scarlet-headed Blackbird	BR	WL	U	R	C	R	C	C	R
Amblyramphus holosericeus									

Family/Species	Status	Habitat	Geographical Regions						
			AC	MG	BC	CC	CP	ÑE	AP
Yellow-rumped Marshbird (320) *Pseudoleistes guirahuro*	BR	GL,WL	-	-	R	U	C	C	R
White-browed Blackbird *Leistes superciliaris*	BR	GL,WL	R	R	U	R	U	U	U
Shiny Cowbird *Molothrus bonariensis*	BR	GL,SF	A	A	A	A	A	A	A
Screaming Cowbird *Molothrus rufoaxillaris*	BR	GL,SF	U	U	U	U	U	U	U
Bay-winged Cowbird *Molothrus badius*	BR	GL,SF	C	U	C	-	R	U	-
Giant Cowbird (321) *Scaphidura oryzivora*	BR	SF,HF	-	H	R	R	R	-	R
Epaulet Oriole *Icterus cayanensis*	BR	WL,SF,HF	C	C	C	C	C	C	C
Troupial *Icterus icterus*	BR	SF	U	-	R	-	-	-	-
Red-rumped Cacique (322) *Cacicus haemorrhous*	BR	HF	-	-	H	C	C	R	C
Golden-winged Cacique *Cacicus chrysopterus*	BR	SF	U	C	C	C	R	U	R
Solitary Black Cacique *Cacicus solitarius*	BR	SF	U	R	U	R	R	U	R
Crested Oropendola *Psarocolius decumanus*	BR	SF,HF	-	U	R	R	R	R	R

FRINGILLIDAE (1 species)

Family/Species	Status	Habitat							
Hooded Siskin *Carduelis magellanica*	BR	SF,HF	R	C	U	C	U	U	R

PASSERIDAE (1 species)

Family/Species	Status	Habitat							
House Sparrow (323) *Passer domesticus*	IB	RE	A	A	A	A	A	A	A

DISTRIBUTIONAL NOTES

Details are provided for selected species (indicated with a number in parenthesis after English name in Annotated Checklist section) for one or more of the following reasons: (1) species with five or fewer records in either the Chaco or Orient (or both); (2) extreme dates, in order of arrival and departure, for migrant species; (3) hypothetical record(s) only in either the Chaco or Orient for species present in the other; (4) species regarded as globally threatened by Collar et al. (1992); or (5) status requires clarification for miscellaneous reasons. Additional details are provided for some species reported in either the Chaco or the Orient for the first time. Species with more than five records in either the Chaco or Orient presumably occur (or have occurred) in adequate numbers; because listing each record would be cumbersome, they are referred to as many records. Additional data on eastern or western limits (relative to Paraguay River) of many species are presented in Appendices 4 and 5.

When sufficient information is available, each record (recorded occurrence of a species) is classified as one of six categories, abbreviated as follows:

(SI) Sight record
(SP) Specimen record
(LSP) Lost specimen record (or not located)
(PH) Photographic record
(VO) Vocalization record (heard)
(NE) Nesting record (eggs)

Records based on uncertain criteria are referred to as reported. Published or unpublished sources (including page number, when applicable) are provided for each record. When available, the institution and catalog number of the record are also provided. Institutional acronyms for specimen, photographic or band records include:

AMNH American Museum of Natural History, New York City, USA

ANSP Academy of Natural Sciences of Philadelphia, Philadelphia, USA

BMNH British Museum (Natural History), London, United Kingdom (recently renamed Natural History Museum)

FMNH Field Museum of Natural History, Chicago, USA

IML Instituto Miguel Lillo, Tucumán, Argentina

MACN Museo Argentino de Ciencias Naturales B. Rivadavia, Buenos Aires, Argentina

MAK Museum Alexander Koenig, Bonn, Germany

MCZ Museum of Comparative Zoology, Harvard University, Cambridge, USA

MFA Museo Félix de Arara, Corrientes, Argentina

MM Münchener Museum, München, Germany

MHNIB Museo de Historia Natural de Itaipú Binacional, Hernandarias, Paraguay

MHNP Museo de Historia Natural del Paraguay, Asunción, Paraguay

MHNSCP Museo de Historia Natural de la Sociedad Científica del Paraguay, Asunción, Paraguay

MNHN Muséum National d'Histoire Naturelle, Paris, France

MNHNP Museo Nacional de Historia Natural del Paraguay, San Lorenzo, Paraguay

MVZ Museum of Vertebrate Zoology, University of California at Berkeley, Berkeley, USA

MZT Museo Zoologico di Torino, Università di Torino, Torino, Italy

RMNH Rijksmuseum van Natuurlijke Historie, Leiden, Denmark.

SMF Natur-museum Senckenberg, Frankfurt, Germany

UMMZ	University of Michigan Museum of Zoology, Ann Arbor, USA
USNM	National Museum of Natural History (formerly United States National Museum), Washington D.C., USA
USFWS	United States Fish and Wildlife Service, Office of Migratory Bird Management, Laurel, USA
VIREO	Visual Resources for Ornithology, Academy of Natural Sciences of Philadelphia, Philadelphia, USA

The coordinates, department and geographical region of each locality are summarized in Appendix 8. For the sake of historical records, I have referred to the former Dptos. of Nueva Asunción and Chaco (see explanation for change in Geography, Climate and Vegetation section) as exNAS and exCHA, respectively. The departments (Fig. 2) are abbreviated as follows:

Chaco:

exCHA	Chaco (now part of Dpto. Alto Paraguay)
APY	Alto Paraguay
exNAS	Nueva Asunción (now part of Dpto. Boquerón)
BOQ	Boquerón
PHA	Presidente Hayes

Orient:

CON	Concepción
AMA	Amambay
SAP	San Pedro
CAN	Canindeyú (formerly Canendiyú)
COR	Cordillera
CAA	Caaguazú
APN	Alto Paraná
CEN	Central
PAR	Paraguarí
GUA	Guairá
CAP	Caazapá
ÑEE	Ñeembucú
MIS	Misiones
ITA	Itapúa

Most locality names follow local usage, based primarily on a map of the country that was recently published by the Dirección del Servicio Geográfico Militar (1992), and secondarily on Paynter (1989). In many cases the same locality is known by two or more names, depending on which map is used. For example, Puerto Bahía Negra in the above cited map is referred to as Bahía Negra on smaller scale topographic maps published by the same institution. For this reason I have chosen to use the names on the most widely available official map of the country. However, for some localities I have retained the original name on specimen labels (e.g., Fort Wheeler, an unknown locality probably near Fortín Guaraní, PHA; Paynter 1989), or have altered the name to reflect current usage (e.g., 235 km W of Río Negro rather than 235 km W of Riacho Negro ; see Methods section). For those unfamiliar with Spanish, the following Spanish-English vocabulary may be useful:

Arroyo = creek, stream

Bahía = bay (of river)

Cerro = hill, mountain

Colonia = colony

Cordillera = mountain range

Estancia = ranch

Fortín = fort

Lago = lake

Laguna = small lake, pond

Parque Nacional = National Park

Puerto = port

Refugio Biológico = Biological Refuge

Reserva Biológica = Biological Reserve

Reserva Natural del Bosque = Natural Forest Reserve

Riacho = temporary (seasonal) river

Río = river

Salto = waterfall

Most locality names in Paraguay are derived from Guaraní, and are often pronounced slightly differently than they would be in Spanish. Thus, a few grammatical guidelines may be helpful. For example, most words in Guaraní are accented on the last syllable, even if no accent mark is indicated. The letter y when followed by a vowel at the beginning of a word (e.g., yerba), or preceded and followed by a vowel (e.g., Ayolas), is pronounced as j in English; thus, Canindeyú would be pronounced as can-neen-day-JEW with an accent on the last syllable. A y that is followed by a consonant at the beginning of a word (e.g., Ypacarai), preceded by a consonant at the end of a word (e.g., Tebicuary), or preceded and followed by a consonant (e.g., Cambyretá), is pronounced as a guttural oo or short i in English (difficult to pronounce correctly); thus, Tebicuary would be pronounced as teb-ick-wa-ROO with an accent on the last syllable. The letters ch in Guaraní are pronounced as sh in English; thus, Choré would be pronounced as shore-AY with an accent on the last syllable. However, there are some exceptions. Chaco, for example, is always pronounced as it would be in Spanish.

Species Accounts

1. Solitary Tinamou
(*Tinamus solitarius*)
Chaco: hypothetical, one (SI) or more (?) at Río Confuso, PHA (Bertoni 1930b:257), but locality questionable; Orient: many records.

2. Small-billed Tinamou
(*Crypturellus parvirostris*)
Chaco: one (SP) at 235 km W of Río Negro, PHA, 14 August 1933 (Hellmayr and Conover 1942:77; FMNH 414401); one (SP) at 265 km W of Puerto La Victoria, exNAS or BOQ, 28 January 1936 (Hellmayr and Conover 1942:77; FMNH 412102); one (SP) at Orloff, BOQ, 16 February 1945 (FMNH 416490); one (SP) at Orloff, BOQ, 5 July 1945 (FMNH 416489); Orient: many records.

3. Brushland Tinamou
(*Nothoprocta cinerascens*)
Northernmost records at about 22°S (e.g., Hellmayr and Conover 1942:91).

4. White-tufted Grebe
(*Rollandia rolland*)
Chaco: many records; Orient: reported at Encarnación, ITA (Podtiaguin 1941:13); reported at Reserva Natural del Bosque Mbaracayú, CAN (Meisel et al. 1992:1); one (SI) at 1 km N of Valle Apúa, PAR, August 1989 (J. R. Contreras et al. 1989:42).

5. Silvery Grebe
(*Podiceps occipitalis*)
Orient: one (SP) at Hernandarias, APN, 15 June 1979 (Colmán and Pérez 1991:33, unpubl.; MHNIB).

6. Great Grebe
(*Podiceps major*)
Two (SP) at unknown locality (Schlegel 1867:38; RMNH?), but possibly in Argentina or Brazil. Chaco: one (SP) at 235 km W of Río Negro, PHA, 24 June 1939 (Storer 1989:3; UMMZ 105234); one (SP) at 235 km W of Río Negro, PHA, 7 September 1939 (Storer 1989:3; UMMZ 105235); one (SI) at Ruta Trans Chaco km 416, BOQ, 7 December 1990 (Contreras et al. 1992a:2); Orient: one (SI) at Lago Ypoá, PAR, 27 August 1989 (J. R. Contreras et al. 1989:42); one (SI) at Río Paraguay, near mouth of Río Bermejo, ÑEE, 7 July 1992 (Contreras et al. 1992a:1, 2), but possibly in Argentina; one (SI) at Río Paraguay, opposite Naranjito, ÑEE, 17 September 1992 (Contreras et al. 1992a:2); one (SI) at Río Paraná, near Refugio Biológico Mbaracayú, CAN, 28 August and 9 September 1985 (Contreras et al. 1992a:2). Specimen UMMZ 105234, mentioned above, is a young bird with wings too short to fly (R. Storer pers. comm.), indicating nesting.

7. Pinnated Bittern
(*Botaurus pinnatus*)
Chaco: one (SP) at 195 km W of Puerto La Victoria, APY or BOQ, 8 March 1937 (Brodkorb 1938c:1; UMMZ 93052); one (SP) at 60 km SE of Orloff, PHA, 11 April 1940 (USNM 370535); erroneously reported for APY (López 1985:12, pers. comm.); Orient: one (SI) at S of San Ignacio, MIS, 4 September 1982 (R. Ridgely).

8. Stripe-backed Bittern
(*Ixobrychus involucris*)
Chaco: many records; Orient: reported at Asunción, CEN (Bertoni 1939:21); one (SI) at Luque, CEN, 6 July 1977 (R. Ridgely); one (SI) at S of San Patricio, MIS, 8 January 1990 (P. Scharf); one (SI) at Estancia La Golondrina, CAA, 24 August 1992 (Brooks et al. 1993:60).

9. Least Bittern
(*Ixobrychus exilis*)

One (SP) at unknown locality, 1979 (Storer 1989:3; UMMZ 202593). Chaco: one or more (LSP) at Villa Hayes, PHA (Bertoni 1930a:245, 1939:21; MHNSCP), but stated to be common (see comment below); one (SP) at unknown locality, presumably near Orloff, February 1939 (Storer 1989:4; USNM 390678); several (SI, VO) at Ruta Trans Chaco km 79, PHA, 5 September 1990, 27 December 1990, and 28 May 1991 (P. Scharf, R. Ridgely and others). Older reports attributed to this species (e.g., see Laubmann 1939:98), including those of Bertoni (see above), may reflect confusion between this species and either the Stripe-backed Bittern (*Ixobrychus involucris*) or Striated Heron (*Butorides striatus*).

10. Little Blue Heron
(*Egretta caerulea*)

Chaco: several (SI) doubtful at southern PHA, December 1983 (Peris and Suárez 1985a:20); one (PH) at Puerto Bahía Negra, APY, 18 August 1988 (Hayes et al. 1990b:95; VIREO x08/2/001); one (SI) at Ruta Trans Chaco km 79, PHA, 8 August 1994 (R. Ryan).

11. Cattle Egret
(*Bubulcus ibis*)

Recent immigrant. First recorded in 1977, when photographed in PHA (Dunning and Ridgely 1982:4, 329). By 1979, large flocks were observed in both the Chaco and Orient (Storer 1989:3), indicating that it was established throughout the country.

12. Capped Heron
(*Pilherodius pileatus*)

Chaco: one (SI) at Río Verde, PHA, between October 1896 and May 1897 (Kerr 1901:232); one (SP) at 40 km W of Puerto La Victoria, APY or PHA, 10 June 1931 (Laubmann 1933a:288, 1939:92; MM 32.246); one (SP) at 40 km W of Puerto La Victoria, APY, 13 June 1931 (Laubmann 1933a:288, 1939:92; MM 32.248); one (SP) at 190 km W of Puerto La Victoria, APY or BOQ, 9 March 1940 (UMMZ 110981); Orient: one (SP) at Estancia Centurión, CON, 1 October 1931 (Laubmann 1933a:288, 1939:92; MM 32.245); one (SP) at 4 km E of Horqueta, CON, 13 December 1937 (UMMZ 96010); reported at San Lázaro, CON, December 1939 (Podtiaguin 1944:99); one (SI) at Río Apa, CON, 2 August 1977 (R. Ridgely); one (SI) at Río Apa, CON, 3 August 1977 (R. Ridgely).

13. Boat-billed Heron
(*Cochlearius cochlearius*)

Chaco: many records; Orient: two (SI) at San Lázaro, CON, December 1939 (Podtiaguin 1944:100); one (SP) at Concepción, CON, 13 August 1983 (Hayes et al. 1990b:95; MNHNP 762).

14. Green Ibis
(*Mesembrinibis cayennensis*)

Chaco: one (SP) at 235 km W of Río Negro, 19 June 1939 (UMMZ 105248), but locality questionable (see Methods section); one (SP) at Riacho Caballero, PHA, 27 February 1938 (UMMZ 96197); one (SI) at Puerto María Auxiliadora, APY, 10 October 1990 (A. Madroño Nieto); Orient: many records.

15. Plumbeous Ibis
(*Theristicus caerulescens*)

Chaco: many records; Orient: reported at Lago Ypoá, PAR (J. R. Contreras et al. 1989:39).

16. Andean Condor
(*Vultur gryphus*)

Chaco: one (PH) captured and released at General Eugenio A. Garay, BOQ, August 1987 (Contreras 1989:5, Contreras et al. 1993a:2) or October 1987 (Contreras et al. 1990:5), but whereabouts of photo(s) not stated; unverified reports from residents in western BOQ (G. Sequera and A. Taber pers. comm.); Orient: hypothetical, one (LSP) at Bahía de Asunción, CEN, 18 September 1943 (Podtiaguin 1944:115), but possibly an escaped bird. This normally montane species has been recorded as a vagrant in Pantanal lowlands in the state of Mato Grosso, Brazil (Sick 1979), and in Chaco lowlands at Estancia Perforación, Dpto. Santa Cruz, Bolivia (Kratter et al. 1993), only 85 km N of General Eugenio A. Garay. Although Podtiaguin admitted that the Bahía de Asunción record (cited above) may have been an escaped bird, natural vagrancy seems equally likely.

17. Chilean Flamingo
(*Phoenicopterus chilensis*)

Chaco: many records, mostly in northwestern PHA, where wintering population may be increasing; Orient: one (LSP) and several (SI) at Urumburú, CEN, 6 June 1940 (Podtiaguin 1944:116). Extreme dates: February (Hayes et al. 1994:89) and 18 November (Brooks 1991b:3, Hayes et al. 1994:89).

18. Coscoroba Swan
(*Coscoroba coscoroba*)

Chaco: many records, including nesting in the vicinity of Laguna Capitán, PHA (Steinbacher 1962:34, Hayes et al. 1994:94); Orient: hypothetical, two (SI) at Pedro Juan Caballero, AMA, 26 September 1990 (P. Scharf), but may represent escaped birds; however, there appears to be some vagrancy northward from the breeding grounds, with the northernmost record represented by a flock of southwardbound migrants over Riacho Ramos, APY, on 28 September 1988 (Hayes et al. 1990b:96).

19. Orinoco Goose
(*Neochen jubata*)

Chaco: one (PH) at 15 km N of Hito II, near the Bolivian border, exNAS, 11 May 1990 (J. Escobar Argaña; VIREO x08/43/001); two (SI) at Laguna Capitán, PHA, or Estancia Campo María, PHA, July 1992 (López 1992:46).

20. White-cheeked Pintail
(*Anas bahamensis*)

Chaco: no specific records published (Laubmann 1939:73), but numerous specimens (FMNH, USNM) and sight records (up to 75 in a day; F. Hayes and P. Scharf) throughout the year in Alto Chaco region, mostly at Laguna Capitán, PHA; Orient: flock of five (SI) at Bahía de Asunción, CEN, 17 November 1988 (F. Hayes, J. Fox and M. Angel), observed along shoreline for about 5 min, then flew away.

21. Cinnamon Teal
(*Anas cyanoptera*)

Chaco: reported at Fortín Donovan, PHA (Kerr 1892:146); one (SP) female of austral race *cyanoptera* at 170 km W of Puerto La Victoria, APY or BOQ, 1 March 1938 (UMMZ 96201); Orient: hypothetical, two (SI) females or immatures at Bahía de Asunción, CEN, 15 February 1989 (F. Hayes), but possibly Blue-winged Teal (*A. discors*), which has not yet been documented from Paraguay but likely occurs as a Nearctic migrant (as in Argentina).

22. Red Shoveler
(*Anas platalea*)

Chaco: reported at Río Pilcomayo, PHA, probably in the vicinity of Fortín Donovan (Kerr 1892:146, 147); one (SP) at 170 km W of Puerto La Victoria, APY or BOQ, 14 February 1939 (UMMZ 105029); two (SP) at Orloff, BOQ, February 1939 (USNM 390658, 399450); one (SI) at Estancia La Golondrina, PHA, 9 July 1989 (F. Hayes, A. Robinson, group of Peace Corps Volunteers); Orient: two (SI), a male and a female, at Bahía de Asunción, CEN, 11 January 1989, 18 January 1989 (female only), 15 February 1989 (female only; F. Hayes, J. Fox, C. Yahnke, C. Sorenson and M. Hayes).

23. Rosy-billed Pochard
(*Netta peposaca*)

Northernmost records at about 22°S, where specimens (UMMZ) include a downy chick taken at 195-200 km W of Puerto La Victoria, APY or BOQ, 1 March 1937 (UMMZ 93123).

24. Brazilian Merganser
(*Mergus octosetaceus*)

Threatened. Probably extinct in Paraguay. Orient: reported for Alto Paraná [region], lat. 27, 1891" (Bertoni 1901:8-10, 1914a:41, 1939:21); one (SI) at Río Carapá, W of Catueté, CAN, February 1984 (López 1986:208, pers. comm.); none found during searches by canoe along 105 km of the Río Carapá, CAN, 22 km of the Río Ytambey, CAN and APN, and 71 km of the Río Ñacunday, APN, July to September 1989 (Granizo and Hayes 1989:18, Hayes and Granizo Tamayo 1992:256). There may not be enough remaining habitat to support a viable population in Paraguay; the most recent survey (1993) of the population in adjacent Misiones Province, Argentina, found only one bird along 450 km of rivers and streams (Benstead 1994).

25. Lake Duck
(*Oxyura vittata*)

Chaco: one (SI) female observed at close range (ca. 5 m) in a marsh at Estancia La Golondrina, PHA, 27 August 1988 (F. Hayes, A. Robinson and group of Peace Corps Volunteers), but could not be relocated the following day; flock of 22 (SI) males and females, in breeding plumage, at a pond beside the Ruta Trans Chaco at

90

Benjamin Aceval, PHA, 6 and 9 December 1988 (F. Hayes, D. Snider and R. Perrin).

26. Black-headed Duck
(*Heteronetta atricapilla*)
Northernmost records at about 22°S, where nesting occurs (Weller 1967).

27. Osprey
(*Pandion haliaetus*)
Extreme dates: 22 August and 16 June (Hayes et al. 1990a:949).

28. Hook-billed Kite
(*Chondrohierax uncinatus*)
Chaco: many records; Orient: two (LSP) at Villarrica, GUA (Hellmayr and Conover 1949:30), but locality of specimens not known; reported at San Lázaro, CON (Podtiaguin 1944:21), but no details provided; two (SI) at Puerto Valle Mi, CON, 1 August 1977 (R. Ridgely); one (SI) at Estancia La Golondrina, CAA, 25 August 1992 (Brooks et al. 1993:62).

29. American Swallow-tailed Kite
(*Elanoides forficatus*)
Extreme dates: 22 August (Brooks et al. 1993:61) and 14 March (Contreras et al. 1988b:26).

30. Snail Kite
(*Rostrhamus sociabilis*)
Most common during austral spring and fall, when migrating (Hayes 1991, Hayes et al. 1994:89).

31. Rufous-thighed Kite
(*Harpagus diodon*)
Chaco: reported without details (Bertoni 1939:23); one (SI) at Parque Nacional Teniente Enciso, exNAS, 29 August 1982 (Hayes et al. 1994:86); one (SI) at Parque Nacional Teniente Enciso, exNAS, 2 September 1982 (Hayes et al. 1994:86); Orient: many records. Extreme dates: 25 August and 25 February (Hayes et al. 1994:86). Chaco records likely refer to migrants.

32. Mississippi Kite
(*Ictinia mississippiensis*)
Extreme dates: 1 October and 24 March (Hayes et al. 1990a:949, 950).

33. Plumbeous Kite
(*Ictinia plumbea*)
Extreme dates: 27 August and 17 June (Hayes et al. 1994:86).

34. Cinereous Harrier
(*Circus cinereus*)
Chaco: hypothetical, reported at Villa Hayes, PHA (Bertoni 1939:23); Orient: one (SP) at 18 km E of Rosario, SAP, 23 December 1937 (UMMZ 96020); one (SI) at S of San Ignacio, MIS, 4 September 1982 (R. Ridgely); one (SI) at 10 km SE of Villa Florida, MIS, 6 June 1991 (R. Ridgely, P. Scharf et al.).

35. Tiny Hawk
(*Accipiter superciliosus*)
Orient: one (LSP) at Puerto Bertoni, APN, June 1897 (Bertoni 1904:7), and recorded subsequently (Bertoni 1926:398); one (SP) at Cambyretá, ITA, 8 July 1934 (Laubmann 1939:171; MM 35134); one (SP) at Campichuelo, ITA, 29 July 1934 (Laubmann 1939:171; MM 35135); reported (doubtful) at Lago Ypacarai, CEN or COR (González Torres and González Romero 1985:179).

36. Mantled Hawk
(*Leucopternis polionota*)
Orient: one (LSP) and others (SI?) at Puerto Bertoni, APN, and Río Yguazú, CAA or APN, during spring, 3 September (Bertoni 1904:8-9, 1914a:43, 1939:23); one (SI) at Río Carapá, 10 km E of Catueté, CAN, 24 July 1989 (Hayes and Granizo Tamayo 1992:255, unpubl.).

37. Crowned Eagle
(*Harpyhaliaetus coronatus*)
Threatened. Chaco: one (SP) at Río Pilcomayo, PHA, 12 June or July 1890 (Kerr 1892:142; Collar et al. 1992:105, 107; BMNH), but possibly in Argentina; one (SP) at 170 km W of Puerto La Victoria, APY or BOQ, 24 February 1938 (UMMZ 98051); one (SP) at 200 km W of Puerto La Victoria, APY or BOQ, 13 September 1939 (Hellmayr and Conover 1949:199; FMNH 102167); one (SP) at 190 km W of Puerto La Victoria, APY or BOQ, 24 June 1940 (Hellmayr and Conover 1949:199; FMNH 102761); one (SP) at 190 km W of Puerto La Victoria, APY or BOQ, 26 June 1940 (Hellmayr and Conover 1949:199; FMNH 102760); one (SP) at Laguna General Diaz, APY or PHA, 13 June 1945 (Hellmayr and

Conover 1949:199; FMNH 152315); one (SP) at Lichtenau, PHA, 1963 (Steinbacher 1968:330; SMF 47864); reported at Colonia Neuland, BOQ, 1988 or 1989 (Neris and Colmán 1991:4); one (SI) at Estancia San José, PHA, July 1989 (Collar et al. 1992:105); one (SI) at Ruta Trans Chaco km 187, PHA, September 1989 (Collar et al. 1992:105); Orient: reported for Alto Paraná region (Bertoni 1914a:42, 1939:23); one (SP) at Villarrica, GUA, February 1907 (Collar et al. 1992:105; BMNH); two (SP) at 70 km E of Rosario, SAP, 10 and 16 January 1938 (UMMZ 100049, 100050); one (SP) at Cerro Amambay, CON, 14 October 1938 (UMMZ 101669); one (SI) at Río Apa, CON, 3 August 1977 (R. Ridgely); two (SI) at Estancia Centurión, CON, 18 May 1989 (Collar et al. 1992:105, López and Hayes unpubl.); reported at Cerro Acahay, PAR (Acevedo et al. 1990:86); one (SI) at Estancia La Golondrina, CAP, 16 July 1992 (Brooks et al. 1993:47); two (SI) at Lagunita, Reserva Natural del Bosque Mbaracayú, CAN, 13 September 1992 (Brooks et al. 1993:47).

38. Gray Hawk
(*Buteo nitidus*)

Chaco: one (SP) at Puerto María, APY, 24 October 1909 (Grant 1911:331; BMNH); Orient: reported but questionable at Lago Ypoá, CEN or PAR (Podtiaguin 1944:54); one (SI) immature at Estancia Itabó, CAN, 4 June 1991 (R. Ridgely, P. Scharf et al.); one to two (SI) at Estancia La Golondrina, CAP, 8-10 July 1992 (Brooks et al. 1993:62, pers. comm.); one (SI) at Estancia San Antonio, APN, 24 July 1992 (Brooks et al. 1993:62, pers. comm.); one (SI) at Lagunita, Reserva Natural del Bosque Mbaracayú, 13 September 1992 (Brooks et al. 1993:62, pers. comm.).

39. White-rumped Hawk
(*Buteo leucorrhous*)

Orient: one (LSP) and others (SI) well described at 25°S, APN?, and 27°S, ITA?, July 1892 and other years (Bertoni 1901:162, 1914a:43, 1939:23); reported at San Juan de B., presumably San Juan Bautista, MIS (Podtiaguin 1944:62); one (SI) perched adult at S of Ciudad del Este, APN, 22 August 1977 (R. Ridgely); one (SI) perched on fence post at 20 km S of San Juan Bautista, MIS, 4 March 1991 (P. Scharf).

40. Short-tailed Hawk
(*Buteo brachyurus*)

Chaco: one (SP) at 195-200 km W of Puerto La Victoria, APY or BOQ, 7 May 1937 (UMMZ 93550); one (SP) at 240 km W of Puerto La Victoria, exNAS or BOQ, 24 June 1938 (UMMZ 93550); one (SI) at Ruta Trans Chaco km 173, PHA, 21 June 1990 (P. Scharf); Orient: many records.

41. Swainson's Hawk
(*Buteo swainsoni*)

Chaco: one (SP) at Orloff, BOQ, 13 December 1955 (Steinbacher 1962:41; MAK 56919); Orient: one (SI) at 40 km SE of Bella Vista, AMA, 3 December 1987 (Hayes et al. 1990a:950); one (SI) at Parque Nacional Ybycuí, PAR, 25 February 1989 (Hayes et al. 1990a:950).

42. Zone-tailed Hawk
(*Buteo albonotatus*)

Chaco: many records, southernmost at Ruta Trans Chaco km 153, just S of Río Negro, PHA (F. Hayes, P. Scharf and J. Escobar Argaña); Orient: two (SI) at Río Apa, CON, 2 and 4 August 1977 (R. Ridgely).

43. Harpy Eagle
(*Harpia harpyja*)

Chaco: hypothetical, one (SI) possible immature at Cerrito, APY, 27 October 1988 (F. Hayes); Orient: one (LSP) at cordilleras del Norte del Paraguay, late 1800s (Bertoni 1901:153); one (LSP) near Yuty, CAP, late 1800s (Bertoni 1901:154), and elsewhere? (Bertoni 1914a:43, 1939:23); reported at San Lázaro, CON (Podtiaguin 1944:57); reported but doubtful at Villeta, CEN (Podtiaguin 1944:57); one (PH, SP) allegedly hatched in AMA and captured in CON (Anonymous 1981:1), subsequently maintained alive until its death on 6 April 1988 (MHNIB).

44. Black-and-white Hawk-Eagle
(*Spizastur melanoleucus*)

Chaco: one (SP) at 265 km W of Puerto La Victoria, exNAS or BOQ, 16 May 1936 (UMMZ 90779); one (SP) at 190 km W of Puerto La Victoria, APY or BOQ, 2 May 1939 (UMMZ 109726); one (SI) at Picada 108, 36 km WSW of Estancia La Patria, exNAS (González Romero and Contreras 1989c:5); Orient: reported at Puerto Bertoni, APN (Bertoni

1914a:43, 80, 1939:24); one (SP) at 20 km E of Rosario, SAP, 17 August 1937 (UMMZ 96019); reported at Reserva Natural del Bosque Mbaracayú, CAN (Meisel et al. 1992:2); one (SI) at Estancia Itabó, CAN, 12 August 1992 (Brooks et al. 1993:51).

45. Ornate Hawk-Eagle
(*Spizaetus ornatus*)

Orient: one (LSP) at embocadura del Río Monday, September 1898 (Bertoni 1901:156, 1914a:43, 1939:24); one (SP) at Sapucái, PAR, 25 July 1900 (USNM 189371); many (SI) reported for Alto Paraná region (Bertoni 1914a:43, 1928c:188, 1939:24); one (SP) at Nueva Germania, SAP, 23 February 1932 (Laubmann 1939:166; MM 32.89); reported at Parque Nacional Cerro Corá, AMA (López undated:3).

46. Collared Forest-Falcon
(*Micrastur semitorquatus*)

Chaco: one (SP) at 80 km W of Puerto Pinasco, PHA, 9 September 1920 (Wetmore 1926:99; USNM 284797); one (SP) at 80 km SW of Lichtenau, BOQ or PHA, 15 July 1962 (Steinbacher 1968:333; SMF 38156); Orient: many records.

47. Spot-winged Falconet
(*Spiziapteryx circumcinctus*)

Chaco: one (SP) at 100 km W of Orloff, BOQ, 1 June 1956 (Steinbacher 1962:44; MAK 57112); reported at Colonia Neuland, BOQ, 1988 or 1989 (Neris and Colmán 1991:4); one (SI) at Estancia Coé Puajhú, exNAS, 12 September 1989 (Contreras 1989:5).

48. Orange-breasted Falcon
(*Falco deiroleucus*)

Chaco: one (SP) at Orloff, BOQ, 25 May 1938 (Hellmayr and Conover 1949:303; FMNH 101841); one (SI) at Retiro Potrerito, APY, 19 June 1988 (Hayes et al. 1990b:96); Orient: one (LSP) or more (?) at Alto Paraná region (Bertoni 1907:308, 1914a:43, 1939:23); one (SP) at Horqueta, CON, 24 February 1934 (Storer 1989:4; UMMZ 75316); one (SI) at Río Carapá, 10 km S of Mbaracayú, CAN, 25 July 1989 (Hayes and Granizo Tamayo 1992:255).

49. Peregrine Falcon
(*Falco peregrinus*)

Many records for both Chaco and Orient (Hayes et al. 1990a:950). There are four specimens (and probably a fifth, which was stolen) of the austral subspecies (*F. p. cassini*) from the central Chaco, BOQ and PHA, between 27 December and 1 June (Steinbacher 1962:45, Storer 1989:4, 5). Bertoni (1914a:43) reported a juvenile specimen (lost) from Puerto Bertoni, APN, and later identified it as a North American subspecies (*F. p. anatum*; Bertoni 1926:398, 1939:23). A banded specimen from North America (subspecies unknown) was recovered at Asunción, CEN, during late November or early December 1987 (Hayes et al. 1990a:950; USFWS band 576-87545; location of specimen unknown, but photo in Anonymous 1987:15)). Sight records along Río Paraguay from 18 September to 25 March may be of North American birds (Hayes et al. 1990a:950), but field identification of subspecies is difficult.

50. Blue-throated Piping-Guan
(*Pipile cumanensis*)

Chaco: hypothetical, one (LSP) at island near Concepción, border of PHA and CON (Hellmayr and Conover 1942:193), but specimen not located; Orient: many records, southernmost at Horqueta, CON, and Cerro Amambay, AMA (UMMZ). Two specimens (UMMZ 100965, 100966) taken at Cerro Amambay, AMA, in October and November 1938, were apparently taken at the same locality and time as Black-fronted Piping Guan (*P. jacutinga*) specimens (see below), indicating sympatry.

51. Black-fronted Piping-Guan
(*Pipile jacutinga*)

Threatened. Orient: one (SP) at Caaguazú, CAA, August 1893 (Salvadori 1895:23; MZT); one (SP) at Caballero, PAR, August 1893 (Salvadori 1895:23; MZT); reported for Río Acaray, CAA or APN, Río Monday, APN, and other rivers between 23ºS and 26ºS, Alto Paraná region (Bertoni 1901:21, 1914a:35, 1939:17); three (SP) or more at Capitán Meza, ITA, 1912, 1938, 1939 (Collar et al. 1992:131; MACN); one (SP) at Río Yuquerí, CAA, February 1932 (Collar et al. 1992:131; MCZ); one (SP) at Río Yguazú, APN or CAA, March 1932 (Collar et al. 1992:131; MCZ); five (SP) at

Cerro Amambay, AMA, 25 October-6 November 1938 (Hellmayr and Conover 1942:91; FMNH 413693-413697); seven (SP) at Cerro Amambay, AMA, 5 October-2 November 1938 (UMMZ 101673-101675, 100391, 100655, 100966, 100656); one (SP) at Reserva Natural del Bosque Mbaracayú, CAN, 16 February 1988 (Collar et al. 1992:131, Meisel et al. 1992:2; collected by Aché Indians and kept by J. Contreras); reported at Reserva Biológica Limoy, APN (Collar et al. 1992:131); one (SI) at Estancia San Antonio, APN, 2 and 3 August 1992 (Brooks et al. 1993:29); four (SI) at Estancia Itabó, CAN, 7, 19 and 20 August 1992 (Brooks et al. 1993:29); two (SI) at Estancia La Golondrina, CAA, 23 and 25 August 1992 (Brooks et al. 1993:29).

52. Speckled Crake
(*Coturnicops notata*)

Threatened. Chaco: one (SP) at Laguna General Diaz, PHA, 8 June 1945 (Blake 1977:509; FMNH 416547); Orient: one (LSP) at Puerto Bertoni, APN (Bertoni 1907:309, 1914a:37, 1939:18); one (SP) at 7 km E of Horqueta, CON, 25 December 1937 (Brodkorb 1938c:2; UMMZ 96035).

53. Red-and-white Crake
(*Laterallus leucopyrrhus*)

Chaco: one (LSP) at Río Pilcomayo, PHA, between December 1885 and February 1886 (Berlepsch 1887:35); reported at Río Confuso, PHA (Podtiaguin 1945:73); Orient: many records.

54. Rufous-sided Crake
(*Laterallus melanophaius*)

Chaco: no published records; one (SP) at 170 km W of Puerto La Victoria, APY or BOQ, 14 February 1938 (UMMZ 96221); one (SP) at Makthlawaiya, PHA, 20 November 1931 (AMNH 320751); two to six (SI, VO) at Ruta Trans Chaco km 79, PHA, 24 February 1990 (two), 5 September 1990 (one), 27 December 1990 (six), 28 and 31 May 1991 (several; P. Scharf, R. Ridgely et al.); Orient: many records.

55. Rufous-faced Crake
(*Laterallus xenopterus*)

Threatened. Orient: one (SP) at Horqueta, CON, 17 November 1933 (Conover 1934:365; FMNH 411221); one (LSP?) at Lima, SAP

(Podtiaguin 1945:74); one (LSP) at Pedro Juan Caballero, AMA (Podtiaguin 1945:74; MHNSCP 621); one (SP) at 6 km NE of Curuguaty, CAN, 16 July 1976 (Myers and Hansen 1980:901; UMMZ 204295); two (SP) at 13 km NE of Curuguaty, CAN, 17 and 18 August 1978 (Myers and Hansen 1980:901; UMMZ 201113, 200634); one (SP) at 6 km NE of Curuguaty, CAN, 11 July 1979 (Myers and Hansen 1980:901; UMMZ 202595).

56. Gray-breasted Crake
(*Laterallus exilis*)

Chaco: one (SP) at Estancia La Golondrina, PHA, 6 August 1979 (Storer 1981:140; UMMZ 202597); Orient: one (SP) at Riacho Ñeembucú, N of Pilar, ÑEE, 20 January 1994 (Contreras and Contreras 1994:1; MFA). The January record suggests that breeding is possible, but the nearest records outside of Paraguay are far to the north (see Storer 1981).

57. Slaty-breasted Wood-Rail
(*Aramides saracura*)

Chaco: hypothetical, one (LSP) at Río Confuso, PHA (Podtiaguin 1945:71; MHNP), but locality is unusual (no nearby records); Orient: many records.

58. Yellow-breasted Crake
(*Porzana flaviventer*)

Chaco: many records; Orient: one (SP) at 5 km E of Horqueta, CON, 9 February 1937 (Brodkorb 1938c:2; UMMZ 92950); two (SP) at Rosario, SAP, 13 February 1939 (UMMZ 111354, 111355); reported at Nueva Italia, CEN (Podtiaguin 1945:72).

59. Paint-billed Crake
(*Neocrex erythrops*)

Extreme dates: 24 August (Brooks et al. 1993:63) and 12 April (Short 1976a:5).

60. Spotted Rail
(*Pardirallus maculatus*)

Extreme dates: 30 August and 13 April (Hayes et al. 1994:86).

61. Plumbeous Rail
(*Pardirallus sanguinolentus*)

Chaco: one (SP) at Laguna General Diaz, PHA, 13 June 1945 (FMNH 410546); two (SP) at 115 km E of Orloff, PHA, 6 September 1955 (Steinbacher 1962:26; MAK 56118, 56119); Orient: many records.

62. Purple Gallinule
(*Porphyrula martinica*)
Extreme dates: 5 September and 30 May (Hayes et al. 1994:86).

63. Azure Gallinule
(*Porphyrula flavirostris*)
Chaco: two (LSP) at Fortín Page, PHA, 26 November 1890 (Kerr 1892:149), but no specimens located at BMNH (thus, identification questionable); one (SP) at 195-200 km W of Puerto La Victoria, APY or BOQ, 28 January 1937 (UMMZ 92982); Orient: many records, southernmost at 3-18 km E of Rosario, SAP (UMMZ). Extreme dates: October (Remsen and Parker 1990:386, 388) and 28 January (Hayes et al. 1994:86).

64. Spot-flanked Gallinule
(*Gallinula melanops*)
Chaco: many records; Orient: hypothetical, reported at Río Tebicuary, ÑEE, MIS, CAP or ITA (Podtiaguin 1945:75).

65. White-winged Coot
(*Fulica leucoptera*)
Chaco: many records; Orient: one (SI) at Bahía de Asunción, CEN, 22 and 29 March 1988 (F. Hayes and J. Fox); one (SI) at Bahía de Asunción, CEN, 11 January 1989 (F. Hayes et al.); nine (SI) at Bahía de Asunción, CEN, 18 and 23 January 1989, 15 February 1989 (F. Hayes et al.).

66. Red-fronted Coot
(*Fulica rufifrons*)
Chaco: two (SP) at Campo Esperanza, PHA, 16 October 1940 (Short 1975:216; UMMZ 111357, 111358); reported at Hohenau, PHA (Podtiaguin 1945:77); reported at Estero Patiño, PHA (Podtiaguin 1945:77).

67. Sungrebe
(*Heliornis fulica*)
Orient: reported for Alto Paraná region (Bertoni 1914a:37); reported at Asunción, CEN (Bertoni 1922:40, 1939:19); reported at Bosque Pira'y, AMA (Acevedo et al. 1990:86); reported at Reserva Natural del Bosque Mbaracayú, CAN (Acevedo et al. 1990:86); reported at Cuenca del Acaray-mí, CAA or CAA (Acevedo et al. 1990:86); five (SI) at Río Carapá, 22, 23 and 25 July 1989 (Hayes and Granizo Tamayo 1992:256, unpubl.); two (SI)

at Estancia La Golondrina, CAA, 24 (one only) and 27 August 1992 (Brooks et al. 1993:63).

68. Black-legged Seriema
(*Chunga burmeisteri*)
Northernmost records at about 22°S (Brodkorb 1937c:33).

69. Pied Lapwing
(*Hoploxypterus cayanus*)
Chaco: one (SP) at 195-200 km W of Puerto La Victoria, APY or BOQ, 18 February 1937 (UMMZ 93254); one (SI) at Ruta Trans Chaco km 341, near Riacho San Carlos, PHA, 22 April 1990 (P. Scharf); Orient: reported for Alto Paraná region (Bertoni 1914a:38, 1939:20); one (SP) at Río Jejuí-Guazú, SAP, 12 January 1932 (Laubmann 1939:87; MM 32.262); one (SP) at 70 km E of Rosario, SAP, 19 January 1938 (UMMZ 96211); eight or more (SI) at Río Apa, CON, 2 and 3 August 1977 (R. Ridgely).

70. Black-bellied Plover
(*Pluvialis squatarola*)
Orient: one (PH) at Bahía de Asunción, CEN, 11 December 1987 (Hayes et al. 1990a:950; VIREO x08/6/002); one (PH) at Bahía de Asunción, CEN, 2 December 1988 (Hayes et al. 1990a:950; VIREO x08/6/003); one (SI) at Bahía de Asunción, CEN, 5 January 1989 (Hayes et al. 1990a:950).

71. American Golden-Plover
(*Pluvialis dominica*)
Extreme dates: 31 August and 8 March (Hayes et al. 1990a:951). Most common during austral spring (Hayes et al. 1990a:951, Hayes and Fox 1991).

72. South American Painted-Snipe
(*Rostratula semicollaris*)
Chaco: many records, northernmost at 115 km E of Orloff, PHA (Steinbacher 1962:36); Orient: reported for Alto Paraná region (Bertoni 1914a:39, 1939:20); one (SI) at Paso Lengá, ÑEE, 22 January 1992 (Contreras and Contreras 1992:2).

73. Greater Yellowlegs
(*Tringa melanoleuca*)
Extreme dates: late August (Myers and Myers 1979:192) and 30 May (P. Scharf). Most common during austral spring (Hayes et al. 1990a:951, Hayes and Fox 1991).

74. Lesser Yellowlegs
(*Tringa flavipes*)
Extreme dates: 7 August (A. Madroño Nieto and J. Escobar Argaña) and 20 June (P. Scharf and R. Ridgely).

75. Solitary Sandpiper
(*Tringa solitaria*)
Extreme dates: 30 July (Hayes et al. 1990a:952) and 8 April (Podtiaguin 1944:86).

76. Spotted Sandpiper
(*Actitis macularia*)
Chaco: many records; Orient: one (SP) at Parque Nacional Ybycuí, PAR, 22 January 1981 (Hayes et al. 1990a:952; MNHNP 714), representing southernmost record; one (SI) at Bahía de Asunción, CEN, 31 January 1989 (Hayes et al. 1990a:952). Extreme dates: 11 September (Contreras 1989:5) and 28 March (Steinbacher 1968:327).

77. Upland Sandpiper
(*Bartramia longicauda*)
Extreme dates: 17 September (Brooks et al. 1993:117, pers. comm.) and 11 April (Hayes et al. 1990a:952).

78. Eskimo Curlew
(*Numenius borealis*)
Threatened. Two (LSP) at unknown locality, one dated 9 October (Sharpe 1896:371; BMNH), but specimens not located; reported to inhabit both dry and wet fields, arriving in flocks of 15 to 20 in September (Bertoni 1898:387, 1914a:38, 1939:20); no records this century.

79. Hudsonian Godwit
(*Limosa haemastica*)
Extreme dates: 31 August and 21 December (Hayes et al. 1990a:952, 953). Most common during austral spring (Hayes et al. 1990a:952, 953, Hayes and Fox 1991).

80. Red Knot
(*Calidris canutus*)
Orient: one (PH) at Bahía de Asunción, CEN, 29 October 1987 (Hayes et al. 1990a:953; VIREO x08/6/004); one (SI) at Bahía de Asunción, CEN, 10 November 1988 (Hayes et al. 1990a:953).

81. Sanderling
(*Calidris alba*)
Chaco: four (SI) well described at Mariscal Estigarribia, 31 August 1990 (A. Madroño Nieto); Orient: reported at Misiones, Paraguay? (Bertoni 1914a:38), probably referring to Misiones, Argentina, and questionable in Paraguay; one (PH) at Bahía de Asunción, CEN, 17 November 1988 (Hayes et al. 1990a:953; VIREO x08/2/002); one (SI) at Bahía de Asunción, CEN, 25 November 1988 (Hayes et al. 1990a:953).

82. Semipalmated Sandpiper
(*Calidris pusilla*)
Chaco: one (SI) at Puerto Pinasco, PHA, 1 September 1920 (Wetmore 1927:10-11); 12 (SI) at Puerto Pinasco, PHA, 20 September 1920 (Wetmore 1927:11); one (SI) carefully observed and well described at Mariscal Estigarribia, BOQ, 31 August 1990 (A. Madroño Nieto).

83. Least Sandpiper
(*Calidris minutilla*)
Chaco: one (SP) at Lichtenau, PHA, 20 October 1960 (Steinbacher 1962:38; MAK 611036); Orient: one (SI) at Bahía de Asunción, CEN, 5 January 1989 (Hayes et al. 1990a:953).

84. White-rumped Sandpiper
(*Calidris fuscicollis*)
Extreme dates: 9 August (F. Hayes et al.) and 4 May (P. Scharf). Most common during austral spring (Hayes et al. 1990a:953, Hayes and Fox 1991).

85. Baird's Sandpiper
(*Calidris bairdii*)
Chaco: 15 reported but questionable (Hayes et al. 1990a:954) at APY, October-November 1984 (López 1985:9); five (SI) at Estancia Zaragosa, PHA, 19 and 22 (one only) August 1990 (R. Behrstock); nine (PH) at Fortín Teniente E. Ochoa, exNAS, 1 September 1990 (P. Scharf); three (SI) at Estancia Klassen, PHA, 9 August 1994 (F. Hayes et al.); two (SI) at Laguna Capitán, PHA, 9 August 1994 (N. Boyajian); Orient: one (SI) at Isla Talavera, ITA, January 1989 (Contreras and Contreras 1994:3); one (SP) in a flock of 23 (SI) at Isla Jara Cué, Playa Ybycuí, ÑEE, 13 January 1994 (Contreras and Contreras 1994:2; MFA).

86. Pectoral Sandpiper
(*Calidris melanotos*)
Extreme dates: 3 August (Myers and Myers 1979:193) and 7 April (Hayes et al. 1990a:954).

87. Stilt Sandpiper
(*Calidris himantopus*)
Extreme dates: 18 August and 5 January (Hayes et al. 1990a:954). Most common during austral spring (Hayes et al. 1990a, Hayes and Fox 1991).

88. Buff-breasted Sandpiper
(*Tryngites subruficollis*)
Extreme dates: late August (Myers and Myers 1979:193) and 18 April (AMNH 321047). Most common during austral spring (Hayes et al. 1990a:954, Hayes and Fox 1991).

89. Wilson's Phalarope
(*Phalaropus tricolor*)
Chaco: many records; Orient: erroneously cited for GUA (Hayes et al. 1990a:954); three (SI) well observed in ponds at Santa Rosa, SAP, 25 September 1990 (P. Scharf). Extreme dates: 1 September (Hayes et al. 1990a:954) and 24/25 February (P. Scharf).

90. Red Phalarope
(*Phalaropus fulicaria*)
Chaco: one (SP) at 170 km W of Puerto La Victoria, APY or BOQ, 5 March 1938 (Brodkorb 1938c:3; UMMZ 96175).

91. Gray-hooded Gull
(*Larus cirrocephalus*)
One (SP) at unknown locality (Schlegel 1863:36, Storer 1989:5, 6; RMNH), but possibly in Argentina or Brazil; Chaco: two (SP) at 120 km E of Orloff, PHA, 1 September 1940 (Storer 1989:6; USNM 571351, 571352); ten (SI) questionable at Río Paraguay, APY, October-November 1984 (López 1985:12); Orient: hypothetical, reported for MIS (A. O. Contreras et al. 1989:11).

92. Brown-hooded Gull
(*Larus maculipennis*)
Three (SP) at unknown locality (Schlegel 1863, Storer 1989:5, 6; RMNH), but possibly in Argentina or Brazil; Orient: one (LSP) at Puerto Bertoni, APN, July 1916 (Bertoni 1919a:256, 1939:19); one (SP) at Sapucái, PAR, 17 August 1901 (not 1907; Storer 1989:5; UMMZ 1647a).

93. Large-billed Tern
(*Phaetusa simplex*)
Uncommon during high water levels (austral winter) along major rivers (Hayes in press), and rare away from major rivers; westernmost record at Estancia Amalia, PHA (Brooks 1991b:3, pers. comm.).

94. Arctic Tern
(*Sterna paradisaea*)
Orient: one (PH) at Bahía de Asunción, CEN, 9 and 10 May 1989 (Hayes et al. 1990a:955; VIREO x08/17/001), providing the first record for the interior of South America.

95. Yellow-billed Tern
(*Sterna superciliaris*)
Uncommon during high water levels (austral winter) along major rivers (Hayes in press), and rare away from major rivers; westernmost record at Estancia Amalia, PHA (Brooks 1991b:3, pers. comm.).

96. Black Skimmer
(*Rynchops niger*)
Uncommon during high water levels (austral winter) along major rivers (Hayes in press), and rare away from major rivers; westernmost record at Estancia Amalia, PHA (Brooks 1991b:3, pers. comm.).

97. Rock Dove
(*Columba livia*)
Introduced; first specimen obtained on 20 September 1941 at Areguá, COR (UMMZ 111006); widespread in most Paraguayan towns by 1987 (F. Hayes and P. Scharf).

98. Scaled Pigeon
(*Columba speciosa*)
Orient: one (LSP) at Puerto Bertoni, APN, 1915 (Bertoni 1919a:255, 1939:18); one (SI) at Estancia Itabó, CAN, 15 August 1992 (Brooks et al. 1993:64); up to seven (SI) at Reserva Natural del Bosque Mbaracayú, CAN, 5, 8, 11-14 and 16 September 1992 (Brooks et al. 1993:64).

99. Picazuro Pigeon
(*Columba picazuro*)
Most abundant during austral winter, particularly in Alto Chaco region (Hayes et al. 1994:90).

100. Spot-winged Pigeon
(*Columba maculosa*)

Chaco: one (SP) at Fortín Guachalla, BOQ, 18 September 1945 (Willim 1947:2; FMNH 416380); four (SP) at Laguna Escalante, PHA, 4 October 1960 (Steinbacher 1962:29, 1968:322; MAK 611026, 611027; SMF 38231, 38232); two (SP) at Laguna Escalante, PHA, 13 August 1966 (Steinbacher 1968:322; SMF 47852, 47853); reported but questionable at Las Delicias, PHA, March or December 1983 or July 1984 (Peris et al. 1987:30); Orient: hypothetical, reported but questionable at Parque Nacional Cerro Corá, AMA (Anonymous 1982b:58, López undated:4); reported at Asunción, CEN (Contreras and González Romero 1988:32).

101. Plain-breasted Ground-Dove
(*Columbina minuta*)

Chaco: one (LSP) at Río Pilcomayo, PHA, 28 December 1885 (Berlepsch 1887:34), but possibly in Argentina; one (SP) at Lichtenau, PHA, 13 December 1963 (Steinbacher 1968:323; SMF 38239); Orient: many records, southernmost at Villarrica, GUA (Hellmayr and Conover 1942:533).

102. Purple-winged Ground-Dove
(*Claravis godefrida*)

Threatened. Orient: one (LSP) of two pairs (SI) well described at 26°53'S and 25°43'S, APN?, July 1893 and other date? (Bertoni 1901:27, 1914a:36, 1939:18).

103. Gray-fronted Dove
(*Leptotila rufaxilla*)

Resembles White-tipped Dove (*L. verreauxi*) and probably overlooked, best distinguished by voice; both are present in humid forests.

104. Hyacinthine Macaw
(*Anodorhynchus hyacinthinus*)

Threatened. Chaco: three (SI) at Puerto María, APY, 11 August 1988 (Hayes et al. 1990b:96); Orient: one (SP) at Diamantina, possibly Arroyo Trementina, CON, 19 June 1887 (López 1992:4; USNM), but I did not see specimen; one (SI) at 1 km from Puerto Valle Mi, CON, 7 March 1984 (López 1992:4); two (SI?) near Río Apa, CON, 1987 (Collar et al. 1992:253); several (SI) at Estancia Primavera, CON, Estancia Centurión, CON (including two on 17 May 1989; N. López and F. Hayes), and Estan-

cia San Luís, CON (including two on 23 December 1988), between September 1988 and October 1989 (López 1992:4); reported by local residents at Estancia Buena Vista, CON, Estancia Mirabeaud, CON, Estancia Santa Sofía, CON, and Retiro Satí, CON, Estancia Reyes Cué, CON, and Estancia Loma Porá, CON (López 1992:4, 5); several (SI) south of Parque Nacional Cerro Corá, AMA (López 1992:4, 5), but questioned by author.

105. Glaucous Macaw
(*Anodorhynchus glaucus*)

Extinct. No precise locality records, but probably occurred along the banks of the Río Paraná and possibly the lower Río Paraguay (Collar et al. 1992:243-249); specimens from unknown locality include: two at AMNH (one received alive in London on 6 March 1886, AMNH 474109; the other received alive in London on 4 May 1898, AMNH 474110); two at ANSP (Collar et al. 1992:242, 243); two at BMNH (Salvadori 1891:149); two at MACN (Orfila 1936:208); two at RMNH (Finsch 1867:391, 392; Collar et al. 1992:242); reported at Río Pelotas, km 3, CAN (Podtiaguin 1944:14, Collar et al. 1992:243); no convincing records during this century (Collar et al. 1992).

106. Blue-and-yellow Macaw
(*Ara ararauna*)

Probably extirpated in Paraguay. Chaco: hypothetical, reported without details (Bertoni 1939:24); Orient: Brabourne (1914a:186) reported a group of 50 live specimens obtained by a collector about 67 miles (108 km) N of Villarrica, GUA; Bertoni (1922a:40) reported that the species was disappearing due to the persecution, and that it was confined to the area between Caaguazú, CAA, and the Cordillera de Mbaracayú, CAN; Dabbene (1920:56) stated that A. de W. Bertoni had just recently observed the species in the north of Paraguay ; reported at Yhú, CAA (Bertoni 1939:24); one (LSP) at Pedro Juan Caballero, AMA, 5 October 1933 (Podtiaguin 1944:11; MHNP); reported at Bosque Estrella, AMA (Acevedo et al. 1990:86). Podtiaguin (1944:11) also reported the species at the following localities: San Lázaro, CON; Villa Franca, ÑEE (questionable); Desmochados (locality unknown); and Guazú-Cuá (locality unknown). The latter three localities were also listed by Zotta

98

(1937:537) for the Blue-throated Macaw (*A. glaucogularis*), but the basis of these reports and the reason why Podtiaguin assigned the localities to *A. ararauna* are unknown; they may have been based upon reports by local residents, and should be regarded with skepticism. Statements in Bertoni (1922a) and Podtiaguin (1944) indicate that they were aware of the distinctions between *A. ararauna* and *A. glaucogularis*, and were thus unlikely to confuse the two species (see *A. glaucogularis* in Hypothetical Species section). Although the specimen from Pedro Juan Caballero may have been imported from elsewhere, there appears to be ample evidence that *A. ararauna* formerly resided in the Orient and less evidence that *A. glaucogularis* resided in Paraguay (see Hypothetical Species section). López (1992) failed to find this species in CON despite extensive field work between September 1988 and October 1989.

107. Red-and-green Macaw
(*Ara chloropterus*)
Chaco: hypothetical, one (LSP) or more (?) at Río Confuso, PHA (Bertoni 1930b:258), but possibly escaped bird(s); reported at APY (Bertoni 1939:24); reported at Puerto Bahía Negra, APY, and Puerto Guaraní, APY (Podtiaguin 1944:10); Orient: many records, including recent sightings (1987-1992) of many birds from various localities in CON, CAN and CAA (e.g., López 1992:6, Brooks et al. 1993:64, F. Hayes). The Chaco reports from APY are credible, but may be based on birds kept by local residents; the occurrence of wild birds requires substantiation.

108. Blue-winged Macaw
(*Ara maracana*)
Chaco: hypothetical, one (SI) or more (?) at Río Confuso, PHA (Bertoni 1930b:258), but possibly escaped bird(s); Orient: many records, including recent records (1978-1992) of only a few birds in CON, CAN and APN (López 1992:6, 7, Brooks et al. 1993:51, UMMZ).

109. Peach-fronted Parakeet
(*Aratinga aurea*)
Chaco: one (SP) at Puerto Pinasco, PHA, 5 September 1916 (Cherrie and Reichenberger 1923:3; AMNH 149400); one (SP) at Puerto Pinasco, PHA, 20 October 1916 (Cherrie and

Reichenberger 1923:3; AMNH 149401); one (LSP) at Villa Hayes, PHA, August 1925 (Bertoni 1930a:246, Podtiaguin 1944:8; MHNSCP 204); two (SI) at Puerto Cooper, PHA, 29 October 1988 (F. Hayes); Orient: many records, southernmost at just N of Pilar, ÑEE (R. Ridgely, P. Scharf et al.), and at 1 km N of Villa Florida, in PAR (F. Hayes).

110. Blaze-winged Parakeet
(*Pyrrhura devillei*)
Chaco: two (SP) at Puerto Guaraní, APY, 27 August 1928 (Zotta 1950:165; MACN, AMNH 785882); two (SP) at Puerto La Victoria, APY, 17 October 1944 (Zotta 1950:165; MACN); Orient: several flocks (SI) at Río Apa, CON, July 1977 (Ridgely 1981:284); one (SI) at Estancia Centurión, CON, 19 January 1989 (López 1992:11). See Taxonomic Notes section.

111. Reddish-bellied Parakeet
(*Pyrrhura frontalis*)
Westernmost record at Fort Wheeler, PHA (AMNH).

112. Blue-winged Parrotlet
(*Forpus xanthopterygius*)
Chaco: one (LSP) at Villa Hayes, PHA, 29 January 1923 (Bertoni 1930a:246, 1939:25, Podtiaguin 1944:84; MHNSCP 197); one (SP) at 235 km W of Río Negro, PHA, 28 July 1939 (UMMZ 105326), but locality questionable (see Methods section); two (SI) at Retiro Potrerito, APY, 18 June 1989 (Hayes et al. 1990b:96); Orient: many records.

113. Vinaceous-breasted Parrot
(*Amazona vinacea*)
Threatened. Orient: many (SI) in Alto Paraná region, including Yaguarasapá, ITA?, 1890 and subsequently (Bertoni 1927:149, 150, 1914a:45, 1939:25); one (SP) at Villarrica, GUA, July 1893 (Salvadori 1895:19; AMNH 475292); one (SP) at Yhú, CAA, August 1893 (Salvadori 1895:19; MZT); two (SP) at Villarrica, GUA, June 1907 (Collar et al. 1992:417; BMNH); one (SP) at E of Caaguazú, CAA, 19 November 1930 (Collar et al. 1992:417; AMNH 320325); one (LSP) and two small flocks (SI) at 9 km E of mouth of Río Apa, CON, 9 December 1939 (Podtiaguin 1944:103; MHNSCP 1395); six (SP) at Puerto Gibaja, APN, 5 August-14 September 1940

(UMMZ 108728-108731, 109736, 111015); many (SI) in several areas of Alto Paraná region, July and August 1977 (Ridgely 1981:362), including up to eight at E of Celos Parini, CAN, 16-18 July 1977, and several E (presumably W) of Ciudad del Este, APN, 22 August 1977 (Collar et al. 1994:417); about 10 (SI) daily at Arroyo Pozuelo, CAN, 2-5 November 1987 (Collar et al. 1992:471; F. Hayes); several (SI) at Colonia Dorada, APN (Silva 1988:3, 1989:247); about 10 (SI) at Catueté, CAN, 24 July 1989 (Collar et al. 1992:417; F. Hayes and T. Granizo Tamayo); 54 (SI) at Río Carapá, S of Mbaracayú, CAN, 25 July 1989 (Collar et al. 1992:417; Hayes and Granizo Tamayo 1992:256, unpubl.); four (SI) at Puerto Barra, APN, 28 September 1989 (Collar et al. 1992:417); several (SI) at Estancia Centurión, CON, and Estancia Santa María de la Sierra, CON, between September 1988 and October 1989 (López 1992:17); 70 (SI) at 2 km S of Reserva Biológica Limoy, APN, 10 May 1990 (López 1992:17); 28 (SI) between Ygatimí and Curuguaty, including Reserva Natural del Bosque Mbaracayú, CAN, 24-29 June 1990 (Meisel et al. 1992:3; P. Scharf); up to 50 (SI) at Estancia Itabó, CAN, 4 and 5 June 1991 (Collar et al. 1992:417; R. Ridgely and P. Scharf); reported at Reserva Biológica Limoy, APN, Reserva Biológica Itabó, APN, N of Hernandarias, APN, Río Ñacunday basin, APN, and Comandacay, APN (Collar et al. 1992:417); 15 (LSP) at Capitán Meza, ITA (Collar et al. 1992:417); up to 40 at Estancia Itabó, CAN, 4-20 August 1992 (Brooks et al. 1993:32); five (SI) at Reserva Biológica Itabó, APN, 17 August 1994 (F. Hayes et al.).

114. Ash-colored Cuckoo
(*Coccyzus cinereus*)

Chaco: one (SP) at 120 km W of Puerto Pinasco, PHA, 31 October 1937 (UMMZ 96064); one (SP) at Orloff, BOQ, 4 March 1946 (FMNH 153336); one (SP) at Lichtenau, PHA, 15 June 1973 (Short 1976a:6; AMNH 810579); one (SP) at Lichtenau, PHA, 27 December 1973 (Short 1976a:6; AMNH 811358); one (SP) at Lichtenau, PHA, 3 January 1974 (Short 1976a:6; AMNH 811357); reported at Las Delicias, PHA, March or December 1983 or July 1984 (Peris et al. 1987:30); Orient: reported at San Ignacio, MIS (Laubmann

1939:190); one (SP) at 7 km N of Puerto Bertoni, APN, 27 September 1940 (UMMZ 108747); one (SI) at NE of Pilar, ÑEE, 2 March 1991 (P. Scharf). Possibly a northern austral migrant.

115. Black-billed Cuckoo
(*Coccyzus erythropthalmus*)

Chaco: one (SP) at Lichtenau, PHA, 11 December 1970 (Short 1972a:895; AMNH 802827).

116. Yellow-billed Cuckoo
(*Coccyzus americanus*)

Extreme dates: 12 August and 1 May (Short 1976b:6).

117. Dark-billed Cuckoo
(*Coccyzus melacoryphus*)

Rare during austral winter (Hayes et al. 1994:86).

118. Pheasant Cuckoo
(*Dromococcyx phasianellus*)

Orient: cited for Alto Paraná region (e.g., Lynch Arribálzalga 1902:342, Laubmann 1939:193) on the basis of a description by Bertoni (1901:43-46, 1914a:48, 1939:27), but the description (especially of voice) appears to be that of Pavonine Cuckoo (*D. pavoninus*); one (SP) at Sapucái, PAR, 14 August 1904 (Chubb 1910:273; BMNH 1905-10-12-62); reported but questionable at Asunción, CEN (Bertoni 1939:27, Podtiaguin 1941:17); one (SI) probable at Parque Nacional Ybycuí, PAR, 18 April 1990 (P. Scharf); one (SI) at Isla Hú, ÑEE, 12 September 1993 (Contreras 1993:1); one (VO) at Tobatí, COR, 7 August 1994 (S. LaBar et al.; vocalizations recorded); one (VO) at Parque Nacional Ybycuí, PAR, 11 and 12 August 1994 (F. Hayes et al.).

119. Pavonine Cuckoo
(*Dromococcyx pavoninus*)

Chaco: one (SP) at Orloff, BOQ, 17 November 1955 (Steinbacher 1962:56; MAK 56145); Orient: many records.

120. Spectacled Owl
(*Pulsatrix perspicillata*)

Chaco: hypothetical, one (SI) or more (?) at Río Confuso, PHA (Bertoni 1930b:258); Orient: many records, south to 25 km E of Rosario, SAP (UMMZ 93636).

100

121. Tawny-browed Owl
(*Pulsatrix koeniswaldiana*)

Orient: one (LSP) well described for Alto Paraná region (Bertoni 1901:175, 176, 1914a:44, 1939:24); two (VO) at Estancia Itabó, CAN, 9, 18 and 19 August 1992 (Brooks et al. 1993:66); one (SI) at Estancia La Golondrina, CAA, 27 August 1992 (Brooks et al. 1993:66).

122. Great Horned Owl
(*Bubo virginianus*)

Chaco: many records; Orient: two eggs (NE) at Estancia Ytañu, CEN (Dalgleish 1889:83), but not located at BMNH; one (SP) at Estancia San Luis, CON, 28 October 1931 (Laubmann 1939:223; MM 32.343); reported for MIS (Bertoni 1939:24), but may refer to Misiones Province, Argentina, or the Estancia Ytañu record cited above; one (SP) at 2 km W of Horqueta, 18 August 1935 (UMMZ 90195); two (SI) at S of San Ignacio, MIS, 4 September 1982 (R. Ridgely); one (SI) dead on road, 10 km S of Villeta, CEN, 10 August 1993 (J. Escobar Argaña, A. Madroño Nieto, F. Hayes).

123. Brazilian Pygmy-Owl
(*Glaucidium minutissimum*)

Orient: one (LSP) at Puerto Bertoni, APN (Bertoni 1907:307, 1914a:44, 1939:24); one (SI) observed through telescope at Estancia Itabó, CAN, 5 June 1991 (R. Ridgely, P. Scharf et al.).

124. Mottled Owl
(*Ciccaba virgata*)

Orient: one (LSP) well described at Puerto Bertoni, APY, 20 July 1898 (Bertoni 1901:178, 1914a:44, 1939:24); one (SP) at Parque Nacional Ybycuí, PAR, 14 June 1979 (UMMZ 202027); one (SI) at Jejuí-mí, Reserva Natural del Bosque Mbaracayú, CAN, 6 September 1992 (Brooks et al. 1993:66); one (VO) at Estancia Itabó, CAN, 10 August 1992 (Brooks et al. 1993:66).

125. Rusty-barred Owl
(*Strix hylophila*)

Orient: two (LSP) at Río Monday and Río Paraná, APN, 20 May 1896 and no date (Bertoni 1901:174); one (LSP) at Djaguarasapá, ITA?, July 1891 (Bertoni 1901:175) and elsewhere? (Bertoni 1914a:44, 1939:24); one (SP) at 8 km N of Puerto San Rafael, ITA, 23 July 1978 (Storer 1989:7; UMMZ 200673); one

(VO) questionable at Choré, SAP, 2 October 1987 (Hayes and Areco de Medina 1988:62, unpubl.); reported at Reserva Natural del Bosque Mbaracayú, CAN (Acevedo et al. 1990:86, Meisel et al. 1992:4).

126. Stygian Owl
(*Asio stygius*)

Chaco: one (LSP, PH) at Villa Hayes, PHA (Bertoni 1930a:243, 246, 1939:24, Podtiaguin 1944:95; MHNSCP 477-5); Orient: one (SP) at Encarnación, ITA, 2 March 1938 (Partridge 1954:118; MACN 30253); one (VO) at Estancia Itabó, CAN, 13 August 1992 (Brooks et al. 1993:67); two (VO) at Estancia La Golondrina, CAA, 23 and 28 August (one only) 1992 (Brooks et al. 1993:67).

127. Short-eared Owl
(*Asio flammeus*)

Chaco: many records; Orient: reported for MIS (Bertoni 1918b:239, 1939:24), but may refer to Misiones Province, Argentina; one (SI) perched along road at night at Lupii, AMA, 26 September 1990 (P. Scharf).

128. Buff-fronted Owl
(*Aegolius harrisii*)

Chaco: one (SP) at Campo Esperanza, PHA, 11 September 1936 (Storer 1989:7; UMMZ 105353); Orient: one (LSP) at Djaguarasapá, ITA?, June 1892 (Bertoni 1904:5); one (LSP) at Puerto Bertoni, APN (Bertoni 1904:5), and elsewhere? (Bertoni 1914a:44, 1939:24); one (SP) at Sapucái, PAR, 28 September 1902 (Chubb 1910:76; BMNH 1903-12-112); one (SP) at 13 km N of Curuguaty, CAN, 15 July 1979 (Storer 1989:7; UMMZ 202028).

129. Common Nighthawk
(*Chordeiles minor*)

Extreme dates: 27 October (Hayes et al. 1990a:955) and 5 May (P. Scharf).

130. Ocellated Poorwill
(*Nyctiphrynus ocellatus*)

Orient: two (LSP) at Puerto Bertoni, APN (Bertoni 1907:304, 1939:25); reported at Río Yguazú, CAA or APN (Bertoni 1914a:46, 1939:25); one (SP) at 13 km N of Curuguaty, CAN, 21 August 1978 (Storer 1989:7; UMMZ 201117); one (VO) at Choré, SAP, 2 October 1987 (Hayes and Areco de Medina 1988:62, unpubl.).

131. Band-winged Nightjar
(*Caprimulgus longirostris*)
Extreme dates: 29 May (Hayes et al. 1994:90) and 9 September (Contreras and González Romero 1991:1).

132. Sickle-winged Nightjar
(*Eleothreptus anomalus*)
Threatened. Orient: one (SP) between Colonia Risso and Río Apa, CON, between August and November 1893 (Salvadori 1895:14; MZT); one (SP) at Villarrica, GUA, April 1924 (Collar et al. 1992:463; BMNH); reported for MIS (A. O. Contreras et al. 1989:11); reported at Ñu Guazú, Asunción, CEN, between 4 and 10 August 1989 (Contreras and González Romero 1989a:1); reported for Estancia Cerrito Vargas, MIS (Collar et al. 1992:463).

133. Long-tailed Potoo
(*Nyctibius aethereus*)
Orient: reported at Puerto Bertoni, APN (Bertoni 1914a:81, 1939:26); one (PH) at nest with one egg (PH) at Zanja Morotí, CON, December 1931 (Laubmann 1940:1, 16, 32); reported erroneously (should refer to Common Potoo [*N. griseus*]) at Choré, SAP (Hayes and Areco de Medina 1988:62); reported at Río Yguazú, APN or CAA (Bertoni 1939:26); one (SP) at Reserva Natural del Bosque Mbaracayú, CAN, 16 February 1988 (Meisel et al. 1992:4; seen by F. Hayes, collected by Aché Indians, identified and kept by J. Contreras); one (SI) at Estancia Itabó, CAN, 4 June 1991 (R. Ridgely, P. Scharf et al.); one (PH) at Estancia La Golondrina, CAP, between 5 and 21 July 1992 (Brooks et al. 1993:67, 68; VIREO B36/1/001).

134. White-collared Swift
(*Streptoprocne zonaris*)
Orient: specimen records (Zimmer 1953a:5; AMNH) overlooked by Meyer de Schauensee (1970:126); many recent records.

135. Ashy-tailed Swift
(*Chaetura andrei*)
Extreme dates for Chaco: 16 August and 22 April (Hayes et al. 1994:86); status during winter is uncertain in Orient (Hayes et al. 1994:86).

136. Gray-rumped Swift
(*Chaetura cinereiventris*)
Orient: only documented record is a photo of an adult at nest in Alto Paraná region (N. Pérez unpubl.; MHNIB, VIREO); many sight records, apparently present during winter (e.g., Brooks et al. 1993:69).

137. Swallow-tailed Hummingbird
(*Eupetomena macroura*)
Orient: one (SP) at Zanja Morotí, CON, 4 September 1930 (Zimmer 1950:9; AMNH 319680); one (SP) at Zanja Morotí, CON, 8 September 1930 (Zimmer 1950:9; AMNH 319681); one (SP) at Estancia Centurión, CON, 2 October 1931 (Laubmann 1933a:291, 1940:9; MM 32.601); one (SP) at Estancia Centurión, CON, 9 October 1931 (Laubmann 1933a:291, 1940:9; MM 32.602).

138. Black Jacobin
(*Melanotrochilus fuscus*)
Orient: one (SP) at Hernandarias, APN, 2 March 1987 (Colmán and Pérez 1991:33, unpubl.; MHNIB); one (SI) at Hernandarias, APN, 16 and 18 August 1994 (N. Pérez et al.).

139. White-vented Violet-ear
(*Colibri serrirostris*)
Chaco: reported without details (Bertoni 1939:26); Orient: reported but questionable at Encarnación, ITA (Bertoni 1914a:47, 1939:26); one (SP) at Nueva Germania, SAP, 31 January 1932 (Laubmann 1933a:292, 1940:14; MM 32.619).

140. Black-throated Mango
(*Anthracothorax nigricollis*)
Chaco: one (LSP) or more (?) at Villa Hayes, PHA (Bertoni 1930a:247, 1939:26; MHNSCP); one (SP) at 235 km W of Río Negro, PHA, 30 August 1939 (UMMZ 105356); one (SP) at Orloff, BOQ, 10 May 1957 (Steinbacher 1962:55; MAK 57178); Orient: many records.

141. White-throated Hummingbird
(*Leucochloris albicollis*)
Chaco: one (SP) at Parque Nacional Defensores del Chaco, exCHA, 6 August 1980 (Storer 1989:10; MNHNP 555); one (SI) at 2 km W of Laguna Salada, PHA, 1 April 1988 (F. Hayes); Orient: many records.

142. White-tailed Goldenthroat
(*Polytmus guainumbi*)
Chaco: one (SP) at Makthlawaiya, PHA, 24 March 1931 (AMNH 320799); one (SI) at 10 km W of Puerto Militar, PHA, 29 November

1989 (P. Scharf); Orient: many records, south-ernmost at Estancia Ñu Porá, MIS (F. Hayes).

143. Surucua Trogon
(*Trogon surrucura*)

Chaco: hypothetical (see below), one (LSP) at Fortín Nueve, PHA, 10 April 1890 (Kerr 1892:139), but not located at BMNH; reported at Puerto Carayá Vuelta, PHA, 22 October 1896 (Kerr 1901:228); one (SI) or more (?) at Río Confuso, PHA (Bertoni 1930b:258); Orient: many records. All Chaco records probably refer to the Blue-crowned Trogon (*Trogon curucui*).

144. Blue-crowned Motmot
(*Momotus momota*)

Chaco: reported without details (Bertoni 1939:25); one (SI) at Retiro Potrerito, APY, 22 and 26 June 1988, 15 August 1989 (Hayes et al. 1990b:97), presumably the same individual.

145. Green-and-rufous Kingfisher
(*Chloroceryle inda*)

Orient: one (SP) at 4 km W of Horqueta, CON, 2 December 1937 (Brodkorb 1938c:4; UMMZ 96248); one (SP) at Cerro Amambay, AMA, 20 November 1938 (UMMZ 101722); one to two (PH) at Río Jejuí-mí, Reserva Natural del Bosque Mbaracayú, CAN, 3-5 and 7 September 1992 (Brooks et al. 1993:71, pers. comm.; VIREO B36/1/002); one (SI) at Lagunita, Reserva Natural del Bosque Mbaracayú, CAN, 13, 15 and 16 September 1992 (Brooks et al. 1993:71, pers. comm.).

146. Pygmy Kingfisher
(*Chloroceryle aenea*)

Chaco: one (SI) at 5 km N of Bahía Negra, APY, 4 October 1984 (López 1985:12, Hayes et al. 1990b:97); one (SP) at Puerto Ramos, APY, 30 September 1988 (Hayes et al. 1990b:97; UMMZ 226553).

147. White-necked Puffbird
(*Notharchus macrorhynchos*)

Chaco: hypothetical, one (SP) at 235 km W of Río Negro, PHA (Short 1972b:48; UMMZ 105344), but locality is unusual and questionable (see Methods section); Orient: many records.

148. White-eared Puffbird
(*Nystalus chacuru*)

Chaco: one (LSP) or more (?) at Villa Hayes, PHA (Bertoni 1930a:248, 1939:28; MHNSCP), credible because of earlier reports nearby on the east bank (Orient) of the Río Paraguay at Lambaré, CEN (Berlepsch 1887:23), and Asunción, CEN (Bertoni 1922b:41); Orient: many records.

149. Spot-billed Toucanet
(*Selenidera maculirostris*)

Orient: only published records are of specimens at MHNIB (Colmán and Pérez 1991:33) and a report for CAN (Meisel 1992:5); many recent sight records for CAN, CAA, APN and CAP (R. Ridgely et al., Brooks et al. 1993:71), suggest that its distribution may have expanded recently into Paraguay; it seems unlikely that Bertoni would have overlooked such a conspicuous species.

150. Red-breasted Toucan
(*Ramphastos dicolorus*)

Chaco: one (SI) at Retiro Potrerito, APY, 22 June 1989 (Hayes et al. 1990b:97); Orient: many records.

151. White-wedged Piculet
(*Picumnus albosquamatus*)

Orient: one (SP) at Salto del Guairá, CAN, 16 March 1989 (Colmán and Pérez 1991:33, Contreras et al. 1993b:2; MHNIB), plus subsequent sight records to the north of Salto del Guairá, CAN, where it replaces the Ochre-collared Piculet (*P. temminckii*; A. Colmán and N. Pérez pers. comm.). Contreras et al. (1993b) cited the date 15 November 1988, but the specimen I examined was labeled 16 March 1989.

152. Golden-green Woodpecker
(*Piculus chrysochloros*)

Chaco: many records; Orient: one (LSP) at Lambaré, CEN, 7 December 1885 (Berlepsch 1887:20); reported at Asunción, CEN (Bertoni 1914a:49, 1922b:41, 1939:28); one (LSP) at Tayru, ÑEE, 6 August 1909 (Grant 1911:320; BMNH), but specimen not located; one (SI) at Río Salado, CEN, 27 August 1989 (P. Scharf); one (SI) at 15 km S of Villeta, CEN, 10 August 1993 (F. Hayes, J. Escobar and A. Madroño Nieto).

153. Pale-crested Woodpecker
(*Celeus lugubris*) and Blond-crested Woodpecker (*Celeus flavescens*)

The distribution of these two species in the Orient is unclear. Short (1972b:48, 1972c:21) questioned the locality of two specimens of *C. lugubris* from Puerto Gibaja, APN (UMMZ 108774, 108775; see discussion in Methods section), and stated that the two species were allopatric. *Celeus lugubris* occurs as far east as Cerro Amambay, AMA (UMMZ), Zanja Morotí, CON (AMNH), and Ybytymí, PAR (Chubb 1910:282; BMNH); *C. flavescens* has been recorded as far west as Independencia, GUA (AMNH). Recent sight records of *C. flavescens* at Parque Nacional Cerro Corá, AMA (López undated:7, F. Hayes and P. Scharf) require confirmation. The two species appear to be allopatric, unless the Puerto Gibaja records for *C. lugubris* are correct. No hybrids are known, supporting their treatment as separate species (Short 1972c).

154. Helmeted Woodpecker
(*Dryocopus galeatus*)

Threatened. Orient: one (SP) at 25°43'S, presumably at Puerto Bertoni, APN, 11 March 1893 (Bertoni 1901:50, 1914a:49, 1939:28); one (SP) at Coronel Oviedo, CAA, between June and August 1893 (Salvadori 1895:15; MZT); two (SP) at Sapucái, PAR, 7 July and 22 August 1904 (Chubb 1910:284); one (SP) at Sapucái, PAR, July or August 1904 (Collar et al. 1992:569; MACN); two (SP) at Cerro Amambay, AMA, 27, 28 August 1938 (Storer 1989:10; UMMZ 100751, 101040); one (SP) at Puerto Edelira, ITA, July 1948 (Collar et al. 1992:569; MNHN); one (SP) at 13 km N of Curuguaty, CAN, 9 July 1979 (Storer 1989:10; UMMZ 202091); one (SI) of Hernandarias, APN, July 1982 (Collar et al. 1992:569); one (SI) probable at 10 km N of Curuguaty, CAN, 15 September 1989 (Collar et al. 1992:568); one (SI) probable at 7 km N of Curuguaty, 16 September 1989 (Collar et al. 1992:568); one (SI) at Parque Nacional Cerro Corá, AMA, 1 December 1989 (P. Scharf); one (SI) at Estancia La Fortuna, CAN, 1 or 2 June 1991 (Collar et al. 1992:568; R. Ridgely et al.); one (SI) at Estancia Itabó, CAN, 4 or 5 June 1991 (Collar et al. 1992:569; R. Ridgely et al.); two reported at Estancia La Golondrina, CAA, 1991

(Brooks et al. 1993:37); reported near Itaipú hydroelectric dam, Hernandarias, APN (Collar et al. 1992:569); five (SI, one PH) at Estancia San Antonio, APN, 26-30 July 1992 (Brooks et al. 1993:37; VIREO B36/1/003); five (SI) at Estancia Itabó, CAN, 6-20 August 1992 (Brooks et al. 1993:37); one (VO, SI) at Estancia La Golondrina, CAA, 22 and 28 August 1992 (Brooks et al. 1993:37).

155. Lineated Woodpecker
(*Dryocopus lineatus*)

Chaco: three (LSP) at Fortín Page, PHA, 3 July 1890 (Kerr 1892:137; BMNH?); one (SP) at 235 km W of Río Negro, PHA, 29 June 1939 (UMMZ 105369), but locality questionable (see Methods section); one (SI) at Ruta Trans Chaco km 75, PHA, 15 July 1989 (A. Madroño Nieto); Orient: many records. The species has been recorded roughly 130 km W of the Río Paraguay at Fortín Page (cited above), and roughly 120 km W of the Río Paraguay along the Río Bermejo, Chaco Province, Argentina (Nores 1992:350, 351); thus, the Río Negro locality (cited above) may be credible.

156. Crimson-crested Woodpecker
(*Campephilus melanoleucos*)

Chaco: one (SP) at Puerto Pinasco, PHA, 9 September 1916 (Naumburg 1930:185; AMNH 149477); one (LSP) at Fort Wheeler, PHA (Naumburg 1930:185; AMNH), but specimen not located; two (LSP) at Villa Hayes, PHA (Bertoni 1930a:248; MHNSCP); one (SP) at Cerro Galván, APY, 29 May 1931 (Laubmann 1939:218; MM 32.511); Orient: many records.

157. Cream-backed Woodpecker
(*Campephilus leucopogon*)

Chaco: many records; Orient: hypothetical, reported at Yaguarasapá, ITA?, and MIS? (Bertoni 1914a:49, 1939:28); reported at Parque Nacional Cerro Corá, AMA (López undated:8); one (SI) at Arroyo Pozuelo, CAN, 5 November 1987 (F. Hayes, A. Colmán and N. Pérez); reported at Reserva Natural del Bosque Mbaracayú, CAN (Meisel et al. 1992:6); two (SI) at Estancia La Golondrina, CAP, 12 and 17 (one only) July 1992 (Brooks et al. 1993:74). The sight records from the Orient, especially in humid forest, are puzzling and require confirmation.

158. Bar-winged Cinclodes
(*Cinclodes fuscus*)

Orient: two (PH) at San Juan de Ñeembucú, ÑEE, 6 June 1991 (Hayes et al. 1994:90, Ridgely and Tudor 1994:43; VIREO R10/13/070).

159. Canebrake Groundcreeper
(*Clibanornis dendrocolaptoides*)

Orient: reported for Alto Paraná region (Bertoni 1907:303); reported at Río Yguazú, CAA or APN, and at Puerto Bertoni, APN (Bertoni 1914a:51, 1939:29); one (PH) netted at Estancia La Golondrina, CAP, 11 July 1992 (Brooks et al. 1993:53; VIREO B36/1/005).

160. Wren-like Rushbird
(*Phleocryptes melanops*)

Chaco: many records, northernmost at about 22°S (FMNH); Orient: hypothetical, reported at Puerto Bertoni, APN (Bertoni 1914a:52, 1939:30). Extreme dates: 26 March (Hayes et al. 1994:90) and 1 October (Steinbacher 1962:67).

161. Tufted Tit-Spinetail
(*Leptasthenura platensis*)

Chaco: one (SP) at Lichtenau, PHA, 28 August 1971 (Short 1976a:9; AMNH 809613); Orient: two (PH) at 10-15 km N of Pilar, ÑEE, 7 June 1991 (Ridgely and Tudor 1994:58, unpubl.; VIREO R10/13/071, R10/13/072).

162. Lesser Canastero
(*Asthenes pyrrholeuca*)

Chaco: one (SP) at Laguna Escalante, PHA, 3 August 1960 (Steinbacher 1962:68; MAK 601531); two (SI) at Fortín Teniente Ochoa, exNAS, 30 January 1990 (P. Scharf), but date is unusual; two (SI) at N of Filadelfia, BOQ, 17 June 1990 (Hayes et al. 1994:90); Orient: one (SP) at Villa Oliva, ÑEE, 11 August 1909 (Grant 1911:129; BMNH); reported but questionable at Puerto Bertoni, APN (Bertoni 1914a:52, 1939:30).

163. Short-billed Canastero
(*Asthenes baeri*)

Chaco: many records; Orient: two (SI) at Villa Florida, MIS, 11 June 1988 (F. Hayes), foraging on ground, described in field notes as having rufous sides of long tail, brown center; grayish face (and back?), no crest, erect tail also observed.

164. Little Thornbird
(*Phacellodomus sibilatrix*)

Chaco: many records; Orient: one (SP) at 17 km E of Luque, CEN or COR, 2 September 1972 (MVZ 163286).

165. Rufous-fronted Thornbird
(*Phacellodomus rufifrons*)

Southernmost record at about 23°30'S, in Chaco (P. Scharf).

166. Lark-like Brushrunner
(*Coryphistera alaudina*)

Chaco: many records; Orient: one (SI) well observed at Pilar, ÑEE, 12 and 13 March 1990 (P. Scharf); three (SI) at Pilar, ÑEE, 10 January 1991 (P. Scharf).

167. Buff-browed Foliage-gleaner
(*Syndactyla rufosuperciliata*)

Chaco: one (SP) at Puerto Sastre, APY, 4 September 1931 (Laubmann 1936:29, 1940:46; MM 32.819); Orient: many records.

168. Russet-mantled Foliage-gleaner
(*Philydor dimidiatus*)

Orient: one (SP) at Estancia San Luis, CON, 17 September 1931 (Laubmann 1940:47; MM 32.815); one (SP) at Zanja Morotí, CON, 15 December 1931 (Laubmann 1940:47; MM 32.814); reported at Parque Nacional Cerro Corá, AMA (Anonymous 1982b:61).

169. Chestnut-capped Foliage-gleaner
(*Hylocryptus rectirostris*)

Orient: two (SP, SI) at 11 km S of Concepción, SAP, 16 September 1988 (Storer 1989:10; UMMZ 226445).

170. Scimitar-billed Woodcreeper
(*Drymornis bridgesii*)

Northernmost records at about 22°S (e.g., Brodkorb 1937c:34).

171. Black-banded Woodcreeper
(*Dendrocolaptes picumnus*)

Chaco: many records; Orient: hypothetical; Brodkorb (1941b:1-3) described *D. picumnus extimus* on the basis of six specimens taken at Puerto Gibaja, APN, on 26 July and 11, 12 and 14 August 1940 (UMMZ 9157, 9163, 9170, 9298, 9336, 9319). However, Short (1972b:48) questioned the locality of these specimens because: (1) *D. picumnus* has not been recorded elsewhere in the Orient (published descriptions refer to the Planalto Woodcreeper [*D. platyrostris*]; Bertoni 1901:69, 70, Grant 1911:135); (2) 50 specimens (AMNH) of *Dendrocolaptes* from Arroyo Urugua-í, Misiones Province, Argentina (opposite Río Paraná from Puerto Gibaja) are all *D. platyrostris*; (3) *D. picumnus extimus* is not morphologically distinct (in Short's opinion) from *D. picumnus pallescens*; (4) the collectors labeled specimens with a typewriter and sometimes gave irregular field numbers; and (5) specimens of other species from Puerto Gibaja, APN, and 235 km W of the Río [Riacho] Negro, PHA, appear to have been mixed up (see Methods section). I found the specimens of *extimus* to differ marginally (less rufescent colors, as described by Brodkorb) from a single UMMZ specimen of *pallescens* (from 235 km W of Río Negro, PHA); furthermore, the field numbers and dates of these specimens are all sequential (as would be expected), and do not overlap those of the Río Negro specimens. Nevertheless, the Puerto Gibaja records of *D. picumnus* should be considered hypothetical and *extimus* a synonym of *pallescens* unless additional specimens of *extimus* are obtained.

172. Planalto Woodcreeper
(*Dendrocolaptes platyrostris*)

Chaco: one (LSP) or more (?) at Villa Hayes, PHA (Bertoni 1930a:250, 1939:30; MHNSCP); Orient: many records.

173. Black-billed Scythebill
(*Campylorhamphus falcularius*)

Orient: several (LSP, NE) reported at 25°40'S, presumably at Puerto Bertoni, APN (Bertoni 1901:71, 1914a:53, 1939:30), and at Río Yguazú, CAA or APN (Bertoni 1914a:53, 1939:30), December 1893; one (SI) at Hotel El Tirol, ITA, 15 August 1977 (R. Ridgely).

174. Giant Antshrike
(*Batara cinerea*)

Chaco: one (SP) at 265 km W of Puerto La Victoria, exNAS or BOQ, 16 September 1936 (UMMZ 93390); one (SP) at 265 km W of Puerto La Victoria, exNAS or BOQ, 11 October 1936 (UMMZ 93001); one (SP) at 100 km S of Lichtenau, PHA, 23 September 1960 (Steinbacher 1962:63; MAK 611023), possibly in vicinity of Fortín Mariscal López, PHA (Nores 1992:350, 351); Orient: hypothetical, reported at Parque Nacional Cerro Corá, AMA (López undated:8).

175. Large-tailed Antshrike
(*Mackenziaena leachii*)

Orient: several (LSP) at Río Yguazú, CAA or APN, and Puerto Bertoni, APN (Bertoni 1907:303, 1914a:51, 1939:29); one (LSP) at Cambyreta, ITA, 26 November 1936 (Laubmann 1940:19), but location of specimen unknown.

176. Rufous-capped Antshrike
(*Thamnophilus ruficapillus*)

Chaco: reported at Villa Hayes, PHA (Bertoni 1930a:249), but no details provided; Orient: reported at Alto Paraná region (Bertoni 1914a:51, 1930a:249); reported at Asunción, CEN (Bertoni 1939:29); one (SP) at Hernandarias, APN, 25 April 1979 (A. Colmán and N. Pérez unpubl.; MHNIB).

177. Black-bellied Antwren
(*Formicivora melanogaster*)

Chaco: several (PH) measured and well described at Parque Nacional Defensores del Chaco, exCHA, August 1989, July and August 1990 (Madroño N. 1991, unpubl. ms, Contreras et al. 1993a:2, Ridgely and Tudor 1994:301; VIREO v06/16/001, v06/16/002, v06/16/003), and June 1990 (P. Scharf and D. Engelman). Initially identified as White-fringed Antwren (*F. grisea*; Madroño N. 1991), but the photographs clearly refer to *F. melanogaster* (F. Hayes and R. Ridgely).

178. Rusty-backed Antwren
(*Formicivora rufa*)

Chaco: one (LSP) or more (?) at Villa Hayes, PHA (Bertoni 1930a:249; MHNSCP); Orient: many records, southernmost record at bluffs 1 km S of Tobatí, COR (F. Hayes).

179. Bertoni's Antbird
(*Drymophila rubricollis*)

Orient: one (LSP) well described at Puerto Bertoni, APN, 1894 (Bertoni 1901:140, 1914a:50, 1939:29). Willis (1988) provided evidence that this species is distinct from the Ferruginous Antbird (*D. ferruginea*).

180. White-backed Fire-eye
(*Pyriglena leuconota*)
Chaco: two (SP, SI) at Retiro Potrerito, APY, 28 June 1988 (Hayes et al. 1990b:99; MNHNP 839).

181. Speckle-breasted Antpitta
(*Hylopezus nattereri*)
Orient: one (LSP) adequately described at Puerto Bertoni, APN, 1903? (Bertoni 1904:5, 1914a:51, 1939:29).

182. Crested Gallito
(*Rhinocrypta lanceolata*)
Northernmost records at about 22°S (Brodkorb 1938c:5).

183. Collared Crescentchest
(*Melanopareia torquata*)
Orient: one (SP) at Cerro Amambay, AMA, 7 October 1938 (Ridgely and Tudor 1994:423; UMMZ 101788).

184. Olive-crowned Crescentchest
(*Melanopareia maximiliani*)
Northernmost records at about 22°S (Brodkorb 1938c:5).

185. Reiser's Tyrannulet
(*Phyllomyias reiseri*)
Orient: one (SP) at Zanja Morotí, CON, 31 August 1930 (Zimmer 1955:23; AMNH 319794); one (SP) at Zanja Morotí, CON, 7 September 1930 (Zimmer 1955:23; AMNH 319795). Stotz's (1990:186) map showing two localities for Paraguay appears to be an error.

186. Mouse-colored Tyrannulet
(*Phaeomyias murina*)
Chaco: one (SP) at Riacho Negro, PHA, 12 December 1913 (Zimmer 1941:10; AMNH 127024); one (SP) at 80 km W of Puerto Pinasco, PHA, 17 April 1931 (Zimmer 1941:10; AMNH 321120); Orient: many records. Extreme dates: 27 August and 17 April (Hayes et al. 1994:86).

187. Southern Scrub-Flycatcher
(*Sublegatus modestus*)
Extreme dates: 5 August and 18 April (Hayes et al. 1994:86).

188. Greenish Elaenia
(*Myiopagis viridicata*)
Chaco: one (SP) at Riacho Negro, PHA, 14 November 1913 (Hayes et al. 1994:86-87; AMNH 127020); one (SP) at Riacho Negro, PHA, 15 November 1913 (Hayes et al. 1994:86-87; AMNH 127019); Orient: many records. Extreme dates: 3 September and 5 May (Hayes et al. 1994:86).

189. Yellow-bellied Elaenia
(*Elaenia flavogaster*)
Chaco: hypothetical, one (SI) at Laguna Capitán, PHA, 8 December 1988 (F. Hayes, D. Snider and R. Perrin); one (SI) at Puerto Bahía Negra, APY, 16 January 1991 (P. Scharf); Orient: many records.

190. Large Elaenia
(*Elaenia spectabilis*)
Extreme dates: 24 August and 16 April (Hayes et al. 1994:87).

191. White-crested Elaenia
(*Elaenia albiceps*)
Chaco: hypothetical, one (LSP) at Villa Hayes, PHA (Bertoni 1930a:251, 1939:32; MHNSCP), but identification regarded as questionable by the author; Orient: many records. Extreme dates during spring: 26 September (Hayes et al. 1994:90) and 23 November (Partridge 1953:87, 1954:141); during fall: one (SP) at Villarrica, GUA, 5 April 1915 (Hayes et al. 1994:90; FMNH 65617). Sight records during August 1992 at Lagunita, Reserva Natural del Bosque Mbaracayú, CAN (Brooks et al. 1993:83), may have been misidentified.

192. Olivaceous Elaenia
(*Elaenia mesoleuca*)
Chaco: hypothetical, reported at Las Delicias, PHA, March or December 1983 or July 1984 (Peris et al. 1987:30); two (SI) possible at Estancia La Golondrina, PHA, 17 December 1988 (F. Hayes, D. Snider and R. Perrin); Orient: many records.

193. Lesser Elaenia
(*Elaenia chiriquensis*)
Orient: one (LSP) at Curuzú Chica, SAP, 29 October 1909 (Grant 1911:119; BMNH), but specimen not located and possibly misidentifed; one (SP) at E of Caaguazú, CAA?, 20 November 1930 (AMNH 320485); reported at Río Paraguay (Bertoni 1939:32), possibly in reference to the Curuzú Chica record cited above.

Apparently a northern austral migrant (e.g., Fry 1970, Ridgely and Tudor 1994).

194. Sooty Tyrannulet
(*Serpophaga nigricans*)

Chaco: one (LSP) or more (?) at Villa Hayes, PHA (Bertoni 1930a:251; MHNSCP); one (SI) at Laguna Salada, PHA, 1 April 1988 (F. Hayes); one (SI) at Estancia Santa Catalina, PHA, 15 August 1990 (A. Madroño Nieto and J. Escobar Argaña); one (SI) at Pozo Colorado, PHA, 3 September 1990 (P. Scharf); Orient: many records. Possibly a southern austral migrant, but present during summer at least in Alto Paraná region (AMNH).

195. White-crested Tyrannulet
(*Serpophaga subcristata*)

Rare during austral summer (Hayes et al. 1994:90-91).

196. White-bellied Tyrannulet
(*Serpophaga munda*)

Chaco: many records; Orient: one (SI) at Estancia Fonciere, CON, 22 May 1989 (Hayes et al. 1994:91); one (SI) at Río Salado, CEN, 27 August 1989 (Hayes et al. 1994:91); reported at Ñu Guazú, Asunción, CEN, between 4 and 10 August 1989 (1989a:2); one (SI) at Lago Ypacarai, COR, 6 August 1994 (F. Hayes et al.). Rare during austral summer (Hayes et al. 1994:91).

197. Plain Tyrannulet
(*Inezia inornata*)

Chaco: many records; Orient: reported as questionable at Puerto Bertoni, APN (Bertoni 1939:32); one (SP) at Belén, CON, 11 August 1930 (Zimmer 1955:3; AMNH 319783); one (SP) at Zanja Morotí, CON, 31 August 1930 (Zimmer 1955:3; AMNH 319788); one (SP) at Zanja Morotí, CON, 7 September 1930 (Zimmer 1955:3; AMNH 319789). Extreme dates: 11 August and 24 March (Hayes et al. 1994:87).

198. Many-colored Rush-Tyrant
(*Tachuris rubrigastra*)

Orient: two (SI) at Laureles, ÑEE, June or July 1988 (T. Granizo Tamayo and J. Fox).

199. Sharp-tailed Tyrant
(*Culicivora caudacuta*)

Chaco: one (LSP) at Villa Hayes, PHA (Bertoni 1930a:251; MHNSCP), but the identification was regarded as questionable by the author; one (SI) well observed in tall grass at Ruta Trans Chaco km 60, PHA, 9 May 1990 (P. Scharf); Orient: many records (Bertoni 1907:4, Chubb 1910:580, Laubmann 1940:111, AMNH), but none since 1932.

200. Crested Doradito
(*Pseudocolopteryx sclateri*)

Chaco: no published records; one (SP) at Puerto Pinasco, PHA, 17 October 1916 (AMNH 149600); one (SP) at Puerto Pinasco, PHA, 19 October 1916 (AMNH 149601); one (SP) at Makthlawaiya, PHA, 20 March 1931 (AMNH 320910); one (SP) at Laguna General Diaz, PHA, 6 May 1945 (FMNH 152618); one (SI) at Ruta Trans Chaco km 210, Riacho Michí, PHA, 20 July 1989 (A. Madroño Nieto); two (SI) at Ruta Trans Chaco km 103, PHA, 31 May 1991 (R. Ridgely, P. Scharf et al.); one (SI) at Estancia Alegre, PHA, 19 August 1994 (F. Hayes et al.); Orient: many records.

201. Dinelli's Doradito
(*Pseudocolopteryx dinellianus*)

Threatened. Chaco: one (SP) at Laguna Escalante, PHA, 3 August 1960 (Steinbacher 1962:78; MAK 601593); one (SP) at Laguna General Diaz, PHA, 20 July 1945 (Hayes et al. 1994:91; FMNH 152593); two (SI) at Ruta Trans Chaco km 79, PHA, 9 May 1990 (Collar et al. 1992:756, Hayes et al. 1994:91); one (SI) at Ruta Trans Chaco km 100, PHA, 16 June 1990 (Collar et al. 1992:756, Hayes et al. 1994:91). Orient: hypothetical, one (SI) at Estancia Itabó, CAN, 10 August 1992 (Brooks 1993:49).

202. Subtropical Doradito
(*Pseudocolopteryx acutipennis*)

Chaco: one (SP) at Lichtenau, PHA, 9 December 1970 (Short 1972a:895, 1976a:12; AMNH 802830); one (SP) at Lichtenau, PHA, 27 April 1973 (Short 1976b:12; AMNH 810650); one (SI) at Ruta Trans Chaco km 210, Riacho Michi, PHA, 9 December 1988 (F. Hayes, D. Snider and R. Perrin); two (SI) at Ruta Trans Chaco km 249, Estero Pirahau, PHA, 10 August 1994 (F. Hayes et al).

203. Warbling Doradito
(*Pseudocolopteryx flaviventris*)

Extreme dates: 23 March (Hayes et al. 1994:91) and 28 November (Kerr 1901:225).

108

204. Rufous-sided Pygmy-Tyrant
(*Euscarthmus rufomarginatus*)

Threatened. Orient: reported at Encarnación, ITA (Bertoni 1939:32), but no details provided (thus hypothetical); one (SP) at Zanja Morotí, CON, 28 December 1944 (Olrog 1979:6; IML).

205. Sepia-capped Flycatcher
(*Leptopogon amaurocephalus*)

Chaco: one (SP) at Puerto Sastre, APY, 4 September 1931 (Laubmann 1940:122; MM 32.677); Orient: many records.

206. Mottle-cheeked Tyrannulet
(*Phylloscartes ventralis*)

Chaco: hypothetical, reported at San Juan, PHA (Contreras and Mandelburger 1985:335, 336); Orient: many records.

207. Sao Paulo Tyrannulet
(*Phylloscartes paulistus*)

Threatened. Orient: reported at NE del Paraguay (Bertoni 1913:222); reported at Puerto Bertoni, APN (Bertoni 1914a:55, 1939:32); one (SP) at Puerto Bertoni, APN, 8 June 1917 (Collar et al. 1992:766; FMNH 66324); one (SP) at E of Yhú, CAA, 6 January 1931 (Collar et al. 1992:766; AMNH 320546); one (SP) at upper Río Yguazú, CAA, 12 January 1931 (Collar et al. 1992:766; AMNH 320547); five (SP) at Cerro Amambay, AMA, 12 September-15 November 1938 (UMMZ 101109, 101110, 100837, 100429, 101835); one (SI) at Estancia La Fortuna, CAN, 1 or 2 June 1991 (Collar et al. 1992:766; R. Ridgely et al.); three (SI) at Reserva Natural del Bosque Mbaracayú, CAN, 2 or 3 June 1991 (R. Ridgely, P. Scharf et al.); two (SI) at Estancia La Golondrina, CAP, 13 (one) and 21 (one) July 1992 (Brooks et al. 1993:45); two (SI) at Estancia Itabó, CAN, 16 and 19 (one) August 1992 (Brooks et al. 1993:45); one (SI) at Parque Nacional Ybycuí, PAR, 12 August 1994 (R. Ryan and S. LaBar).

208. Common Tody-Flycatcher
(*Todirostrum cinereum*)

Chaco: many records; Orient: no records, but one (SP) on an island in the Río Paraguay, 3.5 km SSW of Puerto Valle Mi, border of APY and CON, 7 October 1988 (Hayes et al. 1990b:99; UMMZ 226592), suggests that it occurs in CON. Southernmost record at Puerto La Victoria, PHA (Zotta 1950:166).

209. Large-headed Flatbill
(*Ramphotrigon megacephala*)

Orient: reported at Puerto Bertoni, APN (Bertoni 1914a:55, 1939:32); one (SP) at Cerro Amambay, AMA, 25 October 1938 (UMMZ 101819); one (SI) at Reserva Natural del Bosque Mbaracayú, 16 February 1988 (Meisel et al. 1992:9; F. Hayes); six (SI) at Estancia Itabó, CAN, between 4 and 20 August 1992 (Brooks et al. 1993:81).

210. White-throated Spadebill
(*Platyrinchus mystaceus*)

Chaco: one (SP) at Villa Hayes, PHA, 23 October 1922 (FMNH 152996), probably the same specimen reported from the same locality by Bertoni (1930a:251, 1939:32; see below); one (SP) at Puerto Sastre, APY, 4 September 1931 (Laubmann 1936:34, 35; 1940:102; MM 32.706); Orient: many records.

211. Russet-winged Spadebill
(*Platyrinchus leucoryphus*)

Threatened. Orient: one (SP) at Sapucái, PAR, 9 September 1904 (Chubb 1910:577; BMNH?); one (SP) at Caaguazú, CAA, 9 November 1930 (Collar et al. 1992:779; AMNH 320530); three (SP) at 13 km N of Curuguaty, CAN, 20, 21 and 23 August 1978 (UMMZ 201134, 200852, 200851); at least three (SI, one PH) at Reserva Natural del Bosque Mbaracayú, CAN, 9, 12, 13 and 15 1992 (Brooks et al. 1992:42; VIREO B36/1/006).

212. Bran-colored Flycatcher
(*Myiophobus fasciatus*)

Chaco: hypothetical, reported at Estancia Coé Puajhú, September 1989 (Contreras 1989:3); one (SI) possible near Filadelfia, BOQ, 22 April 1990 (P. Scharf); Orient: many records. Rare during austral winter (Hayes et al. 1994:87).

213. Euler's Flycatcher
(*Lathrotriccus euleri*)

Rare during austral winter (Hayes et al. 1994:87).

214. Fuscous Flycatcher
(*Cnemotriccus fuscatus*)

Rare during austral winter (Hayes et al. 1994:87).

215. Vermilion Flycatcher
(*Pyrocephalus rubinus*)

Rare during austral summer (Hayes et al. 1994:91).

216. Black-crowned Monjita
(*Xolmis coronata*)

Chaco: many records; Orient: reported at Lago Ypacarai, CEN or COR (Bertoni 1939:31). Extreme dates: 28 January and 4 October (Hayes et al. 1994:91).

217. Gray-bellied Shrike-Tyrant
(*Agriornis microptera*)

Extreme dates: 17 June and 14 October (Hayes et al. 1994:91).

218. Mouse-brown Shrike-Tyrant
(*Agriornis murina*)

Extreme dates: 25 April and 8 September (Hayes et al. 1994:91).

219. Austral Negrito
(*Lessonia rufa*)

Chaco: one (SP) at Carmencita, BOQ, 22 August 1962 (Steinbacher 1968:350; SMF 38177); Orient: several (SI) at Isla Yacyretá, MIS, and north bank of Río Paraná, MIS, June and July 1988 (T. Granizo Tamayo); one (SI) at Curuguaty, CAN, 5 May 1990 (Hayes et al. 1994:91); six (SI) at San Juan de Ñeembucú, ÑEE, 6 June 1991 (Hayes et al. 1994:91).

220. Cinereous Tyrant
(*Knipolegus striaticeps*)

Chaco: many records; Orient: one (SP) at Sapucái, PAR, 25 April 1903 (Chubb 1910:575; BMNH 1905-10-12-974); one (SP) at Horqueta, CON, 18 August 1935 (Hayes et al. 1994:91; UMMZ 90405); one (SP) at Horqueta, CON, 20 August 1935 (Hayes et al. 1994:91; UMMZ 90404); one (SP) at Horqueta, CON, 28 August 1935 (Hayes et al. 1994:91; UMMZ 90406); reported at Asunción, CEN (Bertoni 1914a:54, 1939:31). Rare during austral summer (Hayes et al. 1994:91), possibly only a migrant in Orient.

221. Hudson's Black-Tyrant
(*Knipolegus hudsoni*)

Chaco: one (SP) at Puerto Sastre, APY, 2 September 1931 (Laubmann 1933a:299, 1940:80; MM 32.672); one (SP) at Laguna Escalante, PHA, 30 September 1960 (Steinbacher 1962:73; MAK 611005); one (SP) at Licht-enau, PHA, 1 October 1973 (Short 1976a:10; AMNH 810649); reported at General Eugenio A. Garay, exNAS, September 1989 (Contreras 1989:3).

222. Blue-billed Black-Tyrant
(*Knipolegus cyanirostris*)

Chaco: one (SP) at Estero Patiño, PHA, 15 July 1939 (Hayes et al. 1994:92; UMMZ 111408), but locality questionable (see Methods section); Orient: many records. Extreme dates: 4 April (Hayes et al. 1994:92) and 1 September (Chubb 1910:574).

223. White-winged Black-Tyrant
(*Knipolegus aterrimus*)

Chaco: one (SP) at Laguna General Diaz, PHA, 13 July 1945 (Hayes et al. 1994:92, Ridgely and Tudor 1994:626; FMNH 152530); one (SI) at Parque Nacional Teniente Enciso, exNAS, 1 September 1982 (Hayes et al. 1994:92, Ridgely and Tudor 1994:626); reported but questionable at Las Delicias, PHA, March or December 1983 or July 1984 (Peris et al. 1987:30); reported at Estancia Coé Puajhú, exNAS, September 1989 (Contreras 1989:3); reported at General Eugenio A. Garay, exNAS, September 1989 (Contreras 1989:3).

224. Crested Black-Tyrant
(*Knipolegus lophotes*)

Orient: reported as questionable at Ygatimí, CAN (Bertoni 1914a:54, 1939:31); one (SP) at Cerro Amambay, AMA, 31 August 1938 (UMMZ 100121); three (SP) at Cerro Amambay, AMA, 18 September 1938 (UMMZ 100426, 100828, 101104); one (SP) at Cerro Amambay, AMA, 24 September 1938 (UMMZ 100827; series referred to by Ridgely and Tudor 1994:628).

225. Spectacled Tyrant
(*Hymenops perspicillatus*)

Rare during austral summer (Hayes et al. 1994:92). Most records are of females and immatures.

226. Long-tailed Tyrant
(*Colonia colonus*)

Chaco: one (LSP) or more (?) at Villa Hayes, PHA (Bertoni 1930a:250, 1939:31; MHNSCP); Orient: many records.

110

227. Cock-tailed Tyrant
(*Alectrurus tricolor*)

Chaco: hypothetical, one (SP) at 235 km W of Puerto Rosario, in PHA, 1 September 1939 (UMMZ 105415), but locality questionable (see Methods section; no other Chaco records); Orient: many records.

228. Strange-tailed Tyrant
(*Alectrurus risora*)

Threatened. Chaco: one (LSP) at Villa Hayes, PHA (Bertoni 1930a:250; MHNSCP); one (SP) at Río Pilcomayo, PHA, 29 July 1942 (AMNH 748775); six (SI) at Estancia La Golondrina, PHA, 27 and 28 August 1988, and two (SI) on 6 and 12 November 1988 (Collar et al. 1992:791; F. Hayes et al.); one (SI) at Villa Hayes, PHA, 8 July 1989 (Collar et al. 1992:791; F. Hayes et al.); two (SI) at Ruta Trans Chaco km 103, PHA, between 28 and 31 May 1991 (Collar et al. 1992:791; R. Ridgely and P. Scharf); Orient: one (LSP) at Yaguarasapá, ITA?, 1888 (Bertoni 1930a:250); two (SP) at Villarrica, GUA, August 1893 (Salvadori 1895:9; MZT); one (SP) at 25°47'S, APN?, 28 March 1896, presumably near Puerto Bertoni, APN, where recorded subsequently (Bertoni 1901:128, 1914a:54, 1926:397, 1930a:250, 1939:31); four (SP) at Sapucái, PAR, 17 April 1903 (two), 22 April 1904, 6 June 1904 (Chubb 1910:573; BMNH); three (SP) at Villarrica, GUA, October 1905, August 1923 and July 1924 (Collar et al. 1992:791; BMNH); one (SP) at Villarrica, GUA, September 1924 (UMMZ 87361); reported for MIS (A. O. Contreras et al. 1989:11); many (SI) between Estancia Santa Elisa, MIS, and San Juan Bautista, MIS, 12-14 March 1990 (12); 2-4 March 1991 (15), and 6 and 7 June 1991 (47; Collar et al. 1992:793; P. Scharf et al.).

229. Streamer-tailed Tyrant
(*Gubernetes yetapa*)

Chaco: three (SI) at Estancia Doña Julia (100 m from Río Paraguay, not 100 km as reported), APY, 24 September 1984 (Hayes et al. 1990b:99); Orient: many records.

230. Cliff Flycatcher
(*Hirundinea ferruginea*)

Chaco: one (SP) at Puerto Francia, APY? (Salvadori 1895:10; MZT), but locality unknown; one (SI) well observed at Puerto Bahía Negra, APY, 24 April 1991 (P. Scharf); Orient: many records.

231. Shear-tailed Gray-Tyrant
(*Muscipipra vetula*)

Orient: one (LSP?) at Puerto Bertoni, APN, 1906 (Bertoni 1907:300, 1914a:54, 1939:31); one (SI) at Reserva Natural del Bosque Mbaracayú, CAN, 26 June 1990 (Meisel et al. 1992:9, Ridgely and Tudor 1994:618; P. Scharf).

232. Rufous-tailed Attila
(*Attila phoenicurus*)

Chaco: one (SP) at Fortín Conchitas, BOQ, 2 April 1962 (Steinbacher 1968:348; SMF 38326); Orient: hypothetical, one (SI) at Parque Nacional Ybycuí, PAR, January 1990 (Ridgely and Tudor 1994:637; B. Treiterer); one (SI) at Estancia San Antonio, APN, 30 July 1992 (Brooks et al. 1993:80).

233. Swainson's Flycatcher
(*Myiarchus swainsoni*)

Extreme dates: 28 August and 1 March (Hayes et al. 1994:87).

234. Short-crested Flycatcher
(*Myiarchus ferox*)

Chaco: identification of six specimens from Alto Chaco region (Steinbacher 1962:77, 1968:352; SMF) questioned by Short (1976a:12) and Lanyon (1978:529); however, I confirmed the identification of seven specimens taken from various localities in the Matogrosense, Alto Chaco and Bajo Chaco regions (UMMZ), indicating that it is present throughout the Chaco (Lanyon did not examine UMMZ specimens); Orient: many records.

235. Streaked Flycatcher
(*Myiodynastes maculatus*)

Extreme dates: 27 August (Hayes et al. 1994:88) and 7 April (Steinbacher 1962:76).

236. Piratic Flycatcher
(*Legatus leucophaius*)

Chaco: hypothetical, one (SI) briefly observed (15 sec) in forest canopy at Fortín Toledo, BOQ, 26 January 1988 (F. Hayes), but locality is unusual; Orient: many records. Extreme dates: 5 October and 6 May (Hayes et al. 1994:88).

237. Variegated Flycatcher
(*Empidonomus varius*)

Rare during austral winter (Hayes et al. 1994:87).

238. Crowned Slaty Flycatcher
(*Griseotyrannus aurantioatrocristatus*)

Rare during austral winter (Hayes et al. 1994:87-88).

239. Tropical Kingbird
(*Tyrannus melancholicus*)

Rare during austral winter (Hayes et al. 1994:87).

240. Fork-tailed Flycatcher
(*Tyrannus savana*)

Rare during austral winter (Hayes et al. 1994:87).

241. Eastern Kingbird
(*Tyrannus tyrannus*)

Chaco: many records; Orient: reported at Asunción, CEN (Contreras and González Romero 1988:33). Extreme dates: 26 September and 2 February (Hayes et al. 1990a:955).

242. White-naped Xenopsaris
(*Xenopsaris albinucha*)

Chaco: many records; Orient: one (SP) at Cerro Amambay, AMA, 20 October 1938 (UMMZ 101089); one (SI) briefly observed in forest at Parque Nacional Ybycuí, PAR, 12 August 1994 (R. Ryan and S. LaBar).

243. White-winged Becard
(*Pachyramphus polychopterus*)

Extreme dates: 10 August and 24 April (Hayes et al. 1994:88); a sight record of a female on 7 July 1992 (Brooks et al. 1993:78) may have been misidentified.

244. Black-tailed Tityra
(*Tityra cayana*)

Chaco: one (SP) at Riacho Negro, PHA, 15 November 1913 (AMNH 127034); two (SP) at Orloff, BOQ, 8 September 1949 (Steinbacher 1962:71; SMF 29298, 29299); reported at Las Delicias, PHA, March or December 1983 or July 1984 (Peris et al. 1987:30); Orient: many records.

245. Black-crowned Tityra
(*Tityra inquisitor*)

Chaco: one (LSP) or more (?) at Villa Hayes, PHA (Bertoni 1930a:253, 1939:34; MHNSCP); Orient: many records.

246. Swallow-tailed Cotinga
(*Phibalura flavirostris*)

Orient: two (LSP) at Yaguarasapá, ITA?, 12 and 15 June 1893 (Bertoni 1901:105-108); two (SI) at Río Monday, APN, June 1894 (Bertoni 1901:108), and elsewhere? (Bertoni 1914a:58, 1939:33); two (SP) at Independencia, GUA, 14 October 1930 (AMNH 320179, 320180); one (SI) at E of Celos Parini, CAN, 15 July 1977 (R. Ridgely).

247. Helmeted Manakin
(*Antilophia galeata*)

Orient: seven (SP) records, all at Zanja Morotí, CON (Laubmann 1940:71; MM); southernmost (and only recent) record (dead specimen not preserved) at Reserva Indígena de Chupa Poo, S of Ygatimí, CAN, April 1992 (Contreras et al. 1993a:3).

248. Swallow-tailed Manakin
(*Chiroxiphia caudata*)

Chaco: one (SP) at Puerto Pinasco, PHA, 16 October 1916 (AMNH 149663); one (SP) at Villa Hayes, PHA, December 1944 (FMNH 152971); Orient: many records.

249. Band-tailed Manakin
(*Pipra fasciicauda*)

Chaco: several (LSP) at Villa Hayes, PHA (Bertoni 1930a:252, 1939:33; MHNSCP); one (SP) at Puerto La Victoria, APY, 9 February 1943 or 1945 (FMNH 152970; original label missing, new label says 1943, catalog says 1945); Orient: many records.

250. White-tipped Plantcutter
(*Phytotoma rutila*)

Chaco: many records; Orient: one (SP) at Río Salado, CEN, 8 August 1978 (Hayes et al. 1994:90; UMMZ 200889); one (SP) at east bank of Río Paraguay, 10 km NW of Rosario, SAP, 13 September 1988 (Hayes et al. 1994:90; UMMZ 226411); one (SI) at Estancia La Golondrina, CAP, 7 July 1992 (Brooks et al. 1993:85). Extreme dates: 3 June and 20 October (Hayes et al. 1994:90).

251. Purple Martin
(*Progne subis*)

Chaco: many records; Orient: two (SI) at Parque Nacional Vapor Cué, COR, January 1991 (Contreras et al. 1991:37). Extreme dates: 26 September and 7 February (Hayes et al. 1990a:955).

252. Gray-breasted Martin
(*Progne chalybea*)

Rare during austral winter (Hayes et al. 1994:88).

253. Brown-chested Martin
(*Phaeoprogne tapera*)

Extreme dates: 18 August and 25 May (Hayes et al. 1994:88).

254. White-rumped Swallow
(*Tachycineta leucorrhoa*)

Uncommon during austral summer (Hayes et al. 1994:92).

255. Chilean Swallow
(*Tachycineta meyeni*)

Chaco: two (SI) at Puerto 14 de Mayo, APY, 12 August 1988 (Hayes et al. 1990b:100); Orient: many records. Extreme dates: 6 June and 14 September (Hayes et al. 1994:92). Resembles White-rumped Swallow (*T. leucorrhoa*) and probably overlooked; small numbers probably mix with White-rumped Swallow flocks.

256. Blue-and-white Swallow
(*Notiochelidon cyanoleuca*)

Chaco: one (SP) at 200 km W of Puerto Pinasco, BOQ or PHA, 24 September 1920 (Wetmore 1926:343; USNM 283963); one (SP) at 120 km SE of Orloff, PHA, 2 September 1940 (Hayes et al. 1994:92; USNM 370522); four (SI) at Estancia Klassen, PHA, 9 August 1994 (H. Brodkin et al.); three (SI) at Laguna Capitán, PHA, 9 August 1994 (F. Hayes and N. Boyajian); Orient: many records. Extreme dates: 9 August (H. Brodkin et al.) and 13 December (Hayes et al. 1994:92). Recent observations in the Chaco during August (cited above) and S of Villeta, CEN, on 10 August 1993 (F. Hayes et al.) were of individuals in flocks of White-rumped Swallows (*T. leucorrhoa*); it remains uncertain whether these individuals represent wintering birds or migrants.

257. Black-collared Swallow
(*Atticora melanoleuca*)

Orient: seven (SI) at Salto Ñacunday, APN, 27 September 1989 (F. Hayes, T. Granizo Tamayo, W. Sosa and C. Sorenson), observed for 20 min at top of waterfall.

258. Southern Rough-winged Swallow
(*Stelgidopteryx ruficollis*)

Extreme dates: 2 August and 16 April (Hayes et al. 1994:88).

259. Bank Swallow
(*Riparia riparia*)

Extreme dates: 11 September and 17 April (Hayes et al. 1990a:956).

260. Cliff Swallow
(*Hirundo pyrrhonota*)

Extreme dates:2 September (R. Clay, R. Barnes and J. Vincent) and 17 April (Hayes et al. 1990a:956).

261. Barn Swallow
(*Hirundo rustica*)

Extreme dates: 3 September and 17 April (Hayes et al. 1990a:956).

262. Thrush-like Wren
(*Campylorhynchus turdinus*)

Distribution appears to be expanding southward; southernmost records at Pozo Colorado, PHA (Contreras and Contreras 1986:75); S of Villeta, ÑEE (Contreras et al. 1993a:3), and Curuguaty, CAN (P. Scharf and D. Brooks), and Estancia Olivares, 60 km N of Asunción, SAP? (P. Scharf).

263. Fawn-breasted Wren
(*Thryothorus guarayanus*)

Chaco: recorded only recently, southernmost at Retiro Potrerito, APY, where abundant (Hayes et al. 1990b:101); Orient: one (SP) at Refugio Biológico Mbaracayú, CAN (A. Colmán and N. Pérez unpubl.; MHNIB). I have examined the CAN specimen, whose head (but not the bill) is badly damaged; in the absence of specimens for comparisons, it was impossible to distinguish between the Fawn-breasted Wren (*T. guarayanus*) and Buff-breasted Wren (*T. leucotis*), although *T. leucotis* seems more likely based on range and habitat (Ridgely and Tudor 1994; see Taxonomic Notes section).

264. Sedge Wren
(*Cistothorus platensis*)

Orient: one (SP) at Independencia, GUA, 11 October 1930 (Traylor 1988:24; AMNH 320185); one (SP) at Independencia, GUA, 17 October 1930 (Traylor 1988:24; AMNH 320184).

265. Yellow-legged Thrush
(*Platycichla flavipes*)

Extreme dates: October and November (Bertoni 1901:147), probably a spring transient (Hayes et al. 1994:88). An August report at Lago Ypoá, PAR (J. R. Contreras et al. 1989:40), is questionable; otherwise no records since those of Bertoni (1926:397), who reported that it arrived nearly every summer.

266. Slaty Thrush
(*Turdus nigriceps*)

Possibly a northern austral migrant. Bertoni (1901:148, 1907:298, 1928a:187) stated that it arrived every year, but some remained during winter; only recent records include a report at Parque Nacional Cerro Corá, AMA (López undated:11) and three (SI) at Lagunita, Reserva Natural del Bosque Mbaracayú, CAN, 12 and 16 (one only) September 1992 (Brooks et al. 1993:85); A. Colmán and N. Pérez (pers. comm.) state that it sings during winter in Alto Paraná region.

267. Pale-breasted Thrush
(*Turdus leucomelas*)

Chaco: one (LSP) at Fortín Page, PHA, 26 May 1890 (Kerr 1892:122), but not located at BMNH and identification questionable; one (LSP) at Waikthlatingmayalwa, PHA, 4 November 1896 (Kerr 1901:222), but not located at BMNH and identification questionable; one (LSP) or more (?) at Villa Hayes, PHA (Bertoni 1930a:253; MHNSCP); Orient: many records.

268. White-banded Mockingbird
(*Mimus triurus*)

Extreme dates: 1 March and 17 November (Hayes et al. 1994:92).

269. Short-billed Pipit
(*Anthus furcatus*)

Orient: one (LSP) or more (?) at Puerto Bertoni, APN, 1906 (Bertoni 1913:220, 1914a:60, 1939:35), but no description given; three (PH) at San Juan de Ñeembucú, ÑEE, 6 June 1991 (Hayes et al. 1994:93; VIREO).

270. Chaco Pipit
(*Anthus chacoensis*)

Chaco: two (SP) at Puerto Pinasco, PHA, 3 September 1920 (Zimmer 1952:34; USNM 283948, 284029); Orient: several (SI, VO) at Concepción, CON, 3 October 1920 (Wetmore 1926:364; see below); one (SP) at Villarrica, GUA, May 1924 (Storer 1989:11; UMMZ 88465); one (SP) at Nueva Italia, CEN, 16 August 1941 (Zimmer 1953b:18; AMNH 796904). Wetmore's (1926:364) overlooked description of a high, thin tone in a drawn-out song for Yellowish Pipit (*A. lutescens*) undoubtedly refers to *A. chacoensis* (see Straneck 1987, Taxonomic Notes section), which was undescribed at the time.

271. Correndera Pipit
(*Anthus correndera*)

Orient: reported for southern Paraguay (Bertoni 1913:218, 1914a:60, 1939:35); two (SP) at Villarrica, GUA, June 1924 (Hayes et al. 1994:93; UMMZ 88462, 88463).

272. Ochre-breasted Pipit
(*Anthus nattereri*)

Threatened. Chaco: hypothetical, one (SP) at 235 km W of Río Negro, PHA, 2 September 1939 (UMMZ 105444), but locality questionable (see Methods section); reported at Monte Lindo, PHA, May 1989 (Pearman *in* Collar et al. 1992:807); Orient: one (SP) at Paraguarí, PAR (Salvadori 1895:3; MZT); one or more (SI) at S of San Patricio, MIS, August 1977 (Ridgely and Tudor 1989:141). Chaco records appear to be out of range (see Ridgely and Tudor 1989:141) and require confirmation.

273. Red-eyed Vireo
(*Vireo olivaceus*)

Rare during austral winter (Hayes et al. 1994:88).

274. Golden-crowned Warbler
(*Basileuterus culicivorus*)

Chaco: one (SI?) at Río Pilcomayo, PHA, 3 May 1890 (Kerr 1892:123), but possibly in Argentina; one (SP) at Riacho Negro, PHA, 14 November 1913 (Zimmer 1949:46; AMNH 127058); one (LSP) or more (?) at Villa Hayes, PHA (Bertoni 1930a:253, 1939:35;

114

MHNSCP); one (SP) at 235 km W of Río Negro, PHA, 13 August 1939 (UMMZ 105470), but locality questionable (see Methods section); Orient: many records. The species has been recorded at roughly 170 km W of the Río Paraguay at El Resguardo, Formosa Province, Argentina (Nores 1992:350, 351); thus, the Río Negro locality (cited above) may be credible.

275. White-bellied Warbler
(*Basileuterus hypoleucus*)

Chaco: one (SP) and several (SI) at 25 km W of Puerto Pinasco, PHA, September 1920 (Wetmore 1926:368; USNM 284043); two (SP) at Puerto Sastre, APY, 4 September 1931 (Laubmann 1940:210; MM 32.900, 32901); Orient: many records, southernmost at Zanja Morotí, CON (Laubmann 1940:211).

276. White-browed Warbler
(*Basileuterus leucoblepharus*)

Chaco: one (LSP) or more (?) at Villa Hayes, PHA (Bertoni 1930a:253, 1939:35; MHNSCP); Orient: many records, northernmost at Parque Nacional Cerro Corá, CON (López undated:12).

277. Chestnut-backed Tanager
(*Tangara preciosa*)

Northernmost records at 25 km E of Rosario, SAP (UMMZ) and N of Canindeyú, CAN (P. Scharf).

278. Green-throated Euphonia
(*Euphonia chalybea*)

Orient: one (SP) or more well described at 23°S, AMA?, and 26°30'S, ITA?, 1888, with nesting described but identification of species not confirmed (Bertoni 1901:100, 101, 1918c:243, 1919b:286); one (SP) at Paso Yuvay, GUA?, 11 May 1911 (Dabbene 1912:354); two (SP) at Independencia, GUA, 7 October 1930 (AMNH 320248); four (SP) at Cerro Amambay, AMA, 14 September-13 November 1938 (UMMZ 101168-101170, 101866); one (SI) at E of Celos Parini, CAN, 16 July 1977 (R. Ridgely); one (SI) possible at Jejuí-mí, Reserva Natural del Bosque Mbaracayú, CAN, 15 September 1992 (Brooks et al. 1992:58).

279. Diademed Tanager
(*Stephanophorus diadematus*)

One (SP) at unknown locality (UMMZ 89595); Orient: one (LSP) or more well described at

25°S, APN?, and 27°S, ITA?, July 1891 (Bertoni 1901:87, 1914a:62, 1939:36); one (SP) at Puerto Gibaja, APN, 29 September 1940 (UMMZ 109877); one (SI) at Estancia San Antonio, APN, 29 July 1992 (Brooks et al. 1993:87). Possibly a southern austral migrant.

280. Palm Tanager
(*Thraupis palmarum*)

Chaco: hypothetical, 20 (SI) doubtful at APY, October and November 1984 (López 1985:13); Orient: several (SI) at Puerto Bertoni, APN, August 1917 and during (following?) summer (Bertoni 1919a:258, 1939:37); two (SI) well observed throughout the day at Parque Nacional Cerro Corá, AMA, 30 November 1989 (P. Scharf).

281. Blue-and-yellow Tanager
(*Thraupis bonariensis*)

Chaco: many records, northernmost at Retiro Potrerito, APY (F. Hayes); Orient: one (LSP) at Puerto Bertoni, APN, June 1897 (Bertoni 1904:7, 1914a:63, 1939:36); reported at Ñu Guazú, Asunción, CEN, between 4 and 10 August 1989 (Contreras and González Romero 1989a:2); one (SI) at N of Curuguaty, CAN, 24 June 1990 (Hayes et al. 1994:93). Rare during austral summer (Hayes et al. 1994:93).

282. Gray-headed Tanager
(*Eucometis penicillata*)

Orient: one (SP) at Zanja Morotí, CON, 1 December 1931 (Laubmann 1933a:299, 1940:165; MM 32.1046); two (SI) at Río Apa, CON, 3 August 1977 (R. Ridgely); reported at Parque Nacional Cerro Corá, AMA (Anonymous 1982b:64); four (SI) at Estancia Centurión, CON, 17 May 1989 (F. Hayes and N. López); one (SI) at Estancia Fonciere, CON, 21 May 1989 (F. Hayes).

283. Ruby-crowned Tanager
(*Tachyphonus coronatus*)

Chaco: one (LSP) or more (?) at Villa Hayes, PHA (Bertoni 1930a:254, 1939:36; MHNSCP); one (SP) at 235 km W of Río Negro, PHA, 13 August 1939 (UMMZ 105202), but locality questionable (see Methods section); Orient: many records.

284. Hepatic Tanager
(*Piranga flava*)

Rare during austral summer (Hayes et al. 1994:93).

285. Silver-beaked Tanager
(*Ramphocelus carbo*)

Chaco: two (SI) at 1 km N of Bahía Negra, APY, 30 January 1989 (Hayes et al. 1990b:101); Orient: reported at Puerto Bertoni, APN, where an individual spent two or three summers after 1914 (Bertoni 1914a:62, 1926:397, 1939:36); one (SP) at Puerto Adela, CAN, 8 September 1982 (MHNIB).

286. Black-goggled Tanager
(*Trichothraupis melanops*)

Chaco: one (SP) at Monte Sociedad, PHA, 16 May 1931 (Laubmann 1940:166; MM 32.1000); Orient: many records.

287. White-rumped Tanager
(*Cypsnagra hirundinacea*)

Southernmost records at Rosario, SAP (UMMZ).

288. Guira Tanager
(*Hemithraupis guira*)

Chaco: one (SP) at 25 km W of Puerto Pinasco, PHA, 1 September 1920 (Wetmore 1926:392; USNM 284081); two (SP) at Puerto La Victoria, APY, 3 June 1931 (Laubmann 1940:168; MM 32.989, 32990); two (SP) at 235 km W of Río Negro, PHA, 11 August 1939 (UMMZ 105501, 105502), but locality questionable (see Methods section); Orient: many records.

289. White-banded Tanager
(*Neothraupis fasciata*)

Southernmost records at 5 km E of Caaguazú, CAA (AMNH).

290. Magpie Tanager
(*Cissopis leveriana*)

Chaco: one (SP) at Puerto Pinasco, PHA, 16 August 1943 (FMNH 153102); Orient: many records. The Puerto Pinasco record may be questionable because there are no records (surprisingly) from the adjacent Campos Cerrados region. However, one (SP) at 15 km E of Rosario, SAP, 10 February 1939 (UMMZ 105201), indicates that it may occur within 20 km of the Río Paraguay.

291. Black-faced Tanager
(*Schistochlamys melanopis*)

Orient: one (SP) at Refugio Biológico Mbaracayú, CAN (Colmán and Pérez 1991:33, Contreras et al. 1992b:1; MHNIB).

292. Swallow-Tanager
(*Tersina viridis*)

Chaco: two (SP) at Lichtenau, PHA, 2 May 1970 (Short 1972a:895, 1976a:14; AMNH 802828, 802829); Orient: many records. Extreme dates: 26 July (Hayes et al. 1994:88) and 2 May (Short 1972a:895, 1976a:14).

293. Golden-billed Saltator
(*Saltator aurantiirostris*)

Chaco: many records, but only records from the Bajo Chaco region are from Fortín Page, PHA (Kerr 1892:125), and Waikthlatingmayalwa, PHA (Kerr 1901:223), roughly 65 km from the Río Paraguay; Orient: reported at Río Monday, APN (Bertoni 1914a:64, 1939:38), but locality questionable; one (SI) at Puerto Valle Mi, CON, 1 August 1977 (R. Ridgely); reported at Asunción, CEN (Contreras and González Romero 1988:33), but locality questionable. Although not recorded in the Matogrosense region, the species has been recorded in southwestern Mato Grosso, Brazil (e.g., Naumburg 1930:351); thus, the Puerto Valle Mi record (cited above) is not unusual.

294. Black-throated Saltator
(*Saltator atricollis*)

Chaco: one (SP) at Puerto Pinasco, PHA, 2 September 1916 (AMNH 149739); Orient: many records, southernmost at bluffs 1 km S of Tobatí, COR (F. Hayes); Hellmayr (1938:37) reported three specimens at Bernalcué, near Asunción, CEN.

295. Black-throated Grosbeak
(*Pitylus fuliginosus*)

Orient: one (LSP) well described at Djaguarasapá, ITA?, 16 May 1890, and reported to occur between 23°S, AMA?, and 27°S, ITA? (Bertoni 1901:86, 1914a:64, 1939:37); one (SP) at Puerto Gibaja, APN, 21 September 1940 (UMMZ 108946); reported at Reserva Natural del Bosque Mbaracayú, CAN (Brooks et al. 1993:125).

Lined Seedeater *(Sporophila lineola)*   Dan Brown

296. Indigo Grosbeak
(Cyanoloxia glaucocaerulea)
Chaco: hypothetical, one (SP) at 235 km W of Río Negro, PHA, 12 August 1939 (UMMZ 105512); one (SP) at 235 km W of Río Negro, PHA, 14 August 1939 (UMMZ 105513); one (SP) at 235 km W of Río Negro, PHA, 26 August 1939 (UMMZ 105514), but locality for all Chaco records is questionable (see Methods section); Orient: many records. Extreme dates: 26 March (Chubb 1910:632) and 4 October (Hayes et al. 1994:94).

297. Black-masked Finch
(Coryphaspiza melanotis)
Orient: reported at Encarnación, ITA (Bertoni 1914a:63, 1939:37), but no details provided; one (SP) at E of Caaguzú, CAA, 18 November 1930 (AMNH 320667).

298. Buffy-fronted Seedeater
(Sporophila frontalis)
Threatened. Orient: one (LSP) well described at Puerto Bertoni, APN (Bertoni 1901:83, 1907:300, 1914a:65, 1939:38).

299. Temminck's Seedeater
(Sporophila falcirostris)
Threatened. Orient: many (SI, VO) in flowering bamboo along road W of Salto del Guairá, CAN, 14-18 July 1977 (Ridgely and Tudor 1989:416, Ridgely *in* Collar et al. 1992:855).

300. Lined Seedeater
(Sporophila lineola)
Extreme dates: 2 August and 5 May (Hayes et al. 1994:88).

301. Capped Seedeater
(Sporophila bouvreuil)
Chaco: hypothetical, one (LSP) at Villa Hayes, PHA (Bertoni 1930a:256, 1939:38; MHNSCP), but identification regarded as questionable by author; Orient: many records.

302. Dark-throated Seedeater
(Sporophila ruficollis)
Chaco: many records; Orient: reported as questionable at Puerto Bertoni, APN (Bertoni 1914a:65, 1939:38); one (SP) at Sapucái, PAR, 21 March 1904 (Chubb 1910:635; BMNH 1905-10-12-880); one (SI) at 5 km S of Villeta, CEN, 23 October 1989 (Hayes et al. 1994:88); ten (SI) at W of San Juan Bautista, MIS, 2 March 1991 (Hayes et al. 1994:88). Extreme dates: 21 September (Hayes et al. 1994:88) and 7 April (Steinbacher 1968:359).

303. Marsh Seedeater
(Sporophila palustris)
Threatened. Orient: reported at Concepción, CON, September/October 1896 (Kerr 1901: 217, 223), but record questioned by Collar et al. (1992:872) and specimen (BMNH 1886-8-1-21) reidentified as Tawny-bellied Seedeater (*S. hypoxantha*; P. R. Colston pers. comm.); five (SI) at Carayaó, CAA, 13 July 1977 (Hayes et al. 1994:93); one (SP) at Estancia Guarepyá, near Santiago, MIS (A. O. Contreras et al. 1989:11, Contreras et al. 1993a:4; MFA); two (SI) at Estancia Ñu Porá, MIS, 24 March 1989 (Hayes et al. 1994:93); reported at Surubi-y, CEN, March 1990 (Escobar Argaña *in* Collar et al. 1992:870); one (SI) at Estancia La Fortuna, CAN, 17 October 1990 (Hayes et al. 1994:93), presumably listed for Reserva Natural del Bosque Mbaracayú, CAN (Meisel et al. 1992:12); one (SI) at SW of San Juan Bautista, MIS, 2 March 1991 (Hayes et al. 1994:93); reported at 14 km N of Pilar, ÑEE, January 1992 (Contreras et al. 1993a:4); reported at Nueva Italia, CEN, June 1993 (Contreras et al. 1993a:4). The record for January, if correctly identified, may indicate breeding.

304. Rufous-rumped Seedeater
(*Sporophila hypochroma*)

Threatened. Chaco: one (LSP, PH) well described (as *S. plumbeiceps* [=*ruficollis*] *posneri*) at Villa Hayes, PHA, 22 October 1922 (Bertoni 1930a:256; MHNSCP), identified as this species by Hayes et al. (1994:88-89); reported at Estancia Guy near Ruta Trans Chaco km 75, PHA, 12 February 1991 (Contreras et al. 1993a:5); two (SI) at Ruta Trans Chaco km 100, PHA, 24 February 1991 (Collar et al. 1992:862; Hayes et al. 1994:89); reported at vicinity of Puerto Militar, PHA, 3 September 1991 (Contreras et al. 1993a:5); Orient: three (SP) at Estancia Guarepyá, near Santiago, MIS, 20-23 January 1989 (A. O. Contreras et al. 1989:11, Contreras et al. 1993a:5; MFA); three (SI) at 5 km ESE of Villeta, CEN, 23 October 1989 (Collar et al. 1992:862, 863, Contreras et al. 1993a:5, Hayes et al. 1994:89); several (SI) at 5 km N of Eusebio Ayala, along Río Piribebuy, COR, 18-29 January 1991 (Contreras et al. 1993a:5); reported at Caaby Cupé, along Río Ihagüy, COR, 25 January 1991 (Contreras et al. 1993a:5); reported at Ruta IV and Arroyo Montuoso, ÑEE, January 1992 (Contreras et al. 1993a:5); reported at Nueva Italia, CEN, June 1993 (Contreras et al. 1993a:5). Extreme dates (cited above) are 3 September and 24 February; the June record may be questionable.

305. Chestnut Seedeater
(*Sporophila cinnamomea*)

Orient: three (SP) at E of Caaguazú, CAA?, 13 and 14 November 1930 (Hayes et al. 1994:93; AMNH 320652-320654); one (SI) at Estancia Ñu Porá, MIS, 24 March 1989 (Hayes et al. 1994:94); reported at Ñu Guazú, Asunción, CEN, between 4 and 10 August 1989 (Contreras and González Romero 1989a:2); one (SI) at Estancia La Fortuna, CAN, 2 October 1990 (Hayes et al. 1994:94); one (SI) at Lago Ypacarai, COR, 6 August 1994 (R. Ryan).

306. Lesser Seed-Finch
(*Oryzoborus angolensis*)

Chaco: one (LSP) or more (?) at Villa Hayes, PHA (Bertoni 1930a:255, 1939:37; MHNSCP); Orient: many records.

307. Sooty Grassquit
(*Tiaris fuliginosa*)

Orient: one (PH) at Lagunita, Reserva Natural del Bosque Mbaracayú, CAN, 12 September 1992 (Brooks et al. 1993:89; VIREO B36/1/004).

308. Grassland Yellow-Finch
(*Sicalis luteola*)

Extreme dates: 24 February and 23 October (Hayes et al. 1994:93).

309. Great Pampa-Finch
(*Embernagra platensis*)

Northernmost records at Fortín Guachalla, BOQ (FMNH) and Estancia San Luis, CON (Laubmann 1940:150).

310. Lesser Grass-Finch
(*Emberizoides ypiranganus*)

Orient: one (SP) at Estancia San Luis, CON, 22 September 1931 (Laubmann 1940:148, *fide* Eisenmann and Short 1982:12; MM 32.1056); two (SI) at S of Santiago, MIS, 14 August 1977 (R. Ridgely); one (SP) at 13 km N of Curuguaty, CAN, 19 July 1979, and several (SI) probably in vicinity, 7-22 July 1979 (Storer 1989:12; UMMZ 202657); one or more (SI) at Ruta IV, between Arroyo Dos Hermanas and Arroyo Montuoso, ÑEE, between 11 and 23 January 1992 (Contreras and Contreras 1992:1); three (SI) at 15 km N of Ayolas, MIS, 13 August 1994 (S. LaBar et al.).

311. Ringed Warbling-Finch
(*Poospiza torquata*)

Extreme dates: 7 April (Hayes et al. 1994:93) and 25 September (Wetmore 1926:423).

312. Black-and-rufous Warbling-Finch
(*Poospiza nigrorufa*)

Extreme dates: June and 18 August (Chubb 1910:640).

313. Red-rumped Warbling-Finch
(*Poospiza lateralis*)

Orient: one (SP) at Paso Yuvay, GUA?, 12 January 1911 (Dabbene 1912:364; MACN); one (LSP) at Colonie Guaraní, Alto Paraná region (Laubmann 1940:146), but location of specimen unknown.

314. Long-tailed Reed-Finch
(*Donacospiza albifrons*)

Chaco: three (SP) at 235 km W of Río Negro, PHA, 30 August 1939 (UMMZ 105536-

105538), but locality questionable (see Methods section); reported at Las Delicias, PHA, March or December 1983 or July 1984 (Peris et al. 1987:30); two (SI) at Benjamin Aceval, PHA, 12 June 1987 (F. Hayes, A. Robinson and K. Robinson); Orient: many records.

315. Black-crested Finch
(*Lophospingus pusillus*)
Rare during austral summer (Hayes et al. 1994:93); the record at Laguna Capitán, PHA, 28 January 1990 (Hayes et al. 1994:93), was actually at General Eugenio A. Garay, BOQ (P. Scharf pers. comm.).

316. Stripe-capped Sparrow
(*Aimophila strigiceps*)
Chaco: one (SP) at Lichtenau, PHA, 31 January 1974 (Short 1976a:15, 1976b:189; AMNH 811155); one (SP) at Lichtenau, PHA, 29 March 1974 (Short 1976a:15, 1976b:189; AMNH 811153); reported at Estancia Coé Puajhú, exNAS, September 1989 (Contreras 1989:4).

317. Bobolink
(*Dolichonyx oryzivorus*)
Extreme dates: 20 September (Laubmann 1940:174) and 25 March (Steinbacher 1968:362).

318. Yellow-winged Blackbird
(*Agelaius thilius*)
Reported at Río Paraguay (Bertoni 1939:38), but no details provided; Chaco: 20 (SI) at Pozo Colorado, PHA, 2 September 1982 (R. Ridgely); one (SI) at Puente Remanso, PHA, 8 August 1994 (R. Ryan and J. Escobar); Orient: ten (SI) or more at N of Yabebyry, MIS, 12 August 1977 (Ridgely and Tudor 1989:348, Hayes et al. 1994:94); five (SI) at Río Carapá, 5 km E of Catueté, CAN, 24 July 1989 (Hayes et al. 1994:94); two to three (SI) at Estancia San Antonio, APN, 29 (two only) and 30 July 1992 (Brooks et al. 1993:126, pers. comm.).

319. Saffron-cowled Blackbird
(*Agelaius flavus*)
Threatened. Chaco: hypothetical, reported at Bajo Chaco (Collar et al. 1992:965); Orient: three (SP) at Villarrica, GUA, November 1905 (Collar et al. 1992:965; BMNH); one (SP) at Villarrica, GUA, August 1924 (Collar et al. 1992:965; BMNH); two (SP) at Itapé, GUA,

October 1927 (Hellmayr 1937:185; FMNH 69164, 69165); reported at COR? (Bertoni 1939:38); 75 (SI) at S of Santiago, MIS, 14 August 1977 (R. Ridgely); reported at Itaquyry, APN, March 1987 (Collar et al. 1992:965); five (SI) at 10 km W of San Cosme y Damián, ITA, 23 March 1989 (Collar et al. 1992:965; F. Hayes et al.); one (SI) at Estancia Itabó, CAN, 10 August 1992 (Brooks et al. 1993:49).

320. Yellow-rumped Marshbird
(*Pseudoleistes guirahuro*)
Chaco: three (SP) at 235 km W of Río Negro, PHA, 15 August 1939 (UMMZ 105486-105488), but locality questionable (see Methods section); five (SI) at Estancia Villa Rey, 5 km E of Ruta Trans Chaco km 65, PHA, 22 January 1989 (F. Hayes, A. Robinson, K. Robinson and M. Hayes); one (SI) at Ruta Trans Chaco km 55, PHA, 20 October 1989 (F. Hayes, P. Scharf and J. Escobar Argaña); one (SI) at Ruta Trans Chaco km 30, PHA, 8 August 1994 (R. Ryan et al.); Orient: many records.

321. Giant Cowbird
(*Scaphidura oryzivora*)
Chaco: one (LSP) or more (?) at Villa Hayes, PHA (Bertoni 1930a:256, 1939:39; MHNSCP); one (SP) at Alto Paraguay, Bolivia, 15 October 1909 (Grant 1911:105; BMNH), but possibly south of present Bolivian border in APY, however specimen not located; Orient: many records.

322. Red-rumped Cacique
(*Cacicus haemorrhous*)
Chaco: hypothetical, one (SP) at 235 km W of Río Negro, PHA, 29 July 1939 (UMMZ 105484); one (SP) at 235 km W of Río Negro, PHA, 1 August 1939 (UMMZ 105189); one (SP) at 235 km W of Río Negro, PHA, 12 August 1939 (UMMZ 105485), but locality of all Chaco records questionable (see Methods section); Orient: many records. The species has been recorded a short distance (exact distance not given) west of the Río Paraguay at Riacho Pilagá, Formosa Province, Argentina (Nores 1992:350, 351).

323. House Sparrow
(*Passer domesticus*)
Introduced; first reported at Asunción, CEN, in 1920 (Bertoni 1923b:74); widespread in most Paraguayan towns by 1987.

TAXONOMIC NOTES

The following species (indicated with an upper case letter after English name in Annotated Checklist section) are represented by two or more closely related forms in Paraguay that may or may not represent distinct species; thus, my treatment of their taxonomic status merits further clarification. Abbreviations for geographical departments and museums are defined in the Distributional Notes section.

A. Spotted Nothura
(*Nothura maculosa*)

The Chaco Nothura (*N. m. chacoensis*) is sometimes regarded as a distinct species (e.g., Conover 1950, Sibley and Monroe 1990), differing from *N. m. paludivaga* (distributed primarily to the east and southeast of *chacoensis*) and *N. m. pallida* (distributed primarily to the south of *chacoensis*) by its lighter, buffier coloration both above and below, narrower and more vermiculated dorsal barring, and slightly smaller size. Furthermore, the vocalizations of *chacoensis* appear to differ slightly from other races of *maculosa* (R. S. Ridgely pers. comm.). However, Short (1975) pointed out that the differences between *chacoensis* and other races of *N. maculosa* are minor compared to the differences between other species of *Nothura*. The range of *chacoensis* is apparently restricted to the Alto Chaco region of Paraguay and central Formosa Province, Argentina (Conover 1950, Short 1975). At the eastern edge of its range, *chacoensis* narrowly overlaps that of *paludivaga* by about 50 km (see Conover 1950); *chacoensis* has been recorded as far east as 120 km W of Puerto Pinasco, PHA (≈59°00'W; FMNH, UMMZ), whereas *paludivaga* has been recorded as far west as Fort Wheeler, PHA (59°35'W; AMNH), 30 km NE of Fortín Isla Poi, PHA (≈59°30'W; FMNH), and 235 km W of Río Negro, PHA (≈59°32'W; UMMZ). Steinbacher (1962) reported three specimens of *chacoensis* from Laguna Escalante, PHA (MAK, SMF), but Short (1975) identified these as *pallida*. The apparent sympatry of *chacoensis* and *paludivaga* has been argued as evidence that *chacoensis* is a distinct species (e.g., Sibley and Monroe 1990), yet hybridization appears to occur at least occasionally in the narrow range of overlap. Conover (1950) described two possible hybrid specimens (*chacoensis<paludivaga*), but did not state their localities. One of these appears to be FMNH 417655, collected at Laguna General Diaz, APY or PHA (59°01'W); however, I could find no other specimen at FMNH that stands out as being a possible hybrid. Short (1976a) described another possible hybrid (AMNH 802523; *chacoensis>paludivaga*) collected 60 km E of Orloff, in PHA (59°27'W). I concur with Short (1975, 1976a) that *chacoensis* is best regarded as a race of *N. maculosa*.

B. Blue-throated Piping-Guan
(*Pipile cumanensis*)

Formerly regarded as conspecific with Red-throated Piping-Guan (*P. cujubi*), but differs primarily in throat coloration. The two species are apparently sympatric in Mato Grosso, Brazil, and no hybrids are known, thus supporting their treatment as separate species (Vaurie 1967). *Pipile cujubi* may occur in northeastern APY (see Hypothetical Species section).

C. Blaze-winged Parakeet
(*Pyrrhura devillei*)

This species, which is restricted to northern Paraguay and adjacent Mato Grosso, Brazil, may represent a geographical race of the Maroon-bellied Parakeet (*Pyrrhura frontalis*); it differs from *P. f. chiripepe* by the presence of a reddish, orangish or yellowish patch on the underwing coverts (Forshaw 1989). Although *chiripepe* is found in the eastern Chaco and most of the Orient to the south of *devillei*, the two taxa apparently flock together and hybridize in northern Paraguay (Short 1975, in prep., Ridgely 1981). However, the extent to which the two forms hybridize is unclear; I regard them as distinct species until further data are published.

D. Ochre-collared Piculet
(*Picumnus temminckii*)

This species is sometimes regarded as conspecific with White-barred Piculet (*P. cirratus*; e.g., Short 1982), differing from *P. cirratus* primarily by a buffy wash across the face and nape. Although *P. temminckii* apparently hy-

White-barred Piculet *(Picumnus cirratus pilcomayensis)*
Dan Brown

bridizes (no details published) with *P. c. cirratus* (distributed primarily to the north of *temminckii*) in the Brazilian states of São Paulo and Paraná, it is not known to hybridize with *P. c. pilcomayensis* where their ranges meet in eastern Paraguay and eastern Argentina (Short 1982). In the Orient of Paraguay, the ranges of *temminckii* and *pilcomayensis* appear to overlap. Specimens of *temminckii* have been recorded in the Paraguay River basin as far west as Independencia, GUA (56°15'W; AMNH), and Abaí, CAP (55°57'W; AMNH), whereas *pilcomayensis* specimens have been recorded in the Paraná River basin as far east as the upper Río Iguazú, CAA (AMNH), east of Yhú, CAA (AMNH), Itaquyry, APN (MHNIB), and east of Caaguazú, CAA (AMNH; all localities east of 55°55'W). In 1992, Brooks et al. (1993:74) purportedly observed both taxa at Estancia La Golondrina, CAP (55°30'W), Estancia La Golondrina, CAA (55°22'W), Estancia San Antonio, APN (55°20'W), and at Estancia Itabó, CAN (54°38'W). In extreme southern Paraguay, *temminckii* has been recorded at the eastern end of Isla Yacyreta, ITA (≈56°15'W),

and *pilcomayensis* at the western end (≈56°40'W; Brooks et al. 1993:138, pers. comm.). The systematic relationships of *Picumnus* have not been thoroughly investigated (Short 1982). Because *pilcomayensis* and *temminckii* appear to behave as distinct species in Paraguay with no known hybridization in the zone of contact, I regard them as such.

E. White-wedged Piculet
(*Picumnus albosquamatus*)

This species is closely related to the White-barred Piculet (*P. cirratus pilcomayensis*; distributed primarily to the south and east of *P. albosquamatus*), with which it apparently hybridizes in Bolivia and southern Mato Grosso, Brazil (Short 1982). It differs from *P. cirratus* by having whitish dorsal spots and ventral white wedges, which are absent in *cirratus*. No information is available on the zone of contact in Paraguay, where *P. albosquamatus* has been recorded only recently in extreme northeastern CON (see Distributional Notes section). Until further data are published on the extent of hybridization, I concur with Short (1982) that the two taxa are best regarded as distinct species.

F. Green-barred Woodpecker
(*Colaptes melanochloros*)

The Golden-breasted Woodpecker (*C. m. melanolaimus*) is sometimes regarded as a distinct species (e.g., Narosky and Yzurieta 1987, 1989, Clements 1991), differing from *C. m. melanochloros* primarily by its brighter throat and chest colors (yellowish, orangish, even reddish-orange) contrasting with the paler belly, and by its more terrestrial habits. In an extensive study of geographical variation and intergradation within the species, Short (1972b) recognized three races of the western *melanolaimus* group (*melanolaimus, nigroviridis* and *leucofrenatus* from north to south) and two races of the eastern *melanochloros* group (*nattereri* and *melanochloros* from north to south). The two groups intergrade extensively in Corrientes Province, Argentina, in the state of Rio Grande do Sul, Brazil, and to a lesser extent elsewhere (Short 1972b). In Paraguay, the Chaco is chiefly inhabited by *nigroviridis*, although *nattereri* has been reported recently in northeastern APY (Hayes et al. 1990b), in a region where the two races probably intergrade (Short 1972b). Four specimens of *melanochloros* from 235 km W of the Riacho Negro, PHA (UMMZ), are probably from eastern Paraguay (Short 1972b:46-49; further discussed in Methods section). However, there are some indications of introgression from *melanochloros* in Chaco specimens of *nigroviridis* (Short 1972b). The Orient is inhabited mostly by *melanochloros*, with indications of introgression from *nattereri* in the northern Orient and *nigroviridis* in the southern Orient (Short 1972b); a specimen from Lambaré, CEN (SMF 31857), on the east bank of the Río Paraguay, appears to be intermediate between *nigroviridis* and *melanochloros* (Short 1972b). Based on recent observations in the vicinity of San Juan Bautista, MIS, and Ayolas, MIS, the population in the Ñeembucú region resembles *nigroviridis* (F. Hayes et al.). I concur with Short (1972b) that the two groups are conspecific.

G. Campo Flicker
(*Colaptes campestris*)

The northern race (*C. c. campestris*) has a black throat patch, which is generally absent in the southern race (*C. c. campestroides*); the two races were formerly considered separate species (e.g., Meyer de Schauensee 1966, 1970). In an analysis of geographical variation and hybridization within the species, Short (1972b) found that the two races exhibit little geographical variation, except in the color of the throat patch. The two races meet in central Paraguay and to the east and west of Paraguay, where they form a narrow hybrid zone. In Paraguay, pure black-throated *campestris* specimens range southward to Horqueta, CON (23°24'S), and Capitán Bado, AMA (23°16'S), with a very dark-throated immature at Pastoreo, CAA (25°23'S). Pure white-throated *campestroides* specimens range northward to Asunción, CEN (25°16'S) and the Río Pilcomayo, PHA (farther north, but no northern limit given; Short 1972b). Using character scores for throat color ranging from 0 (pure white throat) to 4 (pure black throat), the average score for five specimens from 14-25 km E of Rosario, SAP (24°27'S), is 2.10 (range=0.5 to 3.5), whereas six specimens from Sapucái, PAR (25°40'S), average 1.25 (range=0 to 2.5; Short 1972b). Although there are indications

of introgression in specimens to the north and south of Paraguay, the proportion of intermediate specimens in Paraguay is much higher (Short 1972b). The extent of hybridization between *campestris* and *campestroides* indicates that they are conspecific (Short 1972b).

H. Black-bodied Woodpecker
(*Dryocopus schulzi*)

This species, whose distribution is restricted to the Chaco of Bolivia, Paraguay and Argentina, is closely related to the Lineated Woodpecker (*D. lineatus*), which is distributed to the north and east of *D. schulzi*. It differs from *lineatus* primarily by unmarked black underparts, grayer ear coverts, long pale nasal tufts, a paler bill, a strong black mark on the underwings, a white line over the eye, and smaller size (Short 1982). The vocalizations also differ (Madroño Nieto and Pearman 1992). Several hybrids are known from Argentina and Bolivia. The only hybrid known from Paraguay is a male specimen from 110 km W of Concepción, in PHA (Short 1982:412; Naturhistoriska Riksmuseet, Stockholm, Sweden). The consistent morphological and vocal differences between *schulzi* and *lineatus* and the scarcity of hybrids suggest that they represent distinct species (Short 1982, Madroño Nieto and Pearman 1992).

I. Olive Spinetail
(*Cranioleuca obsoleta*)

This species may be conspecific with the Stripe-crowned Spinetail (*C. pyrrhophia*), which differs from *C. obsoleta* by its distinctly striped crown and whiter underparts. Although the distributions of the two species are largely allopatric (*pyrrhophia* primarily to the west of *obsoleta*), Belton (1984) reported intermediate plumage characters in specimens from southern Rio Grande do Sul, Brazil (AMNH). Belton (1984) found that the calls were indistinguishable by ear, and that each species responded with the same intensity to taped calls of either species; however, Ridgely and Tudor (1994) reported that many species of *Cranioleuca* have similar voices and might be expected to respond to another's voice. In Paraguay, *pyrrhophia* is restricted to the scrub forests of the Chaco; *obsoleta* occurs only in the humid forests of the eastern Orient, and has not been recorded west of Abaí, CAP (55°57'W; AMNH), and Ayolas, MIS

122

(56°54'W; R. Ridgely), at least 200 km E of the nearest record of *pyrrhophia* at 15 km W of Río Paraguay, between Ríos Confuso and Pilcomayo, PHA (°57°49'W; AMNH). The two taxa are allopatric as well as morphologically and ecologically distinct in Paraguay, and are thus treated as separate species.

J. Variable Antshrike
(*Thamnophilus caerulescens*)

The race inhabiting the Argentinian Chaco (*T. c. dinellii*) differs from other races by its rufous rather than whitish underparts (Short 1975, Narosky and Yzurieta 1987, 1989), and may represent a distinct species (Nores 1992). The only published report of *dinellii* in Paraguay is that of Brodkorb (1937c:34) for specimens (UMMZ) obtained 265 km W of Puerto La Victoria, exNAS or BOQ; however, these specimens apparently refer to *T. c. paraguayensis*, which is distributed throughout the Paraguayan Chaco (Laubmann 1940:22, 23). There have been no detailed studies on the geographical variation of these two forms.

K. Reiser's Tyrannulet
(*Phyllomyias reiseri*)

Known from only a few specimens, this species has often been regarded as conspecific with the Greenish Tyrannulet (*P. virescens*; e.g., Traylor 1982). However, Stotz (1990) demonstrated that *reiseri* differs from *virescens* by its paler yellow underparts, a lighter olive wash across the breast, gray-tipped crown feathers contrasting with the brighter, yellower back and upperparts, paler wingbars, a less prominent facial pattern, and shorter wing and tail. Furthermore, *reiseri* is distributed primarily to the north of *virescens* in drier cerrado habitat. There are no signs of hybridization between the two forms. These differences suggest that *reiseri* and *virescens* represent distinct species.

L. Suiriri Flycatcher
(*Suiriri suiriri*)

The Campo Suiriri, represented by two distinctive races (*S. s. affinis* and *S. s. bahiae*), is sometimes considered to be a distinct species (e.g., Short 1975, Sibley and Monroe 1990). It differs from the Chaco Suiriri (*S. s. suiriri*) by its larger bill, paler upperparts, much brighter yellow underparts and, in the case of *affinis*, by

its paler rump and bases to the rectrices. The southern race *suiriri* occupies most of Paraguay, except for northern CON, where it intergrades with *affinis*. Laubmann (1940) regarded two specimens from Zanja Moratí, CON (MM), as typical *affinis*, and five specimens from Estancia San Luis, CON (MM), as intergrades between *affinis* and *suiriri*. Zimmer (1955) reported an additional seven intergrade specimens from Zanja Moratí (AMNH), and ten from Estancia San Luis (AMNH). Traylor (1982) reexamined these specimens, and reported two additional intergrade specimens from Belén, CON (AMNH), which is south of the other localities; however, I found the Belén specimens to be indistinguishable from *suiriri*. Both the upperparts and underparts of the intergrade specimens are intermediate, with the more variable underparts being paler yellow than *affinis* and sometimes as pale as *suiriri*. The average wing length is intermediate, and bill length approaches that of *affinis*. An additional specimen from Companario, southern Mato Grosso, Brazil (AMNH), shows signs of introgression from *suiriri*. Because the population in northern CON appears to be composed entirely of intergrades with no known parental phenotypes, the two forms appear to be conspecific.

M. Small-billed Elaenia
(*Elaenia parvirostris*)

This species hybridizes with a sedentary population of the austral race of the White-crested Elaenia (*E. albiceps chilensis*) at several localities in the Andes of southern Bolivia, where *parvirostris* generally occurs at lower elevations than *albiceps*, but hybridizes at intermediate elevations (Traylor 1982). The hybrid specimens (FMNH) are generally intermediate in both color and size, with either two or three wingbars. However, populations of the two species breed sympatrically in a large area of northern Argentina, where they occur in different habitats and differ markedly in the construction and placement of their nests (Traylor 1982). Although worn and unsexed specimens of either species are often difficult to identify, fresh specimens of *parvirostris* are readily distinguishable from *albiceps* by their greener upperparts, a smaller and more concealed white crown, and three rather than two whitish wing bars. Because no hybrids are known from Argentina, the two forms appear to represent distinct species whose isolating mechanisms have broken down in a limited part of their range.

N. White-bellied Tyrannulet
(*Serpophaga munda*)

This species is sometimes regarded as conspecific with White-crested Tyrannulet (*S. subcristata*; e.g., Bó 1969, Short 1975), from which it differs by whiter underparts, a grayer back and a relatively longer tail. The two species apparently breed in sympatry in western Argentina (Bó 1969) and in the Paraguayan Chaco (Hayes et al. 1994), where intermediate specimens thought to represent hybrids occur (Zimmer 1955, Bó 1969). However, the vocalizations of the two forms are distinct (Narosky and Yzurieta 1987, 1989, Remsen and Traylor 1989, Hayes et al. 1994), suggesting that *munda* is a distinct species. Remsen and Traylor (1989:54) described the calls of *munda* as a soft, spitting, syncopated 'tsi, tsu-tsu, tsu-tsu, tsu-tsu,' and those of *subcristata* as a soft trill preceded by an inflected introductory note: 'sweee?, titititititi'. Hayes et al. (1994) described the call of *munda* as a relatively monotone trill; the call of *subcristata* is more complex, with two distinct parts. The available evidence suggests that the two forms are distinct species.

O. Fuscous Flycatcher
(*Cnemotriccus fuscatus*)

Belton (1984) provided evidence that *C. f. fuscatus* of southeastern Brazil may be specifically distinct from the more widespread *C. f. bimaculatus*. The latter race differs from *fuscatus* by its generally paler underparts, absence of olive tones and a rufous rump (Short 1975). The two forms appear to be sympatric in Brazil (Zimmer 1938), but allopatric in Rio Grande do Sul, Brazil, where Belton (1984) described their habitat preferences, nest construction and vocalizations as being markedly different. Belton (1984) obtained strong responses from individuals of each race to its own taped calls, but neither race responded to the other's vocalizations. The race *bimaculatus* occurs throughout Paraguay (e.g., Laubmann 1940). Although I could find no specimen records of nominate *fuscatus* from Paraguay, Bertoni (1914a:57, 1939:33) reported it from the Alto Paraná re-

gion, and a specimen has been taken on the east bank of the Río Paraná opposite Paraguay at Guaíra, Paraná, Brazil (Zimmer 1938:31; AMNH).

P. Chilean Swallow
(*Tachycineta meyeni*)

This species may be conspecific with the White-rumped Swallow (*T. leucorrhoa*), from which it differs by the absence of a white supraloral streak, more bluish upperparts and duskier underwing coverts (Narosky and Yzurieta 1987, 1989, Ridgely and Tudor 1989). Although their breeding ranges are largely allopatric, with *meyeni* occurring to the south and west of *leucorrhoa*, there appear to be some hybrid specimens (R. S. Ridgely pers. comm.). Nevertheless, the two forms are probably best considered as distinct species until further information is available.

Q. Fawn-breasted Wren
(*Thryothorus guarayanus*)

This species may be conspecific with the Buff-breasted Wren (*T. leucotis*), from which it is distinguished primarily by its smaller size; however, no intergradation has been demonstrated with *T. l. rufiventris*, a large race distributed to the north of *T. guarayanus* (Ridgely and Tudor 1994). Both taxa may also be conspecific with the Long-billed Wren (*T. longirostris*) of eastern Brazil (Ridgely and Tudor 1994). The extreme northeastern Matogrosense region, in APY, is inhabited by *guarayanus*; the extreme northeastern Alto Paraná region, in CAN, is inhabited by either *guarayanus* or *leucotis* (most likely the latter; see Distributional Notes section). Although the two forms may well be distinct species, I have tentatively regarded the form present in northeastern CAN as conspecific with *guarayanus* pending further confirmation of its identification (see Distributional Notes section).

R. Chaco Pipit
(*Anthus chacoensis*)

Although *A. chacoensis* is usually considered to be a distinct species, its validity is often questioned (e.g., Ridgely and Tudor 1989). It appears to be most closely related to the Yellowish Pipit (*A. lutescens*), from which it differs slightly by paler dorsal streaking, less yellowish underparts, more pronounced streaking on the flanks, and a shorter hind claw. Straneck (1987) found that the territorial display flights and calls of *chacoensis* and *lutescens* differ considerably. The flights of *lutescens* generally comprise a series of swooping ascents and descents, may cover a large area, rarely reach 50 m in height, and usually last no longer than 2 min. In contrast, *chacoensis* flies upward 60-80 m, hovers in one area with some short descents and ascents, and may remain in the air for up to 35 min. The display calls of *lutescens* are short, about 0.85 sec, and are composed of a few tics followed by a descending trill. The calls of *chacoensis* average 50 sec in duration, and consist of a relatively monotone, musical trill. The two species are broadly sympatric, but are not known to hybridize. Straneck (1987) stated that the two species occurred in different habitats, sometimes as close as 500 m apart; *lutescens* occurred in shorter grass, whereas *chacoensis* occurred in taller grass (±50 cm high). The differences in behavior, vocalizations and preferred habitat indicate that *chacoensis* represents a distinct species.

S. White-bellied Warbler
(*Basileuterus hypoleucus*)

Specimens with yellowish underparts have been recorded in Santa Cruz, Bolivia (Remsen and Traylor 1989), Mato Grosso, Brazil (Hellmayr 1935), and in Paraguay at 25 km W of Puerto Pinasco, PHA (Wetmore 1926:133; USNM 284043). Remsen and Traylor (1989) suggested that these specimens may represent local introgression with the broadly sympatric Golden-crowned Warbler (*B. culicivorus*). Although mixed pairs have been observed in Brazil (Willis 1986), *hypoleucus* and *culicivorus* generally occur in different habitats (*culicivorus* in more humid forest) and are sympatric over a wide geographical area (Ridgely and Tudor 1989), suggesting that they are distinct, closely related species (see comments in Remsen and Traylor 1989). The possibility also exists that *hypoleucus* may occasionally hybridize with the broadly sympatric Flavescent Warbler (*Basileuterus flaveolus*). On 20 May 1989, I observed what appeared to be a mixed family of *B. hypoleucus* and *B. flaveolus* (two of each) at Estancia Fonciere, CON; however, I did not take notes on their plumages. The vocalizations of *B. hypoleucus* are apparently more similar to those of *B. flaveolus* than *B. culicivorus* (S. LaBar pers. comm.).

T. Marsh Seedeater
(*Sporophila palustris*)

Short (1975) suggested this poorly known species may be a color phase of the Dark-throated Seedeater (*S. ruficollis*), from which it differs primarily by a white, rather than dark, throat. Short (1975) also suggested the Tawny-bellied Seedeater (*S. hypoxantha*) might be conspecific with *S. ruficollis* and *S. palustris*, but this is unlikely (e.g., Ridgely and Tudor 1989). Because there are no known hybrids between any of these forms, each should be considered as distinct species (e.g., Ridgely and Tudor 1989).

U. Chestnut Seedeater
(*Sporophila cinnamomea*)

This poorly known species may be conspecific with the Gray-and-chestnut Seedeater (*S. hypochroma*), which is distributed primarily to the west of *S. cinnamomea*. The two species differ only in the color of the back, which is gray in *hypochroma* and chestnut in *cinnamomea* (Short 1975). However, there are no known hybrids; thus, they should be considered as distinct species (e.g., Ridgely and Tudor 1989).

HYPOTHETICAL SPECIES

The following 104 species of birds have been reported from Paraguay, but have not been adequately documented or are suspected to represent escaped cagebirds. I have divided these species into two groups: (1) *possible species*, those that are known to occur (or formerly occurred) near Paraguay, which may eventually be confirmed as occurring within the country; and (2) *doubtful species*, those that are unlikely to ever be recorded in Paraguay, based on distribution and lack of migratory habits. Abbreviations for geographical departments are defined in the Distributional Notes section.

POSSIBLE SPECIES

Dwarf Tinamou
(*Taoniscus nanus*)
Orient: often cited for Paraguay (e.g., Laubmann 1939:122) and reported at Alto Paraná region (Bertoni 1939:17), but no details provided.

Fasciated Tiger-Heron
(*Tigrisoma fasciatum*)
Orient: one (SP) at Río Monday, APN (Bertoni 1901:15, 16); reported at Reserva Natural del Bosque Mbaracayú, CAN (Meisel et al. 1992:1). Bertoni's specimen, an immature, was originally described as *T.* [*lineatus*] *marmoratum* and later identified by Lynch Arribálzaga (1902:335) and Bertoni (1918e:245) as *T. fasciatum*; however, Bertoni (1939:21) later regarded the species's occurrence in Paraguay as questionable.

Black-necked Swan
(*Cygnus melanocorypha*)
Often cited for Paraguay, but no substantiated records (e.g., Laubmann 1939:68). Possibly occurs in Paraguay as an austral migrant.

Goose sp.
(*Chloephaga* sp.)
Chaco: one (SI) flying across Ruta Trans Chaco km 200, PHA, 20 July 1990 (A. Madroño Nieto), but could not be identified to species, and definitely not an Orinoco Goose (*Neochen jubata*). The bird was dark with the characteristic wing pattern of the genus, and was thought to have been an Ashy-headed Goose (*C. poliocephala*) or Upland Goose (*C. picta*).

Speckled Teal
(*Anas flavirostris*)
Often cited for Paraguay (e.g., Laubmann 1939:73); reported at Río Paraguay (Bertoni 1939:22); Chaco: 80 (SI) at Laguna Millón, PHA, July 1992 (López 1993:46). No details are provided for any of these records; the large numbers reported during 1992 are unsubstantiated. Possibly occurs in Paraguay as an austral migrant.

Southern Wigeon
(*Anas sibilatrix*)
Often cited for Paraguay, but no substantiated records (e.g., Laubmann 1939:73). Possibly occurs in Paraguay as an austral migrant.

Yellow-billed Pintail
(*Anas georgica*)
Chaco: reported at Fortín Donovan, PHA (Kerr 1892:146); 60 (SI) at Laguna Millón, PHA, July 1992 (López 1993:46); 24 (SI) at Laguna Capitán, PHA, or Estancia Campo María, PHA, July 1992 (López 1993:47); Orient: reported at Alto Paraná region (Bertoni 1914a:40), but no details provided. Wetmore (1926:73) referred to specimens from Paraguay, but there are none at the USNM and if such specimens exist, they may have been collected at a time when Paraguay was larger. The large numbers reported during 1992 are unsubstantiated. Possibly occurs in Paraguay as an austral migrant.

Red-backed Hawk
(*Buteo polyosoma*)
Chaco: reported at Las Delicias, PHA, 1983 or 1984 (Peris et al. 1987:29), but no details provided; one (SI) at Mariscal Estigarribia, BOQ, 9 September 1989 (Contreras and González Romero 1989:2, 3, Cabot 1991:207), but no details provided. Although it may occur in Paraguay as an austral migrant, it is similar to the White-tailed Hawk (*Buteo albicaudatus*) and further documentation is needed before this species can be accepted for Paraguay.

126

Crested Eagle
(*Morphnus guianensis*)

Orient: one (SP) in the frontier [border] of Misiones, 27°18'S, October 1887 (Bertoni 1901:154), presumably in Argentina, but perhaps in extreme southern Paraguay; reported for Alto Paraná region (Bertoni 1914a:43, 1939:23), but no details provided; Bertoni (1926:398) also stated that it was recorded only once in 30 years at Puerto Bertoni, APN, but provided no details. Further documentation is needed before this rare species can be accepted for Paraguay.

Black Hawk-Eagle
(*Spizaetus tyrannus*)

Orient: one (SP) at Sapucái, PAR (Bertoni 1914a:43, 1928c:188, 1939:24), but may refer to USNM 189371, which is an Ornate Hawk-Eagle (*S. ornatus*) taken at this locality and was not mentioned by Oberholser (1902); reported at Colonia Nueva Australia (locality unknown) and Caazapá, CAP (Podtiaguin 1944:59); one (SI) at 10 km N of Curuguaty, CAN, 13 September 1990 (P. Scharf), but seen by only one (albeit experienced) observer. Bertoni (1928c:188) observed numerous *S. ornatus* in the Alto Paraná region, but never *S. tyrannus*. Further documentation is needed before this species can be accepted for Paraguay.

Speckled Chachalaca
(*Ortalis guttata*)

Orient: reported as questionable in Alto Paraná region (Bertoni 1939:17); reported at Ygatimí and Curuguaty, CAN, and at mouth of Río Piratíy, CAN (Podtiaguin 1945:653), but no details provided.

Dusky-legged Guan
(*Penelope obscura*)

Chaco: reported at near the mouth of Río Pilcomayo, PHA (Kerr 1892:147), but possibly in Argentina; one (SI) or more (?) at Río Confuso, PHA (Bertoni 1930b:257); reported at Villazón, exNAS, Puesto Estrella, exNAS, Estancia Orihuela, PHA, and Carandayty (not located; Podtiaguin 1945:65); Orient: reported at Asunción, CEN (Bertoni 1939:17); reported at Alto Paraná region (Podtiaguin 1945:65); reported at Lago Ypoá, PAR, CEN or ÑEE (Acevedo et al. 1990:56, 86); reported at Estero Ñeembucú, ÑEE (Acevedo et al. 1990:86). Un-

fortunately no details were given for any of these reports. The only bona fide specimen records that I am aware of are two (SP) from Paraguay obtained in the 1850s during the Page expedition (USNM 256875, 58994), but the specimen labels lack dates and more precise localities, and the specimens were obtained at a time when Paraguay was larger. Storer (1989:15) reported the weight of a male specimen from Paraguay as 960 g. However, the specimen (UMMZ 201975), taken at 13.3 km N of Curuguaty, CAN, is preserved as a skeleton with only a few feathered body parts, including a wing that has light rufous rather than whitish edges to the feathers; thus the specimen represents a Rusty-margined Guan (*Penelope superciliaris*). Although this species may occur in Paraguay (e.g., Vaurie 1966), the lack of specimen records indicates that further documentation is needed before it can be accepted.

Red-throated Piping-Guan
(*Pipile cujubi*)

No published reports (e.g., Vaurie 1967), but the Chamacoco indians of northeastern APY insist that this species, described as having a red throat and white wing patches, is occasionally encountered in the forest.

Red-gartered Coot
(*Fulica armillata*)

Chaco: one (SP) or more at Villa Hayes, PHA (Bertoni 1930a:242), but no description provided that would distinguish this species from the Red-fronted Coot (*F. rufifrons*), which has been adequately documented from Paragauy (see Distributional Notes section).

Two-banded Plover
(*Charadrius falklandicus*)

Reported without details (Bertoni 1914a:38, 1939:19) and attributed to Ihering, but the record is too far out of range to be credible.

Semipalmated Plover
(*Charadrius semipalmatus*)

Chaco: three (SI) at 320 km west (undoubtedly northwest, in PHA) of Asunción, 5 September 1973 (Myers and Myers 1979:191), but no details provided.

Rufous-chested Dotterel
(*Charadrius modestus*)

Chaco: one (SI) between Estancia Coé Puajhú, NAS, and Fortín Nueva Asunción Base Aérea, exNAS, 11 September 1989 (Contreras 1989:5), but no details provided.

Whimbrel
(*Numenius phaeopus*)

Chaco: reported to be muy abundante (very abundant) in the Bajo Chaco region, PHA, December 1983 (Peris and Suarez 1985:20), but there are few records in the interior of South America (e.g., Fjeldså and Krabbe 1990) and no subsequent records for Paraguay (Hayes et al. 1990a:952).

Snowy-crowned Tern
(*Sterna trudeaui*)

Orient: one (SI) at Itá Enramada, CEN, 7 May 1989 (Contreras and Contreras 1992:2); one (SI) at Puerto Nuevo de Pilar, ÑEE, 10 January 1992 (Contreras and Contreras 1992:2); 11 (SI) between Naranjito, ÑEE, and Pilar, ÑEE, 17 September 1992 (Contreras and Contreras 1992:2). Although these sight records are plausible (the authors cite further observations from nearby areas in Argentina), the first sighting was recorded only a few km from where an Arctic Tern (*S. paradisaea*) was photographed two days later (see Distributional Notes section); further documentation of this southern austral migrant is needed.

Royal Tern
(*Sterna maxima*)

Orient: one (SI) at Pilar (along Río Paraguay), ÑEE, 10 September 1992 (Contreras 1992:1), but seen by a single (albeit experienced) observer. Although this record is credible, further documentation is needed before such a rare species can be accepted for Paraguay. Contreras (1992) also cited a published record of the species being captured at Isla Apipé Grande, Corrientes, Argentina, at the southern border of Paraguay, on 24 October 1950.

Plumbeous Pigeon
(*Columba plumbea*)

Orient: several (SI) without details at Puerto Bertoni, APN, July 1917 and July 1918 (Bertoni 1919a:256); two to three (SI) at Lagunita, Reserva Natural del Bosque Mbaracayú, CAN, 10, 13, 16 and 17 September 1992 (Brooks et al. 1993:64), but only seen flying (never perched or carefully studied at close range; T. Brooks pers. comm.). Further documentation is needed before this species can be accepted for Paraguay.

Blue-throated Macaw
(*Ara glaucogularis*)

Bertoni (1922a:39, 40) stated that Azara's Canindé referred to the Blue-and-yellow Macaw (*Ara ararauna*) and that there were no confirmed records of *A. glaucogularis* in Paraguay. Thus far the only confirmed records of *A. glaucogularis* are from Bolivia (Ingels et al. 1981, Collar et al. 1992). However, Podtiaguin (1944:10, 115) reported two specimens taken by E. Avilla at Colonia Esperanza (exact locality unknown) on 18 June 1939; the female was described as having a greenish blue throat...with a few very dark feathers, and the male was stated to represent the typical form (p. 115, translated from Spanish). Podtiaguin also reported an undated specimen taken by P. Willim at Nueva Italia, CEN (probably during the 1930s or early 1940s). Although Podtiaguin's identification is unquestionably correct, the origin of these birds is uncertain. The proximity of Nueva Italia to Asunción suggests that the Nueva Italia specimen may represent an escaped cagebird. The Colonia Esperanza locality is even more problematic; although many localities in the Chaco include the name Esperanza, they are always preceded by a prefix other than Colonia (e.g., Puerto, Campo, Puesto, Estancia). If these specimens came from the northern Chaco, they could be considered a valid record; however, Colonia Esperanza is apparently located in the Orient because, in reference to the scarcity of records in Paraguay, Podtiaguin (1944:115) stated that besides the eastern part of Paraguay it is completely unknown (translated from Spanish). If Colonia Esperanza is in the Orient or even along the Río Paraguay (e.g., Puerto Esperanza), the specimens most likely represent escaped cagebirds or may have been obtained elsewhere.

Golden-capped Parakeet
(*Aratinga auricapilla*)

Orient: two (LSP, SI) at Puerto Bertoni, APN, 11 November 1918 (Bertoni 1918b:239), poorly described but measurements of female

128

seem correct. This record is the most south-westerly for the species (Collar et al. 1992). Numerous specimens were taken from the eastern part of the adjacent state of Paraná, Brazil, between 1901 and 1927 (Collar et al. 1992); although natural vagrancy is plausible, the origin of the birds may be questionable (i.e., escaped cagebirds).

Green-cheeked Parakeet
(*Pyrrhura molinae*)

Orient: one (SP) at unknown locality, June 1859 (Short 1975:227; USNM 16417); three or four (SI) at 50 km W of Ciudad del Este, mid-July 1985 (L. Joseph *in* Forshaw 1989:482). The USNM specimen was collected during Page's second expedition, at a time when Paraguay was larger. The absence of records in the Chaco and northern Orient, which are closest to the species' known range (Forshaw 1989), suggests that the specimen may have been obtained as a cagebird in Asunción, CEN. The 1985 sight record (cited above) is even farther from the species' range.

Red-spectacled Parrot
(*Amazona pretrei*)

Orient: three (SP) at Río Piraty-y (Alto Paraná), possibly referring to the Río Piratíy, CAN, or Arroyo Piratiy, CAA and APN, June 1928 (Podtiaguin 1944:24, 114, 115; MHNSCP 672); several (SI) flying across the Río Paraná, 2 km from Candelaria, Misiones Province, Argentina (and presumably seen in Paraguay near Campichuelo, ITA), July 1987 (Collar et al. 1992:403); one (SI) at Estancia Itabó, CAN, 15 August 1992 (Brooks et al. 1993:35). The specimens reported by Podtiaguin were purportedly obtained by Dr. J. Varinger in 1923 (probably 1933, unless the date of collection is wrong) from F. Posner, who had obtained the specimens from a collector for European museums, and one of these specimens was obtained by the MHNSCP in 1938 and examined by Podtiaguin. Unfortunately the specimen was not described. Bertoni (1927) described variant specimens of the Vinaceous-breasted Parrot (*A. vinacea*, as a new subspecies, *paranensis*) *with relatively green underparts and little (if any) red in the tail and wings. His descriptions are similar to those of A. pretrei,* yet a few obvious plumage characters of *pretrei* were not mentioned by

Bertoni (e.g., red feathers on the legs). Bertoni also reported seeing individuals that were intermediate between typical *vinacea* and *paranensis*, which would be highly unlikely if *paranensis* represented *pretrei*. Furthermore, Bertoni must have been aware of *pretrei*'s existence in Brazil and Argentina, yet he never reported it from Paraguay. Considering the potential for confusion regarding the original source of the *pretrei* specimens, and also the possibility that the specimens represent variant *vinacea*, Podtiaguin's (1944) report must be regarded with skepticism. The Campichuelo birds (cited above) were seen in flight (Collar 1992); thus, identification may be questionable. The Estancia Itabó bird (cited above) was perched and was well described, but was seen by a single observer. There is evidence that the species moves northward from its southernmost breeding locality in the state of Rio Grande do Sul, Brazil (Collar et al. 1992). The three Paraguayan records occurred during the austral winter and may well be valid, but because there are no records from the adjacent state of Paraná, Brazil (Collar et al. 1992), I feel that further documentation is needed before the species can be accepted for Paraguay.

Black-banded Owl
(*Ciccaba huhula*)

Orient: reported at northeastern Paraguay (Short 1975:234), but basis of report unknown; two (VO) at Estancia Itabó, CAN, 9 and 14 August 1992 (Brooks et al. 1993:66), but too distant to be tape-recorded. Further documentation is needed before the species can be accepted for Paraguay.

Lesser Nighthawk
(*Chordeiles acutipennis*)

Reported to occur in Paraguay (Short 1975:238), but basis of report unknown. Chaco: five (SI, VO) hawking low over a brushy field at Fortín Toledo, BOQ, 21 January 1988, and one bird heard emitting a low-pitched trilling call unlike the typical call of the Common Nighthawk (*Chordeiles minor*; F. Hayes), but seen by only one (albeit experienced) observer. Further documentation is needed before the species can be accepted for Paraguay.

129

White-winged Nightjar
(Caprimulgus candicans)

Often cited for Paraguay on the basis of Azara (e.g., Laubmann 1940:5); reported by Short (1975:236) as a subspecies of the White-tailed Nightjar (*C. cayennensis*; Short 1975:236), which it is not (R. S. Ridgely pers. comm.). Although it could conceivably occur in the Campos Cerrados region of Paraguay, there are no substantiated records from the country (Collar et al. 1992).

Sooty Swift
(Cypseloides fumigatus)

Orient: reported at Paraná (Bertoni 1939:26), presumably referring to the Alto Paraná region, or perhaps the Río Paraná; many (SI) at Estancia San Antonio, APN, Estancia Itabó, CAN, Estancia La Golondrina, CAA, and Reserva Natural del Bosque Mbaracayú, CAN, July-September 1992 (Brooks et al. 1993:69). Although the reports may be valid, further documentation is needed before this species can be accepted for Paraguay.

Rufous-throated Sapphire
(Hylocharis sapphirina)

Chaco: one or two (SP) at Fortín Page, PHA (Kerr 1892:135; BMNH), but specimens not described and apparently lost; Orient: reported at Sapucái, PAR (Bertoni 1939:26), but no details provided; one (SI) at Estancia San Antonio, APN, 26 July 1992 (Brooks et al. 1993); two (SI) at Estancia Itabó, CAN, 7 August 1992 (Brooks et al. 1993). Although some or all of these records (especially the most recent) are likely valid (the species is almost certainly present within the country), I feel that further documentation is needed before the species can be accepted for Paraguay.

Glittering-throated Emerald
(Amazilia fimbriata)

Reported for Paraguay by Meyer de Schauensee (1970:144), but basis of report unknown.

Rufous-tailed Jacamar
(Galbula ruficauda)

Reported by Bertoni (1914a:48), but no details provided. However, it does occur in nearby areas of Departamento Santa Cruz, Bolivia (J. V. Remsen pers. comm.).

Common Miner
(Geositta cunicularia)

Orient: one (LSP) at Villarrica, GUA (Vaurie 1980:16), but location of specimen unknown.

Ochre-cheeked Spinetail
(Poecilurus scutatus)

Chaco: one (SI) at APY (presumably near Puerto Bahía Negra), between 18 October and 4 November 1984 (López 1985:12), but no details provided. This species has been recorded in the adjacent departamentos of Bolivia (Santa Cruz, Chuquisaca and Tarija; Remsen and Traylor 1989), and may well occur in Paraguay.

Hudson's Canastero
(Asthenes hudsoni)

Orient: reported at southeastern Paraguay (Vaurie 1980:186), but basis of record unknown.

Freckle-breasted Thornbird
(Phacellodomus striaticollis)

Chaco: two (SP) at Fortín Donovan, PHA, 3 May 1890 (Kerr 1892:132; BMNH?); reported at Waikthlatingmayalwa, PHA, November 1896 (Kerr 1901:226); reported at Río Pilcomayo, PHA (Bertoni 1914a:53, 1939:30); Orient: reported at Concepción, CON, October 1896 (Kerr 1901:226). All of these reports likely refer to the Greater Thornbird (*P. ruber*; Laubmann 1940:44).

White-browed Foliage-gleaner
(Anabacerthia amaurotis)

Orient: one (SI) at Estancia La Golondrina, CAA, 8 July 1992 (Brooks et al. 1993:55); one to three (SI) at Estancia San Antonio, APN, 23, 24, 26 and 27 July 1992 (Brooks et al. 1993:55, pers. comm.); one (SI) at Reserva Biológica Itabó, APN, 17 August 1994 (F. Hayes et al.). Although these records are likely valid, this species is similar to the Buff-browed Foliage-gleaner (*Syndactyla rufosuperciliata*); further documentation is needed before it can be accepted for Paraguay.

Mouse-colored Tapaculo
(Scytalopus speluncae)

Orient: one (SI), possibly the same individual (?), at Estancia La Golondrina, CAA, 12-14 and 19 July 1993 (Brooks et al. 1993:77). Bertoni (1919a:258, 1939:28) specifically stated that this species occurred along the bank of the

Río Paraná opposite Paraguay, but it was never recorded in Paraguay. If correctly identified, the recent sighting(s) may represent a recent range extension, but further documentation is needed before this species can be accepted for Paraguay.

Rusty-fronted Tody-Flycatcher
(*Todirostrum latirostre*)

Reported for Paraguay by Meyer de Schauensee (1970:307), but basis of report unknown.

Black-and-white Monjita
(*Heteroxolmis dominicana*)

Chaco: reported at Fortín Page, PHA (Kerr 1892:129); reported at Waikthlatingmayalwa, PHA (Kerr 1901:225); Orient: reported at Lago Ypoá, PAR, August 1986 (J. R. Contreras et al. 1989:40). No details or any indication of a collected specimen were provided in any of these reports. Although the species may well occur in Paraguay, further documentation is needed before it can be accepted.

Southern Martin
(*Progne modesta*)

Chaco: reported at Estancia Coé Puajhú, exNAS, September 1989 (Contreras 1989:4), but no details reported; Orient: reported at Asunción, CEN, between 1985 and 1988 (Contreras and González Romero 1988:33), but no details reported. Often cited for Paraguay (e.g., Laubmann 1939:198), but there are no substantiated records.

Azure Jay
(*Cyanocorax caeruleus*)

Chaco: hypothetical, several (LSP) at Fortín Page, PHA, 10 September 1890 (Kerr 1892:128), and Waikthlatingmayalwa, PHA, 15 and 21 January 1897 (Kerr 1901:225), but no specimens located at BMNH and probably refer to Purplish Jay (*C. cyanomelas*); Orient: many published records (Salvadori 1895:9, 1900:17, Kerr 1901:225, Chubb 1910:646, Grant 1911:109), but all probably refer to Purplish Jay, which was not reported, and there are no Paraguay specimens at BMNH; one (SP) labeled in Paraguay, 1868, with Brazil crossed out (AMNH 501250), but locality and origin of specimen questionable; two (SI) at W of Ciudad del Este, APN?, August 1977 (Ridgely and Tudor 1989:44); reported at Lago Ypoá, PAR, August 1986 (J. R. Contreras et al.

1989:40). An example of the confusion caused by earlier reports is Oberholser's (1902:140) report of *C. heckelii* from Sapucái, PAR, referred to as *C. caeruleus* by Laubmann (1940:192), but it is definitely *C. cyanomelas* (specimen examined at USNM). In spite of a few recent (and credible) records, I feel that further documentation is needed before this species can be accepted for Paraguay.

Swainson's Thrush
(*Catharus ustulatus*)

Orient: reported at Puerto Bertoni, APN (Bertoni 1914a:58), where it was recorded only once (Bertoni 1926:398), but no details provided.

Chiguanco Thrush
(*Turdus chiguanco*)

Chaco: reported at Fortín Linares (locality unknown; Podtiaguin 1944:116), but no details provided to separate it from any other *Turdus* spp. (melanism may be possible in other species).

Hellmayr's Pipit
(*Anthus hellmayri*)

Chaco: reported at Villazón, exNAS (Podtiaguin 1944:116); two (SP) at Estancia Orihuela, PHA (Podtiaguin 1944:116; MHNP), but no description provided. This species is similar to the Short-billed Pipit (*A. furcatus*) and Correndera Pipit (*A. correndera*), both of which have been documented from Paraguay but not in the Chaco. Podtiaguin may not have had adequate material for comparing his specimens; thus, his identification may be incorrect.

Red-necked Tanager
(*Tangara cyanocephala*)

Orient: one (SI) at E of Celos Parini, CAN, 15 July 1977 (Ridgely and Tudor 1989:257; R. Ridgely), but seen by only one (albeit experienced) observer. Further documentation is needed before the species can be accepted for Paraguay.

Buff-throated Saltator
(*Saltator maximus*)

Orient: reported at Puerto Bertoni, APN (Bertoni 1914a:64, 1939:38), but no details provided.

Thick-billed Saltator
(*Saltator maxillosus*)
Orient: reported at Alto Paraná region (Bertoni 1907:299, 300, 1914a:65); reported at Puerto Bertoni, APN, and Yaguarasapá, ITA? (Bertoni 1939:38); reported at Reserval Natural del Bosque Mbaracayú, CAN (Meisel et al. 1992:12). No details were provided for any of these reports, which may well have been valid.

Yellow Cardinal
(*Gubernatrix cristata*)
Reported without details (Bertoni 1939:37); two (SP) at unknown localities (Collar et al. 1992:883; BMNH, MCZ), the BMNH specimen prior to 1886. Orient: one (SP) at Villarrica, GUA, 12 May 1905 (Collar et al. 1992:883; BMNH); one (SP) at Villarrica, GUA, 10 October 1905, with label stating fairly common (Collar et al. 1992:883; BMNH). There have been no subsequent records of the species for Paraguay. Because this species was a popular cagebird well before 1905 (e.g., Collar et al. 1992), and Villarrica was known to be a center of avicultural trade during the early 1900s (Brabourne 1914), all records from Paraguay likely represent cagebirds. Furthermore, if the species was fairly common in Paraguay in 1905, it should have been recorded at nearby Sapucái, PAR, where a large collection of birds was obtained at the same time by W. Foster (Oberholser 1902, Chubb 1910).

Black-and-tawny Seedeater
(*Sporophila nigrorufa*)
Reported at N. Chaco (Bertoni 1914a:65, 1939:38), but no details provided.

Stripe-tailed Yellow-Finch
(*Sicalis citrina*)
Orient: several (SI) at S of Arroyo Tagatyjá, Serranía de San Luis, CON, first days of September 1991 (Contreras et al. 1994:5).

Brown-and-yellow Marshbird
(*Pseudoleistes virescens*)
Orient: reported at Encarnación, ITA (Bertoni 1939:39), but no details provided.

DOUBTFUL SPECIES

Lesser Rhea
(*Rhea pennata*)
Chaco: several skins examined from Villazón, General Eugenio A. Garay, and Puesto Estrella, exNAS, and reported to occur in small flocks during winter (Podtiaguin 1944:115), but no measurements or descriptions were provided. In Bolivia its distribution is entirely Andean; because there are no records from the adjacent departamentos in Bolivia (Santa Cruz, Chuquisaca and Tarija; Remsen and Traylor 1989), it is extremely unlikely to occur in Paraguay.

Rufous Crab-Hawk
(*Buteogallus aequinoctialis*)
Orient: often cited for Paraguay at San Ignacio, MIS (e.g., Laubmann 1939:163), on the basis of Azara; reported at S. Cosme, presumably referring to San Cosme y Damián, ITA (Podtiaguin 1944:56).

Lined Forest-Falcon
(*Micrastur gilvicollis*)
Orient: one (SP) at Djaguarasapá, ITA?, 1891 (Bertoni 1901:163), a female described as *Accipiter virgatus* (new species) and later thought to represent an immature *M. gilvicollis* (Bertoni 1907:307, 1918e:247, 1939:23). However, Bertoni's measurements indicate a wing:tail ratio of 1.0, which is within the range of variation in the Barred Forest-Falcon (*M. ruficollis*; 0.95-1.15) and well beyond the range of variation in *M. gilvicollis* (1.18-1.35; Schwartz 1972).

Killdeer
(*Charadrius vociferus*)
Often cited for Paraguay (e.g., Laubmann 1939:90) based on a specimen reported by Sharpe (1896:742; BMNH), but the bird was apparently collected by Seebohm, who is not known to have collected in Paraguay (see Ornithological History section).

American Oystercatcher
(*Haematopus palliatus*)
Often cited for Paraguay (e.g., Laubmann 1939:86) on the basis of an earlier citation attributed to Rengger (Berlepsch 1887:126), and reported at Alto Paraná region (Bertoni

1914a:38), but any Paraguayan locality is too far out of range to be credible.

Andean Avocet
(*Recurvirostra andina*)

Berlepsch (1887:126) cited a record of *Recurvirostra* sp.? as fide Rengger.

Common Ground-Dove
(*Columbina passerina*)

Chaco: one (SP) and several (SI) at Puerto Juan Barbero (locality unknown) and Villa Hayes, Remancito and Chaco-í, PHA (Podtiaguin 1941:23, 1944:114); Orient: reported at Alto Paraná region (Bertoni 1914a:36). These reports presumably refer to the Scaled Dove (*C. squammata*), which was not mentioned by the authors.

Pearly Parakeet
(*Pyrrhura perlata*)

Chaco: reported at Puerto Pinasco, PHA (Bertoni 1939:25), but if correctly identified, the record undoubtedly represents escaped cagebirds or were imported from elsewhere.

Pygmy Nightjar
(*Caprimulgus hirundinaceus*)

Orient: reported at Puerto Bertoni, APN (Bertoni 1939:25).

Red-tailed Comet
(*Sappho sparganura*)

Chaco: reported at S.W. Paraguay (Bertoni 1939:27), but no details provided; one (SP) at Paraguay (FMNH 46377), with the specimen label indicating it was collected by White, but nobody of that name has been known to collect in Paraguay (see Ornithological History section) and no other information was provided on the specimen label. Although recorded in the adjacent departamentos of Bolivia (Santa Cruz, Chuquisaca and Tarija; Remsen and Traylor 1989), all records are from the Andes (J. V. Remsen pers. comm.).

Spot-breasted Woodpecker
(*Colaptes punctigula*)

Chaco: one (SI?) at APY, between 18 October and 4 November 1984 (López 1985:12); two (SI) at 58°32'N, 23°30'W (undoubtedly 23°30'S, 58°32'W; east of Pozo Colorado), PHA, December 1983 (Peris and Suarez 1985:132). These records are far south of the nearest known records in Bolivia (Remsen and Traylor 1989).

Ringed Woodpecker
(*Celeus torquatus*)

Reported without details by Bertoni (1914a:49).

Sulphur-bearded Spinetail
(*Cranioleuca sulphurifera*)

Orient: reported at Reserva Natural del Bosque Mbaracayú, CAN (Meisel et al. 1992:6).

Pallid Spinetail
(*Cranioleuca pallida*)

Orient: reported for N.E. Paraguay (Bertoni 1939:30).

White-fringed Antwren
(*Formicivora grisea*)

Chaco: several (PH) measured and well described at Parque Nacional Defensores del Chaco, exCHA, August 1989, July and August 1990 (Madroño N. 1991, pers. comm.), but the photographs (VIREO VO6/16/001, VO6/16/002, VO6/16/003) clearly refer to the Black-bellied Antwren (*F. melanogaster*; R. S. Ridgely pers. comm.), which was previously unrecorded for Paraguay (see Distributional Notes section).

Mottle-backed Elaenia
(*Elaenia gigas*)

Orient: reported at Puerto Bertoni, APY (Bertoni 1939:32).

Plain-crested Elaenia
(*Elaenia cristata*)

Orient: reported at Alto Paraná?, Campos N.W. (Bertoni 1914a:56, 1939:32).

White-throated Tyrannulet
(*Mecocerculus leucophrys*)

Orient: reported at Parque Nacional Cerro Corá, AMA (López undated:10).

Smoke-colored Pewee
(*Contopus fumigatus*)

Orient: several (SI) thought to represent large *Contopus* at Estancia San Antonio, APN, Estancia Itabó, CAN, Estancia La Golondrina, CAA, and Lagunita, Reserva Natural del Bosque Mbaracayú, CAN, July-September 1992 (Brooks et al. 1993:80).

Dusky-capped Flycatcher
(Myiarchus tuberculifer)

Chaco: reported at Las Delicias, PHA, 1983 or 1984 (Peris et al. 1987:30), but no details provided and no other *Myiarchus* sp. reported.

Black-capped Becard
(Pachyramphus marginatus)

Orient: one (SP) at Sapucái, PAR, 15 March 1904 (Chubb 1910:606; BMNH?), but identification questionable.

Black-billed Thrush
(Turdus ignobilis)

Chaco: reported at N.W. Chaco? (Bertoni 1939:34).

Cocoa Thrush
(Turdus fumigatus)

Orient: one (SP) at Puerto Bertoni, APN, 1917 (Bertoni 1919a:257, 1926:398). The description of a juvenile female is inadequate.

White-striped Warbler
(Basileuterus leucophrys)

Orient: reported at Río Paraná (Bertoni 1939:23), perhaps referring to records farther north in Brazil.

Azure-shouldered Tanager
(Thraupis cyanoptera)

Orient: reported at Puerto Bertoni, APN (Bertoni 1926:397), but later regarded as doubtful (Bertoni 1939:37).

Yellow-green Grosbeak
(Caryothraustes canadensis)

Orient: reported at Jejuí, presumably the Río Jejuí Guazú, SAP and CAN (Bertoni 1939:37), but no details provided; if a valid record, it probably represented an escaped cagebird.

Red-capped Cardinal
(Paroaria gularis)

Orient: one (SP) at Puerto Pagani, CON, August-November 1893 (Salvadori 1895:6; MZT), but the description of bill color clearly refers to the Yellow-billed Cardinal (*P. capitata*).

Yellow-striped Brush-Finch
(Atlapetes citrinellus)

Orient: one (SP?) at Río Aguaray-Guazú, SAP or CAN, April 1920 (Bertoni 1924:279); reported at Jejuí (Bertoni 1939:37), presumably referring to the Río Jejuí-Guazú, SAP and

CAN, of which the Río Aguaray Guazú is a tributary. There is also a Río Aguaray-Guazú in southern PHA (Fig. 2), but because both reports probably refer to the same record, the river in the Central Paraguay region is more probable. If the record is valid, the specimen probably represented an escaped cagebird.

Variable Seedeater
(Sporophila americana)

Chaco: reported at 58°32'N, 23°30'W (undoubtedly 23°30'S, 58°32'W; east of Pozo Colorado), PHA, December 1983 (Peris and Suarez 1985:132), but probably refers to Lined Seedeater (*S. lineola*), which is very similar.

Hooded Seedeater
(Sporophila melanops)

Orient: reported at Asunción, CEN (Bertoni 1914a:65, 1939:38), based in part on Azara's description of bird number 126 (also referred to as Chestnut Seedeater [*S. cinnamomea*; Bertoni 1914a:65, 1939:38]). This species is known only from the type specimen and may not even be a valid species (Ridgely and Tudor 1989).

White-throated Seedeater
(Sporophila albogularis)

Reported as questionable in Paraguay (Bertoni 1914a:64, 1939:38).

Red-backed Sierra-Finch
(Phrygilus dorsalis)

Reported without details (Bertoni 1939:37) and attributed to Pereyra.

Yellow-hooded Blackbird
(Agelaius icterocephalus)

Chaco: one (SP) female at Fortín Conchitas, BOQ, 28 March 1962 (Steinbacher 1968:363; SMF 38312). Steinbacher (pers. comm.) stated that the identification is questionable and that the specimen may be an odd Unicolored Blackbird (*A. cyanopus*), but the published measurements appear to be too small. If correctly identified, the record may represent an escaped cagebird. Because the nearest known locality is in the Amazon Basin (Ridgely and Tudor 1989) and there are no records from Bolivia (Remsen and Traylor 1989), vagrancy to Paraguay seems unlikely, although it has been recorded in the Caribbean at Curaçao and Bonaire (Ridgely and Tudor

134

1989:347). Ridgely and Tudor (1989:347) reported a small population of escaped cagebirds established at Villa, in southern Peru, during the 1960s.

Finally, in a recently published checklist of the birds of Paraguay, Contreras et al. (1990) uncritically accepted an additional 19 species for which no details have been published; many of these have been listed in general works such as Dunning and Ridgely (1982), Mason and Steffee (1982), Wendelken (1983), Altman and Smith (1986, 1989, 1993), and Narosky and Yzurieta (1987, 1989). These include: Darwin's Nothura (*Nothura darwinii*), Solitary Eagle (*Harpyhaliaetus solitarius*), Ocellated Crake (*Micropygia schomburgkii*), Willet (*Catoptrophorus semipalmatus*), Band-tailed Nighthawk (*Nyctiprogne leucopyga*), Biscutate Swift (*Streptoprocne biscutata*), White-chinned Sapphire (*Hylocharis cyanus*), White-bellied Hummingbird (*Amazilia chionogaster*), Mottled Piculet (*Picumnus nebulosus*), Scale-throated Earthcreeper (*Upucerthia dumetaria*), Araucaria Tit-Spinetail (*Leptasthenura setaria*), Bay-capped Wren-Spinetail (*Spartanoica maluroides*), Spot-breasted Antvireo (*Dysithamnus stictothorax*), Spotted Bamboowren (*Psilorhamphus guttatus*), Plumbeous Tyrant (*Knipolegus cabanisi*), Black-capped Manakin (*Piprites pileatus*), Bare-necked Fruitcrow (*Gymnoderus foetidus*), Blackpoll Warbler (*Dendroica striata*), and Coal-crested Finch (*Charitospiza eucosma*).

Planalto Hermit *(Phaethornis pretrei)*   Dan Brown

BIOGEOGRAPHY

"...the faunal distinctness of the Chaco from the country east of the Río Paraguay becomes increasingly apparent."

P. Brodkorb (1938c:1)

"Many genera of the Oriental Region...are completely absent in the Chaco Region..."
B. Podtiaguin (1941:34), translated from Spanish

"The only apparent physical barrier [in the Chaco], the rather broad Paraguay-Paraná river system, serves as an eastern limit for some birds, but many species cross the river..."
L. L. Short (1975:167, 168)

As a synthetic discipline, biogeography endeavors to explain the distributional patterns of plants and animals. However, organisms differ greatly in their ecological requirements, and as a consequence their spatial and temporal distribution varies greatly, even among closely related taxa, often resulting in complex patterns that can be difficult to explain. Birds are no exception, and numerous hypotheses have been proposed to explain their distribution. Although the complex distributional patterns of South American birds have been the subject of much debate during the last few decades, most studies have focused on avifaunas of the Andean highlands (e.g., Fjeldså and Krabbe 1990) and tropical lowlands (e.g., Haffer 1985, 1987). In contrast, there have been relatively few biogeographical studies of avifaunas in the subtropical lowlands of South America (e.g., Short 1975, 1980, Nores 1992).

This section is intended to augment our knowledge of the patterns of bird distribution in Paraguay and the factors that may affect them. I begin by reviewing the current hypotheses regarding the origin and diversification of the South American avifauna. I then document patterns of bird distribution in the seven geographical regions of Paraguay by comparing species richness, faunal similarity, faunal uniqueness, affinities with other South American areas, and body sizes of birds in the different regions. I further attempt to evaluate the relative importance of geographical and ecological barriers to bird dispersal by testing a suite of predictions regarding the efficacy of the Paraguay River and the forest/savanna transition as potential barriers to bird dispersal.

ORIGINS

Biological Diversification

Numerous hypotheses have been proposed to explain the diversification of the South American avifauna. These hypotheses can be grouped into three general models of differentiation: (1) vicariance models, which postulate that differentiation occurred in allopatry following fragmentation of contiguous ancestral populations by physiographic or ecological barriers; (2) dispersal models, which postulate that differentiation occurred in allopatry following long-distance dispersal of "founder" individuals across pre-existing barriers; and (3) parapatric models, which postulate that differentiation occurred in parapatric populations situated along ecological gradients, with zones of reduced gene flow coinciding with relatively abrupt environmental changes. All three types of explanations likely contributed to the diversification of the South American avifauna. However, the relative contribution of each remains uncertain and has been the subject of considerable controversy. Currently the most widely discussed hypotheses include three vicariance models and a parapatric model; each of these is briefly described below.

Refuge Hypothesis. Among the various hypotheses proposed, the most widely accepted is the "refuge hypothesis," which was formally proposed by Haffer (1969) and further refined during his studies of bird distribution in the Neotropics (e.g., Haffer 1974, 1978, 1982, 1985, 1987). The refuge hypothesis postulates that climatic oscillations during the Tertiary and particularly during the Quaternary caused forests and savannas to alternately expand and contract, thus fragmenting species' ranges and isolating portions of formerly contiguous ancestral biotas in ecological refugia where species either became extinct, survived unchanged, or differentiated. A return of favorable conditions allowed isolated populations to expand and achieve secondary contact. Because not all species would be expected to disperse at the same rate, the present centers of high diversity and endemism are postulated to represent the localities of paleoecological refugia; theoretically these should be situated between present faunal "suture zones," which represent zones of secondary contact between closely related taxa. The refuge hypothesis invokes differentiation in allopatry following vicariance and thus represents a vicariance model of differentiation.

An abundance of biological, geophysical and paleoecological evidence has been marshalled in support of the refuge hypothesis (e.g., Prance 1982, Whitmore and Prance 1987). However, the hypothesis is frequently challenged by critics, who have contended that: (1) there is substantial evidence of cyclic changes of vegetation during the Quaternary in areas peripheral to the Amazon, but only meager evidence of vegetation changes in the Amazon basin (e.g., Colinvaux 1989); (2) the locations of postulated paleoecological refugia can only be inferred from present distributional patterns of plants and animals, and these patterns do not always support predictions of the hypothesis (e.g., Beven et al. 1984); (3) congruent area cladograms for diverse clades combined with paleogeographical evidence indicate that differentiation of present taxa occurred throughout the Cenozoic, not primarily during the Quaternary (e.g., Cracraft and Prum 1988); and (4) differentiation and congruent area cladograms can be explained by current peripheral isolation and current ecological factors without invoking historical factors (e.g., Endler 1982a, b).

The extent to which differentiation of Paraguayan birds may have occurred in the postulated refugia can only be speculated. Most of the forest refugia postulated for South America by Haffer (1969, 1974) are primarily in the tropical latitudes, far from Paraguay, with the nearest refugia comprising the "Goiás refuge" in south-central Brazil and the "Serra do Mar refuge" in subtropical southeastern Brazil. However, forest refugia apparently occurred, and still occur, in the mountains of northwestern Argentina (Nores and Cerana 1990) and presumably in other portions of subtropical and temperate South America (e.g., Brown and Prance

1987). Haffer (1985) suggested that the postulated forest and non-forest "areas of endemism" (see discussion below) in Neotropical lowlands, including the non-forest Chaco (including western Paraguay) and Campos Cerrados (adjacent to northeastern Paraguay), "may be linked historically to the formation of Quaternary ecological refugia and may indicate their general geographical location" (p. 137).

River Hypothesis. Two other vicariance models provide alternatives to the refuge hypothesis. The first of these is the "river hypothesis" (Haffer 1982) or "riverine-barrier hypothesis" (Capparella 1988, 1991), which was implicit in the writings of early naturalists who studied the distribution of Amazonian animals (e.g., see Sick 1967, Haffer 1974), later dismissed by proponents of other hypotheses (e.g., Croizat 1958, Haffer 1969, 1974, 1982), partially resurrected by Cracraft and Prum (1988), and further developed by Capparella (1988, 1991). The river hypothesis postulates that the formation of Amazonian rivers, initiated by orogenic events in the Andes, effectively fragmented the distribution of forest birds by forming riverine barriers to gene flow between formerly contiguous populations. The vicariant agent of the river hypothesis (Amazonian rivers) is directly observable (Capparella 1991); in contrast, the vicariant agent of the refuge hypothesis (alternating expansions and contractions of forest and savanna) can only be inferred. The refuge hypothesis also recognizes the importance of riverine barriers, but postulates that rivers merely limit the dispersal of birds from refugia, and conveniently provide locations where secondary contact zones can form by reducing gene flow between closely related species that would otherwise cross the river if not for a closely related competitor on the other side.

The river hypothesis predicts that rivers form substantial dispersal barriers and that the contact zones between sister taxa should coincide with major rivers. These predictions are upheld by the well-documented pattern of Amazonian rivers delimiting the ranges of numerous taxa of birds and separating many pairs of closely related taxa, in particular understory *terra firme* forest birds such as manakins, woodcreepers and antbirds (e.g., see reviews by Sick 1967, Haffer 1974, 1979, 1982, 1985, 1987, Capparella 1988, 1991). However, the distribution of many species appears to be unaffected by large rivers. Other species circumvent larger rivers by crossing farther upstream, where the rivers cease to be barriers and where hybridization often occurs between sister taxa at the subspecies level. Also, the contact zones between closely related taxa often occur between rivers, in the middle of the forest, which would not be expected if the rivers are the principal vicariant agents in Amazonia.

The river hypothesis predicts that genotypic differentiation should occur between populations of *terra firme* forest understory birds separated by major Amazonian rivers, regardless of taxonomic affinity or level of phenotypic differentiation (Capparella 1991). Capparella (1988) and others have documented genetic differentiation between river-divided populations of at least five monotypic species (lacking phenotypic differentiation) and between three pairs of closely related, phenotypically differentiated taxa whose ranges are delimited by Amazonian rivers (see Capparella 1991). As Capparella pointed out, this evidence does not rule out the refuge hypothesis, but it obviates the need of postulating paleoecological refugia for differentiation in *terra firme* forest understory birds.

According to Capparella (1991), the river hypothesis also predicts that the time-calibrated genetic distance values (interpreted as a time estimate) between sister taxa separated by major Amazonian rivers will cluster around 1-2 million years ago (m.y.a.), when the Amazonian rivers are thought to have formed. In contrast, the refuge hypothesis predicts a spread of values of up to 6 m.y.a., when the climatic fluctuations of the Quaternary and late Tertiary are thought to have begun (Capparella 1991). The studies by Capparella (1988) and others found a median value of 1.6 m.y.a., which supports the river hypothesis at least for the few pairs of taxa studied thus far. However, the exact time frames for the formation of Amazonian Rivers and for the initiation of climatic oscillations are equivocal, as is the assumption of constant mutation rates in the neutral mutation model for the evolution of electrophoretic character states.

The possibility of riverine barriers serving as a potential vicariant agent farther south, in subtropical South America, has also been suggested by several authors, in particular for the Paraguay-Paraná River system (e.g., Brodkorb 1939b, Gallardo 1979, Myers 1982). However, this hypothesis has not been thoroughly analyzed. In general the major river systems in subtropical South America are not as large and wide as the Amazonian rivers, and fewer species have ranges that are known to be delimited by major

rivers (e.g., see Short 1975 for birds). The potential role of the Paraguay River as a vicariant agent is further addressed in my analyses of dispersal barriers to bird distribution in Paraguay (see below).

Paleogeography Hypothesis. A second vicariance model that provides an alternative to the refuge hypothesis is the "paleogeography hypothesis" (Haffer and Sick 1993; previously referred to as the "island hypothesis" [Haffer 1982]), which was proposed by Chapman (1917) to explain the disjunction of Chocó-Central American taxa on the west side of the Andes from closely related taxa east of the Andes. This hypothesis was widely accepted during the early 20th century (e.g., Croizat 1958), but dismissed by Haffer (1969, 1974, 1982) and resurrected in a modified form by Cracraft and Prum (1988). The paleogeography hypothesis postulates that multiple geotectonic events (e.g., uplift of the Andes, marine transgressions, etc.), occurring throughout the Cenozoic, alternately fragmented and fused contiguous populations of organisms.

Cracraft and Prum (1988) and Prum (1988) documented congruence in the geographical patterns of speciation for several diverse clades of Neotropical birds. The congruence of area cladograms for these clades, combined with paleogeographical evidence, suggest that differentiation of extant taxa occurred through a series of vicariance events operating at various times during the Cenozoic, not just during the late Tertiary and Quaternary as predicted by both the refuge and river hypotheses. These events likely included uplift of the Andes, which apparently occurred intermittently throughout the Cenozoic, and the formation of riverine barriers in Amazonia.

In subtropical South America, Quaternary climatic changes and accompanying changes in vegetation are generally thought to be the vicariance events leading to the isolation and subsequent differentiation of birds to the east of the Andes in the Chaco (e.g., Short 1975, Nores 1992) and southeastern Brazil (e.g., Sick 1985), but events during both the Tertiary and Quaternary have been invoked to explain speciation phenomena of birds in Patagonia (e.g., Vuilleumier 1991). Thus far the best documented patterns of vicariance in Paraguay are the disjunct distributions of closely related taxa separated by the xerophytic Chaco and the coincident occurrence of contact zones along the eastward-flowing Pilcomayo River (Nores 1992). The implications of these vicariant patterns are further addressed in my analyses of dispersal barriers to bird distribution in Paraguay (see below).

Parapatric Differentiation Hypothesis. The "parapatric differentiation hypothesis" was proposed by Endler (1982a, b) as an alternative to the vicariance models of biological diversification in the Neotropics. This hypothesis postulates that differentiation occurred in parapatric populations situated along ecological gradients, and that current ecological barriers reduced gene flow between populations of closely related taxa that exhibit "step clines" (rather than "suture zones"), which are interpreted as zones of primary intergradation (rather than secondary intergradation). The hypothesis postulates that congruent area cladograms result from shared patterns of selection regimes on characters, rather than by vicariance, and thus provide no information about historical relationships (e.g., vicariance).

This hypothesis has been challenged by various workers, who generally contend that divergence occurs primarily in allopatric populations (e.g., Mayr and O'Hara 1986). Cracraft and Prum (1988) and Prum (1988) contended that large suites of postulated derived characters in diverse clades are unlikely to have evolved by parallel selection, and argued that congruent area cladograms among diverse taxa refute the hypothesis of parapatric differentiation.

In summary, several hypotheses have been advanced to explain the diversity of the South American avifauna, but the evidence for each is circumstantial. Much more information is needed about the geotectonic and paleoecological history of South America before the biogeographical history of the South American avifauna can be accurately reconstructed.

Centers of Endemism

Although determining the geographical origin of a taxon is fraught with theoretical problems (e.g., Brown and Gibson 1983), taxa whose distributions are confined to a relatively small geographical area are generally assumed to have evolved there. An extension of this assumption is that areas characterized by congruent distributions of narrowly endemic taxa constitute "centers of endemism" where these taxa are postulated to have differentiated. Although centers of endemism may also represent paleoecologi-

cal refugia (see discussion above), the concept of refugia is derived in part from observable patterns of endemism and includes additional assumptions about the origin of refugia as a result of climatic changes during the Quaternary.

The scale-dependent concept of endemic centers can be useful in testing hypotheses about the historical biogeography of a continental biota, such as the avifauna of tropical South America (e.g., Cracraft 1985, Cracraft and Prum 1988, Prum 1988). Thus far there have been no rigorous analyses or critiques of the postulated centers of endemism in subtropical South America (Müller 1973, Cracraft 1985, Haffer 1985, Ridgely and Tudor 1989), and I do not intend to do so here. However, several of these centers are postulated to occur in the proximity of Paraguay and merit further comment.

Because of the low degree of endemism of Chaco birds, Short (1975) argued that its avifauna was largely derived from other areas in South America. However, Short (1975) and others (e.g., Müller 1973, Cracraft 1985, Haffer 1985, Ridgely and Tudor 1989) have recognized the Chaco (west of the Paraguay River) as a center of endemism for at least a handful of birds. Furthermore, the distribution of numerous subspecies of Paraguayan birds is restricted to the Chaco and nearby areas, including several disjunct taxa with sister groups in the similarly arid Caatinga of eastern Brazil (Short 1975, Cracraft 1985).

The Campos Cerrados center of endemism is postulated to occur to the northeast of Paraguay (Müller 1973, Cracraft 1985, Haffer 1985, Ridgely and Tudor 1989). In Paraguay, several species of narrowly endemic Campos Cerrados birds occur in the Campos Cerrados region and adjacent portions of the Matogrosense and Central Paraguay regions.

The Paraná center of endemism is postulated to occur just to the east and southeast of Paraguay (Müller 1973, Cracraft 1985). The distribution of several species of breeding birds in Paraguay is restricted to this center and nearby areas; most of these species are distributed in the Alto Paraná region and the eastern Central Paraguay region of Paraguay. Cracraft (1985) pointed out that the distribution of numerous species of birds is restricted to the Serra do Mar center (forests and mountains of coastal southern Brazil) and Paraná centers of endemism, which together comprise a distinct center of endemism (unnamed). A large number of breeding birds in Paraguay, occurring primarily in the Central Paraguay and Alto Paraná regions, are representative of the "narrow endemics" of this larger combined center (see Cracraft 1985).

Presumably a large proportion of the breeding birds of Paraguay originated in the proposed centers of endemism of subtropical South America. However, many of these species are broadly distributed on the continent, and it is useless to speculate where each species originated. Rather than attempting to pinpoint the center of origin for each species, an analysis of bird distribution on a much broader scale may be more useful in revealing general trends about the origin of birds in the different regions of Paraguay. I have attempted to do this under the "regional affinities" subheading in the following analyses of regional comparisons.

Red-crested Cardinal *(Paroaria coronata)*

Dan Brown

Table 4: Comparison of species richness of breeding birds among geographical regions

Geographical regions: AC=Alto Chaco; AP=Alto Paraná; BC=Bajo Chaco; CC=Campos Cerrados; CP=Central Paraguay; MG=Matogrosense; ÑE=Ñeembucú.

Ecological/Taxonomic Group	Paraguay	Geographical Regions						
		AC	MG	BC	CC	CP	ÑE	AP
All breeding birds combined*	576	304	270	314	387	469	305	428
Ground-dwelling non-passerines	14	9	4	7	8	9	8	8
Waterbirds	82	69	48	63	57	68	55	53
Raptors/scavengers	62	43	32	37	44	47	30	52
Frugivorous non-passerines*	45	20	26	23	37	39	21	37
Insectivorous non-passerines	54	24	25	27	36	47	29	41
Nectarivorous non-passerines	16	5	3	5	12	14	6	14
Insectivorous passerines	189	83	79	90	117	152	93	133
Omnivorous passerines	114	51	53	62	76	93	63	90

*Glaucous Macaw (*Anodorhynchus glaucus*) excluded from geographical regions

REGIONAL COMPARISONS

Thus far there have been no published comparisons of the avifaunas on opposite sides of the Paraguay River. Although Short (1975) compared the avifauna of the Gran Chaco, which encompasses portions of Bolivia and Argentina in addition to Paraguay, with other geographical regions of South America, he did not compare the Chaco avifauna with that of eastern Paraguay because the latter region was regarded as "ecotonal between campo (north, northeast), pantanal and chaco (west), southeastern Brazilian forest (east, southeast), and pampas (south-central)" (p. 333). However, now that reasonably accurate lists have been compiled for the different regions of Paraguay, thorough comparisons of the component bird faunas of Paraguay can be made. Furthermore, the patterns derived from such comparisons may be indicative of the processes affecting bird distribution in Paraguay, in particular the relative importance of geographical and ecological factors.

Species Richness

Species richness (defined as the number of breeding species) of all breeding birds combined ranks highest in the heavily forested Central Paraguay and Alto Paraná regions, respectively (Table 4). This is presumably due to a greater diversity of foraging niches, food items, nesting sites, etc., in taller humid forests than in the relatively open savannas and shorter scrub forests elsewhere in Paraguay (e.g., Haffer 1990). The moderately forested Campos Cerrados region ranks third (Table 4). The Matogrosense and Ñeembucú regions rank lower than or roughly equal to the relatively arid Alto Chaco and Bajo Chaco regions (Table 4), but this may in part be an artifact of less sampling in the Matogrosense and Ñeembucú regions. The Matogrosense region, which is the most depauperate, has 58% of the number of species recorded in the Central Paraguay region, which is the richest (Table 4).

Regional comparisons of species richness for each of the eight ecological/taxonomic groups of birds (see Table 3, p.48 for list of families) indicate that species richness of ground-dwelling non-passerines (mostly tinamous) is highest in the semiarid Alto Chaco and humid Central Paraguay regions, lowest in the Matogrosense region, and moderately high in the other regions (Table 4). Species richness of the most depauperate region is only 44% of that in the richest region (Table 4); however, further field work will likely add several species, such as the Small-billed Tinamou (*Crypturellus parvirostris*), Tataupa Tinamou (*Crypturellus tataupa*) and Red-winged Tinamou (*Rhynchotus rufescens*), to the Matogrosense region. Species richness of ground-dwelling non-passerines is equally high in regions of the Chaco and Orient, in contrast with the other ecological/taxonomic groups of birds (except waterbirds) in which species richness is highest (marginally so in raptors/scavengers) in regions of the Orient (Table 4).

The number of waterbird species is relatively constant among the regions, with species richness in the most depauperate region (Matogrosense) being 70% of that in the Alto Chaco region, which is relatively arid but marginally the richest region in Paraguay (Table 4). The relatively depauperate waterbird fauna of the Alto Paraná region may be due to a paucity of wetlands. The relatively low number of waterbirds recorded in the Matogrosense and Ñeembucú regions (Table 4), both of which have an abundance of wetlands, is undoubtedly due to less sampling in these regions (fewer species of the rarer waterbirds, such as ducks and rails, have been recorded).

Species richness of raptors and scavengers is highest in the forested regions of the Orient (Alto Paraná, Central Paraguay and Campos Cerrados regions, respectively; Table 4). Because many species of raptors are rare (large-bodied, top-level carnivores generally occur in low densities), the lower numbers of raptors in the Matogrosense and Ñeembucú regions (Table 4) can be attributed to incomplete sampling in these regions. Species richness in the most depauperate region (Ñeembucú) is 58% of that in the richest region (Table 4).

The number of species of frugivorous non-passerines (mostly doves and parrots) is highest in the forested regions of the Orient (Central Paraguay, Alto Paraná and Campos Cerrados regions; Table 4). A moderate number of frugivorous non-passerines occur in the heavily forested but subhumid Matogrosense region of the Chaco (Table 4). Species richness is lowest in the semiarid Alto Chaco region, with only 51% of that in the richest region (Table 4). Myers and Wetzel (1983) noted a similar reduction in frugivorous phyllostomid bats in the Chaco Boreal, reflecting a reduced diversity of fruiting plants (Sarmiento 1972, Esser 1982).

Species richness of insectivorous non-passerines is highest in the Central Paraguay, Alto Paraná and Campos Cerrados regions, respectively, lowest in the Alto Chaco region, and relatively equivalent in the other regions (Table 4). Species richness in the most depauperate region is 51% of that in the richest region (Table 4).

Nectarivorous non-passerines (hummingbirds) are richest in the heavily forested regions of the Orient (Central Paraguay and Alto Paraná regions), and slightly less in the moderately forested Campos Cerrados region (Table 4). The Ñeembucú region has only half as many species as the Campos Cerrados region, whereas the more arid Chaco regions (Matogrosense, Alto Chaco and Bajo Chaco) are exceptionally depauperate (Table 4). Species richness in the most depauperate region (Alto Chaco) is merely 21% of that in the richest regions (Table 4), reflecting a reduced diversity of flowering plants in the drier portions of the Chaco (Sarmiento 1972, Esser 1982).

Species richness of insectivorous passerines and omnivorous passerines, which form the two largest ecological/taxonomic groups, is highest in the forested regions of the Orient (Central Paraguay, Alto Paraná and Campos Cerrados regions, respectively) and lowest in the more arid Chaco regions (Matogrosense, Alto Chaco and Bajo Chaco) and non-forested Ñeembucú region (Table 4). Species richness of insectivorous passerines in the most depauperate region (Matogrosense) is 52% of that in the richest region (Central Paraguay; Table 4). Of the omnivorous passerines, species richness in the depauperate Alto Chaco region is 55% of that in the richest Central Paraguay and Alto Paraná regions (Table 4).

142

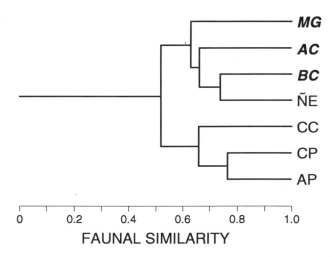

FAUNAL SIMILARITY

Figure 24. UPGMA cluster of Jaccard coefficients of similarity among the seven geographical regions of Paraguay for all breeding birds combined (573 species). Geographical regions are abbreviated as follows: AC=Alto Chaco; AP=Alto Paraná; BC=Bajo Chaco; CC=Campos Cerrados; CP=Central Paraguay; MG=Matogrosense; ÑE=Ñeembucú. The Chaco regions are indicated by bold and italicized type.

Faunal Similarity

A comparison among the different coefficients of similarity for all breeding birds combined in each pair of regions indicated that the Jaccard and Dice coefficients were highly correlated ($r=0.997$, $n=21$, $P<0.001$), whereas the Simpson coefficient showed a weaker but significant correlation with both the Jaccard ($r=0.630$, $n=21$, $P<0.01$) and Dice coefficients ($r=0.643$, $n=21$, $P<0.01$). The weaker correlation of the Simpson coefficient, which is based on the number of species in the most depauperate region, reflects the disparity in species richness among the different regions. In many comparisons among the ecological/taxonomic groups, the Simpson coefficient was equal to 1.0, whereas the Jaccard and Dice coefficients were considerably less. The Simpson coefficient of similarity was generally less informative than the Jaccard and Dice coefficients, whereas the latter two coefficients yielded results that were virtually identical. The Jaccard coefficient, which simply represents a percentage of the species shared between two faunas, is perhaps the most commonly used and most intuitive measure of faunal similarity, and is the one I chose to use in my biogeographical analyses.

A cluster analysis of faunal similarity for all breeding birds combined indicated that the Chaco regions did not cluster separately from the Orient

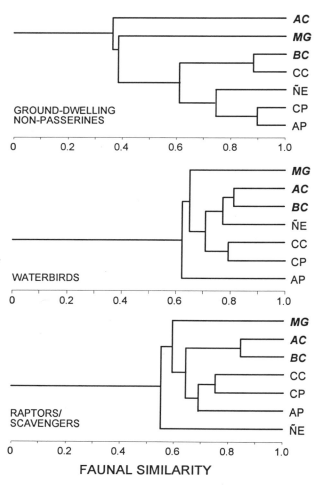

FAUNAL SIMILARITY

Figure 25. UPGMA clusters of Jaccard coefficients of similarity among the seven geographical regions of Paraguay for the ecological/taxonomic groups of birds and forest understory birds. Abbreviations for geographical regions are given in Fig. 24. The Chaco regions are indicated by bold and italicized type.

regions, with the Chaco-like Ñeembucú region of the Orient being more similar to the Chaco regions than to the other regions of the Orient (Fig. 24). Separate cluster analyses for each of the ecological/taxonomic groups indicated that the Chaco regions clustered separately from the Orient regions for only two of the eight groups: insectivorous non-passerines and omnivorous passerines (Fig. 25). The Chaco-like Ñeembucú region clustered with the Chaco regions for three of the eight groups: frugivorous non-passerines, nectarivorous non-passerines and insectivorous passerines (Fig. 25).

The avifauna of the Ñeembucú region was most similar to that of the Bajo Chaco region for all breeding birds combined (Fig. 24), but for only one of the eight ecological/taxonomic groups: nectarivorous

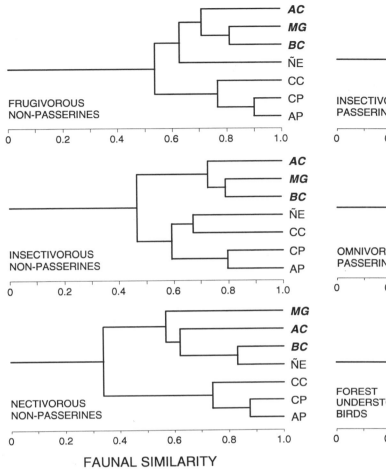

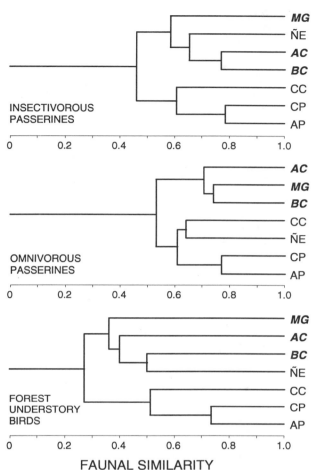

FAUNAL SIMILARITY

FAUNAL SIMILARITY

non-passerines (Fig. 25). In contrast, the Bajo Chaco was most similar to the Alto Chaco for three of the eight groups: waterbirds, raptors/scavengers and insectivorous passerines (Fig. 25).

The heavily forested Central Paraguay and Alto Paraná regions had the most similar avifaunas of any two regions in Paraguay for all breeding birds combined (Fig. 24) and for six of the eight ecological/taxonomic groups: ground-dwelling non-passerines, frugivorous non-passerines, insectivorous non-passerines, nectarivorous non-passerines, insectivorous passerines and omnivorous passerines (Fig. 25). The moderately forested Campos Cerrados region clustered with the Central Paraguay and Alto Paraná regions for all breeding birds combined (Fig. 24) and for four of the eight groups: raptors/scavengers, frugivorous non-passerines, nectarivorous non-passerines and insectivorous passerines (Fig. 25).

The cluster patterns for all breeding birds combined and for the frugivorous non-passerines, insectivorous non-passerines, nectarivorous non-pas-

serines, insectivorous passerines and omnivorous passerines emphasize the faunal similarity of the Ñeembucú region to the Chaco regions, and the distinctness of the Chaco regions and the Chaco-like Ñeembucú region from the more heavily forested regions of the Orient (Figs. 24 and 25). The cluster patterns for ground-dwelling non-passerines, waterbirds, and raptors/scavengers (Fig. 25) differed from the other ecological/taxonomic groups in that no clear pattern emerged.

For all breeding birds combined, the mean Jaccard coefficient value for 21 pairwise comparisons among the seven geographical regions was 0.59 (SD=0.10). Faunal similarity among the regions was greatest for the waterbirds ($\bar{x}$=0.68, SD=0.08), raptors/scavengers ($\bar{x}$=0.62, SD=0.09) and frugivorous non-passerines ($\bar{x}$=0.62, SD=0.13), indicating that the species in these groups were the most widespread in Paraguay. The taxonomic/ecological groups with the lowest mean values, and thus the least widespread in Paraguay, were the nectarivorous non-passerines ($\bar{x}$=0.48, SD=0.20) and the ground-dwelling non-passerines ($\bar{x}$=0.52, SD= 0.20). The mean value was even lower for the forest understory birds ($\bar{x}$=0.35, SD=0.14). The mean values of faunal similarity were intermediate for the remaining groups: 0.54 (SD=0.13) for insectivorous non-passerines; 0.54 (SD=0.13) for insectivorous passerines; and 0.59 (SD=0.11) for omnivorous passerines.

Faunal Uniqueness

The "centers of endemism" concept discussed above deals with postulated areas of endemism in South America, some of which are located in or near Paraguay. I now discuss patterns of faunal "uniqueness" within Paraguay, especially in each of the seven geographical regions of Paraguay.

There are no species of birds that occur exclusively in Paraguay, presumably due to an absence of major dispersal barriers between Paraguay and neighboring countries. Only one currently recognized subspecies, the northern race of the Quebracho Crested-Tinamou (*Eudromia formosa mira*), is endemic to Paraguay (Banks 1977).

Within Paraguay there are many species whose distribution is restricted to a specific area of the country. Each of the seven geographical regions is characterized by one or more species not occurring elsewhere in Paraguay.

As the westernmost (and most arid) region of Paraguay, the Alto Chaco is characterized by numerous resident bird species not recorded elsewhere in Paraguay. These include: Brushland Tinamou (*Nothoprocta cinerascens*), White-bellied Nothura (*Nothura boraquira*), Quebracho Crested-Tinamou (*Eudromia formosa*), Black-headed Duck (*Heteronetta atricapilla*), Black-legged Seriema (*Chunga burmeisteri*), Chaco Earthcreeper (*Upucerthia certhioides*), Scimitar-billed Woodcreeper (*Drymornis bridgesii*), Black-bellied Antwren (*Formicivora melanogaster*), Crested Gallito (*Rhinocrypta lanceolata*), Black-backed Grosbeak (*Pheucticus aureoventris*), Black-crested Finch (*Lophospingus pusillus*), and Stripe-capped Sparrow (*Aimophila strigiceps*). Other species, such as the Crested Hornero (*Furnarius cristatus*), Brown Cacholote (*Pseudoseisura lophotes*), Greater Wagtail-Tyrant (*Stigmatura budytoides*), Golden-billed Saltator (*Saltator aurantiirostris*), Many-colored Chaco-Finch (*Saltatricula multicolor*), and Troupial

(*Icterus icterus*), are nearly restricted to the Alto Chaco region, occurring only marginally in other Chaco regions. Many species occurring in the eastern Chaco (Matogrosense or Bajo Chaco regions) are absent in the more arid Alto Chaco region.

The Matogrosense region's proximity to the Pantanal ecosystem of adjacent Bolivia and Brazil is reflected by a variety of breeding birds occurring only in this part of Paraguay. Each of these birds also occurs on the east bank of the Paraguay River in Brazil, but none has been recorded as far south as the Campos Cerrados region of Paraguay. These include: Pygmy Kingfisher (*Chloroceryle aenea*), Blue-crowned Motmot (*Momotus momota*), Rufous Cacholote (*Pseudoseisura cristata*), Mato Grosso Antbird (*Cercomacra melanaria*), White-backed Fire-eye (*Pyriglena leuconota*), Common Tody-Flycatcher (*Todirostrum cinereum*), and probably the Fawn-breasted Wren (*Thryothorus guarayanus*; see Distributional Notes section).

As the most heavily forested region of the Chaco, numerous species occurring in eastern Paraguay have been recorded in the Matogrosense region but not elsewhere in the Chaco. Most of these presumably breed in this region; some may only stray across the river. These include: Gray-headed Kite (*Leptodon cayanensis*), Gray Hawk (*Buteo nitidus*), Collared Forest-Falcon (*Micrastur semitorquatus*), Hyacinthine Macaw (*Anodorhynchus hyacinthinus*), Golden-collared Macaw (*Ara auricollis*), Pauraque (*Nyctidromus albicollis*), Red-breasted Toucan (*Ramphastos dicolorus*), Plain- crowned Spinetail (*Synallaxis gujanensis*), Buff-browed Foliage-Gleaner (*Syndactyla rufosuperciliata*), Streaked Xenops (*Xenops rutilans*), Sepia-capped Flycatcher (*Leptopogon amauro- cephalus*), Streamer-tailed Tyrant (*Gubernetes yetapa*), Cliff Flycatcher (*Hirundinea ferruginea*), White-winged Swallow (*Tachycineta albiventer*), Silver-beaked Tanager (*Ramphocelus carbo*), White-bellied Warbler (*Basileuterus hypoleucus*), Guira Tanager (*Hemithraupis guira*), Magpie Tanager (*Cissopis leveriana*), and Black-throated Saltator (*Saltator atricollis*).

The Bajo Chaco region has only one presumably resident species found nowhere else in Paraguay. This is the Lake Duck (*Oxyura vittata*), which is distributed primarily to the south of Paraguay.

The Bajo Chaco region's proximity to the Chaco Austral of Argentina and the Orient of Paraguay are reflected by the presence of numerous species of breeding birds not recorded elsewhere in the Chaco: Red-winged Tinamou (*Rhynchotus rufescens*), Red-and-white Crake (*Laterallus leucopyrrhus*), Stygian Owl (*Asio stygius*), White-tailed Goldenthroat (*Polytmus guainumbi*), White-eared Puffbird (*Nystalus chacuru*), Lineated Woodpecker (*Dryocopus lineatus*), Planalto Woodcreeper (*Dendrocolaptes platyrostris*), Rusty-backed Antwren (*Formicivora rufa*), Greenish Elaenia (*Myiopagis viridicata*), Sharp-tailed Tyrant (*Culicivora caudacuta*), Long-tailed Tyrant (*Colonia colonus*), Strange-tailed Tyrant (*Alectrurus risora*), Black-crowned Tityra (*Tityra inquisitor*), Pale-breasted Thrush (*Turdus leucomelas*), Tawny-headed Swallow (*Alopochelidon fucata*), Golden-crowned Warbler (*Basileuterus culicivorus*), White-browed Warbler (*Basileuterus leucoblepharus*), Ruby-crowned Tanager (*Tachyphonus coronatus*), Rufous-rumped Seedeater (*Sporophila hypochroma*), Lesser Seed-Finch (*Oryzoborus angolensis*), Wedge-tailed Grass-Finch (*Emberizoides herbicola*), Long-tailed Reed-Finch (*Donacospiza albifrons*), and Yellow-rumped Marshbird (*Pseudoleistes guirahuro*). Some of these birds may represent migrants or vagrants from the Orient rather than resident breeders.

The Campo Cerrado region's affinities with the Cerrado ecosystem of adjacent Brazil is reflected by several species of resident birds recorded nowhere else in Paraguay. These include: Swallow-tailed Hummingbird (*Eupetomena macroura*), Russet-mantled Foliage-Gleaner (*Philydor dimidiatus*), Reiser's Tyrannulet (*Phyllomyias reiseri*), Rufous-sided Pygmy-Tyrant (*Euscarthmus rufomarginatus*), White-rumped Monjita (*Xolmis velata*), Helmeted Manakin (*Antilophia galeata*), Curl-crested Jay (*Cyanocorax cristatellus*), and Gray-headed Tanager (*Eucometis penicillata*).

Several species of resident birds reach their southernmost limits in the Campos Cerrados region and the adjacent Paraguayan Chaco, and have not been recorded elsewhere in the Orient. These include: Capped Heron (*Pilherodius pileatus*), Hyacinthine Macaw (*Anodorhynchus hyacinthinus*), Golden-collared Macaw (*Ara auricapillus*), Spot-backed Puffbird (*Nystalus maculatus*), Plain-crowned Spinetail (*Synallaxis gujanensis*), Plain Tyrannulet (*Inezia inornata*), and White-bellied Warbler (*Basileuterus hypoleucus*). The only Short-eared Owl (*Asio flammeus*) record from the

Orient is from the Campos Cerrados region, but it likely occurs in other regions of the Orient.

Several species of resident birds have been recorded only in the Central Paraguay region. These include: Pheasant Cuckoo (*Dromococcyx phasianellus*), White-vented Violet-ear (*Colibri serrirostris*), Chestnut-capped Foliage-gleaner (*Hylocryptus rectirostris*), Collared Crescentchest (*Melanopareia torquata*), Russet-winged Spadebill (*Platyrinchus leucoryphus*), Crested Black-Tyrant (*Knipolegus lophotes*), Sedge Wren (*Cistothorus platensis*), and Sooty Grassquit (*Tiaris fuliginosa*). Most of these species are distributed primarily to the east of Paraguay.

Several species of birds that are resident in the Chaco have been recorded in the Central Paraguay region, but not elsewhere in the Orient. These include: Ringed Teal (*Callonetta leucophrys*), Red Shoveler (*Anas platalea*), White-winged Coot (*Fulica leucoptera*), Little Thornbird (*Phacellodomus sibilatrix*), and White-naped Xenopsaris (*Xenopsaris albinucha*). Some of these species are probably vagrants rather than breeders in the Orient. Thus far all Orient records of the Red-and-white Crake (*Laterallus leucopyrrhus*) are from the Central Paraguay region, but it likely occurs in other regions of the Orient.

In spite of its distinction as the most southerly region in Paraguay, the Ñeembucú region has only one presumably breeding species, the Many-colored Rush-Tyrant (*Tachuris rubrigastra*), that has not been recorded elsewhere in Paraguay.

The physiographic resemblance of the Ñeembucú region to the Chaco is reflected by several Chaco species not recorded elsewhere in the Orient. These include: Lesser Canastero (*Asthenes pyrrholeuca*), Short-billed Canastero (*Asthenes baeri*; but possibly a vagrant), Lark-like Brushrunner (*Coryphistera alaudina*), and Rufous-rumped Seedeater (*Sporophila hypochroma*).

The heavily forested Central Paraná and Alto Paraná regions share many species of resident birds not recorded elsewhere in Paraguay; these species are generally distributed to the east of Paraguay, and reach their western distributional limits in the Orient (e.g., Appendix 5). The Alto Paraná region possesses many resident (or formerly resident) species that have not been recorded elsewhere in Paraguay. These include: Brazilian Merganser (*Mergus octosetaceus*), Gray-bellied Hawk (*Accipiter poliogas-*

ter), Tiny Hawk (*Accipiter superciliosus*), Mantled Hawk (*Leucopternis polionota*), Purple-winged Ground-Dove (*Claravis godefrida*), Tawny-browed Owl (*Pulsatrix koeniswaldiana*), Brazilian Pygmy-Owl (*Glaucidium minutissimum*), Rusty-barred Owl (*Strix hylophila*), Black Jacobin (*Melanotrochilus fuscus*), White-wedged Piculet (*Picumnus albosquamatus*), Canebrake Groundcreeper (*Clibanornis dendrocolaptoides*), Black-billed Scythebill (*Campylorhamphus falcularius*), Large-tailed Antshrike (*Mackenziaena leachii*), Rufous-capped Antshrike (*Thamnophilus ruficapillus*), Bertoni's Antbird (*Drymophila rubricollis*), Speckle-breasted Antpitta (*Hylopezus nattereri*), Black-collared Swallow (*Atticora melanoleuca*), Yellow-legged Thrush (*Platycichla flavipes*), Bananaquit (*Coereba flaveola*), Diademed Tanager (*Stephanophorus diadematus*), Black-faced Tanager (*Schistochlamys melanopis*), Black-masked Finch (*Coryphaspiza melanotis*), Buffy-fronted Seedeater (*Sporophila frontalis*), Temminck's Seedeater (*Sporophila falcirostris*), and Blackish-blue Seedeater (*Amaurospiza moesta*).

Three species have been recorded in the Paraguayan Chaco and the Alto Paraná region, but nowhere else in the Orient. These include: Gray Hawk (*Buteo nitidus*), Stygian Owl (*Asio stygius*) and Silver-beaked Tanager (*Ramphocelus carbo*). Each of these species is distributed primarily to the north of Paraguay.

Regional Affinities

The percentage of species occurring in eight broad geographical regions of South America is given for each geographical region of Paraguay in Table 5. The Alto Chaco and Bajo Chaco regions share a high percentage of species with the adjacent Chaco Austral/Pampas to the south and a slightly lower percentage with the Mesopotamia region to the southeast. The Matogrosense region shares a high percentage of species with the adjacent Cerrado region to the north, and a lower percentage with the Chaco Austral/Pampas region farther south. The birds of the Paraguayan Chaco show a high affinity with birds in the adjacent regions of the "arid diagonal" (Caatinga, Campos Cerrados and Chaco, from north to south) of South America, as previously demonstrated by Short (1975).

The Campos Cerrados region of Paraguay shares a high percentage of birds with the Southeastern Brazil region to the southeast and a slightly lower percentage with the adjacent Cerrado region to the northeast. The Central Paraguay and Alto Paraná regions share a high percentage of species with the adjacent Southeastern Brazil region to the east, and a much lower percentage with the Cerrado region farther north. The Ñeembucú region shares a roughly equal percentage of species occurring in the adjacent Mesopotamia region to the south and the more distant Southeastern Brazil region to the east.

Table 5: Percentage of species in each geographical region of Paraguay shared with each of eight broad geographical regions of South America

Geographical regions of South America: AMA=Amazonia; CER=Campos Cerrados; CAA=Caatinga; SEB=Southeastern Brazil; AND=Andean highlands; CHP=Chaco Austral/Pampas; MES=Mesopotamia; PAT=Patagonia (see Methods section)

	Geographical Regions of South America							
Geographical Regions of Paraguay	*AMA*	*CER*	*CAA*	*SEB*	*AND*	*CHP*	*MES*	*PAT*
Alto Chaco	63	81	64	84	25	93	86	19
Matogrosense	71	93	69	87	23	87	85	14
Bajo Chaco	66	87	64	88	22	90	89	17
Campos Cerrados	68	89	63	92	18	68	72	10
Central Paraguay	61	79	55	93	18	62	68	11
Ñeembucú	67	87	63	93	23	85	91	15
Alto Paraná	61	76	55	97	19	58	66	10

Table 6: Comparison of mean body size class of breeding birds among geographical regions

Geographical regions: AC=Alto Chaco; AP=Alto Paraná; BC=Bajo Chaco; CC=Campos Cerrados; CP=Central Paraguay; MG=Matogrosense; ÑE=Ñeembucú

Ecological/Taxonomic Group	AC	MG	BC	CC	CP	ÑE	AP	H
All breeding birds combined								
$\bar{x}$ body size	5.05	4.85	4.84	4.63	4.41	4.59	4.40	14.96*
SD body size	2.96	2.99	2.94	2.87	2.84	2.88	2.80	
Ground-dwelling non-passerines								
$\bar{x}$ body size	8.44	9.00	8.57	8.50	8.56	8.75	8.50	0.65
SD body size	1.42	1.41	1.51	1.41	1.33	1.49	1.41	
Waterbirds								
$\bar{x}$ body size	7.68	8.17	7.78	7.46	7.54	7.80	7.55	3.95
SD body size	2.28	2.28	2.21	2.44	2.27	2.26	2.29	
Raptors/scavengers								
$\bar{x}$ body size	8.05	8.22	8.22	8.18	8.09	8.00	7.92	1.08
SD body size	1.79	1.76	1.75	1.77	1.78	1.76	1.80	
Frugivorous non-passerines								
$\bar{x}$ body size	5.95	6.08	6.00	6.46	6.49	5.95	6.32	1.85
SD body size	1.96	2.13	2.07	2.28	2.20	1.94	2.14	
Insectivorous non-passerines								
$\bar{x}$ body size	4.50	4.68	4.70	4.64	4.49	4.45	4.42	1.32
SD body size	1.38	1.46	1.44	1.42	1.43	1.38	1.45	
Nectarivorous non-passerines								
$\bar{x}$ body size	1.00	1.00	1.00	1.00	1.00	1.00	1.00	-
SD body size	-	-	-	-	-	-	-	
Insectivorous passerines								
$\bar{x}$ body size	2.46	2.32	2.37	2.41	2.32	2.37	2.33	1.21
SD body size	1.12	0.97	0.99	0.98	0.97	0.96	0.91	
Omnivorous passerines								
$\bar{x}$ body size	2.90	2.98	2.97	3.13	2.88	2.89	2.96	1.76
SD body size	1.20	1.31	1.37	1.51	1.39	1.36	1.37	
Forest understory birds								
$\bar{x}$ body size	3.46	2.64	3.29	3.58	3.56	4.39	3.42	4.28
SD body size	2.21	2.02	2.53	2.23	2.43	2.96	2.27	

*P<0.05 (Kruskal-Wallis test)

148

Of the tropical regions, the highest percentage of Amazonia birds occurs in the Matogrosense and Campos Cerrados regions, respectively, and not in the more humid Central Paraguay and Alto Paraná regions. The highest percentage of Cerrado birds occurs in the adjacent Matogrosense and Campos Cerrados regions, respectively. The highest percentage of Caatinga birds occurs in the Matogrosense, with a lower but similar percentage in the other less forested regions. The highest percentage of subtropical Southeastern Brazil birds occurs in the Alto Paraná and Central Paraguay region, with a lower but similar percentage in the other regions.

Of the temperate regions, the highest percentage of Andes birds occurs in the Alto Chaco region, and a slightly lower percentage occurs in the Matogrosense and Ñeembucú regions, respectively; less than a quarter of the avifauna in each geographical region in Paraguay occurs in the Andes. The highest percentage of Chaco Austral/Pampas birds occurs in the Alto Chaco and Bajo Chaco, respectively. The highest percentage of Mesopotamia birds occurs in the Ñeembucú and Bajo Chaco regions, respectively. The highest percentage of Patagonia birds occurs in the Alto Chaco and Ñeembucú regions, respectively, representing less than a fifth of the avifauna of each region.

The Chaco's climate is harsher and less predictable, with more pronounced cycles of rainfall and drought, than that of the Orient (Anonymous 1985). Myers (1982) showed that the rodents inhabiting the Paraguayan Chaco were most closely related to taxa occurring in more temperate areas to the west and south of Paraguay, whereas the rodents inhabiting the Orient were most closely related to taxa occurring in more tropical and subtropical climates to the north and east of Paraguay. The birds of each region in Paraguay occur most frequently in adjacent regions that are ecologically similar. Each region of Paraguay is well represented by tropical, subtropical and temperate species. There is only a slight pattern of temperate species being predominant in the Chaco and tropical/subtropical species in the Orient, with the Matogrosense inhabited by relatively more tropical species than the other Chaco regions and the Ñeembucú region being inhabited by relatively more temperate species than the other Orient regions (Table 5).

A high percentage of species co-occurring in a geographical region of Paraguay and an adjacent geographical region of South America may indicate that many species are derived from these regions. However, modern ecological factors may easily obscure historical patterns of bird distribution, especially in lowlands where there are few physical barriers to bird dispersal.

Body Size

Mean body size varied among the regions (Kruskal-Wallis test, H=14.94, $P<0.05$; Table 6), and was negatively correlated with species richness (Pearson correlation, r=-0.813, n=7 regions, $P<0.05$), indicating that the richer regions had a higher proportion of small-bodied species (Table 7). Presumably a higher diversity of niches is available within the multiple strata of tall forest than within the sparser strata of short forest, which may explain the higher number of small-bodied species in regions with humid forest. Mean body size did not vary significantly among regions for any of the ecological/taxonomic groups of birds or for the forest understory birds (Table 6), which may be expected since a lower diversity of body sizes occurs within groups than among groups.

DISPERSAL BARRIERS

Paraguay River vs Forest-Savanna Barriers

Naturalists have long recognized the peculiar distinctions in the geography, climate, flora and fauna on the opposite sides of the Paraguay River (e.g., M. S. Bertoni 1918). But are the marked differences between the faunas of these regions related to present ecological conditions on each side of the river, or are they the consequence of the river forming a barrier to dispersal? Because of Paraguay's low topographic relief (<800 m), there are no high montane barriers to plant and animal dispersal; thus, the relatively broad Paraguay River is the most likely geographical feature that may have formed a barrier to plant and animal dispersal in Paraguay (e.g., Brodkorb 1939b, Short 1972b, 1975). Alternatively one or more environmental factors, such as a relatively abrupt spatial change in vegetation, may be more of a barrier to bird dispersal than any single geographical feature.

The most plausible ecological barrier to bird dispersal in Paraguay is an abrupt transition from

Table 7: Frequency and percent (below) of breeding birds in different body size classes for each geographical region

Geographical regions: AC=Alto Chaco; AP=Alto Paraná; BC=Bajo Chaco; CC=Campos Cerrados; CP=Central Paraguay; MG=Matogrosense; ÑE= Ñeembucú.

Geographical Region	Body Size Class									
	1	2	3	4	5	6	7	8	9	10
Alto Chaco	22	58	46	32	22	22	20	25	20	37
	7.2	19.1	15.1	10.5	7.2	7.2	6.6	8.2	6.6	12.2
Matogrosense	20	59	46	29	15	17	14	21	15	34
	7.4	21.9	17.0	10.7	5.6	6.3	5.2	7.8	5.6	12.6
Bajo Chaco	25	65	51	34	21	21	20	23	18	36
	8.0	20.7	16.2	10.8	6.7	6.7	6.4	7.3	5.7	11.5
Campos Cerrados	32	88	63	44	27	29	23	23	16	42
	8.3	22.7	16.3	11.4	7.0	7.5	5.9	5.9	4.1	10.9
Central Paraguay	46	119	76	44	36	32	25	28	20	43
	9.8	25.4	16.2	9.4	7.7	6.8	5.3	6.0	4.3	9.2
Ñeembucú	28	67	53	33	22	18	20	20	11	33
	9.2	22.0	17.4	10.8	7.2	5.9	6.6	6.6	3.6	10.8
Alto Paraná	39	111	65	46	34	28	26	27	12	40
	9.1	25.9	15.2	10.7	7.9	6.5	6.1	6.3	2.8	9.3

forest to savanna, which roughly coincides with the course of the upper Paraguay River to the north of Asunción (Dpto. Central), but shifts to the east of the river farther south (Esser 1982; Fig. 6, p. 12). Because the course of the upper Paraguay River roughly coincides with the forest-savanna transition, it may be difficult to distinguish which factor is more important in affecting the distribution of birds in Paraguay. However, the eastward shift of the forest-savanna transition to the south of Asunción provides a convenient distinction between the two potential barriers, and thus makes it easier to test predictions regarding the relative efficacy of geographical and ecological barriers to bird dispersal in Paraguay.

Numerous authors have demonstrated that the Amazon River and some of its larger tributaries delimit the ranges of many taxa of birds, especially farther downstream where the rivers are wider, suggesting that these rivers form a partial, or even complete, barrier to bird dispersal (e.g., Sick 1967, Haffer 1974, 1979, 1985, 1987, Haffer and Fitzpatrick 1985, Capparella 1988, 1991). The rivers also form a partial barrier to gene flow between some

intraspecific bird populations separated by rivers, even between populations lacking phenotypic differentiation (Capparella 1988, 1991). Because the habitats on each side of the Amazon River are similar (mostly rainforest), genotypic and phenotypic differentiation of bird populations separated by Amazonian rivers cannot be attributed to ecological differences alone. As part of the second largest river system in South America, the Paraguay River's potential as a barrier to bird dispersal also merits evaluation.

Myers's (1982) analysis of rodent and bat distribution in Paraguay was the first to reveal an unusually sharp faunal discontinuity coinciding with the Paraguay River. Because the river is only moderately wide and no evidence exists of seas or extensive lakes during the Cenozoic (e.g., Eckle 1959, Putzer 1962), Myers argued that the patterns of mammal distribution in Paraguay reflected dispersal rather than vicariance. Myers concluded that the distinctive rodent and bat faunas on each bank of the Paraguay River did not result from the river being a dispersal barrier, but rather were the result of different edaphic factors (i.e., different soils and vegetation) on each side of the river selectively influencing the immigration of species preadapted to the ecological conditions in adjacent areas. However, the possibility that the river is a dispersal barrier was not rigorously tested and rejected.

Published analyses of Chaco faunas have indicated a fairly high degree of endemism (relative to adjacent areas) for anurans, lizards (Gallardo 1979) and rodents (Myers 1982), but not for butterflies (Brown 1987), snakes (Gallardo 1979), birds (Short 1975) and bats (Myers and Wetzel 1983), suggesting that the Paraguay River may be more of a barrier to dispersal for terrestrial animals (except for snakes, enigmatically) than for volant animals. Myers's (1982) data indicating that faunal similarity was greater for bats than for rodents on each bank of the river would support this hypothesis. Brodkorb (1939b) and Short (1972b, 1975) noted that the ranges of several pairs of closely related taxa (semispecies or subspecies) of birds are separated along the Paraguay River, suggesting that the river could be a partial barrier to gene flow.

Seven predictions of a river barrier hypothesis were tested (see Methods section) to evaluate the relative importance of the Paraguay River and other potential barriers, in particular the forest-savanna transition, to bird dispersal in Paraguay. The results and implications of each test are presented below.

Prediction 1: Regional Cluster Prediction. Because the avifaunas of the Chaco and Orient regions did not cluster separately for all breeding birds combined (Fig. 24), for six of the eight ecological/taxonomic groups and for the forest understory birds (Fig. 25), the Paraguay River does not appear to be a major factor influencing patterns of regional similarity in Paraguay. Furthermore, because the avifauna of the Chaco-like Ñeembucú region was more similar to that of the Chaco regions than to other regions in the Orient for all breeding birds combined (Fig. 24), for three of the eight ecological/taxonomic groups of birds and for forest understory birds (Fig. 25), similarity of habitat appears to be a more important factor than a river barrier in explaining faunal similarity among the regions.

Prediction 2: Distributional Limits Prediction. The distributional limits of an unusually large number of "eastern" and "western" birds occurred within 10 km of the Paraguay River, indicating an abrupt faunal change coinciding with the river (Fig. 26, Appendices 4 and 5). However, of the species

whose distributional limits occurred within 10 km of the river, more species of "western" birds reached their eastern limits on the east side than on the west side (Fig. 26, Appendix 4), which is the opposite of what would be expected if the river formed a dispersal barrier. Although more "eastern" birds reached their western limits within 10 km east of the river than within 10 km west of the river, the large number of species recorded on the west bank (Fig. 26, Appendix 5) suggests that the river is not a substantial dispersal barrier.

The eastern distributional limits of the various ecological/taxonomic groups of "western" birds (Fig. 27) suggest that the river may be more of a barrier to insectivorous non-passerines than for any other group, but the sample size of the group (six species) is too limited to be conclusive. None of the nectarivorous non-passerines was restricted primarily to the Chaco, and the few forest undergrowth species occurring primarily in the Chaco (e.g., Fawn-breasted Wren [*Thryothorus guarayanus*]) were restricted to the Matogrosense region; thus, no comparisons could be made on their distributional limits relative to the Paraguay River.

The western distributional limits of the various ecological/taxonomic groups of "eastern" birds (Fig. 27) suggest that the river may be more of a barrier to the nectarivorous non-passerines (hummingbirds) than for any other group, with only one of nine species (White-tailed Goldenthroat [*Polytmus guainumbi*], which is not a humid forest species) crossing the river into the Chaco, but again the sample size is too limited to be conclusive. The distributional limits of the forest understory birds (Fig. 27), which presumably are less likely to cross an open river than the other groups, do not suggest that the river is an obstacle to their dispersal.

Many forest species have been recorded only as far west as Horqueta (Dpto. Concepción), Nueva Germania (Dpto. San Pedro) and Sapucái (Dpto. Paraguarí), roughly 40-70 km E of the Paraguay River (Fig. 26, Appendix 5). Vast areas of humid forest formerly extended to the east of these localities (Esser 1982; Fig. 6); thus, it is not surprising that so few "eastern" species reach their western limits between 70 and 150 km east of the river. However, to the west of these localities the humid forest becomes fragmented by seasonally flooded savanna and subhumid forest, and extends to the Paraguay River only in the more elevated areas of western Dpto. Concepción and in the vicinity of Asunción,

Dpto. Central (Esser 1982; Fig. 6), where nearly all of the species whose limits occur within 10 km east of the river have been recorded (Appendix 5).

Of the "eastern" forest birds whose distribution extends westward less than 150 km into the Chaco, nearly all have been recorded in the isolated pockets of subhumid forest on hills along the bank of the Paraguay River (e.g., Villa Hayes, Dpto. Presidente Hayes), in gallery forest along Chaco tributaries (e.g., Verde and Pilcomayo Rivers, Dpto. Presidente Hayes), or in the more extensive subhumid forest of the Matogrosense region in Dpto. Alto Paraguay and northern Dpto. Presidente Hayes (Appendix 5). Many "eastern" birds have also been recorded along the gallery forest of Chaco tributaries in Formosa Province and northern Chaco Province, Argentina (Nores 1992; Appendix 5). It thus appears that the distribution of most "eastern" birds is limited more by the absence of adequate forest habitat than by the presence of a moderately wide river.

The numerous records of "eastern" forest birds in patches of appropriate habitat in the eastern Chaco suggest that small populations breed in these areas. Although the "eastern" birds in these areas may represent relict populations that are sedentary, no morphologically differentiated races have been described (e.g., Short 1975); thus, it seems plausible that dispersing individuals freely cross the river in both directions.

Prediction 3: Faunal Similarity Prediction. For all breeding birds combined, faunal similarity for two of the three pairs of adjoining regions divided by the Paraguay River (Matogrosense/Campos Cerrados, Bajo Chaco/Central Paraguay) was lower than that for the six pairs of adjoining regions not divided by the river (Table 8). However, faunal similarity for the river-divided Bajo Chaco/Campos Cerrados regions was higher than that of one and nearly equal to another of the six pairs of adjoining regions not divided by the river (Table 8). Furthermore, faunal similarity between the Bajo Chaco/Ñeembucú regions, which are on opposite sides of the Paraguay River but do not adjoin, was greater than that for three of the six pairs of adjoining regions not divided by a river (Table 8). These patterns indicate that regions divided by the Paraguay River are not necessarily characterized by a reduction in faunal similarity.

The data for each of the eight ecological/taxonomic groups and for the forest understory birds fur-

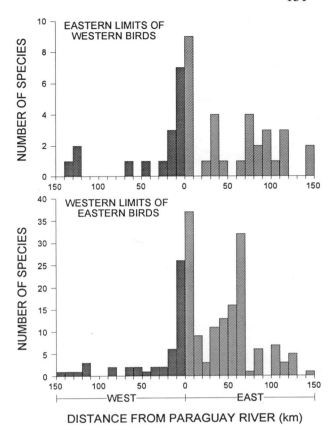

Figure 26. Distributional limits (relative to Paraguay River) of "eastern" and "western" birds whose limits occur within 150 km of the river. Species restricted to Matogrosense and Ñeembucú regions are excluded. Data based on Appendices 4 and 5.

ther indicate that adjoining regions divided by the Paraguay River often have more similar avifaunas than adjoining regions not divided by the river (Table 8). The data for ground-dwelling non-passerines, which presumably have weak dispersal abilities, indicate that faunal similarity between the Bajo Chaco/Campos Cerrados regions, which are divided by the Paraguay River, is higher than that for five of the six pairs of adjoining regions not divided by a river (Table 8). The data for forest understory birds, which presumably includes the species that are least likely to cross an open river, indicate that faunal similarity between the Bajo Chaco/Ñeembucú regions, which are on opposite sides of the Paraguay River but do not adjoin, is higher than that for four of the six pairs of adjoining regions not divided by a river (Table 8). These results suggest that the Paraguay River is no more of a barrier for birds with low dispersal abilities (e.g., ground-dwelling non-passerines and forest understory birds) than for any other group of birds.

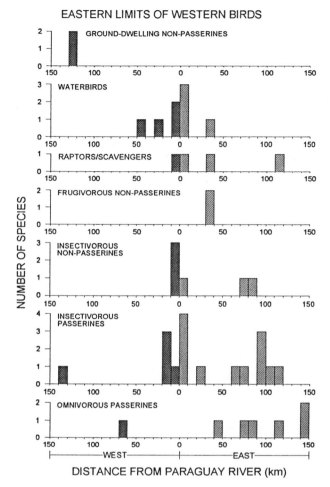

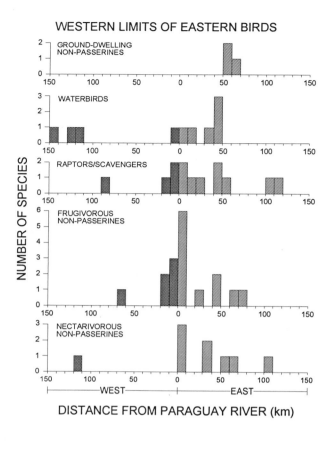

Figure 27. Eastern distributional limits (relative to Paraguay River) of "western" birds and western distributional limits of "eastern" birds by ecological/taxonomic group and forest understory group. Species restricted to Matogrosense and Ñeembucú regions are excluded.

The adjoining Central Paraguay/Alto Paraná regions had a higher or equally high degree of faunal similarity compared with all other pairs of adjoining regions for all breeding birds combined, for five of the eight ecological/taxonomic groups and for the forest understory birds (Table 8). This indicates that the hilly ranges (<800 m high) separating these regions are at best a minor barrier to bird dispersal. The high degree of faunal similarity between these regions is presumably due to similarity of habitat (mostly humid forests).

For all breeding birds combined, the adjoining pair of regions with the lowest degree of faunal similarity is the Bajo Chaco/Central Paraguay regions, the second lowest pair is the Matogrosense/Campos Cerrados regions, and the third lowest is the Central Paraguay/Ñeembucú regions (Table 8). The first two pairs of regions are divided by the Paraguay

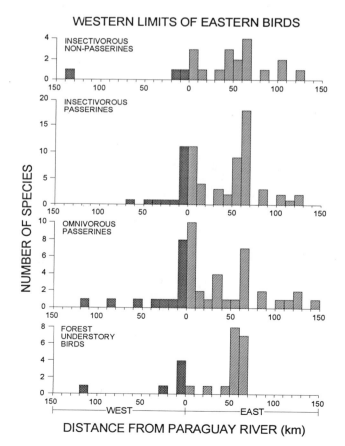

River, and the first and third pairs represent the most abrupt transition from savannas to forests (Figs. 6 and 7, pp 12 and 14). Because faunal similarity between the Ñeembucú/Bajo Chaco regions (separated by Paraguay River) is greater than that for the Ñeembucú/Central Paraguay regions (forest-savanna transition) for all breeding birds combined, for seven of the eight ecological/taxonomic groups and for forest understory birds (Table 8), a relatively abrupt change in habitat appears to be the most important factor in explaining reduced faunal similarity between adjoining regions, and appears to be more of a barrier to bird dispersal than the Paraguay River.

Prediction 4: Body Size Prediction. For all breeding birds combined, the body size class and number of regions in which each breeding species occurred were significantly correlated (Spearman rank correlation, $r_S=0.155$, $n=574$ species, $P<0.001$), indicating that large-bodied birds were

more widely distributed in Paraguay than small-bodied birds.

A comparison of mean body size class ratios for shared:non-shared species between adjoining regions for all breeding birds combined indicated that the ratios for the three pairs of regions divided by the Paraguay River were higher than the ratios for all but one (Campos Cerrados/Central Paraguay) of the six pairs of adjoining regions not divided by the Paraguay River (Table 9). However, the difference in mean body weight between shared and non-shared species was significant (Mann-Whitney U test, $P<0.05$) for only two pairs of regions: Bajo Chaco/Central Paraguay and Campos Cerrados/Central Paraguay (Table 9). The first of these pairs is divided by the Paraguay River, whereas the second is divided by the narrower Ypané River. These results indicate that a lower proportion of small-bodied birds are shared among these pairs of regions and suggest that the rivers may prevent

Table 8: Comparisons of Jaccard coefficients of similarity between adjoining regions that are either divided by the Paraguay River or not divided by the Paraguay River
A comparison between the Bajo Chaco and Ñeembucú regions, which are divided by the Paraguay River but do not adjoin, is also given

Geographical regions: AC=Alto Chaco; AP=Alto Paraná; BC=Bajo Chaco; CC=Campos Cerrados; CP=Central Paraguay; MG=Matogrosense; ÑE=Ñeembucú.

Ecological/ Taxonomic Group	*Adjoining Regions Divided by Paraguay River*				*Adjoining Regions not Divided by Paraguay River*					
	MG x CC	BC x CC	BC x CP	BC x ÑE	AC x MG	AC x BC	MG x BC	CC x CP	CP x ÑE	CP x AP
All breeding birds combined	0.59	0.62	0.56	0.70	0.63	0.76	0.68	0.72	0.61	0.76
Ground-dwelling non-passerines	0.50	0.88	0.60	0.67	0.30	0.45	0.57	0.70	0.70	0.89
Waterbirds	0.67	0.64	0.75	0.79	0.63	0.81	0.66	0.79	0.73	0.68
Raptors/scavengers	0.65	0.69	0.62	0.68	0.63	0.82	0.64	0.75	0.54	0.74
Frugivorous non-passerines	0.70	0.58	0.55	0.69	0.64	0.79	0.81	0.81	0.54	0.90
Insectivorous non-passerines	0.52	0.57	0.45	0.65	0.69	0.76	0.79	0.73	0.58	0.80
Nectarivorous non-passerines	0.25	0.42	0.36	0.83	0.60	0.67	0.60	0.73	0.43	0.87
Insectivorous passerines	0.56	0.58	0.48	0.66	0.59	0.77	0.63	0.67	0.57	0.77
Omnivorous passerines	0.57	0.64	0.59	0.72	0.70	0.71	0.74	0.70	0.65	0.73
Forest understory birds	0.33	0.43	0.32	0.50	0.32	0.47	0.47	0.59	0.33	0.71

Table 9: Comparisons of mean body size class and mean body size class ratios for shared and non-shared species between adjoining regions that are either divided by the Paraguay River or not divided by the Paraguay River

A comparison between the Bajo Chaco and Ñeembucú regions, which are
divided by the Paraguay River but do not adjoin, is also given

Geographical regions: AC=Alto Chaco; AP=Alto Paraná; BC=Bajo Chaco; CC=Campos Cerrados; CP=Central Paraguay; MG=Matogrosense; ÑE=Ñeembucú.

Ecological/ Taxonomic Group	Adjoining Regions Divided by Paraguay River				Adjoining Regions not Divided by Paraguay River					
	MG x CC	BC x CC	BC x CP	BC x ÑE	AC x MG	AC x BC	MG x BC	CC x CP	CP x ÑE	CP x AP
All breeding birds combined										
Shared ($\bar{x}$ size)	4.89	4.83	4.82	4.82	4.99	4.99	4.89	4.63	4.55	4.42
Non-shared ($\bar{x}$ size)	4.24	4.40	4.00	4.27	4.86	4.68	4.66	3.87	4.29	4.32
Shared:non-shared	1.15	1.10	1.21*	1.13	1.03	1.07	1.05	1.20*	1.06	1.02
Ground-dwelling non-passerines										
Shared ($\bar{x}$ size)	9.00	8.57	8.33	8.50	9.00	8.20	9.00	8.29	8.57	8.50
Non-shared ($\bar{x}$ size)	8.00	8.00	9.25	9.33	8.29	9.00	8.00	9.67	9.00	9.00
Shared:non-shared	1.13	1.07	0.90	0.91	1.09	0.91	1.13	0.86	0.95	0.94
Waterbirds										
Shared ($\bar{x}$ size)	8.24	7.88	7.79	8.06	8.27	7.80	8.36	7.53	7.83	7.67
Non-shared ($\bar{x}$ size)	5.95	6.56	6.53	6.13	6.59	7.14	6.29	7.21	6.74	7.00
Shared:non-shared	1.38*	1.20*	1.19*	1.32*	1.25*	1.09	1.33*	1.04	1.16	1.10
Raptors/scavengers										
Shared ($\bar{x}$ size)	8.23	8.15	8.09	8.04	8.14	8.19	8.11	8.10	7.93	8.02
Non-shared ($\bar{x}$ size)	8.06	8.40	8.33	8.46	8.06	7.50	8.60	8.31	8.35	7.87
Shared:non-shared	1.02	0.97	0.97	0.95	1.01	1.09	0.94	0.97	0.95	1.02
Frugivorous non-passerines										
Shared ($\bar{x}$ size)	6.08	5.91	5.91	5.94	6.00	6.11	5.91	6.44	5.95	6.36
Non-shared ($\bar{x}$ size)	7.36	7.31	7.28	6.13	6.10	5.00	7.20	6.75	7.11	7.25
Shared:non-shared	0.83	0.81	0.81	0.97	0.98	1.22	0.82	0.95	0.84	0.88
Insectivorous non-passerines										
Shared ($\bar{x}$ size)	4.57	4.61	4.65	4.59	4.55	4.59	4.65	4.66	4.46	4.49
Non-shared ($\bar{x}$ size)	4.84	4.82	4.43	4.50	4.78	4.71	5.00	4.00	4.50	4.20
Shared:non-shared	0.94	0.96	1.05	1.02	0.95	0.97	0.93	1.16	0.99	1.07
Nectarivorous non-passerines										
Shared ($\bar{x}$ size)	1.00	1.00	1.00	1.00	1.00	1.00	1.00	1.00	1.00	1.00
Non-shared ($\bar{x}$ size)	1.00	1.00	1.00	1.00	1.00	1.00	1.00	1.00	1.00	1.00
Shared:non-shared	1.00	1.00	1.00	1.00	1.00	1.00	1.00	1.00	1.00	1.00
Insectivorous passerines										
Shared ($\bar{x}$ size)	2.30	2.37	2.36	2.43	2.33	2.39	2.32	2.45	2.38	2.30
Non-shared ($\bar{x}$ size)	2.55	2.44	2.30	2.14	2.55	2.57	2.41	2.00	2.22	2.49
Shared:non-shared	0.90	0.97	1.02	1.14	0.92	0.93	0.96	1.22*	1.07	0.92
Omnivorous passerines										
Shared ($\bar{x}$ size)	3.00	3.07	2.98	2.98	2.91	2.89	2.96	3.10	2.91	3.01
Non-shared ($\bar{x}$ size)	3.26	3.00	2.77	2.62	3.11	3.16	3.06	2.55	2.87	2.41
Shared:non-shared	0.92	1.02	1.08	1.14	0.93	0.92	0.97	1.22	1.01	1.25
Forest understory birds										
Shared ($\bar{x}$ size)	2.90	3.58	3.39	3.33	2.17	3.38	2.89	3.75	4.39	3.50
Non-shared ($\bar{x}$ size)	3.60	3.13	3.59	4.78	3.77	3.33	3.10	3.06	3.15	3.46
Shared:non-shared	0.81	1.08	0.94	0.70	0.57	1.01	0.93	1.23	1.39	1.01

*P<0.01 (Mann-Whitney U-test)

small-bodied species from occurring in both regions. However, the significant differences among the regions in mean body size class may complicate the interpretation of results. Because the Campos Cerrados/Central Paraguay regions have relatively similar avifaunas whereas the Bajo Chaco/Central Paraguay regions do not (e.g., Table 8, Fig. 24), the differences in body size between the shared and non-shared birds of the Bajo Chaco/Central Paraguay and Campos Cerrados/Central Paraguay regions does not appear to be related to habitat similarity.

None of the ecological/taxonomic groups of birds or the forest understory birds had higher shared:non-shared body size ratios for the three pairs of adjoining regions divided by the Paraguay than for the six pairs of adjoining regions not divided by the Paraguay River (Table 9). Furthermore, only two of the ecological/taxonomic groups of birds showed significant differences in mean body weight between shared and non-shared species for any pair of adjoining regions. The first group was the waterbirds, in which mean body size of shared species was significantly larger than that of non-shared species for five of the nine pairs of adjoining regions (Table 9). The larger species of waterbirds (e.g., herons, storks) are widespread in Paraguay, whereas many of the smaller species (e.g., rails, bitterns) have been recorded in only a few regions (see Annotated Checklist section). Because many species of rails and bitterns are nocturnal marsh residents and are difficult to collect, the differences in body size between shared and non-shared species may reflect sampling bias. In any event, a river is unlikely to be a dispersal barrier for any species of waterbird. The body size of insectivorous passerines averaged higher for shared species than for non-shared species in the Campos Cerrados/Central Paraguay regions, but not for any other pair of adjoining regions (Table 9). Because fewer small-bodied birds are shared between these two regions, the Ypané River may be a dispersal barrier to smaller birds, or perhaps some other factor may be involved. It seems unlikely, however, that the Ypané River would be

Pied-billed Grebe (*Podilymbus podiceps*)

Dan Brown

any more of a barrier to smaller birds than the much broader Paraguay River.

Prediction 5: Migrant Prediction. For all breeding birds combined, species that are long-distance migrants occurred in more regions on average ($\bar{x}$=5.47 regions, SD=1.78, n=49 species) than relatively sedentary non-migrant species ($\bar{x}$=4.20 regions, SD=2.17, n=526 species; Mann-Whitney U test, z=3.86, P<0.001), indicating that migrant species are relatively more widespread in Paraguay than non-migrant species. Faunal similarity between adjoining regions was generally higher for migrants than for non-migrants (Table 10).

I compared the ratios of faunal similarity for migrant and non-migrant species (Table 10). For all breeding birds combined, the three adjoining regions divided by the Paraguay River had higher migrant:non-migrant ratios of faunal similarity than the six adjoining regions not divided by the Paraguay River (Table 10), suggesting that the Paraguay River may be more of a barrier for relatively sedentary species than for long-distance migrants. The insectivorous passerines accounted for 55% of the breeding bird species that are long-distance migrants. The migrant species of this group occurred in more regions on average ($\bar{x}$=5.93 regions, SD=1.47, n=27 species) than the non-migrant species ($\bar{x}$=4.62 regions, SD=2.09, n=162 species; Mann-Whitney U test, z=4.96, P<0.001), indicating that migrant species are more widespread in Paraguay. The migrant:non-migrant ratios of faunal similarity for the three pairs of adjoining regions divided by the Paraguay River were as high or higher than the corresponding ratios for the six pairs of adjoining regions not divided by the Paraguay River (Table 10), suggesting that the river may be more of a barrier to sedentary species of insectivorous passerines.

The omnivorous passerines accounted for 20% of the breeding birds that are long-distance migrants. Unlike the insectivorous passerines, the migrant species of omnivorous passerines did not occur in more regions on average ($\bar{x}$=3.80 regions, SD=2.04, n=10 species) than the non-migrant species ($\bar{x}$=4.33 regions, SD=2.24, n=104 species; Mann-Whitney U test, z=0.77, P>0.40). Nevertheless, two of the three adjoining pairs of regions divided by the Paraguay River had the highest migrant:non-migrant ratios of faunal similarity, but the third pair had a lower ratio than four of the six adjoining pairs of regions not divided by the Para-

guay River (Table 10). None of the other ecological/taxonomic groups or the forest understory group had more than five breeding species of long-distance migrants; thus, no further within-group comparisons could be made.

The data suggest that the Paraguay River may be a dispersal barrier to sedentary species, especially insectivorous passerines. However, an alternative explanation may exist. Migrant species are more likely to be recorded in unfavorable habitats than non-migrants; thus, the migrant:non-migrant ratios of faunal similarity may be related to habitat differences between adjoining regions. If so, a high ratio for adjoining regions divided by the Paraguay River may be explained by habitat differences. This is supported by the observation that the lowest migrant:non-migrant ratios of faunal similarity (i.e., more similar) for all breeding birds combined occurred between pairs of regions with similar habitat: Alto Chaco/Bajo Chaco, Bajo Chaco/Ñeembucú and Central Paraguay/Alto Paraná regions (Table 10). Furthermore, the low ratio for the superficially similar Bajo Chaco/Ñeembucú regions might not be expected since they are not adjoining. These three pairs of regions also had the lowest ratios for insectivorous passerines, but not for omnivorous passerines (Table 10).

Prediction 6: Distributional Crossover Prediction. Of the breeding birds in Paraguay that occur primarily in the Chaco (some occur marginally on the east bank of the Paraguay River), five species (excluding those occurring only in the Matogrosense region) cross the upper Paraguay River into Mato Grosso do Sul, Brazil, whereas 23 species cross the Paraná River into Corrientes and Entre Ríos, Argentina, or marginally cross the Paraguay River in the Ñeembucú region (Appendix 6). The Chaco Chachalaca (*Ortalis canicollis*) is restricted to the Chaco in Argentina, but crosses the Paraguay River into the northern Orient and could thus be considered a sixth Chaco species that crosses the upper Paraguay River. An additional four species of Chaco birds cross the river both to the north and south of the Orient (Appendix 6).

In contrast with the Chaco birds, 79 species of breeding birds in Paraguay that occur primarily in the Orient (some occur marginally on the west bank of the Paraguay River) cross the upper Paraguay River into Santa Cruz, Bolivia, or marginally cross the Paraguay River into the Matogrosense region, whereas only seven species cross the Paraná River

Table 10: Jaccard coefficients of similarity and coefficient ratios for migrant and non-migrant breeding birds

Comparisons are between pairs of adjoining regions that are either divided
by the Paraguay River or not divided by the Paraguay River
A comparison between the Bajo Chaco and Ñeembucú regions, which are divided
by the Paraguay River but do not adjoin, is also given

Geographical regions: AC=Alto Chaco; AP=Alto Paraná; BC=Bajo Chaco; CC=Campos Cerrados; CP=Central Paraguay; MG=Matogrosense; ÑE=Ñeembucú.

Ecological/ Taxonomic Group	— Adjoining Regions — Divided by Paraguay River				— Adjoining Regions not Divided by Paraguay River —					
	MG x CC	BC x CC	BC x CP	BC x ÑE	AC x MG	AC x BC	MG x BC	CC x CP	CP x ÑE	CP x AP
All breeding birds combined										
Migrants	0.74	0.83	0.76	0.71	0.74	0.83	0.81	0.78	0.75	0.76
Non-migrants	0.57	0.59	0.54	0.70	0.61	0.75	0.67	0.72	0.59	0.76
Migrants:non-migrants	1.30	1.41	1.41	1.01	1.21	1.11	1.21	1.08	1.27	1.00
Insectivorous passerines										
Migrants	0.80	0.92	0.81	0.76	0.83	0.88	0.87	0.89	0.81	0.88
Non-migrants	0.50	0.50	0.41	0.64	0.52	0.73	0.56	0.63	0.52	0.75
Migrants:non-migrants	1.60	1.84	1.98	1.19	1.60	1.21	1.55	1.41	1.56	1.17
Omnivorous passerines										
Migrants	0.60	0.43	0.63	0.57	0.57	0.63	0.67	0.38	0.50	0.33
Non-migrants	0.57	0.66	0.60	0.73	0.72	0.72	0.75	0.74	0.67	0.76
Migrants:non-migrants	1.05	0.65	1.05	0.78	0.79	0.88	0.89	0.51	0.75	0.43

into the Argentinian Chaco to the south of Paraguay (Appendix 6). An additional three species of Orient birds cross the river both to the north and south of the Paraguayan Chaco (Appendix 6).

The higher number of Chaco birds crossing the Paraguay-Paraná River to the south of Paraguay, where it is wider, suggests that the river is not much of a barrier to dispersal. Because the east bank of the Paraná River in Corrientes and Entre Ríos, Argentina, resembles that of the Chaco (e.g., Short 1975, Nores 1987, 1989), habitat appears to be a more important factor in bird distribution than a putative river barrier. Moreover, the scarcity of humid forests on the west bank of the Paraná River in Argentina (e.g., Nores 1987, 1989, 1992) is the most likely reason why so few forest birds of the Orient cross the Paraná River farther south.

The humid forests of the Orient extend northward into the Brazilian Pantanal, where they occur intermingled with wetlands, grasslands and rela-

tively xeric cerrado vegetation (Prance and Schaller 1982). From the Pantanal a wide swath of semihumid forest extends westward across Santa Cruz, Bolivia, and then southward through Chuquisaca and Tarija, Bolivia (Remsen and Traylor 1989), to the Yungas of northwestern Argentina on the east slope of the Andes (Nores 1987, 1989). This fairly continuous belt of semihumid forest marks the western, northern and eastern limits of the relatively arid Chaco Boreal. Thus, it is not surprising that 79 species of Paraguayan birds restricted primarily to the Orient cross the upper Paraguay River into Bolivia (Appendix 6). Furthermore, 24 of these species have a relatively continuous distribution westward across Bolivia and southward to the Yungas forests of northwestern Argentina; these species, all of which occur primarily in humid forest and are absent in the relatively xeric western Chaco, have a distributional pattern that can be described as circum-Chaco (Appendix 6). An additional seven species of birds have an essentially circum-Chaco distribution, but have been recorded at a few scattered localities in the Alto Chaco region; these include: Scaly-headed Parrot (*Pionus maximiliani*), Squirrel Cuckoo (*Piaya cayana*), Tawny-crowned Pygmy-Tyrant (*Euscarthmus meloryphus*), Yellow-olive Flycatcher (*Tolmomyias sulphurescens*), Euler's Flycatcher (*Lathrotriccus euleri*), Crested Becard (*Pachyramphus validus*), and Hooded Tanager (*Nemosia pileata*). The Bran-colored Flycatcher (*Myiophobus fasciatus*), although considered a Chaco resident by Short (1975) and Ridgely and Tudor (1994), has not been recorded in the Paraguayan Chaco; thus, its distribution could also be considered circum-Chaco. An additional 17 species of humid forest birds occurring primarily in the Orient have a disjunct population occurring to the west of the Chaco, in the Yungas of southern Bolivia and northwestern Argentina (Appendix 6). The absence of these species in the intervening dry Chaco, coupled with their occasional presence in gallery forest and subhumid forest in certain areas of the eastern Chaco (Appendix 5), strongly suggest that an arid environment is a more effective dispersal barrier to forest birds than the Paraguay River.

Prediction 7: Phenotypic Differentiation Prediction. Only eight pairs of closely related avian taxa have contact zones that roughly coincide with the Paraguay River. However, Capparella (1988, 1991) demonstrated that phenotypically similar populations of species divided by Amazonian rivers may exhibit genotypic divergence, indicating that genetic studies would be required to fully evaluate the Paraguay River's effect on dispersal and gene flow between intraspecific populations of birds separated by the river. Unfortunately there have been no genetic studies thus far of bird populations in Paraguay. Nevertheless, the information presently known about the contact zones of several closely related taxa provides evidence of the relative importance of the Paraguay River and the forest-savanna transition as potential barriers to gene flow. The contact zones of these taxa are described below:

Spotted Tinamou (*Nothura maculosa*). The Paraguayan Chaco is inhabited by at least three races, of which only *paludivaga* occurs within 100 km of the Paraguay River (Conover 1950, Short 1975, 1976a; see Taxonomic Notes section); the Orient is inhabited by *maculosa*. The race *paludivaga* is notably darker than the other races occurring in Paraguay. Conover (1950) indicated that *paludivaga* and *maculosa* are separated by the Paraguay

River and the Paraná River just south of Paraguay; however, four specimens from the west side of the Paraná River in Santa Fe Province, Argentina, were referred to *maculosa* by Conover. In regard to the Santa Fe specimens, Conover stated that three specimens from western Santa Fe were dark above and approached *paludivaga* in coloration, but that a specimen from farther east at Gálvez, roughly 50 km W of the Paraná River, was very rufescent as in typical *maculosa*. Farther south, *paludivaga* is replaced by *annectens*, which is also dark above, on the west bank of the Paraná River, whereas *maculosa* occurs on the east bank of the Paraná River in eastern Argentina and Uruguay. In Paraguay, Conover (1950) noted that five specimens of *maculosa* from the east bank of the Paraguay River at Rosario, western Dpto. San Pedro, were darker than typical *maculosa*, approaching *paludivaga* in coloration, but that 12 specimens from Horqueta, in southwestern Dpto. Concepción, were rather variable. The zone of contact between *paludivaga* and *maculosa* appears to coincide with the course of the Paraguay and Paraná Rivers (except in Santa Fe Province, Argentina), suggesting that a river barrier may reduce gene flow between these taxa.

Greater Rhea (*Rhea americana*). The various races of this species were discussed by Brodkorb (1939b:137), who wrote: "The large rivers of South America seem to be impassable faunal barriers for these flightless birds, for it appears that the Pilcomayo, the Paraguay, and the Paraná, at least, form boundaries of the ranges of different races." According to Brodkorb (1938a, 1939b), the Paraguayan Chaco is inhabited by *araneipes*, whereas the Orient is inhabited by *nobilis*, which differs from *araneipes* by a darker brown interscapular region and by more rusty coloring on the flanks and upper neck. To the south of Paraguay, *albescens* occurs to the west of the Paraná River and *intermedia* occurs to the east of the river (Brodkorb 1939b). However, few specimens were available for study. Podtiaguin (1944) disputed the distinction between *araneipes* and *nobilis*, stating that the gray tones varied greatly among individuals and that light gray individuals resembling *araneipes*, although rare, could be found throughout Paraguay, not just in the Chaco. Storer (1988) pointed out that only two of the four specimens (including the holotype) of *nobilis* had the rusty hues described by Brodkorb (1939b), and suggested that the rusty colors may be adventitious, but the rusty colors remained after prolonged washing of the feathers with a detergent and after two weeks of soaking in dilute hydrochloric acid, and no ferric hydroxide precipitated when the acid wash was neutralized with ammonia. Storer (1989) later reported seeing grayish rheas in an area of the Orient characterized by gray, rather than red, soils. Although the distinction between *araneipes* and *nobilis* remains obscure, rheas are flightless and are unlikely to ever cross the Paraguay and Paraná Rivers (unless assisted by humans). Further studies would likely reveal phenotypic and genotypic differentiation between populations that are separated by the Paraguay and Paraná Rivers.

Green-barred Woodpecker (*Colaptes melanochloros*). The Chaco is inhabited by the *melanolaimus* group (three races) and the Orient is inhabited by the *melanochloros* group (two races). Short (1972b) studied geographical variation within the species, and I have summarized his findings in the Taxonomic Notes section. The contact zone between the two groups roughly coincides with the upper Paraguay River, but shifts eastward in the southern Orient and continues southward along the forest-savanna transition, well to the east of the Paraná River in Argentina. Short (1972b:49) stated that "the Paraguay River is somewhat of a barrier to interbreeding between *nigroviridis* and *melanochlorosnattereri*, especially in the north," but admitted that "specimens are lacking from the banks of the river." However, it seems unlikely that the Paraguay River would be any more of a barrier to gene flow than the considerably wider portion of the Paraná River in Argentina. Because the forest-savanna transition in the northern Orient roughly corresponds with the course of the upper Paraguay River (Esser 1982; Fig. 6, p. 12), a relatively abrupt change of habitat in this region is a more plausible barrier to gene flow in this species than the Paraguay River.

Black-banded Woodcreeper (*Dendrocolaptes picumnus*) and Planalto Woodcreeper (*D. platyrostris*). The ranges of these closely related species closely approach each other along the upper Paraguay River to the north of Villa Hayes (Dpto. Presidente Hayes; see Distributional Notes section). In the eastern Argentinian Chaco, Narosky and Yzurieta (1987, 1989) and Nores (1992) indicated that *D. platyrostris* occurs in eastern Formosa and Chaco Provinces, Argentina, whereas Ridgely and Tudor (1994) indicated that *D. picumnus* occurs in the area; Chebez and Heinonen Fortabat (1987) recently observed *D. picumnus* in eastern Formosa

Province. In Paraguay, the distribution of the two species appears to be divided by the Paraguay River. This may also be the case farther south, where the possible sympatry of the two species in the Argentinian Chaco requires clarification.

Swainson's Flycatcher (*Myiarchus swainsoni*). The Chaco is inhabited by *ferocior* whereas the Orient is inhabited by *swainsoni*; the latter differs from *ferocior* by darker coloration and several vocal characters (Lanyon 1978). The two races hybridize along a zone corresponding roughly with the Paraguay River and extending southward through Corrientes Province, Argentina, and along the Argentinian-Uruguayan border (Lanyon 1978). Because the contact zone occurs along the forest-savanna transition along the upper Paraguay River and to the east of the Paraná River in Argentina, the Paraguay and Paraná Rivers appear to have a minor or negligible effect on gene flow between the races.

Rufous-collared Sparrow (*Zonotrichia capensis*). All specimens taken from the Paraguayan Chaco have been ascribed to *hypoleuca* (includes *mellea* of the Matogrosense region, which was described by Wetmore [1922] but is not distinct from *hypoleuca* [Short 1976a]), a relatively pale race with the yellow in the bend of the wing usually absent (Chapman 1940). Nearly all specimens taken from the Orient have been diagnosed as *subtorquata*, which is darker and has a distinct yellowish bend to the wing (Chapman 1940). J. R. Contreras et al. (1989:46) reported that one of seven specimens taken at Lago Ypoá (Dpto. Paraguarí), roughly 35 km east of the Paraguay River, appeared to represent an intergrade, whereas the other six were typical *subtorquata*. In eastern Argentina, Bó (1972) found it difficult to diagnose specimens as either *hypoleuca* or *subtorquata*. Bó reported that only four of 13 specimens from Corrientes Province (east of the Paraná River) had yellow in the bend of the wing (referable to *subtorquata*), whereas 25 of 111 in Buenos Aires Province (west of Paraná River) had yellow in the wing. Although the contact zone between *hypoleuca* and *subtorquata* roughly coincides with the Paraguay and Paraná Rivers, specimens diagnosable as either race apparently occur on both sides, suggesting that substantial gene flow occurs between populations separated by the Paraguay and Paraná Rivers.

Ultramarine Grosbeak (*Cyanocompsa brissonii*). The distribution map of Short (1975) indicates that the Chaco is inhabited by *argentina* whereas the Orient is inhabited by *sterea*. Hellmayr (1938) described *argentina* as larger than *sterea* with a heavier bill, a paler plumage in males and more rufescent plumage in females. Hellmayr diagnosed specimens from Mato Grosso, Brazil (east of the Paraguay River), as *argentina*, and stated that specimens from the eastern Argentinian Chaco were "truly intermediate" (p. 101). Short (1976a) considered specimens from Lichtenau (Dpto. Presidente Hayes) as *sterea>argentina*. I examined several hundred specimens and was unable to discern a distinct contact zone between *argentina* and *sterea*, whose characters appear to vary clinally from west to east (Hayes in prep.). There is no evidence that the Paraguay-Paraná River system forms a barrier to gene flow between these putative taxa.

Red-crested Finch (*Coryphospingus cucullatus*). The Chaco is inhabited by *fargoi*, which is generally more brownish-gray than *rubescens* of the Orient (Brodkorb 1938a). I examined several hundred specimens, but did not attempt to quantify plumage coloration (Hayes in prep.). Nevertheless, a few specimens from west of the Paraguay and Paraná Rivers are fairly bright red and may represent *rubescens*, whereas several specimens from east of the Paraguay River are rather brownish and are diagnosable as *fargoi*; several of these specimens were taken during the summer months, at a time when migrants would not be expected. The reddish tones of the species tend to fade gradually from east to west, with no abrupt change; specimens taken within 50 km of the Paraguay River appear to be somewhat intermediate between *fargoi* and *rubescens*. Specimens from throughout Corrientes Province, Argentina, are almost invariably diagnosable as *rubescens*, suggesting that the zone of contact between *fargoi* and *rubescens* is situated to the west of the forest-savanna transition, roughly coinciding with the course of the Paraguay and Paraná Rivers. Specimens from eastern Bolivia and eastern Peru are generally bright red and are thus referable to *rubescens*, indicating that the zone of contact shifts westward from the Paraguay River in Bolivia. The evidence that the Paraguay-Paraná River system forms a barrier to gene flow between *fargoi* and *rubescens* is equivocal.

The available phenotypic evidence, although rather scant, suggests that the Paraguay River may reduce gene flow between a few closely related taxa separated by the river, but the evidence is circumstantial at best. In contrast, the forest-savanna transition clearly separates several pairs of closely related taxa. The forest-savanna transition appears to be a more important barrier to gene flow than the Paraguay and Paraná Rivers. However, genotypic differentiation may occur in the absence of phenotypic differentiation in river-divided populations of birds (Capparella 1988, 1991).

Prediction 8: Contact Zone Prediction. As discussed above, only eight pairs of closely related taxa have contact zones that roughly coincide with the Paraguay River or the forest-savanna transition. In contrast, numerous pairs of closely related taxa have reasonably well documented contact zones in Paraguay that do not coincide with these potential barriers.

At least four pairs of closely related taxa exhibiting west-east variation have contact zones occurring at variable distances to the west of the Paraguay River. These include (west/east): Spotted Nothura (*Nothura maculosa chacoensis/paludivaga*); Black-bodied Woodpecker (*Dryocopus schulzi*)/Lineated Woodpecker (*D. lineatus*); Cream-backed Woodpecker (*Campephilus leucopogon*)/Crimson-crested Woodpecker (*C. melanoleucos*); and Great Pampa-Finch (*Embernagra platensis olivascens/platensis*).

At least 13 pairs of closely related taxa exhibiting west-east variation have contact zones occurring at variable distances to the east of the Paraguay River. These include (west/east): Blue-throated Piping-Guan (*Pipile pipile*)/Black-fronted Piping-Guan (*P. jacutinga*); Golden-collared Macaw (*Ara auricollis*)/Blue-winged Macaw (*A. maracana*); Turquoise-fronted Parrot (*Amazona aestiva*)/Vinaceous-breasted Parrot (*Amazona vinacea*); Blue-crowned Trogon (*Trogon curucui*)/Surucua Trogon (*T. surrucura*); White-barred Piculet (*Picumnus cirratus*)/Ochre-collared Piculet (*Picumnus temminckii*); Pale-crested Woodpecker (*Celeus lugubris*)/Blond-crested Woodpecker (*C. flavescens*); Olivaceous Woodcreeper (*Sittasomus griseicapillus griseicapillus/sylviellus*), Red-billed Scythebill (*Campylorhamphus trochilirostris*)/Black-billed Scythebill (*C. falcularius*); Variable Antshrike (*Thamnophilus caerulescens paraguayensis/caerulescens*); Brown-crested Flycatcher (*Myiarchus tyrannulus tyrannulus/bahiae*); Masked Gnatcatcher (*Polioptila dumicola*)/Cream-bellied Gnatcatcher (*P. lactea*); Rufous-browed Peppershrike (*Cyclarhis gujanensis viridis/ochrocephala*);

and White-lined Tanager (*Tachyphonus rufus*)/ Ruby-crowned Tanager (*T. coronatus*).

At least six pairs of closely related taxa exhibit north/south variation within Paraguay. These include (north/south): Blaze-winged Parakeet (*Pyrrhura devillei*)/Reddish-bellied Parakeet (*P. frontalis*); Campo Flicker (*Colaptes campestris campestris/campestroides*); Rufous-fronted Thornbird (*Phacellodomus rufifrons*)/Little Thornbird (*P. sibilatrix*); Rufous Cacholote (*Pseudoseisura cristata*)/Brown Cacholote (*P. lophotes*); Reiser's Tyrannulet (*Phyllomyias reiseri*)/Greenish Tyrannulet (*Phyllomyias virescens*); and Suiriri Flycatcher (*Suiriri suiriri suiriri/suiriri* x *affinis*).

The high number of contact zones not coinciding with either the Paraguay River or forest-savanna transition suggests that other ecological barriers in Paraguay may be equally effective in reducing dispersal and gene flow between closely related taxa.

Alternative Ecological Barriers

West/East Barriers. The west/east contact zones between the four pairs of taxa to the west of the Paraguay River (see Prediction 8 above) roughly coincide with the fairly abrupt transition from thorn scrub forest in the west to palm savannas and subhumid forest in the east (Fig. 6), suggesting that this transition may be a partial barrier to gene flow between subspecies and that borders between competing species may have stabilized along thresholds of ecological tolerance. However, the cluster analysis in Fig. 24, the distributional limits analysis in Fig. 26, the faunal similarity analysis in Table 8, the body size analysis in Table 9, and the migrant analysis in Table 10 do not demonstrate a marked faunal change (for all breeding birds combined) along this transition.

The west/east contact zones between the 13 pairs of taxa east of the Paraguay River (see Prediction 8 above) occur at varying distances from the Paraguay River, and do not appear to coincide with any abrupt environmental changes. However, the eastern taxa generally occur in taller, more humid forest than their western counterparts, suggesting that borders between closely related taxa may have stabilized along intrinsic thresholds of ecological tolerance, which may reduce gene flow between putative subspecies and competition between species.

The most likely geographical barrier to bird dispersal in the Orient is the tall hilly divide between the Central Paraguay and Alto Paraná regions (Fig. 3, p. 11). However, no contact zones appear to coincide with the divide, and the analyses discussed above indicate a high degree of faunal similarity between the Central Paraguay and Alto Paraná regions (e.g., Figs. 24 and 26, Tables 8-10). These hills and their passes are obviously too low (<800 m) to be effective barriers to bird dispersal.

A west-east direction of geographical replacement by closely related taxa appears to be the dominant pattern in Paraguay, which would be expected since most environmental gradients in the country change in a west-east direction (Table 2).

North/South Barriers. Several environmental changes may be associated with the north/south contact zones between the six pairs of closely related taxa (see Prediction 8 above). The contact zones in the Chaco between Rufous-fronted Thornbird (*Phacellodomus rufifrons*)/Little Thornbird (*P. sibilatrix*) and between Rufous Cacholote (*Pseudoseisura cristata*)/Brown Cacholote (*P. lophotes*) taxa roughly coincide with the transition from subhumid forest to thorn scrub and palm savanna along the boundaries between the Matogrosense/Alto Chaco and Matogrosense/Bajo Chaco regions. However, there does not appear to be a marked faunal change along this transition (e.g., Fig. 24, Tables 8-10).

The contact zones in the Orient between Blaze-winged Parakeet (*Pyrrhura devillei*)/Reddish-bellied Parakeet (*P. frontalis*), Reiser's Tyrannulet (*Phyllomyias reiseri*)/Greenish Tyrannulet (*Phyllomyias virescens*), and Suiriri Flycatcher (*Suiriri suiriri suiriri/suiriri* x *affinis*) roughly coincide with the transition from campos cerrados to humid forest along the boundary between the Campos Cerrados and Central Paraguay regions. The analyses discussed above provide either little evidence (Fig. 24, Table 8) or fair (but perhaps equivocal) evidence (Tables 9 and 10) of a marked faunal change along this transition.

The contact zone between the two races of Campo Flicker (*Colaptes campestris campestris/ campestroides*), which are non-forest birds, has been attributed to recent deforestation between their ranges, which may have permitted secondary contact (Short 1972b). Their contact zone occurs to the south of the campos cerrados/humid forest transition (see Taxonomic Notes section).

The eastward-flowing Pilcomayo River (and Bermejo River, situated just south of the Pilcomayo River in Argentina), which divides Paraguay and Argentina (Fig. 2), separates several taxa in the Paraguayan Chaco from conspecific taxa in the Argentinian Chaco (Nores 1992). The pairs of taxa separated by these rivers include (north/south): Spotted Tinamou (*Nothura maculosa chacoensis/pallida*); Quebracho Crested-Tinamou (*Eudromia formosa mira/formosa*); Greater Rhea (*Rhea americana araneipes/albescens*); Campo Flicker (*Colaptes campestris campestris/campestroides*); Short-billed Canastero (*Asthenes baeri chacoensis/baeri*); Red-billed Scythebill (*Campylorhamphus trochilirostris lafresnayanus/hellmayri*); Variable Antshrike (*Thamnophilus caerulescens paraguayensis/dinellii*); and Crested Gallito (*Rhinocrypta lanceolata saturata/lanceolata*). Nores (1992) also indicated that the contact zones between the Rufous-fronted Thornbird (*Phacellodomus rufifrons*)/Little Thornbird (*P. sibilatrix*) and Rufous Cacholote (*Pseudoseisura cristata*)/Brown Cacholote (*P. lophotes*) occurred near the Pilcomayo River, but their zones of contact actually occur far to the north of the Pilcomayo River (discussed above).

Because the Pilcomayo and Bermejo rivers are relatively narrow (<500 m wide), Nores (1992) argued that these rivers could not possibly represent dispersal barriers and thus could not be the agents of vicariance. Nores studied the distribution of mesophytic forest along these rivers, and found that gallery forests extended westward about 200 km from the Paraguay River. To the west of this point, the shortest distance to the humid Yungas forest in the Andean foothills is roughly 450 km. Scattered patches of forest were encountered along the intervening stretches of these rivers and in nearby dry riverbeds. Nores proposed that more extensive forest occurred along these rivers during periods of Quaternary interglacial phases when the temperature and precipitation were higher than at present. A broad belt of humid forest across the relatively arid Chaco would have subdivided the Chaco into northern and southern components, and presumably would have separated the closely related avian taxa currently separated by the Pilcomayo and Bermejo rivers (Nores 1992).

Nores (1992) also reported that 42 pairs of closely related taxa in the Yungas (west of the Chaco) and Paranense (east of the Chaco) forests are separated by the relatively xeric Chaco. However, five of these taxa occur at least sporadically throughout the Paraguayan Chaco: Scaly-headed Parrot (*Pionus maximiliani*), Squirrel Cuckoo (*Piaya cayana*), Giant Antshrike (*Batara cinerea*), Crested Becard (*Pachyramphus validus*), and Purplish Jay (*Cyanocorax cyanomelas*; see Annotated Checklist section). Moreover, the White-barred Piculet (*Picumus cirratus*) has a race in the Chaco (*P. c. pilcomayensis*) between the Yungas race (*P. c. thamnophiloides*) and the Paranense race (*P. c. temminckii*), and the Paranense race of the Black-banded Woodcreeper (*Dendrocolaptes picumnus extimus*) is not a valid taxon (see Distributional Notes section). Furthermore, many of the intraspecific pairs of taxa are joined by relatively continuous populations to the north of the Chaco (Appendix 6), which presumably permit gene flow between populations in the Yungas and Paranense forests. Nevertheless, at least 17 pairs of intraspecific taxa (Appendix 6) and several pairs of allospecies (Nores 1992) have disjunct populations in Yungas and Paranense forests that are separated by the relatively xerophytic Chaco.

Nores (1992) postulated that a humid forest bridge along the Pilcomayo and Bermejo Rivers provided a dispersal corridor between the humid forest biotas of the Yungas and Paranense forests during humid periods of interglacial phases. Nores attributed the varying levels of differentiation between the Chaco-separated taxa to alternating advances and retreats of humid forest along the Pilcomayo and Bermejo Rivers, and speculated that the least differentiated taxa may have crossed the bridge during the last connection. Nores rejected the possibility that these taxa crossed the relatively arid Chaco and Cerrados without the Pilcomayo-Bermejo forest bridge, but conceded that some taxa may have reached the Yungas and Paranense forests from the north during more humid interglacial periods when the Amazonian and Paranense forests were connected (the Yungas and Amazonian forests are still connected; e.g., Remsen and Traylor 1989, Nores 1992).

Nores (1992) did not discuss where the possible Amazonian-Paranense connections may have occurred. However, such a connection may well have occurred along the upper Paraguay River in northern Paraguay and southwestern Brazil, where humid gallery forest still occurs (e.g., Prance and Schaller 1982). The sources of the Paraguay River are located near the sources of the Guaporé, Juruena, Arinos, Xingú and Manso Rivers of Amazonia in the state of Mato Grosso, Brazil, and humid forest may well have connected these river systems during humid periods of interglacial phases. Many taxa of Chaco birds have sister taxa in the Cerrado that are more or less separated by the upper Paraguay River (e.g., Short 1975), but this phenomenon has not been studied in detail.

Nores's conclusions were challenged by Silva (1994), who argued that: (1) the pairs of Chaco taxa separated by the Pilcomayo and Bermejo rivers may be the result of primary intergradation rather than secondary contact; (2) the degree of differentiation between disjunct Yungas and Paranense taxa may not be proportional to the duration of the disjunction; (3) the courses of the Pilcomayo and Bermejo rivers were not constant during the Quaternary, and as a consequence (4) the gallery forests may have been too unstable to function as dispersal corridors between Yungas and Paranense forests during the Quaternary. These criticisms were rebutted by Nores (1994).

Another alternative explanation for the presence of closely related forest birds on each side of the Chaco is that much of the Chaco was covered by humid forest during periods of higher temperatures and precipitation, and that a return of arid conditions in the Chaco split apart contiguous populations of forest birds. Although Lüders (1961) found evidence (a podzolic soil horizon) that a relatively arid portion of the Paraguayan Chaco was covered by humid forest at times during the Quaternary, additional paleoecological evidence is needed before the postulated presence of humid Chaco forests during the Quaternary can be confirmed.

Conclusions

Unfortunately no statistical tests are available to test rigorously the predictions regarding the effectiveness of potential barriers to bird dispersal in Paraguay. Nevertheless, the patterns of bird distribution in Paraguay suggest that: (1) habitat similarity is the most important factor in explaining faunal similarity among regions; (2) a relatively abrupt forest-savanna transition may be the most important barrier to bird dispersal and gene flow in Paraguay; (3) the relatively broad Paraguay River at best appears to be a weak barrier to bird dispersal, and does not appear to have been an important vicariance agent; (4) there is no evidence that the tall hilly ranges of eastern Paraguay form a dispersal barrier; (5) several zones of fairly abrupt changes in habitat in both the Chaco and Orient may reduce gene flow between closely related taxa of birds; and (6) the Pilcomayo River may have formed a forest bridge between Yungas and Paranense forests, and subdivided the Chaco avifauna, during more humid interglacial periods.

White-winged Becard
(*Pachyramphus polychopterus*)   Dan Brown

CONSERVATION

"Today more than ever before, the birds of this region, and perhaps of many others, need to be protected..."

A. de W. Bertoni (1918a:188, 189), translated from Spanish

The populations of several species of Paraguayan birds apparently began to decline dramatically during the late 1800s and early 1900s, particularly in the Orient. For example, Bertoni (1927:150) described "flocks of thousands" of Vinaceous-breasted Parrots (*Amazona vinacea*) "that began to darken the sky" during the late 1890s, but became much scarcer afterwards (translated from Spanish). By then the Glaucous Macaw (*Anodorhynchus glaucus*) was probably already extinct (Collar et al. 1992) and the Brazilian Merganser (*Mergus octosetaceus*) was "very rare" (Bertoni 1901:10). At the turn of the century, large numbers of birds believed to be agricultural pests were indiscriminately killed (e.g., Bertoni 1898, 1903b) while more attractive cagebirds were captured and sold to collectors in foreign countries (e.g., Brabourne 1914).

Beginning with his first publication on the birds of Paraguay, Bertoni (1898) recognized the need to protect the birds of Paraguay. Although strict laws were subsequently enacted to prohibit the hunting of birds and other wildlife in Paraguay, there has been little enforcement of these laws. More recently, a number of national parks and reserves have been set aside to preserve pristine habitat; however, the vegetation and wildlife within most "preserved" areas have not been adequately protected from human encroachment.

ENVIRONMENTAL THREATS

Numerous causes have been attributed to the decline of bird populations in Paraguay, beginning with the Spanish colonization of the region. Although the uncontrolled hunting of gamebirds may have contributed to the decline of some threatened species, such as the Black-fronted Piping-Guan (*Pipile jacutinga*), the loss or degradation of pristine habitat is undoubtedly the major cause of decline for all species of birds.

The early introduction of livestock (especially cattle) altered the habitat of the savannas, thus contributing to the demise of specialized grassland or savanna species. For example, the extinction of the Glaucous Macaw (*Anodorhynchus glaucus*), a palm-nut specialist, has been attributed to the grazing of chatay palm (*Butia yatay*) seedlings by livestock, which prevented regeneration of the palms (remnant groves are more than 200 years old) and effectively eliminated the macaw's major source of food (Yamashita and Valle 1993). The massive conversion of natural grasslands to agriculture, which requires the removal of all natural vegetation, has been even more detrimental to specialized grassland birds. The decline of grassland and wetland species of birds has been further exacerbated by the annual burning, primarily during the dry season, of many grasslands and marshes throughout the country.

The most serious threat to the forest birds of Paraguay has been the accelerated pace of deforestation during the last few decades, especially in the Orient. This has been facilitated by the construction of two large hydroelectric dams along the Paraná River and smaller ones along the Yguazú and Acaray rivers; plans are in progress for the construction of an additional dam along the Paraná River and even a dam along the upper Paraguay River. In addition to flooding vast tracts of pristine forest, the dams produced the electrical energy needed to fuel the rapidly expanding human population, whose chainsaws and heavy machinery have rapidly deforested most of the Orient. In 1945, approximately 55% of the Orient was covered by forest. The amount was reduced to 34% in 1976 and 25% in 1985; by 1991, only 15% of the Orient was covered by forest (Carlstein Quiñónez 1993). As a consequence, the humid Paranense forests of the Alto Paraná and eastern Central Paraguay regions have largely been fragmented into small, isolated units, thus disrupting the complex ecological relationships of the original forest. No doubt many Paranense forest species will soon become extinct in Paraguay unless drastic measures are taken to curb the destruction of the remaining forest habitat.

The deforestation of the sparsely populated Chaco is far less critical than that of the Orient. Nevertheless, it has been estimated that 30,000 ha of thorn scrub forest are cleared annually from the Mennonite colonies (mostly in eastern Dpto. Boquerón and northwestern Dpto. Presidente Hayes) and 5,000 ha are cleared elsewhere in the Chaco (Carlstein Quiñónez 1993). These figures will certainly increase as humans expand the frontiers of civilization and agriculture within the Chaco (Solbrig 1986).

The deforested regions of Paraguay are used primarily for agriculture and livestock. The timber is mostly used for lumber and fuel. In the Mennonite colonies of the Chaco, several ha of forest are burned daily to generate electricity. It has been estimated that the domestic demand for timber is 30,000 ha annually, yet only 10,000 ha of land have been reforested thus far, mostly with exotic pine and eucalyptus (Carlstein Quiñónez 1993). Clearly the rate of reforestation, preferably by native species, must be increased dramatically if Paraguay hopes to sustainably harvest its dwindling forest resources.

In recent years the uncontrolled use of agricultural pesticides and the unregulated disposal of sewage and industrial effluents have had a negative impact on wetland ecosystems, where toxic chemicals become biomagnified as they move up the food chain. High concentrations of toxic compounds have been documented in the tissues of fish, kingfishers and raptors along the upper Paraguay River watershed (Alho et al. 1988). Mass mortalities of fish occur periodically, which undoubtedly have a negative impact on bird populations. A looming threat is the development of an ambitious project, referred to as the Hidrovia, which proposes to develop a complex navigation system along the Paraná and Paraguay rivers (Bucher et al. 1993). The plan envisions damming the upper Paraguay River to control flooding, dredging and channeling the river's course to enhance navigation, and diverting the river's water into the agricultural areas of the Chaco through irrigation canals. Much of the Pilcomayo River has already been diverted for agricultural purposes in both Paraguay and Argentina. If implemented along the Paraguay River watershed, the proposed Hidrovia projects will only exacerbate the environmental problems of the region.

DISTRIBUTION OF THREATENED SPECIES

During the last decade there have been several attempts at compiling lists of the threatened birds of Paraguay (e.g., Anonymous 1985, Collar and Andrew 1988, Collar et al. 1992). The most recent and comprehensive attempt classified 22 species of birds as globally "threatened" and 35 species as "near-threatened" (all are hereafter referred to as "threatened") in Paraguay (Collar et al. 1992; see Appendix 7). Unfortunately the status of many of these species is poorly known in Paraguay; more species will undoubtedly be added to the list as the remaining natural habitats in Paraguay dwindle. Nevertheless, the information given by Collar et al. (1992) provides a convenient basis by which comparisons can be made and conservation priorities established.

A comparison of the number of threatened species in each geographical region of Paraguay is given in Table 11. The Central Paraguay and Alto Paraná regions are the only geographical regions in which more than half of the threatened species occur; most of these species inhabit humid forests. The Central Paraguay and Ñeembucú regions have a high number of threatened grassland or wetland species. The less disturbed Chaco regions have fewer threatened and near-threatened species, especially the relatively pristine Matogrosense region.

The avifauna of Paraguay is increasingly threatened by the loss or degradation of habitat as the frontiers of civilization and agriculture expand. The most critically threatened birds of the country are the species inhabiting the humid forests of the eastern Orient. Others have already recognized that the few remaining large patches of forest in the Central Paraguay and Alto Paraná regions merit the highest priority for conservation programs (e.g., Acevedo et al. 1990, Brooks et al. 1993, Keel et al. 1993). However, the threatened species of birds occurring elsewhere in the country should not be neglected.

Thus far less than 5% of the land area in Paraguay has been officially set aside for conservation. A list of the officially protected areas by region is provided in Table 12. Unfortunately most of the protected areas are too small and isolated to maintain viable populations of some threatened species such as the Crowned Eagle (*Harpyhaliaetus coronatus*), Harpy Eagle (*Harpia harpyja*), Black-

Table 11: Comparison of the number of threatened (n=22) and near-threatened species (n=35; see Appendix 7) in each geographical region

Geographical regions: AC=Alto Chaco; AP=Alto Paraná; BC=Bajo Chaco; CC=Campos Cerrados; CP=Central Paraguay; MG=Matogrosense; ÑE=Ñeembucú.

	Geographical Regions						
Habitat	*AC*	*MG*	*BC*	*CC*	*CP*	*ÑE*	*AP*
Threatened species	3	1	3	8	12	6	12
Forests	1	1	1	5	6	0	8
Grasslands/wetlands	2	0	2	3	6	6	4
Near-threatened species	10	5	7	13	24	9	22
Forests	5	2	2	6	15	1	19
Grasslands/wetlands	5	3	5	7	9	8	3
Threatened and near-threatened species	13	6	10	21	36	15	34
Forests	6	3	3	11	21	1	27
Grasslands/wetlands	7	3	7	10	15	14	7

fronted Piping-Guan (*Pipile jacutinga*) and Helmeted Woodpecker (*Dryocopus galeatus*). The amount of protected land in Paraguay should be at least doubled and an effort should be made to preserve large tracts of undisturbed habitat. The natural restoration of disturbed areas adjacent to undisturbed areas should also be considered.

Unfortunately there have been few studies thus far of bird populations in Paraguay (e.g., Hayes 1991, in press, Hayes and Fox 1991, Hayes and Granizo Tamayo 1992, Brooks et al. 1993, López 1993).

Furthermore, little information is available on the ecological requirements of the threatened species (e.g., Collar et al. 1992, Brooks et al. 1993). Studies focusing on the ecological requirements and population dynamics of birds in Paraguay are urgently needed to monitor the long-term responses of bird populations to environmental changes and to design protected areas large enough to maintain viable populations.

King Vulture *(Sarcoramphus papa)*   Dan Brown

Table 12: Protected areas of Paraguay by region
(note that Matogrosense region has none), in order of size

Departamentos: AMA=Amambay; APN=Alto Paraná; CAN=Canindeyú; CAP=Caazapá; CEN=Central; CON=Concepción; COR=Cordillera; exCHA=Chaco (part of Alto Paraguay since 1992); exNAS=Nueva Asunción (part of Boquerón since 1992); GUA=Guairá; ITA=Itapúa; PAR=Paraguarí; PHA=Presidente Hayes

Data mostly from Ríos and Zardini (1989) and leaflet provided by the Dirección de Parques Nacionales y Vida Silvestre, obtained in 1993 (courtesy F. Areco de Medina). This table does not include a recently established network of privately owned nature reserves organized by the Fundación Moisés Bertoni.

Geographical Region/protected area	Departamento	Size (ha)
Alto Chaco region		
Parque Nacional Defensores del Chaco	exCHA	780,000
Parque Nacional Teniente Enciso	exNAS	40,000
Bajo Chaco region		
Parque Nacional Tinfunque	PHA	280,000
Campos Cerrados region		
Parque Nacional Cerro Corá	AMA	12,038
Parque Nacional Serranías de San Luís	CON	10,273
Central Paraguay region		
Reserva Natural del Bosque Mbaracayú	CAN	145,000
Parque Nacional Serranía San Rafael*	ITA	78,000
Parque Nacional Ybyturuzú*	GUA	24,000
Parque Nacional Caaguazú*	CAP	16,000
Parque Nacional Ypacaraí	COR	16,000
Parque Nacional Ybycuí	PAR	5,000
Monumento Natural Cerro Acahay	PAR	2,500
Cerro Lambaré	CEN	3
Ñeembucú region		
Parque Nacional Lago Ypoá	PAR	100,000
Alto Paraná region		
Reserva Biológica Limoy	APN	14,828
Reserva Biológica Itabó	APN	11,200
Refugio Biológico Tati Yupi	APN	2,536
Refugio Biológico Mbaracayú	CAN	1,150
Bosque Protector Ñacunday	APN	1,000
Bosque Protector Yakuy	ITA	1,000
Reserva Nacional Kuriy	APN	1,000
Monumento Científico Moises S. Bertoni	APN	200

* occurs on border of Central Paraguay and Alto Paraná regions

ACKNOWLEDGMENTS

I thank K. Able, V. Remsen, and R. Ridgely for reviewing the submitted draft of this monograph. Portions of this monograph formed the basis of my Ph.D. dissertation at Loma Linda University; I thank my committee members, L. Brand, R. Carter, D. Cowles, J. Galusha, J. Gibson, and my major professor, T. Goodwin, for their guidance and encouragement during my research and for reviewing earlier versions of the manuscript. C. Velázquez assisted in translating the Spanish "resumen." H. Brodkin and J. Clements pointed out several previously undetected errors in the submitted draft.

Field work during 1987-1989 was funded by grants from the Pan American Section of BirdLife International (formerly the International Council for Bird Preservation), Sigma Xi, and the United States Fish and Wildlife Service, while I served as a United States Peace Corps Volunteer for the Museo Nacional de Historia Natural del Paraguay (formerly the Inventario Biológico Nacional). Additional funds for field work were provided directly or indirectly by the Asociación de Apoyo a las Comunidades Indígenas, Center for Human Potential, J. Escobar, Evany, German Technical Mission, Itaipú Binacional, Japanese International Cooperation Agency, Ministerio de Agricultura y Ganadería, New York Zoological Society, R. Perrin, A. and K. Robinson, P. Scharf, G. Sequera, D. Snider, The Nature Conservancy, U. S. Peace Corps, and my meager Peace Corps living allowance. Field work during 1993 was personally financed. Field work during 1994 was conducted while guiding a birding trip for Neotropic Bird Tours.

Numerous persons assisted with the field work, most notably C. Aguilar, F. Areco de Medina, N. Boyajian, H. and P. Brodkin, A. Colmán, G. Commeau, J. Escobar, T. Granizo Tamayo, J. Fox, M. Hayes, S. LaBar, N. López de Kochalka, N. Pérez, R. Perrin, J. Ramirez, R. Ryan, P. Scharf, D. Snider, and R. Thorsell. Others included C. Acevedo Gómez, M. Angel, J. Contreras, K. Ericsson, B. Fostervold, J. Kochalka, A. Madroño Nieto, D. Mandelburger, N. Neris, A. and K. Robinson, V. and B. Roth, C. Sorenson, W. Sosa, A. Taber, C. Yahnke, and numerous others who made life interesting.

Museum work during 1992 was funded by grants from the American Museum of Natural History (AMNH), Field Museum of Natural History (FMNH), and Loma Linda University. The following museum personnel provided assistance: A. Andors, M. LeCroy, L. Short, and F. Vuilleumier (AMNH); A. Maurer, T. Schulenberg, and D. Willard (FMNH); P. Chu, D. Golden, J. Hinshaw, R. Payne, and R. Storer (University of Michigan Museum of Zoology); R. Browning, B. Farmer, M. Foster, and G. Graves (National Museum of Natural History). N. K. Johnson of the University of California at Berkeley provided a printout of Paraguayan specimens at the Museum of Vertebrate Zoology, and permission to cite several specimen records. P. Colston provided information on a number of specimen records from the (British) Natural History Museum. A. Colmán and N. Pérez allowed me to examine specimens at the Museo de Historia Natural de Itaipú Binacional in 1994, and to include pertinent specimen records in this monograph.

Unpublished observations of birds in Paraguay were kindly provided by R. Behrstock, D. Brooks, T. Brooks, R. Clay, J. Escobar, D. Finch, J. Fox, S. Goodman, A. Taber, T. Granizo Tamayo, H. Loftin, A. Madroño Nieto, R. Ridgely, A. and K. Robinson, R. Ryan and the clients of Neotropic Bird Tours. I am especially indebted to P. Scharf, whose detailed notes on the numbers of birds observing during his numerous trips and additional information on the rarer species have assisted me greatly.

Drawings of birds were provided by D. Brown.

S. Holt and D. Wechsler kindly provided catalog numbers of rare bird photographs deposited at VIREO (Visual Resources for Ornithology, Academy of Natural Sciences of Philadelphia).

Assistance in obtaining literature was provided by H. and P. Brodkin, T. Brooks, N. Collar, A. Colmán, J. Contreras, J. Escobar, M. Foster, K. Garrett, J. Gibson, S. Goodman, T. Goodwin, J. Hinshaw, N. López de Kochalka, A. Madroño, R. Paynter, N. Pérez, T. Schulenberg, R. Storer, D. Stotz, F. Vuilleumier, and E. Willis. Interlibrary loans were paid for by the Graduate School of Loma Linda University and patiently processed by F. Alemozaffer.

I thank the many Paraguayans, too many to name, who have made life in their country so interesting and adventurous. And finally, I thank my wife, Marta, for cheerfully following me to some of the more remote regions of Paraguay (even during our honeymoon), for patience during the many hours I spent in my office or traveling, and for unwavering emotional support.

LITERATURE CITED

Acevedo Gómez, C. (ed.). 1989. Resumenes y Programa, II Encuentro Paraguayo-Argentino de Ornitología. Imprenta Graphis S. R. L., Asunción. 51 pp.

Acevedo [Gómez], C., J. Fox, R. Gauto, T. Granizo, S. Keel, J. Pinazzo, L. Spinzi, W. Sosa, and V. Vera. 1990. Areas Prioritarias para la Conservación en la Región Oriental del Paraguay. Centro de Datos para la Conservación, Asunción. 99 pp.

Alho, C. J. R., T. E. Lacher, Jr., and H. C. Gonçalves. 1988. Environmental degradation in the Pantanal ecosystem. BioScience 38:164-171.

Altman, A., and B. Swift. 1986. Checklist of the Birds of South America. ZiPrint Parchment (Oxford) Ltd., Oxford, England. 64 pp.

Altman, A., and B. Swift. 1989. Checklist of the Birds of South America. 2nd ed. St. Mary's Press, Washington, D.C. 82 pp.

Altman, A., and B. Swift. 1993. Checklist of the Birds of South America. 3rd ed. BookMasters, Inc., Ashland, Ohio. 84 pp.

American Ornithologists' Union. 1983. Check-list of North American Birds. 6th ed. American Ornithologists' Union, Washington, D.C. 826 pp.

American Ornithologists' Union. 1985. Thirty-fifth supplement to the American Ornithologists' Union Check-list of North American Birds. Auk 102:680-686.

American Ornithologists' Union. 1987. Thirty-sixth supplement to the American Ornithologists' Union Check-list of North American Birds. Auk 104:591-596.

American Ornithologists' Union. 1989. Thirty-seventh supplement to the American Ornithologists' Union Check-list of North American Birds. Auk 106:532-538.

American Ornithologists' Union. 1991. Thirty-eighth supplement to the American Ornithologists' Union Check-list of North American Birds. Auk 108:750-754.

American Ornithologists' Union. 1993. Thirty-ninth supplement to the American Ornithologists' Union Check-list of North American Birds. Auk 110:675-682.

Anonymous. 1981. El taguató ruvichá ganó popularidad. Hoy, Asunción, 25 Sep., p. 1.

Anonymous. 1982a. Guía de Algunos Vertebrados del Parque Nacional Ybycuí. Ministerio de Agricultura y Ganadería and Servicio Forestal Nacional, Asunción. 47 pp.

Anonymous. 1982b. Plan de Manejo y Desarrollo Conceptual del Parque Nacional Cerro Corá. Ministerio de Defensa Nacional, Dirección Técnica, Ministerio de Agricultura y Ganadería and Servicio Forestal Nacional, Asunción. 79 pp.

Anonymous. 1985. Environmental Profile of Paraguay. International Institute for Environment and Development, Technical Planning Secretariat and United States Agency for International Development, Washington, D.C. 162 pp.

Anonymous. 1987. Rara especie de ave llegó hasta Paraguay. El Diario, Asunción, 11 Dec., p. 15.

Anonymous. 1990. Statistix Manual. Analytical Software, St. Paul, Minnesota. 280 pp.

Acosta, E. (ed.). 1991. Encuentro de Ornitología de Paraguay, Brasil y Argentina. Itaipú Binacional, Universidad Nacional de Asunción, and Sociedad de Biología del Paraguay, Ciudad del Este. 43 pp.

Argüello M. de Masulli, B. S. 1983. Exploraciones zoológicas en el Paraguay. Exposición en el Symposia "Historia de la Zoología Neotropical: Los Viajeros" (Informe Final IX Claz Peru), pp. 127-133.

Azara, F. de. 1802a. Apuntamientos para la Historia Natural de los Páxaros del Paragüay y Rio de la Plata. Vol. 1. Imprenta de la Viuda de Ibarra, Madrid. 534 pp.

Azara, F. de. 1802b. Apuntamientos para la Historia Natural de los Quadrúpedos del Paragüay y Rio de la Plata. Vol. 1. Imprenta de la Viuda de Ibarra, Madrid. 318 pp. (Reprinted 1978, by Arno Press, New York).

Azara, F. de. 1805a. Apuntamientos para la Historia Natural de los Páxaros del Paragüay y Rio de la Plata. Vol. 2. Imprenta de la Viuda de Ibarra, Madrid. 562 pp.

Azara, F. de. 1805b. Apuntamientos para la Historia Natural de los Páxaros del Paragüay y Rio de la Plata. Vol. 3. Imprenta de la Viuda de Ibarra, Madrid. 479 pp. (Vols. 1-3 reprinted 1940-1942, by Biblioteca Americana, Buenos Aires, in 5 volumes).

Banks, R. C. 1977. A review of the crested tinamous (Aves: Tinamidae). Proc. Biol. Soc. Washington 89:529-544.

Beddall, B. G. 1975. "Un naturalista original": Don Félix de Azara, 1746-1821. J. Hist. Biol. 8:15-66.

Beddall, B. G. 1983. The isolated Spanish genius-myth or reality? Félix de Azara and the birds of Paraguay. J. Hist. Biol. 16:225-258.

Belton, W. 1884. Taxonomy of certain species of birds from Rio Grande do Sul, Brazil. Natl. Geogr. Res. Rep. 17:183-188.

Benstead, P. 1994. Brazilian Merganser in Argentina: going, going... Cotinga 1:8.

Berlepsch, H. 1887. Systematisches verzeichniss der von Herrn Ricardo Rohde in Paraguay gesammelten vögel. J. f. Ornithol. 35:1-37, 113-134.

Bernardi, L. 1984. Contribución a la dendrología Paraguaya. Primera parte. Apocynaceae-Bombacaceae-Euphorbiaceae-Flacourtiaceae-Mimoso ideae-Caesalpinioideae-Papilionatae. Boissiera 35:1-341.

Bernardi, L. 1985. Contribución a la dendrología Paraguaya. Segunda parte. Meliaceae-Moraceae-Myrsinaceae-Myrtaceae-Rubiaceae-Vochysia ceae. Boissiera 37:1-294.

Bertoni, A. de W. 1898. Catálogo descriptivo de las aves útiles del Paraguay. Rev. Agron. Cienc. Apl., Asunción 1:377-410, 526-539.

Bertoni, A. de W. 1900. Catálogo descriptivo de las aves útiles del Paraguay. Rev. Agron. Cienc. Apl., Asunción 2:1-11, 55-79.

Bertoni, A. de W. 1901. Aves nuevas del Paraguay. Catálogo de las aves del Paraguay. Anal. Cient. Parag. 1(1):1-216.

Bertoni, A. de W. 1903a. Un loro útil en agricultura. El Agricultor 1(5):3.

Bertoni, A. de W. 1903b. Importancia de las aves en agricultura. El Agricultor 1(7):2-3, (8):33-34, (9):41-42, (10):49.

Bertoni, A. de W. 1904. Contribución para el conocimiento de las aves del Paraguay. Anal. Cient. Parag. 1(3):1-10.

Bertoni, A. de W. 1907. Segunda contribución á la ornitología paraguaya. Nuevas especies paraguayas. Rev. Inst. Parag. 1906:298-309.

Bertoni, A. de W. 1913. Sobre aves del Paraguay, poco conocidas. Rev. Chil. Hist. Nat. 17:217-223.

Bertoni, A. de W. 1914a. Fauna Paraguaya. Catálogos Sistemáticos de los Vertebrados del Paraguay. Gráfico M. Brossa, Asunción. 86 pp.

Bertoni, A. de W. 1914b. Las aves y el naranjo. Agronomía 5:419-421.

Bertoni, A. de W. 1914c. Los buitres y el carbunclo. Agronomía 5:423-424.

Bertoni, A. de W. 1914d. Las aves contra las garrapatas. Bol. Dept. Nac. Fom. 1(4):25-26.

Bertoni, A. de W. 1918a. Apuntes sobre aves del Paraguay. Hornero 1:188-191.

Bertoni, A. de W. 1918b. Adiciones a los vertebrados del Paraguay. Anal. Cient. Parag. 2(3):233-241.

Bertoni, A. de W. 1918c. Aves luminosas en el Paraguay. Anal. Cient. Parag. 2(3):242.

Bertoni, A. de W. 1918d. Sobre nidificación de los eufónidos. Anal. Cient. Parag. 2(3):242-244.

Bertoni, A. de W. 1918e. Indice sistemático de las aves nuevas del Paraguay. Anal. Cient. Parag. 2(3):245-247.

Bertoni, A. de W. 1919a. Especies de aves nuevas para el Paraguay. Hornero 1:255-258.

Bertoni, A. de W. 1919b. Apuntes sobre aves del Paraguay. Hornero 1:284-287.

Bertoni, A. de W. 1922a. Errores sobre el Canindé de Azara. Rev. Soc. Cient. Parag. 1(3):39-40.

Bertoni, A. de W. 1922b. Aves observadas en el Parque y Museo Municipal de Asunción ex-"Quinta Caballero"-1920-1921. Rev. Soc. Cient. Parag. 1(3):40-42.

Bertoni, A. de W. 1923a. Notas zoológicas. II. Observaciones ornitológicas. Rev. Soc. Cient. Parag. 1(4-5):52-53.

Bertoni, A. de W. 1923b. Informe sobre el gorrión importado. Rev. Soc. Cient. Parag. 1(4-5):73-74.

Bertoni, A. de W. 1924. Notas sobre aves del Paraguay. Hornero 3:279.

Bertoni, A. de W. 1925a. Aves paraguayas poco conocidas. Rev. Soc. Cient. Parag. 2(1):68-70.

Bertoni, A. de W. 1925b. Sobre nomenclatura guaraní de *Tapera* y *Dromococcyx*. Rev. Soc. Cient. Parag. 2(1):70.

Bertoni, A. de W. 1926. Apuntes ornitológicos. Hornero 3:396-401.

Bertoni, A. de W. 1927. Notas ornitológicas. Nueva forma de psitácidos [*sic*] del Paraguay. (Descripción y distribución de Parakáu y Paraguá.) Rev. Soc. Cient. Parag. 2(3):149-150.

Bertoni, A. de W. 1928a. Sobre el *Planesticus subalaris* (Lev.). Rev. Soc. Cient. Parag. 2(4):187-188.

Bertoni, A. de W. 1928b. El género *Ridgwayornis* A. W. Bertoni (Aves). Rev. Soc. Cient. Parag. 2(4):188.

Bertoni, A. de W. 1928c. Sobre las aves de rapiña del género *Spizaëtus* Vieill. o taguató apiratî. Rev. Soc. Cient. Parag. 2(4):188.

Bertoni, A. de W. 1929. Notas sobre la *Chunga Burmeisteri* [*sic*] (Hartl.) hallada en el Chaco Paraguayo. Rev. Soc. Cient. Parag. 2(5):228.

Bertoni, A. de W. 1930a. Sobre ornitología del Chaco Paraguayo. Aves colectadas por Félix Posner en la Colonia "Monte Sociedad", hoy Benjamin Aceval (Villa Hayes). Rev. Soc. Cient. Parag. 2(6):241-257.

Bertoni, A. de W. 1930b. Anexo; aves observadas por el Dr. A. Barbero paraje Santa Jacinta en el Confuso (Chaco); especies que no figuran en la colección de Posner. Rev. Soc. Cient. Parag. 2(6):257-258.

Bertoni, A. de W. 1939. Catálagos sistemáticos de los vertebrados del Paraguay. Rev. Soc. Cient. Parag. 4(4):1-59.

Bertoni, M. S. 1918. Condiciones Generales de la Vida Orgánica y División Territorial. Imprenta y Edición "Ex Sylvis," Puerto Bertoni, Paraguay.

Beven, S., E. F. Connor, and K. Beven. 1984. Avian biogeography in the Amazon Basin and the biological model of diversification. J. Biogeogr. 11:383-399.

Blake, E. R. 1949. *Ictinia misisippiensis* collected in Paraguay. Auk 66:82.

Blake, E. R. 1977. Manual of Neotropical Birds. Vol. 1. The University of Chicago Press, Chicago. 674 pp.

Bó, N. A. 1969. Acerca de la afinidad de dos formas de *Serpophaga*. Neotropica 15:54-58.

Bó, N. A. 1972. *Zonotrichia capensis hypoleuca* (Todd). Sistemática y distribución en la Argentina. Neotropica 18:95-102.

Boettner, R. 1973. Reflections on the geology of Paraguay. Pp. 61-64 *in* J. R. Gorham (ed.), Paraguay: Ecological Essays. Academy of the Arts and Sciences of the Americas, Miami.

Brabourne, L. 1914. Aviculture in Paraguay. Avicult. Mag., 3rd ser., 5:185-191.

Brodkorb, P. 1934. Geographic variation in *Belonopterus chilensis* (Molina). Occ. Pap. Mus. Zool., Univ. Michigan 293:1-13.

Brodkorb, P. 1935. A new ovenbird from Paraguay. Occ. Pap. Mus. Zool., Univ. Michigan 316:1-2.

Brodkorb, P. 1937a. New or noteworthy birds from the Paraguayan Chaco. Occ. Pap. Mus. Zool., Univ. Michigan 345:1-2.

Brodkorb, P. 1937b. The southern races of the Great Ant-Shrike, *Taraba major*. Proc. Biol. Soc. Washington 50:7-8.

172

Brodkorb, P. 1937c. Additions to the avifauna of Paraguay. Proc. Biol. Soc. Washington 50:33-34.

Brodkorb, P. 1938a. Five new birds from the Paraguayan Chaco. Occ. Pap. Mus. Zool., Univ. Michigan 367:1-5.

Brodkorb, P. 1938b. A new species of Crested Tinamou from Paraguay. Occ. Pap. Mus. Zool., Univ. Michigan 382:1-4.

Brodkorb, P. 1938c. Further additions to the avifauna of Paraguay. Occ. Pap. Mus. Zool., Univ. Michigan 394:1-5.

Brodkorb, P. 1939a. Three new birds from Paraguay. Proc. Biol. Soc. Washington 52:83-84.

Brodkorb, P. 1939b. Notes on the races of *Rhea americanus* (Linnaeus). Proc. Biol. Soc. Washington 52:137-138.

Brodkorb, P. 1939c. A southern race of the Jacana. Proc. Biol. Soc. Washington 52:185-186.

Brodkorb, P. 1941a. An undescribed woodpecker from the Paraguayan Chaco. Proc. Biol. Soc. Washington 54:23-24.

Brodkorb, P. 1941b. A race of woodhewer from the Alto Parana. Occ. Pap. Mus. Zool., Univ. Michigan 453:1-3.

Brooks, D. 1991a. Some notes on the Ciconiiformes in the Paraguayan Chaco. Spec. Grp. Storks Ibises Spoonbills Newsl. 4(1):1.

Brooks, D. 1991b. Algunos antecedentes sobre las poblaciones del norte de Flamenco Chileno (*Phoenicopterus chilensis*). Bol. Secr. Reg. Grupo Phoenicopteridae Sur Andina 2(6):2-3.

Brooks, T. M., R. Barnes, L. Bartrina, S. H. M. Butchart, R. P. Clay, E. Z. Esquivel, N. I. Etcheverry, J. C. Lowen, and J. Vincent. 1993. Bird surveys and conservation in the Paraguayan Atlantic forest. BirdLife Int. Study Rep. 57:1-145.

Brooks, T. [M.], and E. Esquivel. 1994. The fate of the Isla Yacyreta [*sic*], Ñeembucu [*sic*], Paraguay. Cotinga 2:9.

Brown, K. S., Jr. 1987. Biogeography and evolution of Neotropical butterflies. Pp. 66-104 *in* T. C. Whitmore and G. T. Prance (eds.), Biogeography and Quaternary History in Tropical America. Clarendon Press, Oxford, England.

Brown, K. S., Jr., and G. T. Prance. 1987. Soils and vegetation. Pp. 19-45 *in* T. C. Whitmore and G. T. Prance (eds.), Biogeography and Quaternary History in Tropical America. Clarendon Press, Oxford, England.

Brown, J. H., and A. C. Gibson. 1983. Biogeography. The C. V. Mosby Company, St. Louis. 643 pp.

Bucher, E. H., A. Bonetto, T. P. Boyle, P. Canevari, G. Castro, P. Huszar, and T. Stone. 1993. Hidrovia: An Initial Environmental Examination of the Paraguay-Paraná Waterway. Wetlands for the Americas, Manomet, Massachusetts, and Buenos Aires. 72 pp.

Cabot, J. 1991. Distribution and habitat selection of *Buteo polyosoma* and *B. poecilochrous* in Bolivia and neighbouring countries. Bull. Brit. Ornithol. Club 111:199-309.

Cabrera, A. L. 1970. La vegetación del Paraguay en el cuadro fitogeográfico de América del Sur. Bol. Soc. Arg. Bot. 11:121-129.

Cabrera, C., and M. E. Escobar. 1991. Colección de aves del Museo de Historia Natural de Itaipú Binacional. P. 17 *in* E. Acosta (ed.), Encuentro de Ornitología de Paraguay, Brasil y Argentina. Itaipú Binacional, Universidad Nacional de Asunción, and Sociedad de Biología del Paraguay, Ciudad del Este.

Cadogan, L. 1973. Some plants and animals in Guaraní and Guayakí mythology. Pp. 97-104 *in* J. R. Gorham (ed.), Paraguay: Ecological Essays. Academy of the Arts and Sciences of the Americas, Miami.

Capparella, A. P. 1988. Genetic variation in Neotropical birds: implications for the speciation process. Pp. 1658-1664 *in* H. Ouellet (ed.), Acta XIX Congressus Internationalis Ornithologici. Vol. 2. University of Ottawa Press, Ottawa.

Capparella, A. P. 1991. Neotropical avian diversity and riverine barriers. Pp. 307-316 *in* Acta XX Congressus Internationalis Ornithologici. Vol. 1. New Zealand Ornithological Congress Trust Board, Wellington.

Carlstein Quiñónez, R. M. 1993. Ocaso del bosque paraguayo. ABC Color, Suplemento Rural, Asunción, 25 August, pp. 1-2.

Carman, R. L. 1971. Información sobre el matico *Icterus croconotus*. Hornero 11:127.

Cassin, J. 1859. Appendix J. Notes on the birds collected by the La Plata Expedition. Pp. 599-602 *in* T. J. Page, La Plata, The Argentine Confederation and Paraguay. Harper & Brothers, New York.

Castex, M. N. (ed.). 1968. Sánchez Labrador: Peces y Aves del Paraguay Natural Ilustrado, 1767. Compañia General Fabril Editora, S. A., Buenos Aires. 511 pp.

Chapman, F. M. 1917. The distribution of bird-life in Colombia; a contribution to a biological survey of South America. Bull. Amer. Mus. Nat. Hist. 36:1-729.

Chapman, F. M. 1940. The post-glacial history of *Zonotrichia capensis*. Bull. Amer. Mus. Nat. Hist. 77:381-438.

Chebez, J. C., and S. Heinonen Fortabat. 1987. Novedades ornitogeográficas argentinas. I. Nótul. Fauníst. 2:1-2.

Cheetham, A. H., and J. E. Hazel. 1969. Binary (presence-absence) similarity coefficients. J. Paleontol. 43:1130-1136.

Cherrie, G. K., and E. M. B. Reichenberger. 1921. Descriptions of proposed new birds from Brazil, Paraguay, and Argentina. Amer. Mus. Novit. 27:1-6.

Cherrie, G. K., and E. M. B. Reichenberger. 1923. Descriptions of proposed new birds from Brazil and Paraguay. Amer. Mus. Novit. 58:1-8.

Chubb, C. 1910. On the birds of Paraguay. Ibis, ser. 9, 4:53-78, 263-285, 517-534, 571-647.

Clark, G. A., Jr. 1979. Body weights of birds: a review. Condor 81:193-202.

Clements, J. F. 1991. Birds of the World: A Check List. Ibis Publishing Company, Vista, California. 617 pp.

Colinvaux, P. A. 1989. Ice-age Amazon revisited. Nature 340:188-189.

Collar, N. J., and P. N. Andrew. 1988. Birds to Watch: The ICBP World Checklist of Threatened Birds. International Council for Bird Preservation, Cambridge. 320 pp.

Collar, N. J., L. P. Gonzaga, N. Krabbe, A. Madroño Nieto, L. G. Naranjo, T. A. Parker III, and D. C. Wege. 1992 Threatened Birds of the Americas. The ICBP/IUCN Red Data Book. 3rd ed., pt. 2. International Council for Bird Preservation, Cambridge. 1150 pp.

Colmán, A., and N. Pérez. 1991. Registro de nuevas especies de aves para el Paraguay. P. 33 *in* E. Acosta (ed.), Encuentro de Ornitología de Paraguay, Brasil y Argentina. Itaipú Binacional, Universidad Nacional de Asunción, and Sociedad de Biología del Paraguay, Ciudad del Este.

Comte, D., and Y. Hasui. 1971. Geochronology of eastern Paraguay by the Potassium-Argon method. Rev. Bras. Geoc. 1:33-43.

Conover, H. B. 1934. A new species of rail from Paraguay. Auk 51:365-366.

Conover, H. B. 1937. A new race of the Spotted Tinamou, *Nothura maculosa*, from the Paraguayan Chaco. Proc. Biol. Soc. Washington 50:227-230.

Conover, [H.] B. 1950. A study of the spotted tinamous, genus *Nothura*. Fieldiana (Zool.) 31:339-362.

Contreras, A. O. 1993. Hallazgo del Yasy Yateré Guazú *Dromococcyx phasianellus phasianellus* (Spix, 1824) en Isla Hú, Ñeembucú, sudeste del Paraguay oriental (Aves: Cuculidae, Neomorphinae). Nótul. Fauníst. 41:1-2.

Contreras, A. O., and D. Mandelburger. 1985. Aportes para la ornitología del Paraguay. I. La avifauna de Pozo Colorado, Departamento Presidente Hayes, Chaco Boreal. Hist. Nat. 5:334-336.

174

Contreras, A. O., C. Vitale, Y. E. Davies, and J. L. [Ramírez]. 1989. La avifauna del Departamento de Misiones, República del Paraguay. Nota preliminar acerca de la zona comprendida entre Santiago y Ayolas. Pp. 11-12 *in* C. Acevedo Gómez (ed.), Resumenes y Programa, II Encuentro Paraguayo-Argentino de Ornitología. Imprenta Graphis S. R. L., Asunción.

Contreras, J. R. 1986a. Acerca de la presencia de *Phaetornis* [*sic*] *pretrei* (Lesson & Delattre, 1839) (Aves: Trochilidae) en Paraguay oriental. Hist. Nat. 6:31-32.

Contreras, J. R. 1986b. Nota acerca de la distribución de *Euscarthmus meloryphus* Wied, 1831 (Aves, Tyrannidae). Hist. Nat. 6:48.

Contreras, J. R. (ed.). 1988. Ornitología: Argentina-Paraguay, 1988. Corrientes.

Contreras, J. R. 1989. La avifauna de la Estancia Co'e Pyahú y sus cercanías, Nueva Asunción, República del Paraguay. Nótul. Fauníst. 17:1-6.

Contreras, J. R. 1992. Notas ornitológicas paraguayas. I. *Sterna maxima maxima* Boddaert, 1783 y *Anthracothorax nigricollis nigricollis* (Vieillot, 1817). Nótul. Fauníst. 28:1-4.

Contreras, J. R., C. N. Acevedo Gómez, and N. López Huerta. 1988a. Status y distribución del chimango, *Polyborus chimango chimango* (Viellot, 1816) en la República del Paraguay. Nótul. Fauníst. 10:1-2.

Contreras, J. R., C. N. Acevedo Gómez, and N. López Huerta. 1988b. Acerca de la distribución y el status de conservación de *Elanoides forficatus yetapa* en el Paraguay (Aves, Accipitridae). Pp. 25-27 *in* J. R. Contreras (ed.), Ornitología: Argentina-Paraguay, 1988. Corrientes.

Contreras, J. R., and J. Escobar Argaña. 1993. Acerca de la distribución de *Mesembrinibis cayennensis* (Gmelin, 1789) en el norte Argentino y en el Paraguay (Aves: Threskiornithidae). Nótul. Fauníst. 45:1-4.

Contreras, J. R., and A. O. Contreras. 1986. Acerca de *Campylorhynchus turdinus unicolor* Wied en Paraguay y en la República Argentina (Aves: Trogloditidae [*sic*]). Hist. Nat. 6:75-76.

Contreras, J. R., and A. O. Contreras. 1992. Notas ornitológicas paraguayas. III. *Sterna trudeaui* Audubon, 1838, una especie nueva para el Paraguay y nuevos datos sobre otras tres. Nótul. Fauníst. 31:1-3.

Contreras, J. R., and A. O. Contreras. 1993a. Nuevas consideraciones acerca del Chimango, *Milvago chimango chimango* (Viellot; 1816) en la República del Paraguay (Aves: Falconidae). Nótul. Fauníst. 36:1-4.

Contreras, J. R., and A. O. Contreras. 1993b. Acerca de la distribución de *Pipraeidea melanonota melanonota* (Vieillot, 1819) en la República del Paraguay y en el norte Argentino (Aves, Emberizidae: Thraupinae). Nótul. Fauníst. 46:1-4.

Contreras, J. R., A. O. Contreras, and J. Escobar Argaña. 1993a. Comentarios acerca de algunas especies de aves nuevas o poco conocidas para el Paraguay. Nótul. Fauníst. 43:1-7.

Contreras, J. R., and A. O. Contreras. 1994. Acerca de *Laterallus exilis* (Temminck, 1831) y de *Calidris bairdii* (Coues, 1861) en la República del Paraguay (Aves: Rallidae y Scolopacidae). Nótul. Fauníst. 51:1-4.

Contreras, J. R., and N. González Romero. 1988. Una avifauna intraurbana en la ciudad de Asunción, Departamento Central, República del Paraguay. Pp. 30-34 *in* J. R. Contreras (ed.), Ornitología: Argentina-Paraguay, 1988. Corrientes.

Contreras, J. R., and N. González Romero. 1989a. Nuevos datos acerca de la avifauna intraurbana de Ñu Guazú, Asunción, República del Paraguay. Nótul. Fauníst. 18:1-2.

Contreras, J. R., and N. González Romero. 1989b. Notas ornitológicas paraguayas. La Palomita Escamosa *Columbina squammata squammata* (Lesson, 1831). Nótul. Fauníst. 19:1-3.

Contreras, J. R., and N. González Romero. 1989c. Algunas observaciones acerca de la presencia y abundancia de rapaces (Accipitridae y Falconidae) en una transecta a través del Chaco Boreal, Paraguay. Nótul. Fauníst. 20:1-4.

Contreras, J. R., and N. González Romero. 1991. Notas ornitológicas paraguayas. II. *Caprimulgus longirostris bifasciatus* Gould, 1837, como visitante en el Paraguay. Nótul. Fauníst. 24:1-4.

Contreras, J. R., N. Gonzáles Romero, and L. M. Berry. 1990. Lista preliminar de la avifauna de la República del Paraguay. Cuad. Téc. Félix de Azara 2:1-42.

Contreras, J. R., N. González Romero, and A. O. Contreras. 1991. Las aves del Parque Nacional Vapor Cué [*sic*], Departamento Cordillera, República del Paraguay. P. 37 *in* E. Acosta (ed.), Encuentro de Ornitología de Paraguay, Brasil y Argentina. Itaipú Binacional, Universidad Nacional de Asunción and Sociedad de Biología del Paraguay, Ciudad del Este.

Contreras, J. R., N. González Romero, S. Peris Alvarez, A. O. Contreras, and C. Acevedo Gómez. 1989. Contribución al conocimiento de la avifauna del Lago Ypoá y regiones adyacentes del Departamento Paraguarí, República del Paraguay. Inf. Cient. Inst. Cs. Bás., Asunción 6:35-53.

Contreras, J. R., A. Colmán Jara, and N. Pérez Villamayor. 1992a. Notas ornitológicas paraguayas. II. *Podiceps major major* (Boddaert, 1783) (Aves: Podicipedidae). Nótul. Fauníst. 32:1-3.

Contreras, J. R., N. Pérez Villamayor, and A. Colmán Jara. 1992b. Notas ornitológicas paraguayas. IV. Una especie nueva para el Paraguay y consideraciones sobre otras tres. Nótul. Fauníst. 32:1-3.

Contreras, J. R., N. Pérez Villamayor, and A. Colmán Jara. 1993b. Acerca de *Picumnus albosquammatus* Lafresnaye, 1844, y su presencia en la avifauna paraguaya (Picidae: Picumninae). Nótul. Fauníst. 44:1-4.

Cracraft, J. 1985. Historical biogeography and patterns of differentiation within the South American avifauna: areas of endemism. Ornithol. Monogr. 36:49-84.

Cracraft, J. 1988. Deep-history biogeography: retrieving the historical pattern of evolving continental biotas. Syst. Zool. 37:221-236.

Cracraft, J., and R. O. Prum. 1988. Patterns and processes of diversification: speciation and historical congruence in some Neotropical birds. Evolution 42:603-620.

Croizat, L. 1958. Panbiogeography. Vol. 1. The New World. Published by the author, Caracas.

Dabbene, R. 1912. Contribución a la ornitología del Paraguay; notas sobre las aves colectadas en Villa Rica por el señor Félix Posner. Anal. Mus. Nac., Buenos Aires 23:283-390.

Dabbene, R. 1920. El "Canindé" de Azara es el *Ara ararauna* (Lin.). Hornero 2:56.

Dalgleish, J. J. 1889. Notes on a collection of birds and eggs from the Republic of Paraguay. Proc. Roy. Phys. Soc., Edinburgh 10:73-88.

Dibble, S., and A. Webb. 1992. Paraguay plotting a new course. Natl. Geogr. 182(2):88-113.

Dirección del Servicio Geográfico Militar. 1989. [Map of] Paraguay. Escala 1:2.000.000. 8th ed. Dirección del Servicio Geográfico Militar, Asunción.

Dirección del Servicio Geográfico Militar. 1992. [Map of] Paraguay. Escala 1:2.000.000. 11th ed. Dirección del Servicio Geográfico Militar, Asunción.

Dunning, J. B. (ed.). 1992. CRC Handbook of Avian Body Masses. CRC Press, Boca Raton, Florida. 371 pp.

Dunning, J. S., and R. S. Ridgely. 1982. South American Land Birds. Harrowood Books, Newton Square, Pennsylvania. 364 pp.

Eckle, E. B. 1959. Geology and mineral resources of Paraguay-a reconnaissance. Geol. Surv. Prof. Pap. 327:1-110.

Eisenmann, E., and L. L. Short. 1982. Systematics of the avian genus *Emberizoides* (Emberizidae). Amer. Mus. Novit. 2740:1-21.

Emategui, F. 1977. Atlas Hermes. Compendio Geográfico del Paraguay. Hermes Editorial Pedagógica, Asunción. 63 pp.

Endler, J. A. 1982a. Problems in distinguishing historical from ecological factors in biogeography. Amer. Zool. 22:441-452.

Endler, J. A. 1982b. Pleistocene forest refuges: fact or fancy? Pp. 179-200 in G. Prance (ed.), Biological Diversification in the Tropics. Columbia University Press, New York.

Ereshefsky, M. (ed.). 1992. The Units of Evolution: Essays on the Nature of Species. Massachusetts Institute of Technology Press, Cambridge, Massachusetts. 405 pp.

Escobar E., M. E., and M. J. de Salomón. 1983. Contribución al conocimiento de algunas especies de aves que habitan el campus universitario de San Lorenzo-Paraguay. Pp. 23-25 in F. G. Stiles and P. G. Aguilar F. (eds.), Primer Simposio de Ornitología Neotropical (14-15 octubre 1983, Arequipa-Peru). Asociación Peruana para la Conservación de la Naturaleza, Lima.

Esser, G. 1982. Vegetationsgliederung und Kakteenvegetation von Paraguay. Akademie der Wissenschaften und der Literatur, Mainz. 112 pp.

Fariña Sánchez, T. 1973. The climate of Paraguay. Pp. 33-38 in J. R. Gorham (ed.), Paraguay: Ecological Essays. Academy of the Arts and Sciences of the Americas, Miami.

Fernández Pérez, J. (ed.). 1992. Apuntamientos para la Historia Natural de los Páxaros del Paraguay y del Río de la Plata. Comisión Interministerial de Ciencia y Tecnología, Madrid. 619 pp.

Ferreiro, O. 1965. Naturalistas en el Paraguay. Rev. Soc. Cient. Parag. 7(2):53-69.

Fiebrig, C. 1921. Algunos datos sobre aves del Paraguay. Hornero 2:205-213.

Finsch, O. 1867. Die Papageien, Monographisch Bearbeitet. Vol. 1. E. J. Brill, Leiden.

Fjeldså, J., and N. Krabbe. 1990. Birds of the High Andes. Zoological Museum, University of Copenhagen, Copenhagen. 876 pp.

Forshaw, J. M. 1989. Parrots of the World. 3rd ed. Landsowne Editions, Willoughby, Australia. 672 pp.

Foster, M. S. 1981. Cooperative behavior and social organization of the Swallow-tailed Manakin (Chiroxiphia caudata). Behav. Ecol. Sociobiol. 9:167-177.

Foster, M. S. 1983. Training biologists and resource managers in lesser developed countries. Interciencia 8:289-293.

Foster, M. S. 1985. Social organization and behavior of the Swallow-tailed Manakin, Chiroxiphia caudata. Natl. Geogr. Soc. Res. Rep. 18:313-320.

Foster, M. S. 1987a. Feeding methods and efficiencies of selected frugivorous birds. Condor 89:566-580.

Foster, M. S. 1987b. Delayed maturation, neoteny, and social system differences in two manakins of the genus Chiroxiphia. Evolution 41:547-558.

Foster, M. S. 1990. Factors influencing bird foraging preferences among conspecific fruit trees. Condor 92:844-854.

Foster, M. S., and L. A. Fitzgerald. 1982. A technique for live-trapping cormorants. J. Field Ornithol. 53:422-423.

Foster, M. S., N. E. López H., and M. E. Escobar. 1989. Observations of a nest of Red-crowned Ant-Tanagers in Paraguay. J. Field Ornithol. 60:459-468.

Freeman, S., and W. M. Jackson. 1990. Univariate metrics are not adequate to measure body size. Auk 107:69-74.

Fry, C. H. 1970. Ecological distribution of birds in north-eastern Mato Grosso State, Brazil. An. Acad. Brasil. Ciénc. 42:275-318.

Gallardo, J. M. 1979. Composición, distribución y origen de la herpetofauna chaqueña. Pp. 299-307 in W. E. Duellman (ed.), The South American Herpetofauna: its Origin, Evolution, and Dispersal. Mus. Nat. Hist., Univ. Kansas, Monogr. 7.

Garleff, K., and H. Stingl. 1985. Südamerika Geomorphologie und Paläoökologie im jüngeren Quartär. Fach Geographie an der Universität Bamberg, Bamberg. 394 pp.

Gentry, A. H., and J. López Parodi. 1980. Deforestation and increased flooding of the upper Amazon. Science 210:1354-1356.

Giai, A. G. 1949. Sobre un ejemplar joven de *Dromococcyx pavoninus* Pelzeln. Hornero 9:84-87.

Gibson, J. 1990. Biosim. Geoscience Research Institute, Loma Linda, California. [software program]

González Romero, N., and J. Contreras. 1989. Observaciones ornitológicas en el Chaco Boreal, Paraguay. Inf. Cient. Inst. Cs. Bás., Asunción 6:4-9.

González Romero, N., C. Vitale, A. Olavarrieta, and Y. E. Davies. 1988. Avifauna asunceña. I. Aves observadas en el Jardín Botánico y en la zona de Trinidad, noreste de Asunción, Paraguay. Nótul. Fauníst. 11:1-2.

González Torres, D., and N. González Romero. 1985. Estudio Limnológico del Lago Ypacarai. Instituto de Ciencias Básicas, Universidad Nacional de Asunción, Asunción.

Goodman, S. M., and C. Glynn. 1988. Comparative rates of natural osteological disorders in a collection of Paraguayan birds. J. Zool., London 214:167-177.

Gorham, J. R. (ed.). 1973a. Paraguay: Ecological Essays. Academy of the Arts and Sciences of the Americas, Miami. 296 pp.

Gorham, J. R. 1973b. The Paraguayan Chaco and its rainfall. Pp. 39-60 *in* J. R. Gorham (ed.), Paraguay: Ecological Essays. Academy of the Arts and Sciences of the Americas, Miami.

Gorham, J. R. 1973c. The history of natural history in Paraguay. Pp. 1-8 *in* J. R. Gorham (ed.), Paraguay: Ecological Essays. Academy of the Arts and Sciences of the Americas, Miami.

Gotelli, N. J., and G. R. Graves. 1990. Body size and the occurrence of avian species on land-bridge islands. J. Biogeogr. 17:315-325.

Granizo, T., and F. Hayes. 1989. El Pato Serrucho y su posible extinción en el Paraguay. ABC Color, Asunción, Oct. 12, p. 18.

Grant, C. H. B. 1911. List of birds collected in Argentina, Paraguay, Bolivia, and southern Brazil, with field-notes. Ibis 5:80-137, 317-350, 459-478.

Haffer, J. 1969. Speciation in Amazonian forest birds. Science 165:131-137.

Haffer, J. 1974. Avian speciation in tropical South America. Publ. Nutall Ornithol. Club 14:1-390.

Haffer, J. 1978. Distribution of Amazon forest birds. Bonner Zool. Eitr. 28:48-76.

Haffer, J. 1979. Quaternary biogeography of tropical lowland South America. Pp. 107-140 *in* W. E. Duellman (ed.), The South American Herpetofauna: its Origin, Evolution, and Dispersal. Mus. Nat. Hist., Univ. Kansas, Monogr. 7.

Haffer, J. 1982. General aspects of the refuge theory. Pp. 6-24 *in* G. T. Prance (ed.), Biological Diversification in the Tropics. Columbia University Press, New York.

Haffer, J. 1985. Avian zoogeography of the Neotropical lowlands. Ornithol. Monogr. 36:113-146.

Haffer, J. 1987. Biogeography of Neotropical birds. Pp. 105-150 *in* T. C. Whitmore and G. T. Prance (eds.), Biogeography and Quaternary History in Tropical America. Clarendon Press, Oxford, England.

Haffer, J. 1990. Avian species richness in tropical South America. Stud. Neotrop. Fauna Environ. 25:157-183.

Haffer, J., and J. W. Fitzpatrick. 1985. Geographic variation in some Amazonian forest birds. Ornithol. Monogr. 36:147-168.

Haffer, J., and H. Sick. 1993. Biogeography and speciation. Pp. 56-60 *in* H. Sick, Birds in Brazil: a Natural History. Princeton University Press, Princeton, New Jersey. 703 pp.

Hartlaub, C. J. G. 1847. Systematischer Index zu Don Félix du Azara's Apuntamientos para la Historia Natural de los Páxaros del Paraguay y Río de la Plata. Schünemann, Bremen. 29 pp.

178

Hayes, F. E. 1991. Raptor densities along the Paraguay River: seasonal, geographical and time of day variation. J. Raptor Res. 25:101-108.

Hayes, F. E. 1992. Intraspecific kleptoparasitism in the Great Kiskadee (*Pitangus sulphuratus*). Hornero 13:234-235.

Hayes, F. E. In press. Seasonal, geographical and time of day variation in resident waterbird densities along the Paraguay River. Hornero.

Hayes, F. E., and F. E. Areco de Medina. 1988. Notes on the ecology of the avifauna of Choré, Department of San Pedro, Paraguay. Hornero 13:59-70.

Hayes, F. E., and J. Escobar Argaña. 1990. Vertebrates in the diet of woodcreepers (Aves: Dendrocolaptidae). Hornero 13:162-165.

Hayes, F. E., and J. A. Fox. 1991. Seasonality, habitat use, and flock sizes of shorebirds at the Bahía de Asunción, Paraguay. Wilson Bull. 103:637-649.

Hayes, F. E., S. M. Goodman, J. A. Fox, T. Granizo Tamayo and N. E. López. 1990a. North American bird migrants in Paraguay. Condor 92:947-960.

Hayes, F. E., S. M. Goodman, and N. E. López. 1990b. New or noteworthy bird records from the Matogrosense region of Paraguay. Bull. Brit. Ornithol. Club 110:94-103.

Hayes, F. E., and T. Granizo Tamayo. 1992. Bird densities along three tributaries of the Paraná River in eastern Paraguay. Hornero 13:254-256.

Hayes, F. E., and P. A. Scharf. 1993. Birding in Paraguay. Birding 25:118-125.

Hayes, F. E., P. A. Scharf, and H. Loftin. 1991. A Birder's Field Checklist of the Birds of Paraguay. Russ's Natural History Books, Lake Helen, Florida. 27 pp.

Hayes, F. E., P. A. Scharf, and R. S. Ridgely. 1994. Austral bird migrants in Paraguay. Condor 96:83-97.

Hellmayr, C. E. 1935. Catalogue of birds of the Americas. Field Mus. Nat. Hist., Zool. Ser. 13, pt. 8:1-541.

Hellmayr, C. E. 1938. Catalogue of birds of the Americas. Field Mus. Nat. Hist., Zool. Ser. 13, pt. 11:1-662.

Hellmayr, C. E., and B. Conover. 1942. Catalogue of birds of the Americas. Field Mus. Nat. Hist., Zool. Ser. 13, pt. 1, no. 1:1-636.

Hellmayr, C. E., and B. Conover. 1949. Catalogue of birds of the Americas. Field Mus. Nat. Hist., Zool. Ser. 13, pt. 1, no. 4:1-358.

Hengeveld, R. 1990. Dynamic Biogeography. Cambridge University Press, Cambridge. 249 pp.

Howard, R., and A. Moore. 1991. A Complete Checklist of the Birds of the World. 2nd ed. Academic Press, London. 622 pp.

Hubálek, Z. 1982. Coefficients of association and similarity, based on binary (presence-absence) data: an evaluation. Biol. Rev. 57:669-689.

Hueck, K. 1966. Die Wälder Südamerikas. Ökologie, Zusammensetung und wirtschaftliche Bedeutung. Gustav Fischer Verlag, Stuttgart. 422 pp.

Ihering, H. von. 1904. As aves do Paraguay en comparação com as de São Paulo. Rev. Mus. Paulista 6:310-344.

Ingels, J., K. C. Parkes, and J. Farrand, Jr. 1981. The status of the macaw generally but incorrectly called *Ara caninde* (Wagler). Le Gerfaut 71:283-294.

Insfran, F. R. 1929. Observaciones biológicas sobre la (Sarîa-Hû) *Chunga Burmeisteri*. Rev. Soc. Cient. Parag. 2(5):225-227.

Insfran, F. R. 1930. Anatinae del Paraguay "Ypé-î". Rev. Soc. Cient. Parag. 2(6):260.

Insfran, F. R. 1931. Un caso raro de albinismo en la especie *Crotophaga ani* L., Anó Moroti. Rev. Soc. Cient. Parag. 3(1):33.

Insfran, F. R. 1936. Aportes a la ornitología nacional. Sobre biología de las *Leptotila* o Yeruti. Rev. Soc. Cient. Parag. 3(6):193-194.

Keel, S., A. H. Gentry, and L. Spinzi. 1993. Using vegetation analysis to facilitate the selection of conservation sites in eastern Paraguay. Cons. Biol. 7:66-75.

Kerr, J. G. 1891. Extracts from the letters of Mr. J. Graham Kerr, naturalist to the Pilcomayo expedition. Ibis pp. 13-15, 260-272.

Kerr, J. G. 1892. On the avifauna of the lower Pilcomayo. Ibis, ser. 6, 4:120-152.

Kerr, J. G. 1901. On the birds observed during a second zoological expedition to the Gran Chaco. Ibis, ser. 8, 1:215-236.

Kleefisch, T., Jr. 1983. Vogelbeobachtungen in Paraguay. Trochilus 4:105-113.

Kratter, A. W., T. S. Sillett, R. T. Chesser, J. P. O'Neill, T. A. Parker III, and A. Castillo. 1993. Avifauna of a Chaco locality in Bolivia. Wilson Bull. 105:114-141.

Krieg, H. 1931. Wissenschaftliche Ergebnisse der Deutschen Gran Chaco-Expedition. Geographische Übersicht und illustrierter Routenbericht. Strecker und Schröder, Stuttgart. 95 pp.

Krieg, H. 1948. Zwischen Anden und Atlantik. Carl Hansen Vertag, Munich. 490 pp.

Krieg, H., and E. Schuhmacher. 1936. Beobachtungen an südamerikanischen Wildhühnern. Verh. Ornith. Ges. Bayern 21:1-18.

Lanyon, W. E. 1978. Revision of the *Myiarchus* flycatchers of South America. Bull. Amer. Mus. Nat. Hist. 161:427-628.

Laubmann, A. 1930. Wissenschaftliche Ergebnisse der Deutschen Gran Chaco-Expedition. Vögel. Strecker und Schröder, Stuttgart. 334 pp.

Laubmann, A. 1933a. Beiträge zur Avifauna Paraguay's. Anz. Ornithol. Ges. Bayern 2:287-302.

Laubmann, A. 1933b. Ueber Eisvögel aus Paraguay. Anz. Ornithol. Ges. Bayern 2:267-275.

Laubmann, A. 1935. *Accipiter pectoralis* (Bonaparte), neu für Paraguay. Ornithol. Monatsber. 43:190.

Laubmann, A. 1936. Beiträge zur Avifauna von Santa Catharina, Süd-Brasilien. Verh. Ornithol. Ges. Bayern 21:19-46.

Laubmann, A. 1937. Ein zweiter Nachweis von *Accipiter pectoralis* (Bonaparte) in Paraguay. Anz. Ornithol. Ges. Bayern 2:405-406.

Laubmann, A. 1939. Wissenschaftliche Ergebnisse der Deutschen Gran Chaco-Expedition. Die Vögel von Paraguay. Vol. 1. Strecker und Schröder, Stuttgart. 246 pp.

Laubmann, A. 1940. Wissenschaftliche Ergebnisse der Deutschen Gran Chaco-Expedition. Die Vögel von Paraguay. Vol. 2. Strecker und Schröder, Stuttgart. 228 pp.

Lisboa, R. 1991. Atlas Básico. Paraguay y el Mundo. Ediciones Avon, Asunción. 105 pp.

López, J. A., E. L. Little, Jr., F. G. Ritz, J. S. Rombold, and W. J. Hahn. 1987. Arboles Comunes del Paraguay. Ñande Yvyra Mata Kuera. Peace Corps, Washington, D.C. 425 pp.

López, N. 1985. Avifauna del Departamento de Alto Paraguay. Volante Migratorio 4:9-13.

López, N. 1986a. Aves del Arroyo Mina y zonas aledañas. Bol. Inv. Biol. Nac. 8:4.

López, N. E. 1986b. Paraguay. Pp. 200-208 *in* D. A. Scott and M. Carbonell (eds.), A Directory of Neotropical Wetlands. IUCN Cambridge and IWRB Slimbridge.

López, N. 1992. Observaciones sobre la distribución de psitácidos en el Departamento de Concepción, Paraguay. Bol. Mus. Nac. Hist. Nat. Parag. 11:2-25.

López, N. E. 1993. Paraguay. Pp. 38-48 *in* D. E. Blanco and P. Canevari (eds.), Censo Neotropical de Aves Acuáticas 1992. Humedales para las Américas (Wetlands for the Americas), Buenos Aires.

López, N. Undated. Parque Nacional Cerro Corá: Lista de Aves. Servicio Forestal Nacional de Paraguay, Amambay, Paraguay. 16 pp.

Lüders, R. 1961. Bodenbildungen im Chaco Boreal von Paraguay als Zeugen des spät-und postglazialen Klimaablaufs. Geol. Jahrb. 78:603-608.

Lynch Arribálzaga, E. 1902. Apuntes críticos sobre las aves del Paraguay descritas por el señor A. de Winkelried Bertoni. Anal. Mus. Nac. Buenos Aires 7, ser. 2, 4:329-395.

MacArthur, R. H. 1972. Geographical Ecology. Harper and Row, New York. 269 pp.

Madroño N., A. 1991. Observaciones sobre *Formicivora grisea* en el Parque Nacional Defensores del Chaco, Paraguay. P. 40 *in* E. Acosta (ed.), Encuentro de Ornitología de Paraguay, Brasil y Argentina. Itaipú Binacional, Universidad Nacional de Asunción and Sociedad de Biología del Paraguay, Ciudad del Este.

Madroño Nieto, A., and M. Pearman. 1993. Distribution, status and taxonomy of the near-threatened Black-bodied Woodpecker *Dryocopus schulzi*. Bird Conserv. Int. 2:253-271.

Masi Pallarés, R. 1969. Guía de endoparásitos en animales del Paraguay (peces, batracios, reptiles, aves y mamíferos). Rev. Parag. Microbiol. 4:69-76.

Masi Pallarés, R., and C. A. Benítez Usher. 1972a. Algunos hélmintos en aves del Paraguay. Rev. Parag. Microbiol. 7:33-72.

Masi Pallarés, R., and C. A. Benítez Usher. 1972b. Lista de Helminthes en aves del Paraguay. Rev. Parag. Microbiol. 7:73-78.

Mason, C. R., and N. D. Steffee. 1982. Field Checklist of the Birds of Paraguay. Russ Mason's Natural History Tours, Inc., Kissimmee, Florida. 12 pp.

Maurer, B. A., and J. H. Brown. 1988. Distribution of energy use and biomass among species of North American terrestrial birds. Ecology 69:1923-1932.

Mayr, E. 1970. Populations, Species and Evolution. Belknap Press, Harvard University, Cambridge, Massachusetts. 453 pp.

Mayr, E., and R. J. O'Hara. 1986. The biogeographic evidence supporting the Pleistocene forest refuge hypothesis. Evolution 40:55-67.

McKitrick, M. C., and R. M. Zink. 1988. Species concepts in ornithology. Condor 90:1-14.

Meisel, J. E., A. van Humbeeck, and M. Morales. 1992. Reserva Natural del Bosque del Mbaracayú: Lista Preliminar de las Aves de la Reserva. Fundación Moisés Bertoni para la Conservación de la Naturaleza, Asunción. 13 pp.

Meyer de Schauensee, R. 1966. The Species of Birds of South America and their Distribution. The Academy of Natural Sciences of Philadelphia, Philadelphia. 577 pp.

Meyer de Schauensee, R. 1970. A Guide to the Birds of South America. The Academy of Natural Sciences of Philadelphia, Philadelphia. 470 pp.

Müller, P. 1973. The Dispersal Centres of Terrestrial Vertebrates in the Neotropical Realm. Dr. W. Junk B. V., Publishers, The Hague. 244 pp.

Myers, J. P., and L. P. Myers. 1979. Shorebirds of coastal Buenos Aires Province, Argentina. Ibis 121:186-200.

Myers, P. 1982. Origins and affinities of the mammal fauna of Paraguay. Pp. 85-93 *in* M. A. Mares and H. H. Genoways (eds.), Mammalian Biology in South America. Spec. Publ. Ser. vol. 6, Pymatuning Laboratory of Ecology, University of Pittsburgh, Pittsburgh.

Myers, P., and R. L. Hansen. 1980. Rediscovery of the Rufous-faced Crake (*Laterallus xenopterus*). Auk 97:901-902.

Myers, P., and R. M. Wetzel. 1983. Systematics and zoogeography of the bats of the Chaco Boreal. Misc. Publ. Mus. Zool., Univ. Michigan 165:1-59.

Narosky, T., and D. Yzurieta. 1987. Guía para la Identificación de las Aves de Argentina y Uruguay. Asociación Ornitológica del Plata, Buenos Aires. 345 pp.

Narosky, T., and D. Yzurieta. 1989. Birds of Argentina & Uruguay. A Field Guide. Asociación Ornitológica del Plata, Buenos Aires. 337 pp.

Naumburg, E. M. B. 1930. The birds of Matto Grosso, Brazil. Bull. Amer. Mus. Nat. Hist. 60:1-432.

Naumburg, E. M. B. 1935. Gazetteer and maps showing collecting stations visited by Emil Kaempfer in eastern Brazil and Paraguay. Bull. Amer. Mus. Nat. Hist. 68:449-469.

Naumburg, E. M. B. 1937. Studies of birds from eastern Brazil and Paraguay, based on a collection made by Emil Kaempfer. Bull. Amer. Mus. Nat. Hist. 74:139-205.

Naumburg, E. M. B. 1939. Studies of birds from eastern Brazil and Paraguay, based on a collection made by Emil Kaempfer. Bull. Amer. Mus. Nat. Hist. 76:231-276.

Navas, J. R., T. Narosky, N. A. Bó, and J. C. Chébez. 1991. Lista Patrón de los Nombres Comunes de las Aves Argentinas. Asociación Ornitológica del Plata, Buenos Aires. 39 pp.

Neris, N., and F. Colmán. 1991. Observaciones de aves en los alrededores de Colonia Neuland, Departamento Boquerón, Paraguay. Bol. Mus. Nac. Hist. Nat. Parag. 10:1-10.

Nores, M. 1987. Zonas ornitogeográficas de Argentina. Pp. 295-305 in T. Narosky and D. Yzurieta, Guía para la Identificación de las Aves de Argentina y Uruguay. Asociación Ornitológica del Plata, Buenos Aires.

Nores, M. 1989. Ornithogeographic regions of Argentina. Pp. 295-304 in T. Narosky and D. Yzurieta, Birds of Argentina & Uruguay. A Field Guide. Asociación Ornitológica del Plata, Buenos Aires.

Nores, M. 1992. Bird speciation in subtropical South America in relation to forest expansion and retraction. Auk 109:346-357.

Nores, M. 1994. Quaternary vegetational changes and bird differentiation in subtropical South America. Auk 111:499-503.

Nores, M., and M. M. Cerana. 1990. Biogeography of forest relicts in the mountains of northwestern Argentina. Rev. Chil. Hist. Nat. 63:37-46.

Norusis, M. J. 1990. SPSS Introductory Statistics Student Guide. SPSS Inc., Chicago. 420 pp.

Oberbeck, V. R., J. R. Marshall, and H. Aggarwal. 1993. Impacts, tillites, and the breakup of Gondwanaland. J. Geol. 101:1-19.

Oberholser, H. C. 1901. Seven new birds from Paraguay. Proc. Biol. Soc. Washington 14:187-188.

Oberholser, H. C. 1902. List of birds collected by William T. Foster in Paraguay. Proc. U. S. Natl. Mus. 25:127-147.

Olrog, C. C. 1979. Notas ornitológicas. XI. Sobre la colección del Instituto Miguel Lillo. Acta Zool. Lilloana 33:5-7.

Orfila, R. N. 1936. Los Psittaciformes argentinos. Hornero 6:197-225.

Page, T. J. 1859. La Plata, the Argentine Confederation, and Paraguay. Harper & Brothers, New York. 532 pp.

Paiva, A. 1977. Geografía de la República del Paraguay. 3rd ed. Orbis S.A., Asunción. 229 pp.

Palmieri, J. H., and J. C. Velázquez. 1982. Geología del Paraguay. Colección Apoyo a Cátedra, Serie Ciencias Naturales, Ediciones NAPA, Asunción. 65 pp.

Partridge, W. M. 1953. Notas breves sobre aves del Paraguay. Hornero 10:86-88.

Partridge, W. M. 1954. Estudio preliminar de una colección de aves de Misiones. Rev. Inst. Nac. Invest. Cs. Nat. Mus. Arg. Cs. Nat. B. Rivadavia, Cs. Zool. 3:87-153.

Partridge, W. M. 1956. Un nuevo dormilón para la fauna de Argentina y Paraguay. Hornero 10:169-170.

Paynter, R. A., Jr. 1989. Ornithological Gazetteer of Paraguay. 2nd ed. Museum of Comparative Zoology, Cambridge. 59 pp.

Paynter, R. A., Jr., and A. M. G. Caperton. 1977. Ornithological Gazetteer of Paraguay. Museum of Comparative Zoology, Harvard University, Cambridge. 43 pp.

Pereyra, J. A. 1945. La Obra Ornitológica de Azara. Biblioteca Americana, Buenos Aires. 162 pp.

Perez, N., J. van Humbeck, and J. Ortíz. 1988. Estudios faunísticos. Pp. 117-136 in Anonymous (ed.), 2° Seminario de la Itaipú Binacional sobre Medio Ambiente. Foz do Iguaçu, Paraná, Brasil.

Peris, S. J. 1990. Peso y biometría de algunas aves del Chaco húmedo (Presidente Hayes, Paraguay). Ornitol. Neotr. 1:31-32.

Peris, S., L. A. Cabello, F. Suarez, and B. Peco. 1987. Las aves del bajo Chaco: evaluación preliminar. Inf. Cient. Inst. Cs. Bás., Asunción 5:27-33.

Peris, S. J., and F. Suarez. 1985a. Algunas aves invernantes en el bajo Chaco Paraguayo. Volante Migratorio 5:20.

Peris, S. J., and F. Suarez. 1985b. New data on birds of Paraguay. Hist. Nat. 5:132.

Peters, J. A. 1955. The use and misuse of the biotic province concept. Amer. Nat. 89:21-28.

Podtiaguin, B. 1941. Catálogo sistemático de las aves del Paraguay. Aumentado por las contribuciones al conocimiento de la ornitología paraguaya. Rev. Soc. Cient. Parag. 5(5):1-109.

Podtiaguin, B. 1944. Catálogo sistemático de las aves del Paraguay. Aumentado por las contribuciones al conocimiento de la ornitología paraguaya. Rev. Soc. Cient. Parag. 6(3):7-120.

Podtiaguin, B. 1945. Catálogo sistemático de las aves del Paraguay. Rev. Soc. Cient. Parag. 6(6):63-80.

Prance, G. T. (ed.). 1982. Biological Diversification in the Tropics. Columbia University Press, New York. 714 pp.

Prance, G. T., and G. B. Schaller. 1982. Preliminary study of some vegetation types of the Pantanal, Mato Grosso, Brazil. Brittonia 34:228-251.

Prohaska, F. 1976. The climate of Argentina, Paraguay and Uruguay. Pp. 13-112 in W. Schwerdtfeger (ed.), World Series of Climatology. Vol. 12. Climates of Central and South America. Elsevier Scientific Publishing Company, Amsterdam.

Prum, R. O. 1988. Historical relationships among avian forest areas of endemism in the Neotropics. Pp. 2562-2572 in H. Ouellet (ed.), Acta XIX Congressus Internationalis Ornithologici. Vol. 2. University of Ottawa Press, Ottawa.

Putzer, H. 1962. Geologie von Paraguay. Gebrüder Borntraeger, Berlin.

Remsen, J. V., Jr., and T. A. Parker, III. 1990. Seasonal distribution of the Azure Gallinule (Porphyrula flavirostris), with comments on vagrancy in rails and gallinules. Wilson Bull. 102:380-399.

Remsen, J. V., Jr., and M. A. Traylor, Jr. 1989. An Annotated List of the Birds of Bolivia. Buteo Books, Vermillion, South Dakota. 79 pp.

Ridgely, R. S. 1981. The current distribution and status of mainland Neotropical parrots. Pp. 233-384 in R. F. Pasquier (ed.), Conservation of New World Parrots. Smithsonian Institution Press, Washington, D.C.

Ridgely, R. S., and G. Tudor. 1989. The Birds of South America. Vol. I. The Oscine Passerines. University of Texas Press, Austin, Texas. 516 pp.

Ridgely, R. S., and G. Tudor. 1994. The Birds of South America. Vol. II. The Suboscine Passerines. University of Texas Press, Austin, Texas. 814 pp.

Ríos, E., and E. Zardini. 1989. Conservation of biological diversity in Paraguay. Conserv. Biol. 3:118-120.

Rising, J. D., and K. M. Somers. 1989. The measurement of overall body size in birds. Auk 106:666-674.

Robebar, A. 1930. Coleccionistas de aves del Paraguay. Rev. Soc. Cient. Parag. 2(6):239-240.

Salvadori, T. 1891. Catalogue of the Psittaci, or Parrots, in the Collection of the British Museum. British Museum (Natural History), London.

Salvadori, T. 1894. Viaggio del dott. Alfredo Borelli nella Republica Argentina e nel Paraguay. Intorno alla Pyrrhura chiripepé (Vieill.) e descrizione di una nuova specie del genere Pyrrhura. Boll. Mus. Zool. Anat. Comp., Torino 9(190):1-4.

Salvadori, T. 1895. Viaggio del dott. Alfredo Borelli nella Republica Argentina e nel Paraguay. Uccelli raccolti nel Paraguay, nel Matto Grosso, nel Tucuman e nella Provincia di Salta. Boll. Mus. Zool. Anat. Comp., Torino 10(208):1-24.

Salvadori, T. 1900. Viaggio del Dr. A. Borelli nel Matto Grosso e nel Paraguay. Uccelli. Boll. Mus. Zool. Anat. Comp., Torino 15(378):1-19.

Sanjuro, K. M. 1976. Contribución al estudio ecológico del Paraguay. Formaciones vegetales del área norte de la región oriental. Rev. Soc. Cient. Parag. 16(1,2):111-134.

Schade, F., and R. Masi Pallarés. 1967. Las aves del Paraguay. Ia Parte. Rev. Parag. Microbiol. 2:72-85.

Schade, F., and R. Masi Pallarés. 1968. Las aves del Paraguay. II Parte. Rev. Parag. Microbiol. 3:86-105.

Schade, F., and R. Masi Pallarés. 1969. Las aves del Paraguay. III Parte. Rev. Parag. Microbiol. 4:77-96.

Schade, F., and R. Masi Pallarés. 1970. Las aves del Paraguay y un índice. IV Parte. Rev. Parag. Microbiol. 5:35-58.

Schade, F., and R. Masi Pallarés. 1971. Las aves del Paraguay y un índice. Rev. Parag. Microbiol. 6:103-122.

Schlegel, H. 1863. Hist. d'Hist. Natur. des Pays-Bas. Rev. Méth. Crit. des Coll. Déposées dans cet Etablis IV, 32, Lari:1-52.

Schlegel, H. 1867. Hist. d'Hist. Natur. des Pays-Bas. Rev. Méth. Crit. des Coll. Déposées dans cet Etablis IV, 33, Urinatores:1-50.

Schmitt, G., and J. P. Hubbard. 1974. Eastern Kingbird in Paraguay. Wilson Bull. 86:466.

Schwartz, P. 1972. *Micrastur gilvicollis*, a valid species sympatric with *M. ruficollis* in Amazonia. Condor 74:399-415.

Sclater, P. L. 1897. (Extracts from a letter received from Mr. J. Graham Kerr). Ibis, ser. 7, 3:257.

Selva, M. 1917. Manuscritos inéditos del Padre Noseda sobre aves del Paraguay. Physis 3:180-185.

Sharpe, R. B. 1896. Catalogue of the Limicolae in the collection of the British Museum. British Museum (Natural History), London.

Sharpe, R. B. 1905. (A new species of *Nemosia* from Paraguay). Bull. Brit. Ornithol. Club 15:96.

Short, L. L. 1972a. Two avian species new to Paraguay. Auk 89:895.

Short, L. L. 1972b. Systematics and behavior of South American flickers (Aves, *Colaptes*). Bull. Amer. Mus. Nat. Hist. 149:1-109.

Short, L. L. 1972c. Relationships among the four species of the superspecies *Celeus elegans* (Aves, Picidae). Amer. Mus. Novit. 2487:1-26.

Short, L. L. 1975. A zoogeographic analysis of the South American Chaco avifauna. Bull. Amer. Mus. Nat. Hist. 154:167-352.

Short, L. L. 1976a. Notes on a collection of birds from the Paraguayan Chaco. Amer. Mus. Novit. 2597:1-16.

Short, L. L. 1976b. *Aimophila strigiceps* new to Paraguay. Auk 93:189-190.

Short, L. L. 1980. Chaco woodland birds of South America-some African comparisons. Pp. 147-158 *in* D. N. Johnson (ed.), Proceedings of the Fourth Pan-African Ornithological Congress. Southern African Ornithological Society.

Short, L. L. 1982. Woodpeckers of the World. Delaware Mus. Nat. Hist. Monogr. No. 4. 700 pp.

Sibley, C. G., and J. E. Ahlquist. 1990. Phylogeny and Classification of Birds: a Study in Molecular Evolution. Yale University Press, New Haven, Connecticut. 976 pp.

Sibley, C. G., and B. L. Monroe, Jr. 1990. Distribution and Taxonomy of Birds of the World. Yale University Press, New Haven, Connecticut. 1111 pp.

Sick, H. 1967. Rios e enchentes na Amazônia como obstáculo para a avifauna. Pp. 495-520 *in* H. Lent (ed.), Atas do Simpósio sôbre a Biota Amazônica, vol. 5 (Zoologia). Conselho de Pesquisas, Rio de Janeiro.

Sick, H. 1979. Notes on some Brazilian birds. Bull. Brit. Ornithol. Club 99:115-120.

Sick, H. 1985. Observations on the Andean-Patagonian component of southeastern Brazil's avifauna. Ornithol. Monogr. 36:233-237.

184

Siegel-Causey, D. 1992. [Review of] Distribution and Taxonomy of Birds of the World. Auk 109:939-944.

Silva, J. M. C. 1994. Can avian distribution patterns in northern Argentina be related to gallery-forest expansion-retraction caused by Quaternary climatic changes? Auk 111:495-499.

Silva, T. 1988. Bird watching in Paraguay. Bull. Amazona Soc. 5(4):2-6.

Silva, T. 1989. Bei Vogelfängern in Paraguay. Gefied. Welt 113:247-248.

Simpson, G. G. 1977. Too many lines: the limits of the Oriental and Australian zoogeographic regions. Proc. Amer. Philos. Soc. 121:107-120.

Sneath, P. H. A., and R. R. Sokal. 1973. Numerical Taxonomy. W. H. Freeman and Company, San Francisco. 573 pp.

Solbrig, O. T. 1986. The advance of the agricultural frontier in the Gran Chaco area of South America: an interesting research opportunity. Biol. Int. 13:2-5.

Steinbacher, J. 1962. Beiträge zur Kenntnis der Vögel von Paraguay. Abhandl. Senckenbergischen Naturf. Gesell. 502:1-106.

Steinbacher, J. 1968. Weitere Beiträge über Vögel von Paraguay. Senckenbergiana Biol. 49:317-365.

Storer, R. W. 1981. The Rufous-necked Crake (*Laterallus xenopterus*) and its Paraguayan congeners. Wilson Bull. 93:137-144.

Storer, R. W. 1988. Type specimens of birds in the collections of the Univeristy of Michigan Museum of Zoology. Misc. Publ. Mus. Zool., Univ. Michigan 174:1-69.

Storer, R. W. 1989. Notes on Paraguayan birds. Occ. Pap. Mus. Zool., Univ. Michigan 719:1-21.

Stotz, D. F. 1990. The taxonomic status of *Phyllomyias reiseri*. Bull. Brit. Ornithol. Club 110:184-187.

Straneck, R. J. 1987. Aportes sobre el comportamiento y distribución de la Cachirla Amarillenta, *Anthus lutescens* Pucheran y la Cachirla Chaqueña, *Anthus chacoensis* Zimmer. Rev. Mus. Arg. Cs. Nat. B. Rivadavia Inst. Nac. Cs. Nat., Zool. 14:95-102.

Traylor, M. A., Jr. (ed.). 1979. Check-list of Birds of the World. Museum of Comparative Zoology, Cambridge, Massachusetts. 365 pp.

Traylor, M. A., Jr. 1982. Notes on tyrant flycatchers (Aves: Tyrannidae). Fieldiana Zool., new ser. 13:1-22.

Traylor, M. A., Jr. 1986. Geographic variation and evolution in South American *Cistothorus platensis* (Aves: Troglodytidae). Fieldiana Zool., new ser. 48:1-35.

Vanzolini, P. E., and W. R. Heyer. 1988. Proceedings of a Workshop on Neotropical Distributional Patterns. Academia Brasileira de Ciências, Rio de Janeiro. 488 pp.

Vaurie, C. 1966. Systematic notes on the bird family Cracidae. No. 5. *Penelope purpurascens*, *Penelope jacquaçu*, and *Penelope obscura*. Amer. Mus. Novit. 2250:1-23.

Vaurie, C. 1967. Systematic notes on the bird family Cracidae. No. 7. The genus *Pipile*. Amer. Mus. Novit. 2296:1-16.

Vaurie, C. 1980. Taxonomy and geographical distribution of the Furnariidae (Aves, Passeriformes). Bull. Amer. Mus. Nat. Hist. 166:1-357.

Vogel, C. (ed.). 1984. Late Cainozoic Palaeoclimates of the Southern Hemisphere. A. A. Balkema, Rotterdam. 520 pp.

Vogt, J. G. 1931. Algo sobre los ramphástidos. Rev. Soc. Cient. Parag. 3(1):33-35.

Vuilleumier, B. S. 1971. Pleistocene changes in the fauna and flora of South America. Science 173:771-780.

Vuilleumier, F. 1991. A quantitative survey of speciation phenomena in Patagonian birds. Ornitol. Neotrop. 2:5-28.

Weller, M. W. 1967. Distribution and habitat selection of the Black-headed Duck (*Heteronetta atricapilla*). Hornero 10:299-306.

Wendelken, P. W. 1983. Una Lista Anotada de las Aves del Paraguay. Published by the author. 57 pp.

Wetmore, A. 1922. Description of a *Brachyspiza* from the Chaco of Argentina and Paraguay. Proc. Biol. Soc. Washington 34:39-40.

Wetmore, A. 1926. Observations on the birds of Argentina, Paraguay, Uruguay, and Chile. Bull. U. S. Natl. Mus. 133:1-448.

Wetmore, A. 1927. Our migrant shorebirds in southern South America. U. S. Dept. Agric. Tech. Bull. 26:1-24.

Wetzel, R. M., R. E. Dubos, R. L. Martin, and P. Myers. 1975. *Catagonus*, an "extinct" peccary, alive in Paraguay. Science 189:379-381.

Whitmore, T. C., and G. T. Prance (eds.). 1987. Biogeography and Quaternary History in Tropical America. Clarendon Press, Oxford, England. 214 pp.

Willim, P. 1947. Contribuciones al conocimiento de las aves del Chaco Paraguayo. Rev. Soc. Cient. Parag. 7(2):1-4.

Willis, E. O. 1986. Vireos, wood warblers and warblers as ant followers. Le Gerfaut 76:177-186.

Willis, E. O. 1988. *Drymophila rubricol[l]is* (Bertoni, 1901) is a valid species (Aves, Formicariidae). Rev. Brasil. Biol. 48:431-438.

Yamashita, C., and M. de P. Valle. 1993. On the linkage between *Anodorhynchus* macaws and palm nuts, and the extinction of the Glaucous Macaw. Bull. Brit. Ornithol. Club 113:53-60.

Zar, J. H. 1984. Biostatistical Analysis. 2nd ed. Prentice-Hall, Inc., Englewood Cliffs, New Jersey. 718 pp.

Zimmer, J. T. 1938. Studies of Peruvian birds. No. XXIX. The genera *Myiarchus*, *Mitrephanes*, and *Cnemotriccus*. Amer. Mus. Novit. 994:1-32.

Zimmer, J. T. 1941. Studies of Peruvian birds. XXXVII. The genera *Sublegatus*, *Phaeomyias*, *Camptostoma*, *Xanthomyias*, *Phyllomyias*, and *Tyranniscus*. Amer. Mus. Novit. 1109:1-25.

Zimmer, J. T. 1949. Studies of Peruvian birds. No. 54. The families Catamblyrhynchidae and Parulidae. Amer. Mus. Novit. 1428:1-59.

Zimmer, J. T. 1950. Studies of Peruvian birds. No. 56. The genera *Eutoxeres*, *Campylopterus*, *Eupetomena*, and *Florisuga*. Amer. Mus. Novit. 1450:1-14.

Zimmer, J. T. 1952. A new subspecies of pipit from Argentina and Paraguay. Proc. Biol. Soc. Washington 65:31-34.

Zimmer, J. T. 1953a. Studies of Peruvian birds. No. 64. The swifts: family Apodidae. Amer. Mus. Novit. 1609:1-20.

Zimmer, J. T. 1953b. Studies of Peruvian birds. No. 65. The jays (Corvidae) and pipits (Motacillidae). Amer. Mus. Novit. 1649:1-27.

Zimmer, J. T. 1955. Further notes on tyrant flycatchers (Tyrannidae). Amer. Mus. Novit. 1749:1-24.

Zotta, A. R. 1937. Lista sistemática de las aves argentinas. Hornero 6:531-554.

Zotta, A. R. 1938. Dos pájaros nuevos para la fauna paraguaya. Hornero 7:64.

Zotta, A. R. 1940. Una nueva especie y otra confirmada para la fauna del Paraguay. Hornero 7:364-365.

Zotta, A. R. 1950. Dos aves nuevas para el Paraguay y una para el Uruguay. Hornero 9:165-166.

APPENDIX 1

Chronological sequence of publications primarily on Paraguayan ornithology, or with substantial contributions to Paraguayan ornithology. Omitted publications include newspaper articles, articles within symposia on Paraguayan ornithology, broad systematic reviews of South American birds, field guides, articles dealing almost exclusively with birds of other countries, and articles dealing primarily with anthropology, parasites and the history of ornithology.

1760-1879
Sánchez Labrador 1767, *in* Castex 1968
Azara 1802b
Azara 1805a
Azara 1805b
Hartlaub 1847
Cassin 1859

1880-1889
Berlepsch 1887
Dalgleish 1889

1890-1899
Kerr 1891
Kerr 1892
Salvadori 1894
Salvadori 1895
Sclater 1897
Bertoni 1898

1900-1909
Bertoni 1900
Salvadori 1900
Bertoni 1901
Kerr 1901
Oberholser 1901
Lynch Arribálzaga 1902
Oberholser 1902
Bertoni 1903a
Bertoni 1903b
Bertoni 1904
Ihering 1904
Sharpe 1905
Bertoni 1907

1910-1919
Chubb 1910
Grant 1911
Dabbene 1912
Bertoni 1913
Bertoni 1914a
Bertoni 1914b
Bertoni 1914c
Bertoni 1914d
Brabourne 1914
Bertoni 1918a

Bertoni 1918b
Bertoni 1918c
Bertoni 1918d
Bertoni 1918e
Bertoni 1919a
Bertoni 1919b

1920-1929
Dabbene 1920
Cherrie and Reichenberger 1921
Fiebrig 1921
Wetmore 1922
Cherrie and Reichenberger 1923
Bertoni 1922a
Bertoni 1922b
Bertoni 1923a
Bertoni 1923b
Bertoni 1924
Bertoni 1925a
Bertoni 1925b
Bertoni 1926
Wetmore 1926
Bertoni 1927
Wetmore 1927
Bertoni 1928a
Bertoni 1928b
Bertoni 1928c
Bertoni 1929
Insfran 1929

1930-1939
Bertoni 1930a
Bertoni 1930b
Insfran 1930
Laubmann 1930
Insfran 1931
Vogt 1931
Laubmann 1933a
Laubmann 1933b
Brodkorb 1934
Conover 1934
Brodkorb 1935
Laubmann 1935
Naumburg 1935
Insfran 1936
Krieg and Schuhmacher 1936

Conover 1937
Laubmann 1937
Brodkorb 1937a
Brodkorb 1937b
Brodkorb 1937c
Naumburg 1937
Brodkorb 1938a
Brodkorb 1938b
Brodkorb 1938c
Zotta 1938
Bertoni 1939
Brodkorb 1939a
Brodkorb 1939b
Brodkorb 1939c
Laubmann 1939
Naumburg 1939

1940-1949
Laubmann 1940
Zotta 1940
Brodkorb 1941a
Brodkorb 1941b
Podtiaguin 1941
Podtiaguin 1944
Podtiaguin 1945
Willim 1947
Krieg 1948
Blake 1949
Giai 1949

1950-1959
Conover 1950
Zotta 1950
Zimmer 1952
Partridge 1953
Partridge 1954
Zimmer 1955
Partridge 1956

1960-1969
Steinbacher 1962
Schade and Masi Pallarés 1967
Weller 1967
Schade and Masi Pallarés 1968
Steinbacher 1968

Schade and Masi Pallarés 1969

1970-1979
Schade and Masi Pallarés 1970
Schade and Masi Pallarés 1971
Carman 1971
Short 1972a
Short 1972b
Short 1972c
Schmitt and Hubbard 1974
Short 1975
Short 1976a
Short 1976b
Paynter and Caperton 1977
Myers and Myers 1979

1980-1989
Myers and Hansen 1980
Foster 1981
Ridgely 1981
Storer 1981
Anonymous 1982a
Anonymous 1982b
Eisenmann and Short 1982
Foster and Fitzgerald 1982
Mason and Steffee 1982
Traylor 1982
Escobar and Salomón 1983
Kleefisch 1983
Wendelken 1983
Anonymous 1985
Contreras and Mandelburger 1985
Foster 1985
González Torres and González Romero 1985
López 1985
Peris and Suarez 1985a
Peris and Suarez 1985b

Altman and Swift 1986
Contreras 1986a
Contreras 1986b
Contreras and Contreras 1986
López 1986a
López undated
Foster 1987a
Foster 1987b
Peris et al. 1987
Stäbler 1987
Contreras 1988
Contreras et al. 1988a
Contreras and González Romero 1988
González Romero et al. 1988
Goodman and Glynn 1988
Hayes and Areco de Medina 1988
Perez et al. 1988
Silva 1988
Altman and Swift 1989
Acevedo Gómez 1989
Contreras 1989
Contreras and González Romero 1989a
Contreras and González Romero 1989b
Contreras et al. 1989
Foster et al. 1989
González Romero and Contreras 1989
Paynter 1989
Silva 1989
Storer 1989

1990-present
Acevedo et al. 1990
Contreras et al. 1990
Foster 1990

Hayes and Escobar Argaña 1990
Hayes et al. 1990a
Hayes et al. 1990b
Peris 1990
Remsen and Parker 1990
Acosta 1991
Brooks 1991a
Brooks 1991b
Contreras and González Romero 1991
Hayes 1991
Hayes and Fox 1991
Hayes et al. 1991
Neris and Colmán 1991
Contreras 1992
Contreras and Contreras 1992
Contreras et al. 1992a
Contreras et al. 1992b
Fernández Pérez 1992
Hayes 1992
Hayes and Granizo Tamayo 1992
López 1992
Meisel et al. 1992
Nores 1992
Brooks et al. 1993
Contreras 1993
Contreras and Argaña 1993
Contreras and Contreras 1993a
Contreras and Contreras 1993b
Contreras et al. 1993a
Contreras et al. 1993b
López 1993
Hayes and Scharf 1993
Brooks and Esquivel 1994
Contreras and Contreras 1994
Hayes et al. 1994
Hayes in press

APPENDIX 2

Summary of field work in Paraguay during 1987-1994. Days spent observing birds in the vicinity of Asunción, San Lorenzo and Guarambaré (all in Dept. Central) are excluded, except for trips to the Bahía de Asunción. Abbreviations for departments are given in Distributional Notes section.

January 1987

25   Villeta, CEN

February 1987

03   Villeta, CEN

19   Ruta Trans Chaco from Puente Remanso to Río Negro, PHA

21-22   Cerro Acahay, PAR

23-25   Tobatí, COR

March 1987

13-15   Parque Nacional Ybycuí, PAR

22   Paraguarí, PAR

28   Parque Nacional Ybycuí, PAR

April 1987

05   Parque Nacional Ybycuí, PAR

11   Hernandarias, APN

May 1987

01-03   Hernandarias, APN

14   Paraguarí, PAR

15-18   Hernandarias, APN

June 1987

07   Villeta, CEN

12   Ruta Trans Chaco from Puente Remanso, PHA, to Fortín Toledo, BOQ

13   Fortín Toledo, BOQ

14   Ruta Trans Chaco from Fortín Toledo, BOQ, to Puente Remanso, PHA

28   Tobatí, COR

July 1987

05   Puente Remanso, PHA

07   Puente Remanso, PHA

10   Puente Remanso, PHA

13-16   Choré, SAP

28-31   Parque Nacional Ybycuí, PAR

August 1987

09   Tobatí, COR

14   Puente Remanso, PHA

18   Puente Remanso, PHA

22   Ruta Trans Chaco from Puente Remanso, PHA, to Filadelfia, BOQ

23   Ruta Trans Chaco from Filadelfia, BOQ, to Puente Remanso, PHA

26-28   Parque Nacional Cerro Corá, AMA

29-30   Pedro Juan Caballero, AMA

September 1987

14-17   Choré, SAP

18   Areguá, COR

19   Nueva Italia, CEN

27   Puente Remanso, PHA

29-30   Choré, SAP

October 1987

01-04   Choré, SAP

09-12   Puentecita, CAA (not misspelled)

16   Ruta Trans Chaco from Puente Remanso to Río Negro, PHA

20   Bahía de Asunción, CEN

25   Bahía de Asunción, CEN

29   Bahía de Asunción, CEN

November 1987

01   Hernandarias, APN

02-05   Arroyo Pozuelo, CAN

December 1987

06   Bahía de Asunción, CEN

11   Bahía de Asunción, CEN

16   Bahía de Asunción, CEN

23   Bahía de Asunción, CEN

January 1988

03   Bahía de Asunción, CEN

15   Bahía de Asunción, CEN

17   Ruta Trans Chaco from Puente Remanso, PHA, to Fortín Toledo, BOQ

18-31   Fortín Toledo and Filadelfia, BOQ

February 1988

01-02   Fortín Toledo and Filadelfia, BOQ

03	Ruta Trans Chaco from Fortín Toledo, BOQ, to Puente Remanso, PHA
09	Bahía de Asunción, CEN
11	Bahía de Asunción, CEN
15-18	Reserva Natural del Bosque Mbaracayú, CAN
25	Bahía de Asunción, CEN
28	Bahía de Asunción, CEN

March 1988

01	Areguá, CEN
08	Bahía de Asunción, CEN
11	Bahía de Asunción, CEN
15	Bahía de Asunción, CEN
17	Puente Remanso, PHA
22	Bahía de Asunción, CEN
23-24	Cerro Acahay, PAR
25	Puente Remanso, PHA
29	Bahía de Asunción, CEN
31	Ruta Trans Chaco from Puente Remanso, PHA, to Fortín Toledo, BOQ

April 1988

01	Filadelfia, BOQ, Laguna Capitán and Laguna Salada, PHA
02	Ruta Trans Chaco from Filadelfia, BOQ, to Puente Remanso, PHA
07	Bahía de Asunción, CEN
13-18	Villa Florida, PAR and MIS

May 1988

| 25 | Bahía de Asunción, CEN |

June 1988

02	Bahía de Asunción, CEN
10-12	Villa Florida, PAR and MIS
14-17	Río Paraguay by boat from Asunción, CEN, to Puerto Bahía Negra and Retiro Potrerito, APY
18-22	Retiro Potrerito, APY
23	Retiro Potrerito to Puerto Bahía Negra, APY
24	Puerto Bahía Negra, APY
25	Puerto Bahía Negra, APY to Retiro Potrerito, APY
26-29	Retiro Potrerito, APY
30	Retiro Potrerito to Puerto Bahía Negra, APY

July 1988

01-03	Río Paraguay by boat from Puerto Bahía Negra, APY, to Asunción, CEN
12	Bahía de Asunción, CEN
17	Tobatí, PAR
20-22	Parque Nacional Cerro Corá, AMA
23-24	Pedro Juan Caballero, AMA

August 1988

05	Bahía de Asunción, CEN
09-11	Río Paraguay by boat from Asunción, CEN, to Puerto Bahía Negra and Puerto 14 de Mayo, APY
12	Puerto 14 de Mayo, APY
13	Puerto 14 de Mayo to Retiro Potrerito, APY
14-16	Retiro Potrerito, APY
17	Retiro Potrerito to Puerto Bahía Negra, APY
18-19	Puerto Bahía Negra, APY
22	Bahía de Asunción, CEN
27-28	Estancia La Golondrina and Puente Remanso, PHA

September 1988

| 09 | Bahía de Asunción, CEN |

October 1988

10	Bahía de Asunción, CEN
21	Bahía de Asunción, CEN
25-30	Río Paraguay by boat from Asuncíon, CEN, to Puerto Bahía Negra, APY, to Asunción, CEN

November 1988

06	Estancia La Golondrina, PHA
09	Bahía de Asunción, CEN
10	Bahía de Asunción, CEN
12-14	Estancia La Golondrina, PHA
17	Bahía de Asunción, CEN
19-20	Villa Florida, PAR and MIS
22	Bahía de Asunción, CEN
25	Bahía de Asunción, CEN
26	Lago Ypoá, PAR

December 1988

02	Bahía de Asunción, CEN
06	Ruta Trans Chaco from Puente Remanso, PHA, to Filadelfia, BOQ
07	Filadelfia and Fortín Toledo, BOQ

190

08   Filadelfia and Loma Plata, BOQ, and Laguna Capitán, PHA

09   Ruta Trans Chaco from Filadelfia, BOQ, to Puente Remanso, PHA

10   Parque Nacional Ybycuí, PAR

12   Troncal 2, north of Hernandarias, APN

13   Ciudad del Este, APN, to Hotel El Tirol, ITA

14   Hotel El Tirol, ITA

15   Hotel El Tirol, ITA, to Ayolas, MIS, to Villa Florida, MIS

16   Villa Florida, PAR and MIS, to Bahía de Asunción, CEN

17   Estancia La Golondrina and Puente Remanso, PHA

21   Bahía de Asunción, CEN

January 1989

05   Bahía de Asunción, CEN

11   Bahía de Asunción, CEN

15   Emboscada, COR

17   Bahía de Asunción, CEN

22   Puente Remanso, Villa Hayes and Estancia Villa Rey (5km E of Ruta Trans Chaco km 65), PHA

23   Bahía de Asunción, CEN

24-27   Río Paraguay by boat from Asunción, CEN, to Puerto Bahía Negra, APY

28-31   Puerto Bahía Negra, APY

February 1989

01-07   Puerto Bahía Negra, APY

15   Bahía de Asunción, CEN

24-27   Parque Nacional Ybycuí, PAR

March 1989

08-11   Santiago and Ayolas, MIS

14   Bahía de Asunción, CEN

22   Santiago, MIS

23   Santiago and Ayolas, MIS, to San Cosme y Damián, ITA

24   Ayolas to Estancia Ñu Porá, MIS

25   Ayolas to Yabebyry, MIS

26   Ayolas, MIS, to Asunción, CEN

April 1989

12   Bahía de Asunción, CEN

May 1989

09   Bahía de Asunción, CEN

10   Bahía de Asunción, CEN

13   Concepción to Estancia Santa Sofia, CON

14-15   Estancia Santa Sofia, CON

16   Estancia Santa Sofia to Estancia Centurión, CON

17-18   Estancia Centurión, CON

19   Estancia Centurión to Puerto Fonciere, CON

20-21   Estancia Fonciere, CON

22   Estancia Fonciere to Concepción, CON

23   Concepción, CON, and nearby west bank of Río Paraguay, PHA

31   Bahía de Asunción, CEN

July 1989

03-05   Lago Ypacarai, CEN and COR

08   Estancia La Golondrina and Puente Remanso, PHA

10   Bahía de Asunción, CEN

18   Bahía de Asunción, CEN

21-23   Río Carapá by canoe from 12 km SE of Corpus Cristi to Catueté, CAN

24-26   Río Carapá by canoe from Catueté to 14 km SSE of Mbaracayú, CAN

30   Estancia La Golondrina and Puente Remanso, PHA

August 1989

11   Puerto Bahía Negra and Puerto 14 de Mayo, APY

12-13   Puerto 14 de Mayo, APY

14   Puerto 14 de Mayo to Retiro Potrerito, APY

15-16   Retiro Potrerito, APY

17   Retiro Potrerito to Puerto 14 de Mayo and Puerto Bahía Negra, APY

18   Puerto Bahía Negra, APY

24   Río Ytambey, CAN and APY

25   Río Ytambey by boat from Laurel to "supercarretera" (road from Hernandarias, APN, to Cruce Guaraní, CAN), CAN and APN

26-27   Reserva Biológica Limoy, APN

September 1989

10	Ruta Trans Chaco from Puente Remanso to km 340 and to Estancia Pozo Azul (35 km E of Ruta Trans Chaco km 180), PHA
11	Ruta Trans Chaco from Estancia Pozo Azul to Puente Remanso, PHA
14	Asunción, CEN, to Curuguaty, CAN
15-16	Curuguaty to Yukirí, CAN
19	Bahía de Asunción, CEN
25	Puerto Barra (confluence of Arroyo Yñaró and Río Ñacunday), APN
26-27	Río Ñacunday by canoe from Puerto Barra to bridge (of road between Ciudad del Este, APN, and Capitán Meza, ITA), and Salto Ñacunday, APN
28	Puerto Barra, APN, to Hotel El Tirol, ITA
29	Hotel El Tirol, ITA

October 1989

09	Parque Nacional Ybycuí, PAR
20	Ruta Trans Chaco from Puente Remanso, PHA, to Loma Plata, BOQ
21	Laguna Capitán, PHA, and Ruta Trans Chaco from Loma Plata, BOQ, to Puente Remanso, PHA
23	Villeta to 25 km S, and Nueva Italia, CEN
24	Nueva Italia, CEN

30	Bahía de Asunción, CEN

November 1989

02-03	Parque Nacional Ybycuí, PAR

August 1993

10	Villeta to 15 km S of Villeta, CEN
16-17	Villa Florida, PAR and MIS
19-20	Nueva Italia, CEN

August 1994

06	Lago Ypacarai, COR
07	Tobatí, COR
08	Ruta Trans Chaco from Puente Remanso, PHA, to Filadelfia, BOQ
09	Estancia Klassen, Estancia Santa María and Laguna Capitán, PHA
10	Ruta Trans Chaco from Filadelfia and Fortín Toledo, BOQ, to Puente Remanso, PHA
11	Lambaré, CEN, to Parque Nacional Ybycuí, PAR
12	Parque Nacional Ybycuí, PAR, to Villa Florida, MIS
13	Villa Florida to 20 km W of San Juan Bautista, to Ayolas, MIS
14	Hotel El Tirol, ITA
15	Hotel El Tirol, ITA, to Ciudad del Este, APN
17	Reserva Biológica Itabó, APN
18	Hernandarias and Refugio Biológico Tati Yupi, APN
19	Ruta 12 from Ruta Trans Chaco to Estancia Estrella, PHA
20	Nueva Italia, CEN

APPENDIX 3

Forest understory species of birds that do not typically occur in open or aquatic habitats.

Solitary Tinamou (*Tinamus solitarius*)

Brown Tinamou (*Crypturellus obsoletus*)

Undulated Tinamou (*Crypturellus undulatus*)

Small-billed Tinamou (*Crypturellus parvirostris*)

Tataupa Tinamou (*Crypturellus tataupa*)

Spot-winged Wood-Quail (*Odontophorus capueira*)

Plain-breasted Ground-Dove (*Columbina minuta*)

Blue Ground-Dove (*Claravis pretiosa*)

Purple-winged Ground-Dove (*Claravis godefrida*)

Ruddy Quail-Dove (*Geotrygon montana*)

Violaceous Quail-Dove (*Geotrygon violacea*)

Canebrake Groundcreeper (*Clibanornis dendrocolaptoides*)

Rufous-capped Spinetail (*Synallaxis ruficapilla*)

Sooty-fronted Spinetail (*Synallaxis frontalis*)

Chicli Spinetail (*Synallaxis spixi*)

Pale-breasted Spinetail (*Synallaxis albescens*)

Plain-crowned Spinetail (*Synallaxis gujanensis*)

Gray-bellied Spinetail (*Synallaxis cinerascens*)

Buff-browed Foliage-gleaner (*Syndactyla rufosuperciliata*)

White-eyed Foliage-gleaner (*Automolus leucophthalmus*)

Chestnut-capped Foliage-gleaner (*Hylocryptus rectirostris*)

Rufous-breasted Leaftosser (*Sclerurus scansor*)

Great Antshrike (*Taraba major*)

Stripe-backed Antbird (*Myrmorchilus strigilatus*)

Black-bellied Antwren (*Formicivora melanogaster*)

Rusty-backed Antwren (*Formicivora rufa*)

Bertoni's Antbird (*Drymophila rubricollis*)

White-backed Fire-eye (*Pyriglena leuconota*)

White-shouldered Fire-eye (*Pyriglena leucoptera*)

Short-tailed Antthrush (*Chamaeza campanisona*)

Variegated Antpitta (*Grallaria varia*)

Speckle-breasted Antpitta (*Hylopezus nattereri*)

Rufous Gnateater (*Conopophaga lineata*)

Tawny-crowned Pygmy-Tyrant (*Euscarthmus meloryphus*)

Southern Antpipit (*Corythopis delalandi*)

Drab-breasted Pygmy-Tyrant (*Hemitriccus diops*)

Ochre-faced Tody-Flycatcher (*Todirostrum plumbeiceps*)

Large-headed Flatbill (*Ramphotrigon megacephala*)

White-throated Spadebill (*Platyrinchus mystaceus*)

Russet-winged Spadebill (*Platyrinchus leucoryphus*)

Fawn-breasted Wren (*Thryothorus guarayanus*)

Flavescent Warbler (*Basileuterus flaveolus*)

Golden-crowned Warbler (*Basileuterus culicivorus*)

White-bellied Warbler (*Basileuterus hypoleucus*)

White-browed Warbler (*Basileuterus leucoblepharus*)

Red-crowned Ant-Tanager (*Habia rubica*)

Chestnut-headed Tanager (*Pyrrhocoma ruficeps*)

Saffron-billed Sparrow (*Arremon flavirostris*)

Blackish-blue Seedeater (*Amaurospiza moesta*)

Uniform Finch (*Haplospiza unicolor*)

APPENDIX 4

Eastern distributional limits (relative to Paraguay River) of western breeding birds (distributed primarily in Chaco and westward). Only species whose limits are within 150 km of river are included. Species restricted to the Matogrosense region are excluded.

Distance/Species	Locality	Source
130-140 km W of Paraguay River		
Crested Hornero *Furnarius cristatus*	Ruta Trans Chaco km 302, PHA	F. Hayes and J. Escobar Argaña
120-130 km W of Paraguay River		
White-bellied Nothura *Nothura boraquira*	120 km W of Puerto Pinasco, PHA	Hellmayr and Conover 1942
Quebracho Crested-Tinamou *Eudromia formosa*	120 km W of Puerto La Victoria, PHA	Hellmayr and Conover 1942
90-100 km W of Paraguay River		
Subtropical Doradito *Pseudocolopteryx acutipennis*	Ruta Trans Chaco km 210, PHA	F. Hayes et al.
40-50 km W of Paraguay River		
South American Painted-Snipe *Rostratula semicollaris*	Ruta Trans Chaco km 75, PHA	A. Madroño Nieto
20-30 km W of Paraguay River		
Spot-flanked Gallinule *Gallinula melanops*	Estancia La Golondrina, PHA	F. Hayes et al.
10-20 km W of Paraguay River		
Stripe-crowned Spinetail *Cranioleuca pyrrhophia*	15 km W of Río Paraguay, between Ríos Pilcomayo and Confuso, PHA	AMNH
Stripe-backed Antbird *Myrmorchilus strigilatus*	Retiro Potrerito, APY	F. Hayes
Olive-crowned Crescentchest *Melanopareia maximiliani*	W of Villa Hayes, PHA	A. Madroño Nieto
0-10 km W of Paraguay River		
Coscoroba Swan *Coscoroba coscoroba*	Riacho Ramos, APY	Hayes et al. 1990b
Lake Duck *Oxyura vittata*	Benjamin Aceval, PHA	F. Hayes et al.
Rufous-legged Owl *Strix rufipes*	Puerto La Victoria, APY	Laubmann 1939
White-fronted Woodpecker *Melanerpes cactorum*	Puerto 14 de Mayo, APY	F. Hayes
Cream-backed Woodpecker *Campephilus leucopogon*	Puerto 14 de Mayo, APY	F. Hayes
Black-banded Woodcreeper *Dendrocolaptes picumnus*	Puerto Guaraní, APY	Zotta 1938

194

Distance/Species	Locality	Source
Many-colored Chaco-Finch *Saltatricula multicolor*	Puerto Sastre, APY	Laubmann 1940
0-10 km E of Paraguay River		
White-cheeked Pintail *Anas bahamensis*	Bahía de Asunción, CEN	Hayes in press
Ringed Teal *Callonetta leucophrys*	Asunción, CEN	Contreras and González Romero 1988
Zone-tailed Hawk *Buteo albonotatus*	Río APA, CON	R. Ridgely
White-winged Coot *Fulica leucoptera*	Bahía de Asunción, CEN	Hayes in press
Golden-green Woodpecker *Piculus chrysochloros*	Lambaré, CEN	Berlepsch 1887
Lesser Canastero *Asthenes pyrrholeuca*	Villa Oliva, ÑEE	Grant 1911
Lark-like Brushrunner *Coryphistera alaudina*	Pilar, ÑEE	P. Scharf
White-bellied Tyrannulet *Serpophaga munda*	Estancia Fonciere, CON	Hayes et al. 1994
Golden-billed Saltator *Saltator aurantiirostris*	Valle Mi, CON	R. Ridgely
20-30 km E of Paraguay River		
Little Thornbird *Phacellodomus sibilatrix*	17 km E of Luque, CEN	MVZ
30-40 km E of Paraguay River		
Plumbeous Ibis *Theristicus caudatus*	Lago Ypoá, PAR	J. R. Contreras et al. 1989
Golden-collared Macaw *Ara auricollis*	Estancia Centurión, CON	N. López and F. Hayes
Great Horned Owl *Bubo virginianus*	Estancia San Luis, CON	Laubmann 1939
40-50 km E of Paraguay River		
Bay-winged Cowbird *Molothrus badius*	1 km N of Villa Florida, PAR	F. Hayes
60-70 km E of Paraguay River		
Cinereous Tyrant *Knipolegus striaticeps*	Sapucái, PAR	Chubb 1910
70-80 km E of Paraguay River		
Checkered Woodpecker *Picoides mixtus*	Estancia Sofia, CON	F. Hayes
Rufous-fronted Thornbird *Phacellodomus rufifrons*	Estancia Sofia, CON	F. Hayes
Black-capped Warbling-Finch *Poospiza melanoleuca*	Estancia Sofia, CON	F. Hayes

Distance/Species	Locality	Source
80-90 km E of Paraguay River		
Blue-crowned Trogon *Trogon curucui*	Zanja Morotí, CON	Laubmann 1939
Dark-throated Seedeater *Sporophila ruficollis*	SW of San Juan Bautista, MIS	Hayes et al. in prep.
90-100 km E of Paraguay River		
Chotoy Spinetail *Schoeniophylax phryganophila*	1 km N of Villa Florida, PAR	F. Hayes
Yellow-throated Spinetail *Certhiaxis cinnamomea*	1 km N of Villa Florida, PAR	F. Hayes
Short-billed Canastero *Asthenes baeri*	Villa Florida, MIS	F. Hayes
100-110 km E of Paraguay River		
Great Rufous Woodcreeper *Xiphocolaptes major*	Parque Nacional Ybycuí, PAR	P. Scharf
110-120 km E of Paraguay River		
Harris' Hawk *Parabuteo unicinctus*	Coronel Oviedo, CAA	Podtiaguin 1944
Crested Doradito *Pseudocolopteryx sclateri*	Villarrica, GUA	Bertoni 1914
Chestnut-capped Blackbird *Agelaius ruficapillus*	Villarrica, GUA	Hellmayr 1937
140-150 km E of Paraguay River		
Yellow-billed Cardinal *Paroaria capitata*	Estancia Ñu Porá, MIS	F. Hayes
Unicolored Blackbird *Agelaius cyanopus*	Estancia Ñu Porá, MIS	F. Hayes

APPENDIX 5

Western distributional limits (relative to Paraguay River) of eastern breeding birds (distributed primarily in Orient and eastward). Only species whose limits are within 150 km of river are included. Species restricted to the Ñeembucú region are excluded. Species indicated with an asterisk have been recorded west of the Paraguay River in Formosa Province or northeastern Chaco Province, Argentina (Nores 1992).

Distance/Species	Locality	Source
140-150 km W of Paraguay River		
Large-billed Tern *Phaetusa simplex*	Ruta Trans Chaco km 236, PHA	F. Hayes
130-140 km W of Paraguay River		
Lineated Woodpecker* *Dryocopus lineatus*	Fortín Page, PHA	Kerr 1892
120-130 km W of Paraguay River		
Yellow-billed Tern *Sterna superciliaris*	Estancia Amalia, PHA	D. Brooks
110-120 km W of Paraguay River		
Plumbeous Rail *Pardirallus sanguinolentus*	Laguna General Diaz, PHA	FMNH
White-tailed Goldenthroat *Polytmus guainumbi*	Makthlawaiya, PHA	AMNH
Saffron-billed Sparrow* *Arremon flavirostris*	Fortín Donovan, PHA	Kerr 1892
80-90 km W of Paraguay River		
Collared Forest-Falcon* *Micrastur semitorquatus*	80 km W of Puerto Pinasco, PHA	Wetmore 1926
Chestnut-vented Conebill *Conirostrum speciosum*	80 km W of Puerto Pinasco, PHA	Wetmore 1926
70-80 km W of Paraguay River		
Rufous-rumped Seedeater *Sporophila hypochroma*	Ruta Trans Chaco km 100, PHA	Collar et al. 1992
60-70 km W of Paraguay River		
Yellow-chevroned Parakeet *Brotogeris chiriri*	Waikthlatingmayalwa, PHA	Kerr 1901
Tawny-headed Swallow *Alopochelidon fucata*	Waikthlatingmayalwa, PHA	Kerr 1901
50-60 km W of Paraguay River		
Crested Oropendola* *Psarocolius decumanus*	Estancia Orihuela, PHA	Hayes et al. 1990b
40-50 km W of Paraguay River		
Greenish Elaenia* *Myiopagis viridicata*	Riacho Negro, PHA	AMNH

Distance/Species	Locality	Source
30-40 km W of Paraguay River		
Sharp-tailed Tyrant *Culicivora caudacuta*	Ruta Trans Chaco km 60, PHA	P. Scharf
Yellow-rumped Marshbird *Pseudoleistes guirahuro*	Estancia Villa Rey, PHA	F. Hayes et al.
20-30 km W of Paraguay River		
White-bellied Warbler *Basileuterus hypoleucus*	25 km W of Puerto Pinasco, PHA	Wetmore 1926
Guira Tanager* *Hemithraupis guira*	25 km W of Puerto Pinasco, PHA	Wetmore 1926
10-20 km W of Paraguay River		
Gray-headed Kite* *Leptodon cayanensis*	Retiro Potrerito, APY	Hayes et al. 1990b
Blue-winged Parrotlet* *Forpus xanthopterygius*	Retiro Potrerito, APY	Hayes et al. 1990b
Pauraque* *Nyctidromus albicollis*	Retiro Potrerito, APY	Hayes et al. 1990b
Red-breasted Toucan* *Ramphastos dicolorus*	Retiro Potrerito, APY	Hayes et al. 1990b
Streaked Xenops *Xenops rutilans*	Retiro Potrerito, APY	Hayes et al. 1990b
Long-tailed Reed-Finch *Donacospiza albifrons*	Benjamin Aceval, PHA	F. Hayes, A. and K. Robinson
0-10 km W of Paraguay River		
Gray Hawk *Buteo nitidus*	Puerto María, APY	Grant 1911
Red-and-white Crake *Laterallus leucopyrrhus*	Río Pilcomayo, PHA	Berlepsch 1887
Hyacinthine Macaw *Anodorhynchus hyacinthinus*	Puerto María, APY	Hayes et al. 1990b
Peach-fronted Parakeet *Aratinga aurea*	Villa Hayes, PHA	Bertoni 1930a
Blaze-winged Parakeet *Pyrrhura devillei*	Puerto Guaraní, APY	Zotta 1950
Stygian Owl *Asio stygius*	Villa Hayes, PHA	Bertoni 1930a
White-eared Puffbird *Nystalus chacuru*	Villa Hayes, PHA	Bertoni 1930a
Buff-browed Foliage-gleaner* *Syndactyla rufosuperciliata*	Puerto Sastre, APY	Laubmann 1940
Planalto Woodcreeper* *Dendrocolaptes platyrostris*	Villa Hayes, PHA	Bertoni 1930a
Rusty-backed Antwren *Formicivora rufa*	Villa Hayes, PHA	Bertoni 1930a
Sepia-capped Flycatcher *Leptopogon amaurocephalus*	Puerto Sastre, PHA	Laubmann 1940
White-throated Spadebill *Platyrinchus mystaceus*	Villa Hayes, PHA	Bertoni 1930a

Distance/Species	Locality	Source
Long-tailed Tyrant* *Colonia colonus*	Villa Hayes, PHA	Bertoni 1930a
Streamer-tailed Tyrant *Gubernetes yetapa*	Estancia Doña Julia, APY	Hayes et al. 1990b
Cliff Flycatcher *Hirundinea ferruginea*	Puerto Bahía Negra, APY	P. Scharf
Black-crowned Tityra* *Tityra inquisitor*	Villa Hayes, PHA	Bertoni 1930a
Swallow-tailed Manakin *Chiroxiphia caudata*	Puerto Pinasco, PHA	AMNH
Band-tailed Manakin *Pipra fasciicauda*	Villa Hayes, PHA	Bertoni 1930a
White-winged Swallow *Tachycineta albiventer*	Estancia Doña Julia, APY	Hayes et al. 1990b
Pale-breasted Thrush* *Turdus leucomelas*	Villa Hayes, PHA	Bertoni 1930a
White-browed Warbler* *Basileuterus leucoblepharus*	Villa Hayes, PHA	Bertoni 1930a
Ruby-crowned Tanager *Tachyphonus coronatus*	Villa Hayes, PHA	Bertoni 1930a
Black-goggled Tanager *Trichothraupis melanops*	Monte Sociedad, PHA	Laubmann 1940
Magpie Tanager *Cissopis leveriana*	Puerto Pinasco, PHA	FMNH
Black-throated Saltator *Saltator atricollis*	Puerto Pinasco, PHA	AMNH
Lesser Seed-Finch *Oryzoborus angolensis*	Villa Hayes, PHA	Bertoni 1930a

0-10 km E of Paraguay River

Distance/Species	Locality	Source
Harpy Eagle *Harpia harpyja*	San Lázaro, CON	Podtiaguin 1944
Barred Forest-Falcon *Micrastur ruficollis*	San Lázaro, CON	Podtiaguin 1944
Rusty-margined Guan *Penelope superciliaris*	San Lázaro, CON	Podtiaguin 1944
Blue-throated Piping-Guan *Pipile pipile*	Cerro Concurrencia, CON	Grant 1911
Sungrebe* *Heliornis fulica*	Asunción, CEN	Bertoni 1922
Red-and-green Macaw *Ara chloropterus*	San Lázaro, CON	Podtiaguin 1944
Blue-winged Macaw *Ara maracana*	San Lázaro, CON	Podtiaguin 1944
Vinaceous-breasted Parrot *Amazona vinacea*	San Lázaro, CON	Podtiaguin 1944
Sickle-winged Nightjar *Eleothreptus anomalus*	Colonia Risso/Río Apa, CON	Salvadori 1895
Fork-tailed Woodnymph *Thalurania furcata*	San Lázaro, CON	Podtiaguin 1944

Distance/Species	Locality	Source
Violet-capped Woodnymph *Thalurania glaucopis*	Asunción, CEN	Contreras and González Romero 1988
Versicolored Emerald *Amazilia versicolor*	Asunción, CEN	Bertoni 1922
Surucua Trogon* *Trogon surrucura*	15 km S of Villeta, CEN	A. Madroño Nieto et al.
Rufous-capped Motmot *Baryphthengus ruficapillus*	Asunción, CEN	Nores 1992
Chestnut-eared Aracari *Pteroglossus castanotis*	Asunción, CEN	Bertoni 1901
Buff-fronted Foliage-gleaner *Philydor rufus*	San Lázaro, CON	Podtiaguin 1944
Chestnut-capped Foliage-gleaner *Hylocryptus rectirostris*	11 km S of Concepción, CON	Storer 1989
White-throated Woodcreeper *Xiphocolaptes albicollis*	Asunción, CEN	Nores 1992
Greenish Tyrannulet *Phyllomyias virescens*	Asunción, CEN	Nores 1992
Gray Elaenia *Myiopagis caniceps*	Asunción, CEN	Bertoni 1922
Olivaceous Elaenia *Elaenia mesoleuca*	Asunción, CEN	Bertoni 1922
Lesser Elaenia *Elaenia chiriquensis*	Curuzú Chica, SAP	Grant 1911
Highland Elaenia *Elaenia obscura*	Asunción, CEN	Bertoni 1922
Bran-colored Flycatcher *Myiophobus fasciatus*	Bahía de Asunción, CEN	F. Hayes
Tropical Pewee *Contopus cinereus*	Colonia Risso, CON	Salvadori 1895
White-rumped Monjita *Xolmis velata*	Puerto Fonciere, CON	F. Hayes
Chestnut-crowned Becard* *Pachyramphus castaneus*	Asunción, CEN	Bertoni 1939
Bare-throated Bellbird *Procnias nudicollis*	Asunción, CEN	Bertoni 1926
Curl-crested Jay *Cyanocorax cristatellus*	San Lázaro, CON	Podtiaguin 1944
White-necked Thrush *Turdus albicollis*	Cerro Lorito, CON	Wetmore 1926
Burnished-buff Tanager *Tangara cayana*	Asunción, CEN	UMMZ
Fawn-breasted Tanager *Pipraeidea melanonota*	Estancia Pasó Pucú, ÑEE	Contreras and Contreras 1993b
Chestnut-backed Tanager *Tangara preciosa*	Asunción, CEN	Nores 1992
Golden-rumped Euphonia* *Euphonia cyanocephala*	Asunción, CEN	Bertoni 1939
Gray-headed Tanager *Eucometis penicillata*	Estancia Fonciere, CON	F. Hayes

Distance/Species	Locality	Source
White-rumped Tanager *Cypsnagra hirundinacea*	Rosario, SAP	UMMZ
Capped Seedeater *Sporophila bouvreuil*	Asunción, CEN	Bertoni 1922
Marsh Seedeater *Sporophila palustris*	15 km N of Pilar, ÑEE	Contreras et al. 1993a
Red-rumped Cacique* *Cacicus haemorrhous*	Asunción, CEN	Bertoni 1939

10-20 km E of Paraguay River

Distance/Species	Locality	Source
Cinereous Harrier *Circus cinereus*	18 km E of Rosario, SAP	UMMZ
Ash-throated Crake *Porzana albicollis*	N end of Lago Ypacarai, COR	S. LaBar et al.
Rufous Nightjar *Caprimulgus rufus*	Estancia Estrellas, CON	Laubmann 1940
Ochre-breasted Foliage-gleaner *Philydor lichtensteini*	18 km E of Rosario, SAP	UMMZ
Yellow-bellied Elaenia *Elaenia flavogaster*	Nueva Italia, CEN	AMNH
Cock-tailed Tyrant *Alectrurus tricolor*	15 km E of Rosario, SAP	UMMZ
Lined Seedeater *Sporophila lineola*	15 km E of Rosario, SAP	UMMZ
Chestnut Seedeater *Sporophila cinnamomea*	NE of Lago Ypacarai, COR	R. Ryan

20-30 km E of Paraguay River

Distance/Species	Locality	Source
Violaceous Quail-Dove *Geotrygon violacea*	Areguá, COR	UMMZ
Spectacled Owl *Pulsatrix perspicillata*	25 km E of Rosario, SAP	UMMZ

30-40 km E of Paraguay River

Distance/Species	Locality	Source
Pheasant Cuckoo *Dromococcyx pavoninus*	Tobatí, COR	S. LaBar et al.
Planalto Hermit *Phaethornis pretrei*	Tobatí, COR	Storer 1989
Swallow-tailed Hummingbird *Eupetomena macroura*	Estancia Centurión, CON	Laubmann 1933a
Green-and-rufous Kingfisher *Chloroceryle inda*	4 km W of Horqueta, CON	Brodkorb 1938c
Russet-mantled Foliage-gleaner *Philydor dimidiatus*	Estancia San Luis, CON	Laubmann 1940
Sharp-billed Treehunter *Heliobletus contaminatus*	Lago Ypoá, PAR	J. R. Contreras et al. 1989
Eared Pygmy-Tyrant *Myiornis auricularis*	Tobatí, COR	F. Hayes et al.
Red-ruffed Fruitcrow *Pyroderus scutatus*	5 km W of Horqueta, CON	UMMZ

Distance/Species	Locality	Source
Lesser Grass-Finch *Emberizoides ypiranganus*	Estancia San Luis, CON	Laubmann 1940
Plumbeous Seedeater *Sporophila plumbea*	Estancia San Luis, CON	Laubmann 1940
Giant Cowbird* *Scaphidura oryzivora*	Estancia San Luis, CON	Laubmann 1940

40-50 km E of Paraguay River

American Swallow-tailed Kite *Elanoides forficatus*	Horqueta, CON	UMMZ
Rufous-thighed Kite *Harpagus diodon*	Horqueta, CON	Hayes et al.1994
Rufous-faced Crake *Laterallus xenopterus*	Horqueta, CON	Conover 1934
Blackish Rail *Pardirallus nigricans*	Horqueta, CON	Hellmayr and Conover 1942
Giant Snipe *Gallinago undulata*	5 km E of Horqueta, CON	UMMZ
Gray-fronted Dove *Leptotila rufaxilla*	Horqueta, CON	UMMZ
Ruddy Quail-Dove *Geotrygon montana*	Horqueta, CON	Hellmayr and Conover 1942
Short-tailed Nighthawk* *Lurocalis semitorquatus*	5 km E of Horqueta, CON	UMMZ
White-necked Puffbird *Notharchus macrorhynchos*	Horqueta, CON	UMMZ
Rusty-breasted Nunlet *Nonnula rubecula*	Horqueta, CON	UMMZ
Black-capped Antwren *Herpsilochmus atricapillus*	Horqueta, CON	UMMZ
Piratic Flycatcher* *Legatus leucophaius*	Horqueta, CON	UMMZ
Blue Dacnis *Dacnis cayana*	Horqueta, CON	UMMZ

50-60 km E of Paraguay River

Solitary Tinamou *Tinamus solitarius*	Nueva Germania, SAP	Krieg and Schumacher 1936
Ornate Hawk-Eagle *Spizaetus ornatus*	Nueva Germania, SAP	Laubmann 1939
Spot-winged Wood-Quail *Odontophorus capueira*	Nueva Germania, SAP	Laubmann 1939
White-vented Violet-ear *Colibri serrirostris*	Nueva Germania, SAP	Laubmann 1933a
Black-throated Trogon *Trogon rufus*	Nueva Germania, SAP	Laubmann 1939
Yellow-fronted Woodpecker *Melanerpes flavifrons*	Nueva Germania, SAP	Laubmann 1939
Rufous-capped Spinetail *Synallaxis ruficapilla*	Nueva Germania, SAP	Laubmann 1940

Distance/Species	Locality	Source
White-eyed Foliage-gleaner *Automolus leucophthalmus*	Nueva Germania, SAP	Laubmann 1940
Thrush-like Woodcreeper *Dendrocincla turdina*	Nueva Germania, SAP	Laubmann 1940
Short-tailed Antthrush *Chamaeza campanisona*	Nueva Germania, SAP	Laubmann 1940
Rufous Gnateater *Conopophaga lineata*	Nueva Germania, SAP	Laubmann 1940
Southern Antpipit *Corythopis delalandi*	Nueva Germania, SAP	Laubmann 1940
Social Flycatcher *Myiozetetes similis*	Cerro Acahay, PAR	F. Hayes
Greenish Schiffornis *Schiffornis virescens*	Nueva Germania, SAP	Laubmann 1940
Sharpbill *Oxyruncus cristatus*	Nueva Germania, SAP	Laubmann 1940
Red-crowned Ant-Tanager *Habia rubica*	Nueva Germania, SAP	Laubmann 1940
60-70 km E of Paraguay River		
Brown Tinamou *Crypturellus obsoletus*	Choré, SAP	Hayes and Areco de Medina 1988
Red-capped Parrot *Pionopsitta pileata*	Sapucái, PAR	Chubb 1910
Ocellated Poorwill *Nyctiphrynus ocellatus*	Choré, SAP	Hayes and Areco de Medina 1988
Scale-throated Hermit *Phaethornis eurynome*	Choré, SAP	Hayes and Areco de Medina 1988
White-spotted Woodpecker *Veniliornis spilogaster*	Sapucái, PAR	Chubb 1910
White-browed Woodpecker *Piculus aurulentus*	Sapucái, PAR	Chubb 1910
Helmeted Woodpecker *Dryocopus galeatus*	Sapucái, PAR	Chubb 1910
Robust Woodpecker *Campephilus robustus*	Choré, SAP	Hayes and Areco de Medina 1988
Chicli Spinetail *Synallaxis spixi*	Sapucái, PAR	Oberholser 1902
Gray-bellied Spinetail *Synallaxis cinerascens*	Sapucái, PAR	Chubb 1910
Black-capped Foliage-gleaner *Philydor atricapillus*	Sapucái, PAR	Chubb 1910
Rufous-breasted Leaftosser *Sclerurus scansor*	Sapucái, PAR	Chubb 1910
Sharp-tailed Streamcreeper *Lochmias nematura*	Sapucái, PAR	Chubb 1910
Spot-backed Antshrike *Hypoedaleus guttatus*	Sapucái, PAR	Chubb 1910
Plain Antvireo *Dysithamnus mentalis*	Sapucái, PAR	Chubb 1910

Distance/Species	Locality	Source
Rufous-winged Antwren *Herpsilochmus rufimarginatus*	Sapucái, PAR	Chubb 1910
Rough-legged Tyrannulet *Phyllomyias burmeisteri*	Sapucái, PAR	Chubb 1910
Yellow Tyrannulet *Capsiempis flaveola*	Sapucái, PAR	Chubb 1910
Gray-hooded Flycatcher *Mionectes rufiventris*	Sapucái, PAR	Chubb 1910
Southern Bristle-Tyrant *Phylloscartes eximius*	Sapucái, PAR	Chubb 1910
Mottle-cheeked Tyrannulet *Phylloscartes ventralis*	Sapucái, PAR	Chubb 1910
Ochre-faced Tody-Flycatcher *Todirostrum plumbeiceps*	Sapucái, PAR	Chubb 1910
Sirystes *Sirystes sibilator*	Sapucái, PAR	Chubb 1910
Three-striped Flycatcher *Conopias trivirgata*	Sapucái, PAR	Chubb 1910
Wing-barred Manakin *Piprites chloris*	Sapucái, PAR	Chubb 1910
Cream-bellied Gnatcatcher *Polioptila lactea*	Sapucái, PAR	Chubb 1910
Rufous-crowned Greenlet *Hylophilus poicilotis*	Sapucái, PAR	Chubb 1910
Blue-naped Chlorophonia *Chlorophonia cyanea*	Sapucái, PAR	Chubb 1910
Violaceous Euphonia *Euphonia violacea*	Sapucái, PAR	Oberholser 1902
Chestnut-bellied Euphonia *Euphonia pectoralis*	Sapucái, PAR	Chubb 1910
Chestnut-headed Tanager *Pyrrhocoma ruficeps*	Sapucái, PAR	Chubb 1910
Uniform Finch *Haplospiza unicolor*	Sapucái, PAR	Chubb 1910

70-80 km E of Paraguay River

Black-fronted Piping-Guan *Pipile jacutinga*	Caballero, PAR	Salvadori 1895

80-90 km E of Paraguay River

Long-tailed Potoo *Nyctibius aethereus*	Zanja Morotí, CON	Laubmann 1940
Reiser's Tyrannulet *Phyllomyias reiseri*	Zanja Morotí, CON	Zimmer 1955
Mouse-colored Tyrannulet *Phaeomyias murina*	Zanja Morotí, CON	Zimmer 1941
Rufous-sided Pygmy-Tyrant *Euscarthmus rufomarginatus*	Zanja Morotí, CON	Olrog 1979
Helmeted Manakin *Antilophia galeata*	Zanja Morotí, CON	Laubmann 1933a

Distance/Species	Locality	Source
100-110 km E of Paraguay River		
Mottled Owl *Strix virgata*	Parque Nacional Ybycuí, PAR	UMMZ
Great Dusky Swift *Cypseloides senex*	Parque Nacional Ybycuí, PAR	F. Hayes et al.
White-collared Swift *Streptoprocne zonaris*	Parque Nacional Ybycuí, PAR	F. Hayes et al.
Black-breasted Plovercrest *Stephanoxis lalandi*	Parque Nacional Ybycuí, PAR	MVZ
Scaled Woodcreeper *Lepidocolaptes squamatus*	Parque Nacional Ybycuí, PAR	P. Scharf
Lesser Woodcreeper *Lepidocolaptes fuscus*	Parque Nacional Ybycuí, PAR	P. Scharf
Saffron-cowled Blackbird *Agelaius flavus*	Itapé, GUA	Hellmayr 1937
110-120 km E of Paraguay River		
White-rumped Hawk *Buteo leucorrhous*	San Juan Bautista, MIS	Podtiaguin 1944
Planalto Flycatcher *Phyllomyias fasciatus*	Estancia Ñu Porá, CON	AMNH
Red-rumped Warbling-Finch *Poospiza lateralis*	Paso Yuvay [near Villarrica?], GUA	Dabbene 1912
120-130 km E of Paraguay River		
Ochre-collared Piculet *Picumnus temminckii*	Independencia, GUA	AMNH
Streak-capped Antwren *Terenura maculata*	Independencia, GUA	Naumburg 1939
Sedge Wren *Cistothorus platensis*	Independencia, GUA	AMNH
Green-headed Tanager *Tangara seledon*	Independencia, GUA	AMNH
Green-throated Euphonia *Euphonia chalybea*	Independencia, GUA	AMNH
140-150 km E of Paraguay River		
White-banded Tanager *Neothraupis fasciata*	Upper Río Yguazú, CAA	AMNH

APPENDIX 6

Breeding species of Paraguayan birds primarily restricted to the Chaco but crossing the Paraguay River to the north of the Orient. Species restricted to Matogrosense region are excluded.

Spot-backed Puffbird (*Nystalus maculatus*)

Stripe-backed Antbird (*Myrmorchilus strigilatus*)

Black-bellied Antwren (*Formicivora melanogaster*)

Black-backed Grosbeak (*Pheucticus aureoventris*)

Troupial (*Icterus icterus*)

Breeding species of Paraguayan birds primarily restricted to the Chaco but crossing the Paraná River to the south of the Orient.

Coscoroba Swan (*Coscoroba coscoroba*)

White-cheeked Pintail (*Anas bahamensis*)

Silver Teal (*Anas versicolor*)

Cinnamon Teal (*Anas cyanoptera*)

Red Shoveler (*Anas platalea*)

Ringed Teal (*Callonetta leucophrys*)

Lake Duck (*Oxyura vittata*)

Black-headed Duck (*Heteronetta atricapilla*)

Spot-flanked Gallinule (*Gallinula melanops*)

White-winged Coot (*Fulica leucoptera*)

Red-fronted Coot (*Fulica rufifrons*)

South American Painted-Snipe (*Rostratula semicollaris*)

Spot-winged Pigeon (*Columba maculosa*)

Chaco Earthcreeper (*Upucerthia certhioides*)

Crested Hornero (*Furnarius cristatus*)

Stripe-crowned Spinetail (*Cranioleuca pyrrhophia*)

Little Thornbird (*Phacellodomus sibilatrix*)

Lark-like Brushrunner (*Coryphistera alaudina*)

Brown Cacholote (*Pseudoseisura lophotes*)

Scimitar-billed Woodcreeper (*Drymornis bridgesii*)

White-naped Xenopsaris (*Xenopsaris albinucha*)

Stripe-capped Sparrow (*Aimophila strigiceps*)

Many-colored Chaco-Finch (*Saltatricula multicolor*)

Breeding species of Paraguayan birds primarily restricted to the Chaco, but crossing the Paraguay River to the north of the Orient and the Paraná River to the south of the Orient.

Plumbeous Ibis (*Theristicus caerulescens*)

White-fronted Woodpecker (*Melanerpes cactorum*)

Cream-backed Woodpecker (*Campephilus leucopogon*)

Golden-billed Saltator (*Saltator aurantiirostris*)

206

Breeding species of Paraguayan birds primarily restricted to the Orient (some occur in the eastern Chaco but are absent in the xeric western Chaco) but crossing the Paraguay River to the north of the Orient. Species that have a relatively continuous distribution westward across Bolivia and southward to the Yungas forests of northwestern Argentina are indicated with an asterisk; these species have a circum-Chaco distribution.

Gray-headed Kite (*Leptodon cayanensis*)

American Swallow-tailed Kite (*Elanoides forficatus*)*

Rufous-thighed Kite (*Harpagus diodon*)*

Gray-bellied Hawk (*Accipiter poliogaster*)

Tiny Hawk (*Accipiter superciliosus*)

Harpy Eagle (*Harpia harpyja*)*

Ornate Hawk-Eagle (*Spizaetus ornatus*)*

Barred Forest-Falcon (*Micrastur ruficollis*)*

Collared Forest-Falcon (*Micrastur semitorquatus*)*

Rusty-margined Guan (*Penelope superciliaris*)

Blue-throated Piping-Guan (*Pipile pipile*)

Ash-throated Crake (*Porzana albicollis*)

Sungrebe (*Heliornis fulica*)

Scaled Pigeon (*Columba speciosa*)

Gray-fronted Dove (*Leptotila rufaxilla*)

Ruddy Quail-Dove (*Geotrygon montana*)

Violaceous Quail-Dove (*Geotrygon violacea*)

Blue-and-yellow Macaw (*Ara ararauna*)

Red-and-green Macaw (*Ara chloropterus*)

Pheasant Cuckoo (*Dromococcyx phasianellus*)

Spectacled Owl (*Pulsatrix perspicillata*)*

Mottled Owl (*Strix virgata*)

Pauraque (*Nyctidromus albicollis*)*

Ocellated Poorwill (*Nyctiphrynus ocellatus*)

White-collared Swift (*Streptoprocne zonaris*)*

Planalto Hermit (*Phaethornis pretrei*)*

Swallow-tailed Hummingbird (*Eupetomena macroura*)

White-vented Violet-ear (*Colibri serrirostris*)*

Fork-tailed Woodnymph (*Thalurania furcata*)*

Versicolored Emerald (*Amazilia versicolor*)

Amethyst Woodstar (*Calliphlox amethystina*)

Green-and-rufous Kingfisher (*Chloroceryle inda*)

White-necked Puffbird (*Notharchus macrorhynchos*)

Chestnut-eared Aracari (*Pteroglossus castanotis*)

Buff-fronted Foliage-gleaner (*Philydor rufus*)

Streaked Xenops (*Xenops rutilans*)*

Black-capped Antwren (*Herpsilochmus atricapillus*)*

Rusty-backed Antwren (*Formicivora rufa*)

Collared Crescentchest (*Melanopareia maximiliani*)

Planalto Tyrannulet (*Phyllomyias fasciatus*)

Rough-legged Tyrannulet (*Phyllomyias burmeisteri*)

Mouse-colored Tyrannulet (*Phaeomyias murina*)*

Gray Elaenia (*Myiopagis caniceps*)*

Greenish Elaenia (*Myiopagis viridicata*)*

Lesser Elaenia (*Elaenia chiriquensis*)

Sharp-tailed Tyrant (*Culicivora caudacuta*)

Sepia-capped Flycatcher (*Leptopogon amaurocephalus*)*

Southern Antpipit (*Corythopis delalandi*)

White-throated Spadebill (*Platyrinchus mystaceus*)

Tropical Pewee (*Contopus cinereus*)*

White-rumped Monjita (*Xolmis velata*)

Long-tailed Tyrant (*Colonia colonus*)

Cock-tailed Tyrant (*Alectrurus tricolor*)

Streamer-tailed Tyrant (*Gubernetes yetapa*)

Cliff Flycatcher (*Hirundinea ferruginea*)

Sirystes (*Sirystes sibilator*)

Piratic Flycatcher (*Legatus leucophaius*)*

Black-tailed Tityra (*Tityra cayana*)

Black-crowned Tityra (*Tityra inquisitor*)

Helmeted Manakin (*Antilophia galeata*)

Band-tailed Manakin (*Pipra fasciicauda*)

Pale-breasted Thrush (*Turdus leucomelas*)

Golden-crowned Warbler (*Basileuterus culicivorus*)*

Bananaquit (*Coereba flaveola*)

Blue Dacnis (*Dacnis cayana*)

Palm Tanager (*Thraupis palmarum*)

Gray-headed Tanager (*Eucometis penicillata*)

Silver-beaked Tanager (*Ramphocelus carbo*)

White-rumped Tanager (*Cypsnagra hirundinacea*)

Guira Tanager (*Hemithraupis guira*)*

White-banded Tanager (*Neothraupis fasciata*)

Black-faced Tanager (*Schistochlamys melanopis*)

Black-throated Saltator (*Saltator atricollis*)

Black-masked Finch (*Coryphaspiza melanotis*)

Saffron-billed Sparrow (*Arremon flavirostris*)*

Plumbeous Seedeater (*Sporophila plumbea*)

Lesser Seed-Finch (*Oryzoborus angolensis*)

Giant Cowbird (*Scaphidura oryzivora*)

Crested Oropendola (*Psarocolius decumanus*)*

Breeding species of Paraguayan birds primarily restricted to the Orient but crossing the Paraná River to the south of the Chaco. Species restricted to the Ñeembucú region are excluded.

Sickle-winged Nightjar (*Eleothreptus anomalus*)

Chicli Spinetail (*Synallaxis spixi*)

Planalto Woodcreeper (*Dendrocolaptes platyrostris*)

Diademed Tanager (*Stephanophorus diadematus*)

Lesser Grass-Finch (*Emberizoides ypiranganus*)

Red-rumped Warbling-Finch (*Poospiza lateralis*)

Saffron-cowled Blackbird (*Agelaius flavus*)

Breeding species of Paraguayan birds restricted to the Orient, but crossing the Paraguay River to the north of the Chaco and the Paraná River to the south of the Chaco.

Rufous Nightjar (*Caprimulgus rufus*)

Bran-colored Flycatcher (*Myiophobus fasciatus*)

Golden-rumped Euphonia (*Euphonia cyanocephala*)

Breeding species of Paraguayan birds primarily restricted to humid forests of the Orient (and in Paranense forests of adjacent Brazil and Argentina) and absent from the western Chaco, but with a disjunct population occurring in the Yungas forests on the east slope of the Andes in southern Bolivia or northwestern Argentina.

Brown Tinamou (*Crypturellus obsoletus*)

Buff-browed Foliage-gleaner (*Syndactyla rufosuperciliata*)

Buff-fronted Foliage-gleaner (*Philydor rufus*)

Sharp-tailed Streamcreeper (*Lochmias nematura*)

Rufous-capped Antshrike (*Thamnophilus ruficapillus*)

Short-tailed Antthrush (*Chamaeza campanisona*)

Rough-legged Tyrannulet (*Phyllomyias burmeisteri*)

Lesser Elaenia (*Elaenia chiriquensis*)

Highland Elaenia (*Elaenia obscura*)

Mottle-cheeked Tyrannulet (*Phylloscartes ventralis*)

Ochre-faced Tody-Flycatcher (*Todirostrum plumbeiceps*)

Cliff Flycatcher (*Hirundinea ferruginea*)

Slaty Thrush (*Turdus nigriceps*)

White-necked Thrush (*Turdus albicollis*)

River Warbler (*Basileuterus rivularis*)

Fawn-breasted Tanager (*Pipraeidea melanonota*)

Golden-rumped Euphonia (*Euphonia cyanocephala*)

APPENDIX 7

Species of birds in Paraguay classified as threatened or even extinct (Collar et al. 1992); species considered to be extinct in Paraguay are indicated with an asterisk.

Brazilian Merganser (*Mergus octosetaceus*)*
Crowned Eagle (*Harpyhaliaetus coronatus*)
Black-fronted Piping-Guan (*Pipile jacutinga*)
Speckled Crake (*Coturnicops notata*)
Rufous-faced Crake (*Laterallus xenopterus*)
Purple-winged Ground-Dove (*Claravis godefrida*)
Hyacinthine Macaw (*Anodorhynchus hyacinthinus*)
Glaucous Macaw (*Anodorhynchus glaucus*)*
Vinaceous-breasted Parrot (*Amazona vinacea*)
Sickle-winged Nightjar (*Eleothreptus anomalus*)
Helmeted Woodpecker (*Dryocopus galeatus*)
Dinelli's Doradito (*Pseudocolopteryx dinellianus*)

Rufous-sided Pygmy-Tyrant (*Euscarthmus rufomarginatus*)
São Paulo Tyrannulet (*Phylloscartes paulistus*)
Russet-winged Spadebill (*Platyrinchus leucoryphus*)
Strange-tailed Tyrant (*Alectrurus risora*)
Ochre-breasted Pipit (*Anthus nattereri*)
Buffy-fronted Seedeater (*Sporophila frontalis*)
Temminck's Seedeater (*Sporophila falcirostris*)
Marsh Seedeater (*Sporophila palustris*)
Rufous-rumped Seedeater (*Sporophila hypochroma*)
Saffron-cowled Blackbird (*Agelaius flavus*)

Species of birds in Paraguay classified as near-threatened (Collar et al. 1992).

Greater Rhea (*Rhea americana*)
Solitary Tinamou (*Tinamus solitarius*)
Orinoco Goose (*Neochen jubata*)
Gray-bellied Hawk (*Accipiter poliogaster*)
Mantled Hawk (*Leucopternis polionota*)
Harpy Eagle (*Harpia harpyja*)
Black-and-white Hawk-Eagle (*Spizastur melanoleucus*)
Orange-breasted Falcon (*Falco deiroleucus*)
Hudsonian Godwit (*Limosa haemastica*)
Blue-winged Macaw (*Ara maracana*)
Red-capped Parrot (*Pionopsitta pileata*)
Buff-fronted Owl (*Aegolius harrisii*)
Saffron Toucanet (*Baillonius bailloni*)
White-browed Woodpecker (*Piculus aurulentus*)
Black-bodied Woodpecker (*Dryocopus schulzi*)
Canebrake Groundcreeper (*Clibanornis dendrocolaptoides*)
Russet-mantled Foliage-gleaner (*Philydor dimidiatus*)

Chestnut-capped Foliage-gleaner (*Hylocryptus rectirostris*)
Reiser's Tyrannulet (*Phyllomyias reiseri*)
Sharp-tailed Tyrant (*Culicivora caudacuta*)
Bearded Tachuri (*Polystictus pectoralis*)
Southern Bristle-Tyrant (*Phylloscartes eximius*)
Bay-ringed Tyrannulet (*Phylloscartes sylviolus*)
Hudson's Black-Tyrant (*Knipolegus hudsoni*)
Cock-tailed Tyrant (*Alectrurus tricolor*)
Shear-tailed Gray-Tyrant (*Muscipipra vetula*)
Swallow-tailed Cotinga (*Phibalura flavirostris*)
Bare-throated Bellbird (*Procnias nudicollis*)
Cream-bellied Gnatcatcher (*Polioptila lactea*)
Chaco Pipit (*Anthus chacoensis*)
Black-masked Finch (*Coryphaspiza melanotis*)
Dark-throated Seedeater (*Sporophila ruficollis*)
Chestnut Seedeater (*Sporophila cinnamomea*)
Blackish-blue Seedeater (*Amaurospiza moesta*)
Lesser Grass-Finch (*Emberizoides ypiranganus*)

APPENDIX 8

Gazetteer of localities mentioned in text for bird records and for field work by ornithologists. Unnamed localities within 10 km of a stated locality are not given. Abbreviations for departments are: AMA=Amambay; APN=Alto Paraná; APY=Alto Paraguay; BOQ=Boquerón; CAA=Caaguazú; CAN=Canindeyú (=Canendiyú); CAP=Caazapá; CEN=Central; exCHA=Chaco (now Alto Paraguay); CON=Concepción; COR=Cordillera; GUA=Guairá; ITA=Itapúa; MIS=Misiones; exNAS=Nueva Asunción (now Boquerón); ÑEE=Ñeembucú; PAR=Paraguarí; PHA=Presidente Hayes; SAP=San Pedro. Abbreviations for geographical regions are: AC=Alto Chaco; AP=Alto Paraná; BC=Bajo Chaco; CC=Campos Cerrados; CP=Central Paraguay; MG=Matogrosense; ÑE=Ñeembucú. Coordinates (degrees, minutes) are for south latitude/west longitude, respectively; many are approximate rather than exact. Additional information for many localities is provided by Paynter (1989).

Locality	Department(s)	Region(s)	Coordinates
Abaí	CAP	CP	26,01/55,57
Areguá	COR	CP	25,18/57,25
Arroyo Dos Hermanas	ÑEE	ÑE	Many
Arroyo Montuoso	ÑEE	ÑE	Many
Arroyo Piratiy	CAA,APN	AP	Many
Arroyo Pozuelo	CAN	AP	Many
Arroyo Tagatyjá (near Serranía de San Luis)	CON	CC	Not located
Arroyo Trementina	CON	CC	Many
Asunción	CEN	CP	25,18/57,38
Ayolas	MIS	ÑE	27,24/56,54
Bahía de Asunción	CEN	CP	25,17/57,38
Belén	CON	CC	23,30/57,06
Bella Vista	AMA	CC	22,08/56,31
40 km SE	AMA	CC	22,17/56,21
Benjamin Aceval	PHA	BC	24,58/57,34
Bernalcué (near Asunción; Hellmayr 1938)	CEN?	CP	Not located
Bosque Estrella	AMA	CP	23,20/56,05
Bosque Pira'y	AMA	CP	23,30/55,45
Caaby Cupé (along Río Yhagüy)	COR	CP	Not located
Caaguazú	CAA	CP/AP	25,26/56,02
Caballero	PAR	CP	25,41/56,50
Cambyretá	ITA	AP	27,20/55,45
Campichuelo	ITA	AP	27,26/55,45
Campo Esperanza	PHA	AC	22,20/59,39
Capitán Bado	AMA	CP	23,16/55,32
Capitán Meza	ITA	AP	27,01/55,34
Capitán Miranda	ITA	AP	27,14/55,49
Carandayty	Unknown	Unknown	Not located
Carayaó	CAA	CP	25,05/56,36
Carmencita	BOQ	AC	22,29/62,16
Catueté	CAN	AP	24,11/54,41
Celos Parini	CAN	AP	Not located

Locality	Department(s)	Region(s)	Coordinates
Cerrito	APY	MG	21,27/57,56
Cerro Acahay	PAR	CP	25,52/57,10
Cerro Amambay	CON	CP	23,10/55,30
(40 km WSW of Capitán Bado)			
Cerro Concurrencia	CON	CC	22,20/58,00
Cerro Galván	APY	MG	22,25/58,05
Cerro Lorito	CON	CC	22,45/57,50
Chaco-í	PHA	BC	25,15/57,38
Choré	SAP	CP	24,10/56,35
Ciudad del Este	APN	AP	25,33/54,37
(formerly Puerto Presidente Stroessner)			
50 km W	APN	AP	Uncertain
Colonia Dorada	APN	AP	Not located
Colonia Esperanza	Unknown	Unknown	Not located
Colonia Fernheim	BOQ	AC	22,20/59,55
(includes Filadelfia and Orloff)			
Colonia Menno	BOQ	AC	22,30/59,45
(includes Loma Plata, Laguna Capitán and Lichtenau)			
Colonia Neuland	BOQ	AC	22,35/60,00
Colonia Nueva Australia	Unknown	Unknown	Not located
Colonia Ñacunday	APN	AC	26,49/54,49
Colonia Risso	CON	CC	22,21/57,50
Colonie Guaraní	Unknown	AP	Not located
Comandacay	Unknown	AP	Not located
Concepción	CON	CC	23,25/57,00
11 km S	SAP	CC	22,30/57,29
Cordillera de Mbaracayú	CAN	AP	Many
Coronel Oviedo	CAA	CP	25,25/56,27
Corpus Cristi	CAN	AP	24,03/54,55
12 km SE	CAN	AP	24,09/54,53
Cuenca del Acaray-mí	CAA	AP	24,40/55,24
Curuguaty	CAN	CP	24,31/55,42
13 km N	CAN	CP	24,22/55,42
Curupayty	ÑEE	ÑE	27,09/58,36
Curuzú Chica	SAP	CP	24,00/57,10
Desmochados	Unknown	Unknown	Not located
Diamantina	CON	CC	Not located
(probably Arroyo Trementina; López 1992)			
Djaguarasapá	ITA?	AP	Not located
(=Yaguarasapá?)			
Embalse de Itaipú	APN,CAN	AP	Many
Emboscada	COR	CP	25,09/57,19
Encarnación	ITA	AP	27,20/55,54
Estancia Alegre	PHA	BC	Uncertain
(near Estancia Estrella)			
Estancia Amalia	PHA	AC	22,34/59,06
Estancia Buena Vista	CON	CC	22,25/57,29

Locality	Department(s)	Region(s)	Coordinates
Estancia Campo María	PHA	AC	59,19/22,37
Estancia Centurión	CON	CC	22,15/57,35
Estancia Cerrito Vargas	MIS	ÑE	Not located
Estancia Coé Puajhú	exNAS	AC	20,38/61,57
Estancia Doña Julia	APY	MG	20,11/58,09
Estancia Estrella	PHA	BC	24,51/58,18
Estancia Estrellas	CON	CC	22,10/57,42
Estancia Fonciere	CON	CC	22,28/57,47
Estancia Guarepyá (near Santiago)	MIS	ÑE	Not located
Estancia Guy (near Ruta Trans Chaco km 75)	PHA	BC	Not located
Estancia Itabó	CAN	AP	24,27/54,38
Estancia Klassen	PHA	AC	59,17/22,15
Estancia La Fortuna	CAN	CP	24,24/55,38
Estancia La Golondrina	CAA	AP	24,43/55,22
Estancia La Golondrina	CAP	AP	25,33/55,30
Estancia La Golondrina	PHA	BC	24,56/57,42
Estancia La Patria	exNAS	AC	21,24/61,25
36 km WSW (on Picada 108)	exNAS	AC	21,32/61,32
Estancia Loma Porá	CON	CC	22,18/58,36
Estancia Mirabeaud, CON	CON	CC	22,29/57,18
Estancia Ñu Porá	CON	CC	23,09/56,19
Estancia Ñu Porá	MIS	ÑE	Not located
Estancia Orihuela	PHA	BC	23,25/58,40
Estancia Pasó Pucú (near Curupayty)	ÑEE	ÑE	27,09/58,36
Estancia Primavera	CON	CC	22,23/57,45
Estancia Reyes Cué	CON	CC	22,19/57,39
Estancia San Antonio	APN	AP	25,18/55,20
Estancia San Jose (15 km SW of Ruta Trans Chaco km 75, near Río Confuso; Collar et al. 1992)	PHA	BC	Not located
Estancia San Luis (=San Luis de la Sierra)	CON	CC	22,25/57,27
Estancia Santa Catalina (W of Villa Hayes; A. Madroño Nieto, pers. comm.)	PHA	BC	Not located
Estancia Santa Elisa	MIS	ÑE	26,55/57,29
Estancia Santa María de la Sierra	CON	CC	24,16/58,36
Estancia Santa Sofia	CON	CC	22,21/57,08
Estancia Villa Rey	PHA	BC	24,44/57,12
Estancia Ytañu	CEN	ÑE	25,50/57,45
Estancia Zaragosa (near Pozo Colorado; R. Behrstock, pers. comm.)	PHA	BC?	Not located
Estero Ñeembucú	ÑEE	ÑE	27,05/57,38
Estero Patiño	PHA	BC	24,05/59,55
Estero Pirahau (at Ruta Trans Chaco km 249)	PHA	BC	23,37/58,42
Eusebio Ayala	COR	CP	25,24/56,56

212

Locality	Department(s)	Region(s)	Coordinates
Filadelfia	BOQ	AC	22,21/60,02
Fort Wheeler (=Fortín Guaraní?)	PHA	AC	22,40/59,35
Fortín Conchitas (=Algarobo)	BOQ	AC	22,44/61,54
Fortín Donovan	PHA	BC	24,52/58,40
Fortín General Caballero	PHA	BC	24,09/59,32
Fortín Guachalla	BOQ	AC	22,27/62,20
Fortín Guaraní	PHA	AC	22,44/59,30
Fortín Linares	Unknown	Unknown	Not located
Fortín Mariscal López	PHA	AC	23,40/59,44
Fortín Nueva Asunción Base Aérea	exNAS	AC	20,47/61,57
Fortín Nueve	PHA	BC	24,53/58,30
Fortín Page	PHA	BC	24,47/58,45
Fortín Teniente Agripino Enciso	exNAS	AC	21,14/61,35
Fortín Teniente E. Ochoa	exNAS	AC	21,42/61,02
Fortín Toledo	BOQ	AC	22,21/60,20
General Eugenio A. Garay	exNAS	AC	20,32/62,09
Guazú-Cuá	Unknown	Unknown	Not located
Hernandarias	APN	AP	25,23/54,38
Hito IIex	exNAS	AC	21,04/62,15
15 km N	exNAS	AC	20,57/62,15
Hohenau	PHA	AC	59,24/22,37
Horqueta	CON	CC	23,24/56,53
Hotel El Tirol (at Capitán Miranda)	ITA	AP	27,11/55,47
Independencia	GUA	CP	25,43/56,15
Isla Jara Cué (Playa Ybycuí, opposite mouth of Río Bermejo)	ÑEE	ÑE	26,52/58,23
Isla Talavera	ITA	ÑE	27,35/56,38
Isla Yacyretá	ITA	ÑE	27,25/56,26
Itá Enramada (hotel in Luque, CEN)	CEN	CP	25,37/57,30
Itapé	GUA	CP	25,51/56,38
Itaquyry	APN	AP	24,58/55,06
Jejuí (probably Río Jejuí-Guazú)	Unknown	Unknown	Not located
Jejuí-mí (within Reserva Natural del Bosque Mbaracayú; Brooks et al. 1993)	CAN	CP	24,07/55,32
Lambaré	CEN	CP	25,21/57,39
Lago Ypacarai	CEN,COR	CP	25,19/57,19
Lago Ypoá	CEN,PAR	ÑE	25,48/57,28
Laguna Capitán	PHA	AC	22,33/59,42
Laguna Escalante	PHA	BC	23,50/60,46
Laguna General Diaz	PHA	AC	22,18/59,01
Laguna Millón (near Ruta Trans Chaco km 375; López 1993)	PHA	AC	22,55/59,31
Laguna Salada	PHA	AC	22,32/59,18

Locality	Department(s)	Region(s)	Coordinates
Lagunita	CAN	CC	24,07/55,26
(within Reserva Natural del Bosque Mbaracayú; Brooks et al. 1993)			
Las Delicias	PHA	BC	Not located
(12 km N of Ruta Trans Chaco km 109; Peris et al. 1987)			
Laurel	APN,CAN	AP	24,38/54,52
Laureles	ÑEE	ÑE	27,16/57,25
Lichtenau	PHA	AC	22,50/59,40
80 km SW	BOQ,PHA?	AC	Uncertain
100 km S	BOQ,PHA?	AC	Uncertain
(near Fortín Mariscal López?; Nores 1992)			
Lima	SAP	CP	23,56/56,28
Loma Plata	BOQ	AC	22,21/59,48
Lupii	CON	CC	Not located
Luque	CEN	CP	25,16/57,34
17 km E	CEN,COR	CP	Uncertain
Makthlawaiya	PHA	BC	23,20/58,50
Mariscal Estigarribia	BOQ	AC	22,02/60,36
Mbaracayú	CAN	AP	24,15/54,31
14 km SSE	CAN	AP	24,16/54,35
Monte Lindo	PHA	BC	23,52/57,27
Monte Sociedad	PHA	BC	25,03/57,35
Naranjito	ÑEE	ÑE	26,56/58,27
Nueva Germania	SAP	CP	23,54/56,34
Nueva Italia	CEN	ÑE	25,37/57,30
Ñu Guazú	CEN	CP	25,16/57,35
(NE of Asunción)			
Orloff	BOQ	AC	22,15/59,50
(between Filadelfia and Loma Plata)			
115 km E (Laguna Salada?)	PHA	AC	Uncertain
120 km E (Laguna Salada?	PHA	AC	Uncertain
60 km SE (Laguna Capitán?)	PHA	AC	Uncertain
120 km SE (Laguna Salada?)	PHA	AC	Uncertain
100 km W	BOQ	AC	Uncertain
Paraguarí	PAR	CP	26,00/57,10
Parque Nacional Cerro Corá	AMA	CC	22,39/56,04
Parque Nacional Defensores del Chaco	exCHA	AC	20,20/60,30
Parque Nacional Teniente Enciso	exNAS	AC	21,08/61,38
Parque Nacional Vapor Cüé	COR	CP	25,13/56,48
Parque Nacional Ybycuí	PAR	CP	26,07/56,49
Paso Lengá	ÑEE	ÑE	26,54/58,22
Paso Yuvay	GUA?	CP?	Not located
Pedro Juan Caballero	AMA	CC	Many
Picada 108	exNAS	AC	Many
at 36 km WSW of Estancia La Patra	exNAS	AC	21,32/61,32
Pilar	ÑEE	ÑE	26,25/58,23
10-15 km N	ÑEE	ÑE	Uncertain
14 km N	ÑEE	ÑE	Uncertain

Locality	Department(s)	Region(s)	Coordinates
N at Riacho Ñeembucú	ÑEE	ÑE	26,52/58,23
Playa Ybycuí	ÑEE	ÑE	26,52/58,23
(Isla Jara Cué, opposite mouth of Río Bermejo)			
Pozo Colorado	PHA	AC,BC	23,28/58,52
Puentecita	CAA	CP	Not located
(NE of Coronel Oviedo; not misspelled; F. Hayes)			
Puente Remanso	CEN,PHA	BC,CP	25,11/57,31
Puerto 14 [Catorce] de Mayo	APY	MG	20,20/58,06
Puerto Bahía Negra	APY	MG	20,14/58,10
Puerto Barra	APN	AP	26,02/55,13
Puerto Bertoni	APN	AP	25,38/54,40
Puerto Carayá Vuelta	PHA	MG	23,09/57,32
Puerto Cooper	PHA	MG	23,02/57,48
Puerto Edelira	ITA	AP	26,54/55,10
Puerto Fonciere	CON	CC	22,29/57,48
Puerto Francia	APY?	MG?	Not located
(possibly in Bolivia)			
Puerto Gibaja	APN	AP	25,33/54,40
Puerto Guaraní	APY	MG	21,18/57,55
Puerto Juan Barbero	Unknown	Unknown	Not located
Puerto La Victoria	APY	MG	22,20/57,55
(formerly Puerto Casado)			
40 km W	APY,PHA	MG	22,14/58,14
170 km W	APY,BOQ	AC	22,03/59,27
190 km W	APY,BOQ	AC	22,03/59,38
195 km W	APY,BOQ	AC	22,03/59,41
200 km W	APY,BOQ	AC	22,03/59,44
240 km W	BOQ,exNAS	AC	22,03/60,08
265 km W	BOQ,exNAS	AC	22,02/60,21
Puerto María	APY	MG	21,37/57,56
Puerto María Auxiliadora	APY	MG	21,43/57,55
Puerto Militar	PHA	BC	23,26/57,27
Puerto Nuevo de Pilar	ÑEE	ÑE	26,52/58,23
Puerto Pagani	CON	CC	Not located
Puerto Pinasco	PHA	MG	22,43/57,50
25 km W	PHA	MG	Uncertain
80 km W	PHA	MG	Uncertain
120 km W	PHA	AC	Uncertain
200 km W	BOQ,PHA	AC	Uncertain
Puerto Ramos	APY	MG	20,16/58,08
Puerto San Rafael	ITA	AP	26,40/54,53
Puerto Sastre	APY	MG	22,06/57,59
Puerto Valle Mi	CON	CC	22,15/57,55
Puesto Estancia-í	PHA	AC	22,22/59,18
(=Estancia-I)			
Puesto Estrella	exNAS	AC	21,03/62,12
Refugio Biológico Mbaracayú	CAN	AP	24,00/54,14

Locality	Department(s)	Region(s)	Coordinates
Remancito	PHA	BC	25,10/57,31
Reserva Biológica Limoy	APN	AP	24,42/54,23
Reserva Indígena de Chupa Poo (S of Ygatimí)	CAN	CP	Not located
Reserva Natural del Bosque Mbaracayú	CAN	AP	24,07/55,30
Retiro Potrerito	APY	MG	20,20/58,13
Retiro Satí	CON	CC	22,26/57,09
Riacho Caballero (30-40 km W of Rosario; Paynter 1989:5)	PHA	BC	Uncertain
Riacho Michi (at Ruta Trans Chaco km 210)	PHA	BC	23,51/58,28
Riacho Ñeembucú	ÑEE	ÑE	Many
Riacho Negro 235 km W (see Río Negro)	PHA	BC	25,04/57,55
Riacho Ramos	APY	MG	20,16/58,07
Riacho San Carlos	PHA	AC,BC	Many
at Ruta Trans Chaco km 341	PHA	AC	23,03/59,15
Riacho Verde (=Río Verde?)	PHA?	MG?,AC?,BC?	Many
Río Acaray	APN,CAA	AP	Many
Río Aguaray-Guazú	CAN,SAP	CP	Many
Río Aguaray-Guazú	PHA	BC	Many
Río Apa	CON	CC	Many
Río Bermejo	Argentina	Many	
mouth at Río Paraguay	ÑE	ÑE	26,52/58,23
Río Carapá	CAN	AP	Many
Río Confuso	PHA	BC	Many
Río Jejuí-Guazú	CAN,SAP	CP	Many
Río Jejuí-mí	CAN	CP	Many
at Reserva Natural del Bosque Mbaracayú	CAN	CP	24,07/55,32
Río Monday	APN	AP	Many
embocadura del (mouth of)	APN	AP	25,35/54,35
Río Negro	PHA	BC	Many
235 km W (of mouth) (near Estero Patiño)	PHA	BC	24,09/59,32
at Ruta Trans Chaco	PHA	BC	24,12/58,19
Río Ñacunday	APN	AP	Many
Río Paraná	APN,CAN,ITA MIS,ÑEE	AP,ÑE	Many
Río Paraguay	APY,CON,COR ÑEE,PHA,SAP	BC,CC,CP MG,ÑE	Many
Río Pelotas	CAN	AP	Many
km 3 (from mouth?)	CAN	AP	Uncertain
Río Pilcomayo	PHA	AC,BC	Many
15 km W of Río Paraguay	PHA	BC	25,05/57,49
Río Piratíy	CAN	AP	Many
Río Piraty-y (possibly Río Piratíy or Arroyo Piratiy)	Unknown	Unknown	Not located

216

Locality	Department(s)	Region(s)	Coordinates
Río Piratíy	CAN	AP	Many
Río Piribebuy	COR	CP	Many
Río Salado	CEN,COR	CP	Many
Río Siete Puntas	PHA	BC	Many
Río Tebicuary	CAP,ITA,MIS ÑEE,PAR	CP,ÑE	Many
Río Verde	PHA	AC,BC,MG	Many
Río Yguazú	APN,CAA	AP	Many
Río Ytambey	CAN,APN	AP	Many
at Supercarretera	CAN,APN	AP	24,38/54,53
(road from Hernandarias, APN, to Cruce Guaraní, CAN)			
Río Yuquerí	CAA	AP	25,15/55,39
(possibly Arroyo Yuquyry)			
Rosario	SAP	CP	24,27/57,03
15 km E	SAP	CP	24,27/56,59
18 km E	SAP	CP	24,27/56,57
20 km E	SAP	CP	24,27/56,56
25 km E	SAP	CP	24,27/56,53
70 km E	SAP	CP	Uncertain
235 km W	PHA	BC	24,09/59,32
Ruta IV	ÑEE,MIS	ÑE	Many
between Arroyo Dos Hermanas			
and Arroyo Montuoso	ÑEE	ÑE	26,47/58,12
at Arroyo Montuoso	ÑEE	ÑE	Not located
Ruta Trans Chaco	BOQ,PHA	AC,BC	Many
km 55 (N of Asunción)	PHA	BC	24,56/57,35
km 60 (N of Asunción)	PHA	BC	24,55/57,38
km 65 (N of Asunción)	PHA	BC	24,54/57,40
km 75 (N of Asunción)	PHA	BC	24,50/57,45
km 79 (N of Asunción)	PHA	BC	24,48/57,47
km 100 (N of Asunción)	PHA	BC	24,39/57,58
km 103 (N of Asunción)	PHA	BC	24,38/57,59
km 153 (N of Asunción)	PHA	BC	24,19/58,12
km 173 (N of Asunción) (near Río Negro)	PHA	BC	24,12/58,19
km 187 (N of Asunción)	PHA	BC	24,03/58,23
km 200 (N of Asunción)	PHA	BC	23,58/58,25
km 210 (N of Asunción) (near Riacho Michi)	PHA	BC	23,51/58,28
km 236 (N of Asunción)	PHA	BC	23,41/58,38
km 249 (N of Asunción) (near Estero Pirahau)	PHA	BC	23,37/58,42
km 302 (N of Asunción)	PHA	AC	23,22/59,07
km 341 (N of Asunción) (near Riacho San Carlos)	PHA	AC	23,03/59,15
km 416	BOQ	AC	22,35/59,51
Salto del Guairá	CAN	AP	24,02/54,16
Salto Ñacunday	APN	AP	26,03/54,40

See above.

Locality	Department(s)	Region(s)	Coordinates
San Cosme y Damián	ITA	ÑE	27,15/56,19
San Ignacio	MIS	ÑE	26,52/57,03
San Juan	PHA	BC	23,25/58,50
San Juan Bautista	MIS	ÑE	26,42/57,05
20 km S	MIS	ÑE	27,05/57,04
San Juan de Ñeembucú	ÑEE	ÑE	26,41/57,52
San Lázaro	CON	CC	22,10/57,55
San Patricio	MIS	ÑE	27,02/56,45
Santa Barbara	CAA	CP	Uncertain
(40 km N of Villarrica, probably near Coronel Oviedo; Field Museum of Natural History unpubl. catalogs)			
Santiago	MIS	ÑE	27,10/56,44
Sapucái	PAR	CP	25,40/56,55
(formerly Sapucay)			
Serranía de San Luis	CON	CC	Many
Surubi-y	CEN	CP?	Not located
Tayru	ÑEE	ÑE	27,00/58,30
Tobatí	COR	CP	25,15/57,04
Troncal 2	APN	AP	Many
(unpaved road)			
Urumburú	CEN	CP	Uncertain
(frente a [across from] Villa Hayes ; Podtiaguin 1944:116)			
Valle Apúa	PAR	ÑE	26,02/57,13
Villa Florida	MIS	ÑE	26,25/57,05
(south bank of Río Tebicuary; north bank is in PAR)			
Villa Franca	ÑEE	ÑE	26,17/58,12
Villa Hayes	PHA	BC	25,06/57,34
Villa Oliva	ÑEE	ÑE	26,01/57,53
Villarrica	GUA	CP	25,45/56,26
108 km N	CAA,SAP	CP	Uncertain
Villazón	exNAS	AC	20,35/62,16
Villeta	CEN	ÑE	25,28/57,36
Waikthlatingmayalwa	PHA	BC	23,25/58,10
(=Misión Inglesa?)			
Yabebyry	MIS	ÑE	27,23/57,08
Yaguarasapá	ITA?	AP	Not located
(=Djaguarasapá?)			
Ybytymí	PAR	CP	25,46/56,47
Ygatimí	CAN	CP	24,05/53,30
Yhú	CAA	AP	24,59/55,59
Yuty	CAP	CP	26,35/56,10
Zanja Morotí	CON	CC	22,30/57,00

INDEX

A

Accipiter
  bicolor   58
  poliogaster   58, 146, 206, 208
  striatus   58
  superciliosus   58, 90, 146, 206
Actitis
  macularia   62, 95
Aegolius
  harrisii   66, 100, 208
Agelaius
  cyanopus   83, 133, 195
  flavus   83, 118, 204, 207, 208
  icterocephalus   133
  ruficapillus   83, 195
  thilius   53, 83, 118
Agriornis
  microptera   75, 109
  murina   75, 109
Aimophila
  strigiceps   83, 118, 144, 205
Ajaia
  ajaja   56
Alectrurus
  risora   76, 110, 145, 208
  tricolor   45, 76, 110, 200, 206, 208
Alopochelidon
  fucata   78, 145, 196
Amaurospiza
  moesta   83, 146, 192, 208
Amazilia
  chionogaster   134
  fimbriata   129
  versicolor   67, 199, 206
Amazona
  aestiva   64, 160
  pretrei   128
  vinacea   64, 98, 128, 160, 164, 198, 208
Amazonetta
  brasiliensis   57
Amblyramphus
  holosericeus   83
Ammodramus
  humeralis   83
Anabacerthia
  amaurotis   129
Anas
  bahamensis   57, 89, 194, 205
  cyanoptera   57, 89, 205
  discors   89
  flavirostris   125
  georgica   125
  platalea   57, 89, 145, 205
  sibilatrix   125
  versicolor   57, 205
Anhinga   55

Anhinga
  anhinga   55
Ani
  Greater   65
  Smooth-billed   65
Anodorhynchus
  glaucus   47, 64, 97, 164, 208
  hyacinthinus   63, 97, 145, 197, 208
Anodorhynchus
  hyacinthinus   144
Ant-Tanager
  Red-crowned   81, 192, 202
Antbird
  Bertoni's   53, 72, 105, 146, 192
  Dusky-tailed   72
  Ferruginous   105
  Mato   72, 144
  Stripe-backed   72, 192, 193, 205
Anthracothorax
  nigricollis   67, 101
Anthus
  chacoensis   79, 113, 123, 208
  correndera   79, 113, 130
  furcatus   79, 113, 130
  hellmayri   130
  lutescens   79, 113, 123
  nattereri   79, 113, 208
Antilophia
  galeata   77, 111, 145, 203, 206
Antpipit
  Southern   74, 192, 202, 206
Antpitta
  Speckle-breasted   53, 72, 106, 146, 192
  Variegated   72, 192
Antshrike
  Barred   72
  Giant   72, 105, 162
  Great   72, 192
  Large-tailed   53, 72, 105, 146
  Rufous-capped   72, 105, 146, 207
  Spot-backed   71, 202
  Tufted   72
  Variable   72, 122, 160, 162
Antthrush
  Short-tailed   72, 192, 202, 207
Antvireo
  Plain   72, 202
  Spot-breasted   134
Antwren
  Black-bellied   72, 105, 132, 144, 192, 205
  Black-capped   72, 201, 206
  Rufous-winged   72, 203
  Rusty-backed   72, 105, 145, 192, 197, 206
  Streak-capped   72, 204

  White-fringed   105, 132
Anumbius
  annumbi   70
Ara
  ararauna   53, 64, 97, 127, 206
  auricapillus   145
  auricollis   64, 144, 160, 194
  chloropterus   64, 98, 198, 206
  glaucogularis   98, 127
  maracana   64, 98, 160, 198, 208
Aracari
  Chestnut-eared   68, 199, 206
Aramides
  cajanea   60
  saracura   60, 93
  ypecaha   60
Aramus
  guarauna   61
Aratinga
  acuticaudata   64
  aurea   64, 98, 197
  auricapilla   127
  leucophthalmus   64
Ardea
  cocoi   55
Arremon
  flavirostris   82, 192, 196, 207
Asio
  clamator   65
  flammeus   66, 100, 145
  stygius   65, 100, 145, 146, 197
Asthenes
  baeri   70, 104, 145, 195
  hudsoni   129
  pyrrholeuca   70, 104, 145, 194
Atlapetes
  citrinellus   133
Atticora
  melanoleuca   53, 78, 112, 146
Attila
  phoenicurus   76, 110
Attila
  Rufous-tailed   76, 110
Automolus
  leucophthalmus   71, 192, 202
Avocet
  Andean   132

B

Baillonius
  bailloni   68, 208
Bamboowren
  Spotted   134
Bananaquit   80, 146, 206
Bartramia
  longicauda   62, 95

Baryphthengus
   ruficapillus 67, 199
Basileuterus
   culicivorus 80, 113, 124, 145,
      192, 206
   flaveolus 80, 124, 192
   hypoleucus 80, 114, 124, 144,
      145, 192, 197
   leucoblepharus 80, 114, 145, 192,
      198
   leucophrys 133
   rivularis 80, 207
Batara
   cinerea 72, 105, 162
Beardless-Tyrannulet
   Southern 73
Becard
   Black-capped 133
   Chestnut-crowned 77, 199
   Crested 77, 158, 162
   Green-backed 77
   White-winged 77, 111
Bellbird
   Bare-throated 77, 199, 208
Bittern
   Least 55, 88
   Pinnated 55, 87
   Stripe-backed 55, 87, 88
Black-Hawk
   Great 58
Black-Tyrant
   Blue-billed 75, 109
   Crested 75, 109, 145
   Hudson's 75, 109, 208
   White-winged 75, 109
Blackbird
   Chestnut-capped 83, 195
   Chopi 83
   Saffron-cowled 83, 118, 204, 207,
      208
   Scarlet-headed 83
   Unicolored 83, 133, 195
   White-browed 84
   Yellow-hooded 133
   Yellow-winged 53, 83, 118
Bobolink 83, 118
Botaurus
   pinnatus 55, 87
Bristle-Tyrant
   Southern 74, 203, 208
Brotogeris
   chiriri 64, 196
Brush-Finch
   Yellow-striped 133
Brushrunner
   Lark-like 70, 104, 145, 194, 205
Bubo
   virginianus 65, 100, 194
Bubulcus
   ibis 55, 88

Busarellus
   nigricollis 58
Buteo
   albicaudatus 59, 125
   albonotatus 59, 91, 194
   brachyurus 59, 91
   leucorrhous 53, 58, 91, 204
   magnirostris 58
   nitidus 58, 91, 144, 146, 197
   polyosoma 125
   swainsoni 59, 91
Buteogallus
   aequinoctialis 131
   meridionalis 58
   urubitinga 58
Butorides
   striatus 55, 88
Buzzard-Eagle
   Black-chested 58

C

Cacholote
   Brown 70, 144, 161, 162, 205
   Rufous 70, 144, 161, 162
Cacicus
   chrysopterus 84
   haemorrhous 84, 118, 200
   solitarius 84
Cacique
   Golden-winged 84
   Red-rumped 84, 118, 200
   Solitary 84
Cairina
   moschata 57
Calidris
   alba 62, 95
   bairdii 62, 95
   canutus 62, 95
   fuscicollis 62, 95
   himantopus 62, 96
   melanotos 62, 96
   minutilla 62, 95
   pusilla 53, 62, 95
Calliphlox
   amethystina 67, 206
Callonetta
   leucophrys 57, 145, 194, 205
Campephilus
   leucopogon 69, 103, 160, 193, 205
   melanoleucos 69, 103, 160
   robustus 69, 202
Camptostoma
   obsoletum 73
Campylorhamphus
   falcularius 53, 71, 105, 146, 160
   trochilirostris 71, 160
Campylorhynchus
   turdinus 78, 112
Canastero
   Hudson's 129
   Lesser 70, 104, 145, 194

Short-billed 70, 104, 145, 162, 195
Caprimulgus
   candicans 129
   cayennensis 129
   hirundinaceus 132
   longirostris 66, 101
   parvulus 66
   rufus 66, 200, 207
   sericocaudatus 66
Capsiempis
   flaveola 73, 203
Caracara
   Chimango 59
   Crested 24, 59
   Yellow-headed 59
Caracara
   plamcus 59
Cardinal
   Red-capped 133
   Red-crested 82
   Yellow 131
   Yellow-billed 82, 133, 195
Carduelis
   magellanica 84
Cariama
   cristata 61
Caryothraustes
   canadensis 133
Casiornis
   rufa 76
Casiornis
   Rufous 76
Casmerodius
   albus 55
Cathartes
   aura 56
   burrovianus 56
Catharus
   ustulatus 130
Catoptrophorus
   semipalmatus 134
Celeus
   flavescens 69, 103, 160
   lugubris 69, 103, 160
   torquatus 132
Cercomacra
   melanaria 72, 144
Certhiaxis
   cinnamomea 70, 195
Ceryle
   torquata 68
Chachalaca
   Chaco 59, 156
   Speckled 126
Chaco-Finch
   Many-colored 82, 144, 194, 205
Chaetura
   andrei 66, 101
   cinereiventris 66, 101
Chamaeza
   campanisona 72, 192, 202, 207

220

Charadrius
    collaris 61
    falklandicus 126
    modestus 127
    semipalmatus 126
    vociferus 131
Charitospiza
    eucosma 134
Chauna
    torquata 56
Chiroxiphia
    caudata 77, 111, 198
Chloephaga
    picta 125
    poliocephala 125
Chloroceryle
    aenea 68, 102, 144
    amazona 68
    americana 68
    inda 68, 102, 200, 206
Chlorophonia
    Blue-naped 80, 203
Chlorophonia
    cyanea 80, 203
Chlorostilbon
    aureoventris 67
Chondrohierax
    uncinatus 57, 90
Chordeiles
    acutipennis 128
    minor 66, 100, 128
Chunga
    burmeisteri 61, 94, 144
Ciccaba
    huhula 128
    virgata 65, 100
Ciconia
    maguari 56
Cinclodes
    Bar-winged 69, 104
Cinclodes
    fuscus 69, 104
Circus
    buffoni 58
    cinereus 58, 90, 200
Cissopis
    leveriana 81, 115, 144, 198
Cistothorus
    platensis 79, 113, 145, 204
Claravis
    godefrida 53, 63, 97, 146, 192, 208
    pretiosa 63, 192
Clibanornis
    dendrocolaptoides 69, 104, 146, 192, 208
Cnemotriccus
    fuscatus 75, 108, 123
Coccyzus
    americanus 64, 99
    cinereus 64, 99
    erythropthalmus 64, 99

    melacoryphus 64, 99
Cochlearius
    cochlearius 56, 88
Coereba
    flaveola 80, 146, 206
Colaptes
    campestris 69, 121
    melanochloros 69, 120, 159
    punctigula 132
Colibri
    serrirostris 67, 101, 145, 201, 206
Colonia
    colonus 76, 109, 145, 198, 206
Columba
    cayennensis 63
    livia 63, 96
    maculosa 63, 97, 205
    picazuro 63, 96
    plumbea 127
    speciosa 53, 63, 96, 206
Columbina
    minuta 63, 97, 192
    passerina 132
    picui 63
    squammata 132
    talpacoti 63
Comet
    Red-tailed 132
Condor
    Andean 56, 88
Conebill
    Chestnut-vented 80, 196
Conirostrum
    speciosum 80, 196
Conopias
    trivirgata 76, 203
Conopophaga
    lineata 72, 192, 202
Contopus
    cinereus 75, 199, 206
    fumigatus 132
Coot
    Red-fronted 61, 94, 126, 205
    Red-gartered 126
    White-winged 61, 94, 145, 194, 205
Coragyps
    atratus 56
Cormorant
    Neotropic 55
Coryphaspiza
    melanotis 82, 116, 146, 207, 208
Coryphistera
    alaudina 70, 104, 145, 194, 205
Coryphospingus
    cucullatus 82, 160
Corythopis
    delalandi 74, 192, 202, 206
Coscoroba
    coscoroba 57, 89, 193, 205

Cotinga
    Swallow-tailed 77, 111, 208
Coturnicops
    notata 60, 93, 208
Cowbird
    Bay-winged 84, 194
    Giant 84, 118, 201, 207
    Screaming 84
    Shiny 84
Crab-Hawk
    Rufous 131
Crake
    Ash-throated 60, 200, 206
    Gray-breasted 60, 93
    Ocellated 134
    Paint-billed 60, 93
    Red-and-white 60, 93, 145, 197
    Rufous-faced 60, 93, 201, 208
    Rufous-sided 60, 93
    Speckled 60, 93, 208
    Yellow-breasted 60, 93
Cranioleuca
    obsoleta 70, 121
    pallida 132
    pyrrhophia 70, 121, 193, 205
    sulphurifera 132
Crax
    fasciolata 60
Crescentchest
    Collared 73, 106, 145, 206
    Olive-crowned 73, 106, 193
Crested-Tinamou
    Quebracho 54, 144, 162, 193
Crotophaga
    ani 65
    major 65
Crypturellus
    obsoletus 54, 192, 202, 207
    parvirostris 54, 87, 140, 192
    tataupa 54, 140, 192
    undulatus 54, 192
Cuckoo
    Ash-colored 64, 99
    Black-billed 64, 99
    Dark-billed 64, 99
    Guira 65
    Pavonine 65, 99
    Pheasant 65, 99, 145, 200, 206
    Squirrel 65, 158, 162
    Striped 65
    Yellow-billed 64, 99
Culicivora
    caudacuta 74, 107, 145, 197, 206, 208
Curassow
    Bare-faced 60
Curlew
    Eskimo 53, 62, 95
Cyanocompsa
    brissonii 82, 159

Cyanocorax
  caeruleus 130
  chrysops 78
  cristatellus 78, 145, 199
  cyanomelas 78, 130, 162
Cyanoloxia
  glaucocaerulea 82, 116
Cyclarhis
  gujanensis 80
Cygnus
  melanocorypha 125
Cypseloides
  senex 66, 204
Cypsnagra
  hirundinacea 81, 115, 200, 207

D

Dacnis
  Blue 80, 201, 206
Dacnis
  cayana 80, 201, 206
Dendrocincla
  turdina 71, 202
Dendrocolaptes
  picumnus 71, 104, 159, 193
  platyrostris 71, 105, 145, 159, 197, 207
Dendrocygna
  autumnalis 57
  bicolor 57
  viduata 57
Dendroica
  striata 134
Dolichonyx
  oryzivorus 83, 118
Donacobius
  atricapillus 78
Donacobius
  Black-capped 78
Donacospiza
  albifrons 83, 117, 145, 197
Doradito
  Crested 74, 107, 195
  Dinelli's 74, 107, 208
  Subtropical 74, 107, 193
  Warbling 74, 107
Dotterel
  Rufous-chested 127
Dove
  Eared 63
  Gray-fronted 63, 97, 201, 206
  Rock 63, 96
  Scaled 63, 132
  White-tipped 63, 97
Dromococcyx
  pavoninus 65, 99, 200
  phasianellus 65, 99, 145, 206
Drymophila
  ferruginea 105
  malura 72
  rubricollis 53, 72, 105, 146, 192

Drymornis
  bridgesii 71, 104, 144, 205
Dryocopus
  galeatus 69, 103, 166, 202, 208
  lineatus 69, 103, 121, 145, 160, 196
  schulzi 69, 121, 160, 208
Duck
  Black-headed 57, 90, 144, 205
  Brazilian 57
  Comb 57
  Lake 53, 57, 89, 144, 193, 205
  Masked 57
  Muscovy 57
Dysithamnus
  mentalis 72, 202
  stictothorax 134

E

Eagle
  Crested 126
  Crowned 58, 90, 165, 208
  Harpy 59, 91, 165, 198, 206, 208
  Solitary 134
Earthcreeper
  Chaco 69, 144, 205
  Scale-throated 134
Egret
  Cattle 55, 88
  Great 55
  Snowy 55
Egretta
  caerulea 55, 88
  thula 55
Elaenia
  albiceps 73, 106
  chiriquensis 73, 106, 199, 206, 207
  cristata 132
  flavogaster 73, 106, 200
  gigas 132
  mesoleuca 73, 106, 199
  obscura 73, 199, 207
  parvirostris 73, 122
  spectabilis 73, 106
Elaenia
  Gray 73, 199, 206
  Greenish 73, 106, 145, 196, 206
  Highland 73, 199, 207
  Large 73, 106
  Lesser 73, 106, 199, 206, 207
  Mottle-backed 132
  Olivaceous 73, 106, 199
  Plain-crested 132
  Small-billed 73, 122
  White-crested 73, 106
  Yellow-bellied 73, 106, 200
Elanoides
  forficatus 58, 90, 201, 206
Elanus
  leucurus 58

Eleothreptus
  anomalus 66, 101, 198, 207, 208
Emberizoides
  herbicola 83, 145
  ypiranganus 83, 117, 201, 207, 208
Embernagra
  platensis 83, 117
Emerald
  Glittering-bellied 67
  Glittering-throated 129
  Versicolored 67, 199, 206
Empidonomus
  varius 76, 111
Eucometis
  penicillata 81, 114, 145, 199, 207
Eudromia
  formosa 54, 144, 193
Eupetomena
  macroura 67, 101, 145, 200, 206
Euphonia
  chalybea 80, 114, 204
  chlorotica 80
  cyanocephala 80, 199, 207
  pectoralis 80, 203
  violacea 80, 203
Euphonia
  Chestnut-bellied 80, 203
  Golden-rumped 80, 199, 207
  Green-throated 80, 114, 204
  Purple-throated 80
  Violaceous 80, 203
Euscarthmus
  meloryphus 74, 158, 192
  rufomarginatus 74, 108, 145, 203, 208

F

Falco
  deiroleucus 59, 92, 208
  femoralis 59
  peregrinus 59, 92
  rufigularis 59
  sparverius 59
Falcon
  Aplomado 59
  Bat 59
  Laughing 59
  Orange-breasted 59, 92, 208
  Peregrine 59, 92
Falconet
  Spot-winged 59, 92
Finch
  Black-crested 83, 118, 144
  Black-masked 82, 116, 146, 207, 208
  Coal-crested 134
  Red-crested 82, 160
  Saffron 83
  Uniform 83, 192, 203

Fire-eye
    White-backed   72, 106, 144, 192
    White-shouldered   72, 192
Firewood-gatherer   70
Flamingo
    Chilean   56, 88
Flatbill
    Large-headed   75, 108, 192
Flicker
    Campo   69, 121, 161, 162
Fluvicola
    albiventer   75
    leucocephala   76
Flycatcher
    Boat-billed   76
    Bran-colored   75, 108, 158, 199,
        207
    Brown-crested   76, 160
    Cliff   76, 110, 144, 198, 206,
        207
    Crowned   76, 111
    Dusky-capped   133
    Euler's   75, 108, 158
    Fork-tailed   77, 111
    Fuscous   75, 108, 123
    Gray-hooded   74, 203
    Piratic   76, 110, 201, 206
    Planalto   204
    Sepia-capped   74, 108, 144, 197,
        206
    Short-crested   76, 110
    Social   76, 202
    Streaked   76, 110
    Suiriri   73, 122, 161
    Swainson's   76, 110, 159
    Three-striped   76, 203
    Variegated   76, 111
    Vermilion   75, 109
    Yellow-olive   75, 158
Foliage-gleaner
    Black-capped   70, 202
    Buff-browed   70, 104, 129, 144,
        192, 197, 207
    Buff-fronted   71, 199, 206, 207
    Chestnut-capped   71, 104, 145,
        192, 199, 208
    Ochre-breasted   70, 200
    Russet-mantled   70, 104, 145, 200,
        208
    White-browed   129
    White-eyed   71, 192, 202
Forest-Falcon
    Barred   59, 131, 198, 206
    Collared   59, 92, 144, 196, 206
    Lined   131
Formicivora
    grisea   105, 132
    melanogaster   72, 105, 132, 144,
        192, 205
    rufa   72, 105, 145, 192, 197,
        206

Forpus
    xanthopterygius   64, 98, 197
Fruitcrow
    Bare-necked   134
    Red-ruffed   77, 200
Fulica
    armillata   126
    leucoptera   61, 94, 145, 194, 205
    rufifrons   61, 94, 126, 205
Furnarius
    cristatus   69, 144, 193, 205
    rufus   69

G

Galbula
    ruficauda   129
Gallinago
    paraguaiae   62
    undulata   62, 201
Gallinula
    chloropus   61
    melanops   60, 94, 193, 205
Gallinule
    Azure   60, 94
    Purple   60, 94
    Spot-flanked   60, 94, 193, 205
Gallito
    Crested   73, 106, 144, 162
Gampsonyx
    swainsonii   58
Geositta
    cunicularia   44, 129
Geothlypis
    aequinoctialis   80
Geotrygon
    montana   63, 192, 201, 206
    violacea   63, 192, 200, 206
Geranoaetus
    melanoleucus   58
Geranospiza
    caerulescens   58
Glaucidium
    brasilianum   65
    minutissimum   53, 65, 100, 146
Gnatcatcher
    Cream-bellied   79, 160, 203, 208
    Masked   79, 160
Gnateater
    Rufous   72, 192, 202
Gnorimopsar
    chopi   83
Godwit
    Hudsonian   62, 95, 208
Golden-Plover
    American   61, 94
Goldenthroat
    White-tailed   67, 101, 145, 150,
        196
Goose
    Ashy-headed   125
    Orinoco   57, 89, 125, 208

    Upland   125
Grallaria
    varia   72, 192
Grass-Finch
    Lesser   83, 117, 201, 207, 208
    Wedge-tailed   83, 145
Grassquit
    Blue-black   82
    Sooty   83, 117, 145
Gray-Tyrant
    Shear-tailed   53, 76, 110, 208
Grebe
    Great   55, 87
    Least   55
    Pied-billed   55
    Silvery   55, 87
    White-tufted   55, 87
Greenlet
    Rufous-crowned   79, 203
Griseotyrannus
    aurantioatrocristatus   76, 111
Grosbeak
    Black-backed   82, 144, 205
    Black-throated   81, 115
    Indigo   82, 116
    Ultramarine   82, 159
    Yellow-green   133
Ground-Dove
    Blue   63, 192
    Common   132
    Picui   63
    Plain-breasted   63, 97, 192
    Purple-winged   53, 63, 97, 146,
        192, 208
    Ruddy   63
Groundcreeper
    Canebrake   69, 104, 146, 192, 208
Guan
    Dusky-legged   126
    Rusty-margined   59, 126, 198, 206
Gubernatrix
    cristata   131
Gubernetes
    yetapa   76, 110, 144, 198, 206
Guira
    guira   65
Gull
    Brown-hooded   62, 96
    Gray-hooded   62, 96
Gymnoderus
    foetidus   134

H

Habia
    rubica   81, 192, 202
Haematopus
    palliatus   131
Haplospiza
    unicolor   83, 192, 203
Harpagus
    diodon   58, 90, 201, 206

Harpia
    harpyja 59, 91, 165, 198, 206, 208
Harpyhaliaetus
    coronatus 58, 90, 165, 208
    solitarius 134
Harrier
    Cinereous 58, 90, 200
    Long-winged 58
Hawk
    Bicolored 58
    Black-collared 58
    Crane 58
    Gray 58, 91, 144, 146, 197
    Gray-bellied 58, 145, 206, 208
    Harris' 58, 195
    Mantled 53, 58, 90, 146, 208
    Red-backed 125
    Roadside 58
    Savanna 58
    Sharp-shinned 58
    Short-tailed 59, 91
    Swainson's 59, 91
    Tiny 58, 90, 146, 206
    White-rumped 53, 58, 91, 204
    White-tailed 59, 125
    Zone-tailed 59, 91, 194
Hawk-Eagle
    Black 126
    Black-and-white 59, 91, 208
    Ornate 59, 92, 126, 201, 206
Heliobletus
    contaminatus 71, 200
Heliomaster
    furcifer 67
Heliornis
    fulica 61, 94, 198, 206
Hemithraupis
    guira 81, 115, 144, 197, 207
Hemitriccus
    diops 74, 192
    margaritaceiventer 74
Hermit
    Planalto 67, 200, 206
    Scale-throated 24, 67, 202
Heron
    Boat-billed 56, 88
    Capped 55, 88, 145
    Cocoi 55
    Little 55, 88
    Striated 55, 88
    Whistling 55
Herpetotheres
    cachinnans 59
Herpsilochmus
    atricapillus 72, 201, 206
    rufimarginatus 72, 203
Heteronetta
    atricapilla 57, 90, 144, 205
Heteroxolmis
    dominicana 130

Himantopus
    mexicanus 61
Hirundinea
    ferruginea 76, 110, 144, 198, 206, 207
Hirundo
    pyrrhonota 78, 112
    rustica 78, 112
Hoploxypterus
    cayanus 61, 94
Hornero
    Crested 69, 144, 193, 205
    Rufous 69
Hummingbird
    Swallow-tailed 67, 101, 145, 200, 206
    White-bellied 134
    White-throated 67, 101
Hydropsalis
    brasiliana 66
Hylocharis
    chrysura 67
    cyanus 134
    sapphirina 129
Hylocryptus
    rectirostris 71, 104, 145, 192, 199, 208
Hylopezus
    nattereri 53, 72, 106, 146, 192
Hylophilus
    poicilotis 79, 203
Hymenops
    perspicillatus 75, 109
Hypoedaleus
    guttatus 71, 202

I

Ibis
    Bare-faced 56
    Buff-necked 56
    Green 56, 88
    Plumbeous 56, 88, 194, 205
    White-faced 56
Icterus
    cayanensis 84
    icterus 30, 84, 144, 205
Ictinia
    mississippiensis 58, 90
    plumbea 58, 90
Inezia
    inornata 74, 107, 145
Ixobrychus
    exilis 55, 88
    involucris 55, 87, 88

J

Jabiru 56
Jabiru
    mycteria 56

Jacamar
    Rufous-tailed 129
Jacana
    jacana 61
Jacana
    Wattled 61
Jacobin
    Black 67, 101, 146
Jay
    Azure 130
    Curl-crested 78, 145, 199
    Plush-crested 78
    Purplish 78, 130, 162

K

Kestrel
    American 59
Killdeer 131
Kingbird
    Eastern 77, 111
    Tropical 76, 111
Kingfisher
    Amazon 68
    Green 68
    Green-and-rufous 68, 102, 200, 206
    Pygmy 68, 102, 144
    Ringed 68
Kiskadee
    Great 76
Kite
    American 58, 90, 201, 206
    Gray-headed 57, 144, 197, 206
    Hook-billed 57, 90
    Mississippi 58, 90
    Pearl 58
    Plumbeous 58, 90
    Rufous-thighed 58, 90, 201, 206
    Snail 58, 90
    White-tailed 58
Knipolegus
    aterrimus 75, 109
    cabanisi 134
    cyanirostris 75, 109
    hudsoni 75, 109, 208
    lophotes 75, 109, 145
    striaticeps 75, 109, 194
Knot
    Red 62, 95

L

Lapwing
    Pied 61, 94
    Southern 61
Larus
    cirrocephalus 62, 96
    maculipennis 62, 96
Laterallus
    exilis 60, 93
    leucopyrrhus 60, 93, 145, 197

224

melanophaius 60, 93
xenopterus 60, 93, 201, 208
Lathrotriccus
euleri 75, 108, 158
Leaftosser
Rufous-breasted 71, 192, 202
Legatus
leucophaius 76, 110, 201, 206
Leistes
superciliaris 84
Lepidocolaptes
angustirostris 71
fuscus 71, 204
squamatus 71, 204
Leptasthenura
platensis 70, 104
setaria 134
Leptodon
cayanensis 57, 144, 197, 206
Leptopogon
amaurocephalus 74, 108, 144, 197, 206
Leptotila
rufaxilla 63, 97, 201, 206
verreauxi 63, 97
Lessonia
rufa 75, 109
Leucochloris
albicollis 67, 101
Leucopternis
polionota 53, 58, 90, 146, 208
Limosa
haemastica 62, 95, 208
Limpkin 61
Lochmias
nematura 71, 202, 207
Lophospingus
pusillus 83, 118, 144
Lurocalis
semitorquatus 66, 201

M

Macaw
Blue-and-yellow 53, 64, 97, 127, 206
Blue-throated 98, 127
Blue-winged 64, 98, 160, 198, 208
Glaucous 47, 64, 97, 164, 208
Golden-collared 64, 144, 145, 160, 194
Hyacinthine 63, 97, 144, 145, 197, 208
Red-and-green 64, 98, 198, 206
Machetornis
rixosus 76
Mackenziaena
leachii 53, 72, 105, 146
severa 72
Manacus
manacus 77

Manakin
Band-tailed 77, 111, 198, 206
Black-capped 134
Helmeted 77, 111, 145, 203, 206
Swallow-tailed 77, 111, 198
White-bearded 77
Wing-barred 77, 203
Mango
Black-throated 67, 101
Marsh-Tyrant
White-headed 76
Marshbird
Brown-and-yellow 131
Yellow-rumped 84, 118, 145, 197
Martin
Brown-chested 78, 112
Gray-breasted 78, 112
Purple 78, 112
Southern 130
Mecocerculus
leucophrys 132
Megarynchus
pitangua 76
Melanerpes
cactorum 69, 193, 205
candidus 68
flavifrons 68, 201
Melanopareia
maximiliani 73, 106, 193, 206
torquata 73, 106, 145
Melanotrochilus
fuscus 67, 101, 146
Merganser
Brazilian 53, 57, 89, 145, 164, 208
Mergus
octosetaceus 53, 57, 89, 145, 164, 208
Mesembrinibis
cayennensis 56, 88
Micrastur
gilvicollis 131
ruficollis 59, 131, 198, 206
schomburgkii 134
semitorquatus 59, 92, 144, 196, 206
Milvago
chimachima 59
chimango 59
Mimus
saturninus 79
triurus 79, 113
Miner
Common 44, 129
Mionectes
rufiventris 74, 203
Mockingbird
Chalk-browed 79
White-banded 79, 113
Molothrus
badius 84, 194
bonariensis 84

rufoaxillaris 84
Momotus
momota 53, 67, 102, 144
Monjita
Black-and-white 130
Black-crowned 75, 109
Gray 75
White 75
White-rumped 75, 145, 199, 206
Moorhen
Common 61
Morphnus
guianensis 126
Motmot
Blue-crowned 53, 67, 102, 144
Rufous-capped 67, 199
Muscipipra
vetula 53, 76, 110, 208
Mycteria
americana 56
Myiarchus
ferox 76, 110
swainsoni 76, 110, 159
tuberculifer 133
tyrannulus 76
Myiodynastes
maculatus 76, 110
Myiopagis
caniceps 73, 199, 206
viridicata 73, 106, 145, 196, 206
Myiophobus
fasciatus 75, 108, 158, 199, 207
Myiopsitta
monachus 64
Myiornis
auricularis 74, 200
Myiozetetes
similis 76, 202
Myrmorchilus
strigilatus 72, 192, 193, 205

N

Nandayus
nenday 64
Negrito
Austral 75, 109
Nemosia
pileata 81, 158
Neochen
jubata 57, 89, 125, 208
Neocrex
erythrops 60, 93
Neothraupis
fasciata 81, 115, 204, 207
Netta
peposaca 24, 57, 89
Night-Heron
Black-crowned 55
Nighthawk
Band-tailed 134
Common 66, 100, 128

Lesser   128
Nacunda   66
Short-tailed   66, 201
Nightjar
Band-winged   66, 101
Little   66
Pygmy   132
Rufous   66, 200, 207
Scissor-tailed   66
Sickle-winged   66, 101, 198, 207,
   208
Silky-tailed   66
White-tailed   129
White-winged   129
Nonnula
rubecula   68, 201
Notharchus
macrorhynchos   68, 102, 201, 206
Nothoprocta
cinerascens   54, 87, 144
Nothura
boraquira   54, 144, 193
darwinii   134
maculosa   54, 119, 158
Nothura
Darwin's   134
Spotted   54, 119, 160
White-bellied   54, 144, 193
Notiochelidon
cyanoleuca   78, 112
Numenius
borealis   53, 62, 95
phaeopus   127
Nunlet
Rusty-breasted   68, 201
Nyctibius
aethereus   66, 101, 203
griseus   66, 101
Nycticorax
nycticorax   55
Nyctidromus
albicollis   66, 144, 197, 206
Nyctiphrynus
ocellatus   66, 100, 202, 206
Nyctiprogne
leucopyga   134
Nystalus
chacuru   68, 102, 145, 197
maculatus   68, 145, 205

O

Odontophorus
capueira   60, 192, 201
Oriole
Epaulet   84
Oropendola
Crested   84, 196, 207
Ortalis
canicollis   59, 156
guttata   126

Oryzoborus
angolensis   82, 117, 145, 198, 207
Osprey   57, 90
Otus
atricapillus   65
choliba   65
Owl
Barn   65
Black-banded   128
Buff-fronted   66, 100, 208
Burrowing   65
Great   65, 100, 194
Mottled   65, 100, 204, 206
Rufous-legged   65, 193
Rusty-barred   65, 100, 146
Short-eared   66, 100, 145
Spectacled   65, 99, 200, 206
Striped   65
Stygian   65, 100, 145, 146, 197
Tawny-browed   53, 65, 100, 146
Oxyruncus
cristatus   77, 202
Oxyura
dominica   57
vittata   53, 57, 89, 193, 144, 205
Oystercatcher
American   131

P

Pachyramphus
castaneus   77, 199
marginatus   133
polychopterus   77, 111
validus   77, 158, 162
viridis   77
Painted-Snipe
South   61, 94, 193, 205
Pampa-Finch
Great   83, 117, 160
Pandion
haliaetus   57, 90
Parabuteo
unicinctus   58, 195
Parakeet
Black-hooded   64
Blaze-winged   64, 98, 119, 161,
   197
Blue-crowned   64
Golden-capped   127
Green-cheeked   128
Maroon-bellied   119
Monk   64
Peach-fronted   64, 98, 197
Pearly   132
Reddish-bellied   64, 98, 161
White-eyed   64
Yellow-chevroned   64, 196
Pardirallus
maculatus   60, 93
nigricans   60, 201
sanguinolentus   60, 93, 196

Paroaria
capitata   82, 133, 195
coronata   82
gularis   133
Parrot
Red-capped   64, 202, 208
Red-spectacled   128
Scaly-headed   64, 158, 162
Turquoise-fronted   64, 160
Vinaceous-breasted   64, 98, 128,
   160, 164, 198, 208
Parrotlet
Blue-winged   64, 98, 197
Parula
pitiayumi   80
Parula
Tropical   80
Passer
domesticus   84, 118
Pauraque   66, 144, 197, 206
Penelope
obscura   126
superciliaris   59, 126, 198, 206
Peppershrike
Rufous-browed   80, 160
Pewee
Smoke-colored   132
Tropical   75, 199, 206
Phacellodomus
ruber   70, 129
rufifrons   70, 104, 161, 162, 194
sibilatrix   70, 104, 145, 161, 162,
   194, 205
striaticollis   129
Phaeomyias
murina   73, 106, 203, 206
Phaeoprogne
tapera   78, 112
Phaethornis
eurynome   24, 67, 202
pretrei   67, 200, 206
Phaetusa
simplex   63, 96, 196
Phalacrocorax
brasilianus   55
Phalarope
Red   62, 96
Wilson's   62, 96
Phalaropus
fulicaria   62, 96
tricolor   62, 96
Pheucticus
aureoventris   82, 144, 205
Phibalura
flavirostris   77, 111, 208
Philydor
atricapillus   70, 202
dimidiatus   70, 104, 145, 200, 208
lichtensteini   70, 200
rufus   71, 199, 206, 207

Phimosus
  infuscatus 56
Phleocryptes
  melanops 69, 104
Phoenicopterus
  chilensis 56, 88
Phrygilus
  dorsalis 133
Phyllomyias
  burmeisteri 73, 203, 206, 207
  fasciatus 73, 204, 206
  reiseri 73, 106, 122, 145, 161, 203, 208
  virescens 73, 122, 161, 199
Phylloscartes
  eximius 74, 203, 208
  paulistus 74, 108, 208
  sylviolus 74, 208
  ventralis 74, 108, 203, 207
Phytotoma
  rutila 78, 111
Piaya
  cayana 65, 158, 162
Picoides
  mixtus 69, 194
Piculet
  Mottled 134
  Ochre-collared 68, 102, 119, 160, 204
  White-barred 68, 119, 160, 162
  White-wedged 68, 102, 120, 146
Piculus
  aurulentus 69, 202, 208
  chrysochloros 69, 102, 194
Picumnus
  albosquamatus 68, 102, 120, 146
  cirratus 68, 119, 160
  nebulosus 134
  temminckii 68, 102, 119, 160, 204
Pigeon
  Pale-vented 63
  Picazuro 63, 96
  Plumbeous 127
  Scaled 53, 63, 96, 206
  Spot-winged 63, 97, 205
Pilherodius
  pileatus 55, 88, 145
Pintail
  White-cheeked 57, 89, 194, 205
  Yellow-billed 125
Pionopsitta
  pileata 64, 202, 208
Pionus
  maximiliani 64, 158, 162
Pipile
  cujubi 119, 126
  cumanensis 92, 119
  jacutinga 60, 92, 160, 164, 166, 203, 208
  pipile 60, 160, 198, 206

Piping-Guan
  Black-fronted 60, 92, 160, 164, 166, 203, 208
  Blue-throated 60, 92, 119, 160, 198, 206
  Red-throated 119, 126
Pipit
  Chaco 79, 113, 123, 208
  Correndera 79, 113, 130
  Hellmayr's 130
  Ochre-breasted 79, 113, 208
  Short-billed 79, 113, 130
  Yellowish 79, 113, 123
Pipra
  fasciicauda 77, 111, 198, 206
Pipraeidea
  melanonota 80, 199, 207
Piprites
  chloris 77, 203
  pileatus 134
Piranga
  flava 81, 115
Pitangus
  sulphuratus 76
Pitylus
  fuliginosus 81, 115
Plantcutter
  White-tipped 78, 111
Platycichla
  flavipes 79, 113, 146
Platyrinchus
  leucoryphus 75, 108, 145, 192, 208
  mystaceus 75, 108, 192, 197, 206
Plegadis
  chihi 56
Plover
  Black-bellied 61, 94
  Collared 61
  Semipalmated 126
  Two-banded 126
Plovercrest
  Black-breasted 67, 204
Pluvialis
  dominica 61, 94
  squatarola 61, 94
Pochard
  Rosy-billed 24, 57, 89
Podager
  nacunda 66
Podiceps
  major 55, 87
  occipitalis 55, 87
Podilymbus
  podiceps 55
Poecilurus
  scutatus 129
Polioptila
  dumicola 79, 160
  lactea 79, 160, 203, 208
Polyborus
  plancus 24

Polystictus
  pectoralis 74, 208
Polytmus
  guainumbi 67, 101, 145, 150, 196
Poorwill
  Ocellated 66, 100, 202, 206
Poospiza
  lateralis 83, 117, 204, 207
  melanoleuca 83, 194
  nigrorufa 83, 117
  torquata 83, 117
Porphyrula
  flavirostris 60, 94
  martinica 60, 94
Porzana
  albicollis 60, 200, 206
  flaviventer 60, 93
Potoo
  Common 101
  Gray 66
  Long-tailed 66, 101, 203
Procnias
  nudicollis 77, 199, 208
Progne
  chalybea 78, 112
  modesta 130
  subis 78, 112
Psarocolius
  decumanus 84, 196, 207
Pseudocolopteryx
  acutipennis 74, 107, 193
  dinellianus 74, 107, 208
  flaviventris 74, 107
  sclateri 74, 107, 195
Pseudoleistes
  guirahuro 84, 118, 145, 197
  virescens 131
Pseudoseisura
  cristata 70, 144, 161, 162
  lophotes 70, 144, 161, 162, 205
Psilorhamphus
  guttatus 134
Pteroglossus
  castanotis 68, 199, 206
Puffbird
  Spot-backed 68, 145, 205
  White-eared 68, 102, 145, 197
  White-necked 68, 102, 201, 206
Pulsatrix
  koeniswaldiana 53, 65, 100, 146
  perspicillata 65, 99, 200, 206
Pygmy-Owl
  Brazilian 53, 65, 100, 146
  Ferruginous 65
Pygmy-Tyrant
  Drab-breasted 74, 192
  Eared 74, 200
  Rufous-sided 74, 108, 145, 203, 208
  Tawny-crowned 74, 158, 192

Pyriglena
    leuconota 72, 106, 144, 192
    leucoptera 72, 192
Pyrocephalus
    rubinus 75, 109
Pyroderus
    scutatus 77, 200
Pyrrhocoma
    ruficeps 81, 192, 203
Pyrrhura
    devillei 64, 98, 119, 161, 197
    frontalis 64, 98, 119, 161
    molinae 128
    perlata 132

Q

Quail-Dove
    Ruddy 63, 192, 201, 206
    Violaceous 63, 192, 200, 206

R

Rail
    Blackish 60, 201
    Plumbeous 60, 93, 196
    Spotted 60, 93
Ramphastos
    dicolorus 68, 102, 144, 197
    toco 68
Ramphocelus
    carbo 81, 115, 144, 146, 207
Ramphotrigon
    megacephala 75, 108, 192
Recurvirostra
    andina 132
Reed-Finch
    Long-tailed 83, 117, 145, 197
Rhea
    americana 54, 158, 162, 208
    pennata 131
Rhea
    Greater 54, 158, 162, 208
    Lesser 131
Rhinocrypta
    lanceolata 73, 106, 144
Rhynchotus
    rufescens 54, 140, 145
Riparia
    riparia 78, 112
Rollandia
    rolland 55, 87
Rostratula
    semicollaris 61, 94, 193, 205
Rostrhamus
    sociabilis 58, 90
Rush-Tyrant
    Many-colored 53, 74, 107
Rushbird
    Wren-like 69, 104
Rynchops
    niger 63, 96

S

Saltator
    atricollis 81, 115, 144, 198, 207
    aurantiirostris 81, 115, 144, 194, 205
    coerulescens 81
    maxillosus 131
    maximus 130
    similis 81
Saltator
    Black-throated 81, 115, 144, 198, 207
    Buff-throated 130
    Golden-billed 81, 115, 144, 194, 205
    Grayish 81
    Green-winged 81
    Thick-billed 131
Saltatricula
    multicolor 82, 144, 194, 205
Sanderling 95
Sandpiper
    Baird's 62, 95
    Buff-breasted 62, 96
    Least 62, 95
    Pectoral 62, 96
    Semipalmated 53, 62, 95
    Solitary 62, 95
    Spotted 62, 95
    Stilt 62, 96
    Upland 62, 95
    White-rumped 62, 95
Sapphire
    Gilded 67
    Rufous-throated 129
    White-chinned 134
Sappho
    sparganura 132
Sarcoramphus
    papa 56
Sarkidiornis
    melanotos 57
Satrapa
    icterophrys 76
Scaphidura
    oryzivora 84, 118, 201, 207
Schiffornis
    Greenish 77, 202
Schiffornis
    virescens 77, 202
Schistochlamys
    melanopis 81, 115, 146, 207
Schoeniophylax
    phryganophila 70, 195
Sclerurus
    scansor 71, 192, 202
Screamer
    Southern 56
Screech-Owl
    Tropical 65

    Variable 65
Scrub-Flycatcher
    Southern 73, 106
Scytalopus
    speluncae 129
Scythebill
    Black-billed 53, 71, 105, 146, 160
    Red-billed 71, 160, 162
Seed-Finch
    Lesser 82, 117, 145, 198, 207
Seedeater
    Black-and-tawny 131
    Blackish-blue 83, 146, 192, 208
    Buffy-fronted 53, 82, 116, 146, 208
    Capped 82, 116, 200
    Chestnut 82, 117, 124, 133, 200, 208
    Dark-throated 82, 116, 124, 195, 208
    Double-collared 82
    Gray-and-chestnut 124
    Hooded 133
    Lined 82, 116, 133, 200
    Marsh 82, 116, 124, 200, 208
    Plumbeous 82, 201, 207
    Rufous-rumped 82, 117, 145, 196, 208
    Rusty-collared 82
    Tawny-bellied 82, 116, 124
    Temminck's 53, 82, 116, 146, 208
    Variable 133
    White-bellied 82
    White-throated 133
Selenidera
    maculirostris 68, 102
Seriema
    Black-legged 61, 94, 144
    Red-legged 61
Serpophaga
    munda 74, 107, 123, 194
    nigricans 73, 107
    subcristata 74, 107, 123
Sharpbill 77, 202
Shoveler
    Red 57, 89, 145, 205
Shrike-Tyrant
    Gray-bellied 75, 109
    Mouse-brown 75, 109
Sicalis
    citrina 131
    flaveola 83
    luteola 83, 117
Sierra-Finch
    Red-backed 133
Sirystes 76, 203, 206
Sirystes
    sibilator 76, 203, 206
Siskin
    Hooded 84

Sittasomus
  griseicapillus 71
Skimmer
  Black 63, 96
Snipe
  Giant 62, 201
  South 62
Spadebill
  Russet-winged 75, 108, 145, 192, 208
  White-throated 75, 108, 192, 197, 206
Sparrow
  Grassland 83
  House 84, 118
  Rufous-collared 83, 159
  Saffron-billed 82, 192, 196, 207
  Stripe-capped 83, 118, 144, 205
Spartanoica
  maluroides 134
Speotyto
  cunicularia 65
Spinetail
  Chicli 70, 192, 202, 207
  Chotoy 70, 195
  Gray-bellied 70, 192, 202
  Ochre-cheeked 129
  Olive 70, 121
  Pale-breasted 70, 192
  Pallid 132
  Plain-crowned 70, 144, 145, 192
  Rufous-capped 70, 192, 201
  Sooty-fronted 70, 192
  Stripe-crowned 70, 121, 193, 205
  Sulphur-bearded 132
  Yellow-throated 70, 195
Spizaetus
  ornatus 59, 92, 126, 201, 206
  tyrannus 126
Spizastur
  melanoleucus 59, 91, 208
Spiziapteryx
  circumcinctus 59, 92
Spoonbill
  Roseate 56
Sporophila
  albogularis 133
  americana 133
  bouvreuil 82, 116, 200
  caerulescens 82
  cinnamomea 82, 117, 124, 133, 200, 208
  collaris 82
  falcirostris 53, 82, 116, 146, 208
  frontalis 53, 82, 116, 146, 208
  hypochroma 82, 117, 124, 145, 196, 208
  hypoxantha 82, 116, 124
  leucoptera 82
  lineola 82, 116, 133, 200
  melanops 133

  nigrorufa 131
  palustris 82, 116, 124, 200, 208
  plumbea 82, 201, 207
  ruficollis 82, 116, 124, 195, 208
Starthroat
  Blue-tufted 67
Stelgidopteryx
  ruficollis 78, 112
Stephanophorus
  diadematus 80, 114, 146, 207
Stephanoxis
  lalandi 67, 204
Sterna
  maxima 127
  paradisaea 63, 96, 127
  superciliaris 63, 96, 196
  trudeaui 127
Stigmatura
  budytoides 74, 144
Stilt
  Black-necked 61
Stork
  Maguari 56
  Wood 56
Streamcreeper
  Sharp-tailed 71, 202, 207
Streptoprocne
  biscutata 134
  zonaris 66, 101, 204, 206
Strix
  hylophila 65, 100, 146
  rufipes 65, 193
  virgata 204, 206
Sublegatus
  modestus 73, 106
Suiriri
  suiriri 73, 122, 161
Sungrebe 61, 94, 198, 206
Swallow
  Bank 78, 112
  Barn 78, 112
  Black-collared 53, 78, 112, 146
  Blue-and-white 78, 112
  Chilean 78, 112, 123
  Cliff 78, 112
  Southern 78, 112
  Tawny-headed 78, 145, 196
  White-rumped 78, 112, 123
  White-winged 78, 144, 198
Swallow-Tanager 81, 115
Swan
  Black-necked 125
  Coscoroba 57, 89, 193, 205
Swift
  Ashy-tailed 66, 101
  Biscutate 134
  Gray-rumped 66, 101
  Great 66, 204
  White-collared 66, 101, 204, 206
Synallaxis
  albescens 70, 192

  cinerascens 70, 192, 202
  frontalis 70, 192
  gujanensis 70, 144, 145, 192
  ruficapilla 70, 192, 201
  spixi 70, 192, 202, 207
Syndactyla
  rufosuperciliata 70, 104, 129, 144, 192, 197, 207
Syrigma
  sibilatrix 55

T
Tachuri
  Bearded 74, 208
Tachuris
  rubrigastra 53, 74, 107
Tachybaptus
  dominicus 55
Tachycineta
  albiventer 78, 144, 198
  leucorrhoa 78, 112, 123
  meyeni 78, 112, 123
Tachyphonus
  coronatus 81, 114, 145, 161, 198
  rufus 81, 161
Tanager
  Azure-shouldered 133
  Black-faced 81, 115, 146, 207
  Black-goggled 81, 115, 198
  Blue-and-yellow 81, 114
  Burnished-buff 80, 199
  Chestnut-backed 80, 114, 199
  Chestnut-headed 81, 192, 203
  Diademed 80, 114, 146, 207
  Fawn-breasted 80, 199, 207
  Gray-headed 81, 114, 145, 199, 207
  Green-headed 80, 204
  Guira 81, 115, 144, 197, 207
  Hepatic 81, 115
  Hooded 81, 158
  Magpie 81, 115, 144, 198
  Orange-headed 81
  Palm 53, 81, 114, 207
  Red-necked 130
  Ruby-crowned 81, 114, 145, 161, 198
  Sayaca 81
  Silver-beaked 81, 115, 144, 146, 207
  White-banded 81, 115, 204, 207
  White-lined 81, 161
  White-rumped 81, 115, 200, 207
Tangara
  cayana 80, 199
  cyanocephala 130
  preciosa 80, 114, 199
  seledon 80, 204
Taoniscus
  nanus 125

Tapaculo
  Mouse-colored 129
Tapera
  naevia 65
Taraba
  major 72, 192
Teal
  Blue-winged 89
  Cinnamon 57, 89, 205
  Ringed 57, 145, 194, 205
  Silver 57, 205
  Speckled 125
Terenura
  maculata 72, 204
Tern
  Arctic 63, 96, 127
  Large-billed 63, 96, 196
  Royal 127
  Snowy-crowned 127
  Yellow-billed 63, 96, 196
Tersina
  viridis 81, 115
Thalurania
  furcata 67, 198, 206
  glaucopis 67, 199
Thamnophilus
  caerulescens 72, 122
  doliatus 72
  ruficapillus 72, 105, 146, 207
Theristicus
  caerulescens 56, 88, 205
  caudatus 56, 194
Thlypopsis
  sordida 81
Thornbird
  Freckle-breasted 129
  Greater 70, 129
  Little 70, 104, 145, 161, 162, 194, 205
  Rufous-fronted 70, 104, 161, 162, 194
Thraupis
  bonariensis 81, 114
  cyanoptera 133
  palmarum 53, 81, 114, 207
  sayaca 81
Thrush
  Black-billed 133
  Chiguanco 130
  Cocoa 133
  Creamy-bellied 79
  Pale-breasted 79, 113, 145, 198, 206
  Rufous-bellied 79
  Slaty 79, 113, 207
  Swainson's 130
  White-necked 79, 199, 207
  Yellow-legged 79, 113, 146
Thryothorus
  guarayanus 78, 112, 123, 144, 150, 192

  leucotis 112, 123
  longirostris 123
Tiaris
  fuliginosa 83, 117, 145
Tiger-Heron
  Fasciated 125
  Rufescent 55
Tigrisoma
  fasciatum 125
  lineatum 55
Tinamou
  Brown 54, 192, 202, 207
  Brushland 54, 87, 144
  Dwarf 125
  Red-winged 54, 140, 145
  Small-billed 54, 87, 140, 192
  Solitary 54, 87, 192, 201, 208
  Spotted 158, 162
  Tataupa 54, 140, 192
  Undulated 54, 192
Tinamus
  solitarius 54, 87, 192, 201, 208
Tit-Spinetail
  Araucaria 134
  Tufted 70, 104
Tityra
  Black-crowned 77, 111, 145, 198, 206
  Black-tailed 77, 111, 206
Tityra
  cayana 77, 111, 206
  inquisitor 77, 111, 145, 198, 206
Todirostrum
  cinereum 75, 108, 144
  latirostre 130
  plumbeiceps 74, 192, 203, 207
Tody-Flycatcher
  Common 75, 108, 144
  Ochre-faced 74, 192, 203, 207
  Rusty-fronted 130
Tody-Tyrant
  Pearly-vented 74
Tolmomyias
  sulphurescens 75, 158
Toucan
  Red-breasted 68, 102, 144, 197
  Toco 68
Toucanet
  Saffron 68, 208
  Spot-billed 68, 102
Treehunter
  Sharp-billed 71, 200
Trichothraupis
  melanops 81, 115, 198
Tringa
  flavipes 62, 95
  melanoleuca 62, 94
  solitaria 62, 95
Troglodytes
  aedon 79

Trogon
  Black-throated 67, 201
  Blue-crowned 67, 102, 160, 195
  Surucua 24, 67, 102, 160, 199
Trogon
  curucui 67, 102, 160, 195
  rufus 67, 201
  surrucura 24, 67, 102, 160, 199
Troupial 30, 84, 144, 205
Tryngites
  subruficollis 96
Turdus
  albicollis 79, 199, 207
  amaurochalinus 79
  chiguanco 130
  fumigatus 133
  ignobilis 133
  leucomelas 79, 113, 145, 198, 206
  nigriceps 79, 113, 207
  rufiventris 79
Tyrannulet
  Bay-ringed 74, 208
  Greenish 73, 122, 161, 199
  Mottle-cheeked 74, 108, 203, 207
  Mouse-colored 73, 106, 203, 206
  Plain 74, 107, 145
  Planalto 73, 206
  Reiser's 73, 106, 122, 145, 161, 203, 208
  Rough-legged 73, 203, 206, 207
  Sao 74, 108, 208
  Sooty 73, 107
  White-bellied 74, 107, 123, 194
  White-crested 74, 107, 123
  White-throated 132
  Yellow 73, 203
Tyrannus
  melancholicus 76, 111
  savana 77, 111
  tyrannus 77, 111
Tyrant
  Cattle 76
  Cinereous 75, 109, 194
  Cock-tailed 45, 76, 110, 200, 206, 208
  Long-tailed 76, 109, 145, 198, 206
  Plumbeous 134
  Sharp-tailed 74, 107, 145, 197, 206, 208
  Spectacled 75, 109
  Strange-tailed 76, 110, 145, 208
  Streamer-tailed 76, 110, 144, 198, 206
  Yellow-browed 76
Tyto
  alba 65

U

Upucerthia
  certhioides 69, 144, 205
  dumetaria 134

V

Vanellus
  chilensis 61
Veniliornis
  passerinus 69
  spilogaster 69, 202
Violet-ear
  White-vented 67, 101, 145, 201, 206
Vireo
  olivaceus 79, 113
Vireo
  Red-eyed 79, 113
Volatinia
  jacarina 82
Vultur
  gryphus 56, 88
Vulture
  Black 56
  King 56
  Lesser 56
  Turkey 56

W

Wagtail-Tyrant
  Greater 74, 144
Warbler
  Blackpoll 134
  Flavescent 80, 124, 192
  Golden-crowned 80, 113, 124, 145, 192, 206
  River 80, 207
  White-bellied 80, 114, 124, 144, 145, 192, 197
  White-browed 80, 114, 145, 192, 198
  White-striped 133
Warbling-Finch
  Black-and-rufous 83, 117
  Black-capped 83, 194
  Red-rumped 83, 117, 204, 207
  Ringed 83, 117
Water-Tyrant
  Black-backed 75
Whimbrel 127
Whistling-Duck
  Black-bellied 57
  Fulvous 57
  White-faced 57
Wigeon
  Southern 125
Willet 134
Wood-Quail
  Spot-winged 60, 192, 201
Wood-Rail
  Giant 60
  Gray-necked 60
  Slaty-breasted 60, 93

Woodcreeper
  Black-banded 71, 104, 159, 162, 193
  Great 71, 195
  Lesser 71, 204
  Narrow-billed 71
  Olivaceous 71, 160
  Planalto 71, 105, 145, 159, 197, 207
  Scaled 71, 204
  Scimitar-billed 71, 104, 144, 205
  Thrush-like 71, 202
  White-throated 71, 199
Woodnymph
  Fork-tailed 67, 198, 206
  Violet-capped 67, 199
Woodpecker
  Black-bodied 69, 121, 160, 208
  Blond-crested 69, 103, 160
  Checkered 69, 194
  Cream-backed 69, 103, 160, 193, 205
  Crimson-crested 69, 103, 160
  Golden-green 69, 102, 194
  Green-barred 69, 120, 159
  Helmeted 69, 103, 166, 202, 208
  Lineated 69, 103, 121, 145, 160, 196
  Little 69
  Pale-crested 69, 103, 160
  Ringed 132
  Robust 69, 202
  Spot-breasted 132
  White 68
  White-browed 69, 202, 208
  White-fronted 69, 193, 205
  White-spotted 69, 202
  Yellow-fronted 68, 201
Woodstar
  Amethyst 67, 206
Wren
  Buff-breasted 112, 123
  Fawn-breasted 78, 112, 123, 144, 150, 192
  House 79
  Long-billed 123
  Sedge 79, 113, 145, 204
  Thrush-like 78, 112
Wren-Spinetail
  Bay-capped 134

X

Xenops
  minutus 71
  rutilans 71, 144, 197, 206
Xenops
  Plain 71
  Streaked 71, 144, 197, 206
Xenopsaris
  albinucha 77, 111, 145, 205

Xenopsaris
  White-naped 77, 111, 145, 205
Xiphocolaptes
  albicollis 71, 199
  major 71, 195
Xolmis
  cinerea 75
  coronata 75, 109
  irupero 75
  velata 75, 145, 199, 206

Y

Yellow-Finch
  Grassland 83, 117
  Stripe-tailed 131
Yellowlegs
  Greater 62, 94
  Lesser 62, 95
Yellowthroat
  Masked 80

Z

Zenaida
  auriculata 63
Zonotrichia
  capensis 83, 159